Human Resource Management in an International Context

The CIPD would like to thank the following members of the CIPD Publishing editorial board for their help and advice:

- Pauline Dibben, Sheffield University
- Edwina Hollings, Staffordshire University Business School
- Caroline Hook, Huddersfield University Business School
- Vincenza Priola, Keele University
- John Sinclair, Napier University Business School

Human Resource Management in an International Context

Rosemary Lucas, Ben Lupton
and Hamish Mathieson

Chartered Institute of Personnel and Development

Published by the Chartered Institute of Personnel and Development,
151 The Broadway, London, SW19 1JQ

First published 2006

Typeset by Kerry Press Ltd, Luton, Bedfordshire

Printed in Great Britain by Cromwell Press, Trowbridge, Wiltshire

British Library Cataloguing in Publication Data

A catalogue of this manual is available from the British Library

ISBN 1-84398-109-2
ISBN-13 978 1-84398-109-1

Chartered Institute of Personnel and Development,
151 The Broadway, London, SW19 1JQ
Tel: 020 8612 6200
email: cipd@cipd.co.uk   website: www.cipd.co.uk
incorporated by royal charter. registered charity no. 1079797

Contents

Chapter 13 – Ethics and organisational justice

Boxes, figures and tables

Chapter 3
Box: P&O Group: business strategy and the human dimension
Box: International HR societies and associations
Table 1: IHRM practices in strategic orientation across ten countries

Chapter 4
Table 2: Comparative public policy approaches to work–life integration
Box: Types of WLI policy and their implications

Chapter 5
Box: Gap Inc.'s international culture
Box: Schein's model of cultural levels

Chapter 7
Box: Unpacking the learning architect role
Box: Key questions to evaluate L&D interventions
Figure 1: Four development types

Chapter 8
Figure 2: Typical performance management cycle
Table 3: The effect of individualism/collectivism and power distance on the performance appraisal process

Chapter 9
Box: Sources of hardship on expatriate placements
Box: Researching national information

Chapter 10
Table 4: Average union density and collective bargaining coverage

Chapter 11
Box: The influence of ILO standards

Chapter 12
Box: Healthy and happy eating at McDonald's
Table 5: Examples of company terms for CSR
Table 6: Handling CSR at boardroom level

Chapter 13
Box: A brief consequentialist analysis of the effectiveness of regulation in business
Box: Utilitarianism – steps of maximising human happiness by minimising unhappiness
Box: Would bribery be acceptable to a Kantian?
Box: Should loyalty come before honesty in business?
Table 7: Changes in social-moral attitudes in the Ukraine

About the contributors

Matthew Allen is Senior Lecturer in International Business at the Manchester Metropolitan University Business School (MMUBS). His research interests include HRM in multinational corporations and the effects of different HRM policies on company performance. This research has been funded by the German Academic Exchange Service, the Hans Böckler Foundation and the Fritz Thyssen Foundation. He has published in leading international journals, including the *Socio-Economic Review* and the *Journal of Public Policy*. He edits the Working Paper Series at MMUBS.

Carol Atkinson is a Senior Lecturer in HRM at MMUBS. She has worked at MMU for six years, having previously held HR practitioner roles in financial services, retail and the voluntary sector. She teaches Employee Resourcing, Performance Management and Professional and Academic Capability to postgraduate HRM students. Her research interests are in working time flexibility, performance management and the small firm employment relationship. She is currently engaged with colleagues on a British Academy-funded project investigating flexible working practices in small firms. She is a Chartered Member of the CIPD.

Paul Brook is Senior Lecturer in the Marketing and Retail Division, MMUBS. He is also UCU MMUBS Convenor. Before joining MMU in 1991 he was a researcher for USDAW, the shop workers' union. He teaches sociology of service work and consumption to a range of students. His research interests are the service labour process and customer service. His current research on emotional labour theory includes a recent article for *Work, Employment & Society* on 'customer-oriented bureaucracy' and front-line worker collectivism.

Susan Curtis is a Senior Lecturer in HRM at MMU Cheshire. She teaches across the spectrum of HRM. Her current research interests are the psychological contract, students working during term-time, actual and preferred working hours and the retail and hospitality industries. She is currently undertaking a PhD examining dimensions of the psychological contract in relation to undergraduates' term-time employment.

Laura Hall is a Senior Lecturer in HRM at MMU Cheshire. After working in personnel management she gained her PhD in human resource management from UMIST. She spent many years as the CIPD national examiner for management development and is co-author, together with Derek Torrington and Stephen Taylor, of a leading Human Resource Management text currently in its sixth edition. She is also engaged with colleagues on a British Academy funded project investigating flexible working practices in small firms. She is a Chartered Fellow of the CIPD.

Maryam Herin is Group Head of Human Resources at United Utilities plc, a FTSE 100 company which provides water, wastewater, gas and electricity services to customers. She is responsible for implementing strategic HR projects across the Group and for Group HR policy and services. Prior to this, Maryam was the HR Executive at the Cheshire Building Society and previously worked at Barclays Bank plc. Maryam has experience of integrating HR and cusiness strategy to enhance business performance. She is a member of the MMUBS Advisory Board and works to maintain relations between Universities and Industry, and often provides guest lectures in HR and OD matters. She is a Chartered Fellow of the CIPD, and has an MBA and a masters degree in HRM.

Gill Homan is a Principal Lecturer in HRM at MMUBS. Areas of specialist expertise in teaching include: Reward Management, Employee and Management Development and Personal Development together with supervision and examining at PhD and Masters level. Active within the CIPD, she is a Past Chair, Treasurer and current member of the Manchester Branch Committee; a national reward examiner and a Quality Management team member. Current research interests in the reward field include pensions; team based pay; and total reward. Consultancy interests lie within the fields of leadership, conflict and reward systems. She is also active within small business networks within the region. She is a co-editor of Strategic Reward Systems and publishes within the fields of development and reward. She is a Chartered Member of the CIPD.

Peter Kidger is a Senior Lecturer in HRM in the Salford Business School at the University of Salford. He worked for a number of years in industry in both HR and line management roles, before joining the University. His main areas of teaching are Strategic and International HRM, and his main research interest is in HRM in multinational companies. He has published in these fields, and most recently has been looking at the HR aspects of knowledge transfer in MNCs.

Rosemary Lucas is Professor of Employment Relations and Research coordinator of HRMOB Division at MMUBS, and worked as a senior practitioner for 10 years before embarking on an academic career. Her main research interests are employment relations in the hospitality industry, minimum wages, the youth labour market and comparative HRM. She has published widely on these topics, including two books of employment relations in the hospitality industry. She teaches HRM and Comparative Employee Relations on postgraduate courses in HRM, IHRM and the MBA, and is a Chartered Fellow of the CIPD.

Ben Lupton is Principal Lecturer in HRM at MMUBS. He is Director of Postgraduate HRM Programmes, and teaches Employee Resourcing, Selection Testing and Employment Equality. He researches and publishes in the areas of employment equality, gender and occupations, and the HR profession. Ben has a Masters degree in HRM and a PhD in Sociology. Before becoming a lecturer, Ben was an HR manager in the NHS and is a Chartered Fellow of the CIPD.

Hamish Mathieson is Senior Lecturer in Employment Relations at MMUBS. He teaches across a range of undergraduate and postgraduate programmes, including the MA in HRM, on which he was Programme Leader, and the MA in International HRM. His research interests are in the fields of employee voice, union commitment and employment relations in the public services. He is currently involved in an international research study of public sector reform. He is also a member of the CIPD Professional Standards Conference Design Team and is a Chartered Member of the CIPD.

Andrew Pendleton is Professor of Human Resource Management and Head of the Master's Programme at the University of York. He is currently teaching comparative HRM and industrial relations at Masters level. He was previously Professor of HRM at MMUBS. He was educated at the universities of Bath and Oxford, and his main research interests are employee stock ownership and corporate governance. His research has been funded by the ESRC, the Nuffield Foundation, European Commission, European Foundation and UK government departments.

Elke Pioch is a Senior Lecturer, Marketing and Retail Division, MMUBS and teaches International Retailing and Organisational Organisational Culture Management (particularly in a retail context) to various student groups. She researches organisational culture management in an international retail context. Recent publications include an article on retail employee perceptions of organisational life following cross-border acquisition in the *International Journal of Human Resource Management.* Her PhD was on retailer internationalisation in the European Union.

Andrew Rowe is a Senior Lecturer in Organisational Behaviour, MMUBS. Teaching responsibilities includes Unit Leader for Social Science, Work and Management and Organisational Behaviour and Management Development. He is active in research relating to collective learning and a recent paper in the prestigious *Journal of Engineering Manufacture* won the IMechE award for Best Short Paper in 2005. Prior to joining MMUBS, Andrew completed a PhD in Management Learning entitled *Exploring the Dance of Team Learning* at the University of Essex. He was also part of a research team at Cranfield University, investigating effective Service Delivery in Public Private Partnerships through the nurturing of teamworking cultures.

Carol Scutt is a Senior Lecturer in Management Development at MMUBS. She has had a number of careers, among them Personnel and Training Officer with an engineering company in West Sussex followed by move to a small consultancy as a manager and director running government funded training programmes. In the early 1990s she became self-employed and spent much of her time teaching management development in academic institutions throughout South London and the south east of England, which led to a senior lectureship in Management Development at South Bank University, a role she has developed further at MMUBS.

Sue Shaw is Head of Human Resource Management and Organisational Behaviour Division at MMUBS. She teaches and researches in the area of HRM and prior to joining MMU worked in both manufacturing and wholesaling. Her areas of specialism are HRM in China, Gender and Performance and the HR function and she has a number of publications in these areas. She is a Chartered Fellow of the CIPD and in 2004 was awarded the Institute's Distinguished Badge of Merit in recognition of her services to the profession.

Stephen Taylor is a Senior Lecturer in HRM at MMUBS and a national examiner for the CIPD. He previously taught at UMIST and worked in a variety of HR management roles in the hotel industry and in the NHS. He teaches courses in Employment Law, Employee Resourcing, Employee Relations and the Business Context at postgraduate and undergraduate level. Research interests include employee retention, occupational pensions and regulatory issues. He is the author / co-author of several books including *People Resourcing* (now in its third edition), *Employment Law: An Introduction* (with Astra Emir), *The Employee Retention Handbook* and three editions of *Human Resource Management* (with Derek Torrington and Laura Hall). He regularly represents parties in employment tribunals and is a Chartered Fellow of the CIPD.

Richard Warren is a Principal Lecturer at MMUBS with responsibility HRMOB Undergraduate Programmes. He holds degrees from the polytechnics of Wolverhampton and Plymouth and the University of Manchester. He teaches at undergraduate and postgraduate level in the areas of Business Ethics and Corporate Governance and Accountability and Comparative Employee Relations. Richard was a merchant seaman for five years before working in the Commercial Department of the shipowners A. P. Moller. He joined MMU in 1984. His research interests are business ethics, corporate governance and industrial relations and he has published a book, *Corporate Governance and Acccountability* (Liverpool Academic Press, 2000) and articles in a wide variety of journals.

Carol Woodhams is a Senior Lecturer in HRM at MMUBS. Her primary research interests include examining equal opportunities within small to medium-sized enterprises, debates of human resources and disability equality and the impact of disability equality legislation. She has published widely on these topics including articles in the *Journal of Social Policy, Human Resource Management Journal* and *British Journal of Industrial Relations*. She teaches

Organisational Behaviour and Human Resource Management on a wide range of programmes at undergraduate and postgraduate level. She also teaches quantitative methods on the Masters in Research programme. She is a Chartered Fellow of the CIPD.

Acknowledgements

We would like to extend thanks to those people who have been instrumental in helping us to bring this book to fruition. Ruth Lake of CIPD Publishing for commissioning the book, prompt advice and helpful assistance throughout. All our fellow-contributors for making the book happen. Sue Shaw for her encouragement, support and assistance. Pat Walker and Tayo Ososipe for their administrative support. Finally, our families without whose patience and support this book would not have been possible.

Rosemary Lucas, Ben Lupton and Hamish Mathieson

Introduction

WHAT IS THIS BOOK ABOUT?

Human Resource Management in an International Context is a theoretical and practical textbook that is critical, analytical and research-based, yet accessible. It explores a number of themes impacting on employment issues worldwide that can be applied globally, from either an international or a comparative perspective. The authors comprise a dedicated team of research active academics, mainly from Manchester Metropolitan University (MMU) which is designated a Chartered Institute of Personnel and Development (CIPD) Centre of Research Excellence. Most teach on the MA in Human Resource Management (HRM) and the MA in International Human Resource Management, have practitioner experience, and maintain ongoing links with the CIPD, HR practitioners and trade unions.

This book will enable students studying international and comparative HRM at undergraduate and postgraduate levels to:

- develop a critical understanding of HRM theory and practice from both an international and a comparative perspective
- understand core and novel HRM topics within a variety of international contexts and geographical locations
- relate these topics to a conceptual framework based on seven international themes, and also to particular sectoral and organisational settings
- apply critical thinking in a practical way through major case studies, smaller case studies, case study tasks and discussion questions.

WHO SHOULD READ IT?

This textbook will serve students at all levels (undergraduate, postgraduate, professional). It is very well suited to particular types of courses – eg MBAs, where HRM is studied as part of a business degree, and postgraduate courses in HRM. It will also have special appeal to international students on MBAs, students on Master's in HRM, and students who wish to develop managerial or HR careers cross-nationally. So while appealing to those on traditional UK home-based specialist courses, it will also serve the growing market of international students coming to the UK to study.

WHAT DOES THE BOOK CONTAIN?

This introductory section is followed by the 13 main chapters that comprise the main body of the book. These chapters are structured into five main parts:

1. Employment and HRM
2. Work organisation, flexibility and culture

3.   Recruiting, managing and developing people

4.   Regulation and employment relations

5.   Corporate governance, justice and equity.

The two chapters in Part 1 set up the seven international themes and they provide a contextual overview of current debates within employment and HRM, thereby setting the scene for remaining 11 chapters. The book closes with a short concluding chapter that draws out the significance of these themes.

HOW TO USE THIS BOOK

The book can be used in two main ways. Firstly, the chapters can be read in sequence to develop a fuller understanding of a range of key HRM issues in an international context. Secondly, although each of the chapters is also self-standing in its own right and may be used selectively, they will be better understood after reading the two chapters in Part 1. Inevitably, each chapter has taken a selective approach to the topic concerned and we do not claim to cover every angle of every topic or to follow a predetermined formula or syllabus.

The broad approach taken in this book

The 13 main chapters begin with a series of learning objectives, followed by a short section outlining the chapter's purpose and scope, which identifies the themes that are to be highlighted within the main body of the chapter. This is followed by a brief introduction to the topic, the main focus of the chapter being upon how the topic is located in an international context, using a wide range of comparative, international and global examples to illustrate how HRM policies and practices are formulated and applied. These chapters contain three to seven main sections, each concluding with a set of discussion questions. Most are also illustrated by boxes and tables. All chapters incorporate a significant proportion of case-based material with discussion tasks, including a major case study located at the end of the chapter and a number of smaller case studies illustrating HR issues and practices in a specific national, international or global context. The accumulation of case studies from different countries and perspectives throughout the text shows how the various national, cultural and regulatory environments influence international HR practice in Europe, Asia, Africa, Australasia and North and South America. The chapters finish with a short section that draws conclusions and raises future issues, followed by a complete reference list, including weblinks.

We also move beyond the large organisation or multinational company (MNC) and trade union emphasis taken in much of the literature, by offering discussion about, and providing practical examples from, a wide range of organisations. These include the public, private and voluntary sectors, large and small firms, and manufacturing and service organisations. Additionally, we move beyond the European and North American contexts by including material from a much wider range of other countries across the world. Particular attention is paid to 'emergent' and 'developing' economies – for example, the EU 'accession states' in Central and Eastern Europe, China, India and Africa.

WHAT IS DIFFERENT ABOUT THIS BOOK?

A thematic conceptual framework

Three primary themes provide the conceptual framework for each of the main chapters and run throughout the book:

1 Globalisation

Globalisation is the movement towards greater worldwide integration of economic and political activities. Globalisation is an economic phenomenon, but there are social and political consequences of the greater integration of the world economy.

2 Convergence and divergence

Convergence is the extent to which HRM policies and practices converge towards a common set of macro western universals. Divergence is where HRM policies and practices differ because they are culturally determined. Cross-vergence may arise from the interaction between economic ideology and national culture, which produces a unique value system that is neither one nor the other.

3 Cultural variation

Culture is used to explain the differences between human groups, and cultural variation becomes significant where it is manifested in different behaviour patterns and tangible objects. Cultural variation may be reflected in different institutional arrangements, the nature of the business environment, types of industrial sector, and organisational contingencies, strategies and policies.

Four subsidiary and related themes also appear in the context of particular chapters:

1 Technological change and the knowledge economy

The main challenge to the West comes from the rise of nations such as China and India for reasons that include flexibility of response, entrepreneurship, adaptability and lower labour costs. The dominance of the English language – for example, in information technology (IT) – has contributed to western nations becoming an important educator for developing nations, particularly in higher-level academic skills, such as PhDs and MBAs. Emerging economies are thus gaining competitive advantage and moving towards dominance in high-technology, high-skill and knowledge work.

2 Demographic trends and labour market change

Many western societies face labour supply problems and skills shortages because of ageing populations and low birth rates, which may be filled by untapped internal labour sources and migrant workers from the enlarged EU and elsewhere across the world, including Africa. However, there is a danger that western economies could become low-skills economies given the emergence of high-technology high-skill knowledge economies elsewhere whose lower labour costs give them an additional competitive edge.

3 European Union (EU) enlargement

This addresses the challenges facing an expanded EU made up of 25 very different economies. It makes the achievement of the EU's objectives of economic and social cohesion even more difficult, particularly as member states can implement measures to suit their own national institutional arrangements. The playing-field is not level, and unemployment remains high in many countries, especially those with the most highly regulated employment systems.

4 Emerging economies

This issue reflects how the dominance of individualised western economies is being competitively challenged by the emergence of collective economies in the East, such as China and India. Additionally, former Communist regimes in Central and Eastern Europe have become market-focused, and this is impacting upon the economic fortunes of Western European nations. The economic prosperity of African and Latin American nations is more diverse.

The importance of particular themes varies in relation to different topics, and some chapters are necessarily more selective than others. For example, Chapter 5, *Culture change management* explores cultural aspects in some depth, with reference to corporate culture, while Chapter 11, *Employment law* focuses heavily on the extent to which the law may converge or diverge across countries. Nevertheless, we draw these themes together in the final chapter and reflect upon their significance.

THE STRUCTURE OF THE BOOK

Part 1 Employment and HRM

Chapter 2, *Employment in a global context* examines how employment is developing in an international context. The authors pay particular attention to the three key themes of cultural variation, globalisation, and convergence and divergence, from which the other four themes of technological change and the knowledge economy, demographic trends and labour market change, EU enlargement, and emerging economies emanate. The focus is thus upon national differences, convergence through globalisation, and the role of MNCs. The first section provides an overview of the nature of employment, with reference to economic, political, psychological and social factors. Section 2 examines how a world of different nation states impacts on the employment practices that shape HRM strategies and policies. Section 3 addresses a world of cultures, highlighting the work of Hofstede, and how cultural differences impact upon human behaviour and the management of employment policies and practices. Section 4 takes a global perspective and discusses why globalisation is tending to promote a convergence of management and employment practices at international and regional levels. Section 5 considers the role of the MNCs, highlighting the strategic choices they can make and the factors that determine the extent to which MNCs promote international employment and HRM policies. The case studies consider different aspects of employment in a global context. The major case study concerns the subsidiaries of US MNCs in Germany. The smaller case studies address managing employment in Nigeria and the subsidiaries of German MNCs in the UK.

Chapter 3, *Human resource management* develops the themes and concepts introduced in Chapter 2 by considering how employment is managed through HRM policies and practices. Strongly underpinned by each of the seven themes, the chapter provides a contextual overview of current debates within HRM, many of which are picked up and developed in subsequent chapters. The first section outlines the nature and scope of HRM, highlighting how the term 'human resources' can be viewed as 'soft', with an emphasis on humans, and 'hard', with an emphasis on resource. It also outlines HRM activity and how different approaches to strategy inform a strategic framework for HRM. The second section discusses comparative models of HRM, beginning with an overview of traditional and other variations of western models and their limitations, before considering how cross-national HRM may be modelled and better understood. The third section explores the differences between international and global HRM and how far and in what way we can expect HRM to diverge, converge or cross-verge. The fourth section addresses the management of HRM and outlines the status of and the changing nature of the HR function, including role of the HR specialist and line manager. It also considers the role of IT in HR and examines the role of HR departments in different countries. The major case study focuses on notions of justice and fairness, the nature of HR strategy and *guanxi* in a joint Chinese and Swiss venture in China. The smaller case studies address HRM in transition in Central and Eastern European culture and the implementation of HR practices and the role of line managers in multinational banking in Pakistan.

Part 2 Work organisation, flexibility and culture

Chapter 4, *Work organisation and flexibility* pays particular attention to the five themes of globalisation, emerging economies, EU enlargement, technological change and the knowledge economy, and demographic trends and labour market change, showing how the combined consequences of these influences have forced well-established western capitalist economies to adopt new forms of work organisation and greater flexibility in employment relationships in the face of greater competition. In addition, the issues of regulated and deregulated economies are explored in order to address how far state-driven initiatives lead to divergence or convergence of practice in matters such as working time and work–life integration (WLI) policies. Underpinned by employer and employee perspectives throughout, the first section provides an overview of work organisation and flexibility. The second section discusses the major influences on work and work organisation, highlighting issues of demand and supply, work intensification, and how changing demographics have altered employees' expectations, including the demand for more WLI policies. In Section 3 the UK's deregulated labour market is compared and contrasted with other more highly regulated frameworks applied elsewhere in the world. Section 4 considers employer perspectives on flexible working practices, including the concepts of core and periphery, trends in flexibility and the implications of part-time working. Section 5 considers employee perspectives on flexible working practices, considering the business case approach and how different types of WLI policy may be implemented. The major case study considers how the issue of work–life balance has been dealt with in Norway. The smaller case studies address working time and deregulation in Australia and New Zealand, the rationale behind the introduction of a 35-hour working week in France and trust-based working time in Germany.

Chapter 5, *Culture change management* focuses heavily on corporate culture, primarily in relation to the themes of globalisation and convergence and divergence, while also addressing labour market change and technological change and the knowledge economy. The first section introduces the concept of culture change management. The second section debates the meaning of culture. The third section explores the relationship between culture and HRM in three respects, providing an outline of why culture should be managed, a review of the place of culture in HRM theory and a discussion of customer-orientation and the 'New Service Management School'. Section 4 focuses on exporting company cultures, taking the specific case of international retailers who have sought to reproduce successful domestic formats and quality of customer service in new national contexts. Section 5 provides an evaluation of culture change programmes from two perspectives – from empirical evidence that highlights aspects of success and failure in general, and from the case of companies that specifically recruit only employees that have a passion for their product. The sixth section returns to culture management and considers the extent to which managing culture is feasible, with reference to the two key theoretical perspectives of Smircich and Martin. The seventh section considers culture as a contested terrain through explorations of customer service in the Customer-Oriented Bureaucracy and emotional labour and the commercialisation of feeling. The major case study is concerned with the efforts of a global retailer to export its culture to a UK food retailer that has been subject to a takeover. The smaller case studies consider whether a generically based 'Anglo-Saxon' model of culture may be applied in Greece, 'from-below' culture management interventions based on the recruitment of employees with a 'passion for product or service' in the UK, and how the consequences of managing 'unpredictable' customers led to strike action among cabin crew at Cathay Pacific airline.

Part 3 Recruiting, managing and developing people

Chapter 6, *Recruitment and selection* begins by exploring how demographic and labour market changes, together with technological change and the emergence of the knowledge economy, have further underlined the key strategic role of recruitment and selection in providing organisations with competitive advantage through their human capital. In Section 2 the authors go on to explore this in the changing international context in which this key area of resourcing activity is undertaken, highlighting – among other things – the impact of globalisation, the tension between the convergence of HR practices internationally and the impact of local culture, and the changing nature of labour markets nationally and internationally. Section 3 follows with a detailed and critical examination of the theory and practice of recruitment and selection, using examples from around the world to illustrate the impact of the different contextual factors identified above. The chapter finishes by focusing on two specific current issues: the use of technology in recruitment and selection, and the recruitment and selection of international staff. The major case study examines the recruitment and selection of senior staff in a utility company in Estonia. The smaller case studies illustrate key recruitment and selection issues arising from the examples of a hospice in Uganda, a hotel in Mali and an Internet recruitment firm operating in Asia-Pacific.

Chapter 7, *Learning and development* draws out a number of themes – particularly convergence and divergence, and cultural variation – in the context of globalisation and the increased significance of working in a knowledge-based economy. The authors examine the theory and practice of learning and development (L&D), highlighting the importance for organisations (and individuals) of effective L&D within the context of a global economy that puts an increasing emphasis on technology and knowledge as sources of competitive advantage. Section 1 introduces L&D in an international context. Section 2 provides a critical review of the debates around the nature and meaning of L&D and of its changing role in organisations. It considers the information-processing view of organisational learning, individual, group and team learning, the learning organisation and learning as participation. Section 3 identifies the key players in L&D and the role of HR practitioners as thinking performers and learning architects. Section 4 discusses the options available for encouraging L&D, including the role of higher education and its best and worst features. The main case study explores the practice of action learning within a multicultural group. The smaller case studies consider the cultural context of L&D, learning as participation within communities of practice, and L&D in a major IT company in India.

Chapter 8, *Managing performance* focuses primarily on the themes of globalisation, technological change and cultural variation. The authors argue that managing performance is a key source of competitive advantage for organisations and show how these three themes, in particular, present challenges to organisations in achieving it. Section 1 provides a conceptual overview of performance management, which includes a critical examination of the debates in this area, the differences in approach and the assumptions that lie behind them. In Section 2 the authors go on to examine the processes of performance management and the issues arising for organisations at each part of the performance cycle. Section 3 focuses on performance management and reward, both financial and non-financial, and how this may vary cross-nationally. Section 4 discusses performance management and teams, including a review of developments in managing team performance. Section 5 explores expatriate performance management in terms of developments and challenges. Section 6 explains the method of 360-degree feedback, identifying its purpose, process and limitations. The major case study assesses the role of 360-degree feedback in managing performance in a New Zealand utility company. The smaller case studies address the ever controversial issue of the link between performance management and reward systems in Australian local government, the issue of managing the performance of teams in Egypt, and the management of expatriate staff's performance in a Finnish MNC.

Chapter 9, *Reward* is focused around the themes of globalisation and cultural variation, but also explores the impact of technological change and emerging economies on reward strategies. The chapter examines three aspects of international reward management: the impact of national differences on approaches to reward, the management of expatriate reward, and global reward management. The first section explores the strategic significance of reward, before looking at the context in which reward strategies are developed. The authors explain how and why cultural, political, socio-economic and legal differences between nations and regions must be considered in developing different aspects of reward strategy. Having provided this context, the authors examine strategies for rewarding expatriate workers, exploring the different categories of expatriate worker and the factors that impact on their remuneration. The constituent elements of expatriate reward strategies are examined, and different approaches to combine them are evaluated. The third section identifies the different influences that impact on multinational firms in developing global reward systems and the strategic choices that have to be made. This section also looks in detail at the different elements that make up such a reward system. The chapter offers case studies for analysis and discussion based around the expatriate reward strategy and global reward strategy of major multinational companies.

Part 4 Regulation and employment relations

Chapter 10, *Employee voice* focuses primarily on the themes of globalisation and convergence and divergence, but also touches on cultural variation, emerging economies and EU enlargement. Section 1 opens by considering the multiple meanings of 'employee voice' and how voice can be expressed in either conflictual or integrative ways. It goes on to examine the varying rationales for employee voice and the links between these and the interests of the parties in the employment relationship. Section 2 follows with a review of direct and indirect forms of voice and the different kinds of mechanisms by which voice may be articulated, before the focus turns to voice in an international comparative context. In Section 3 an analytical framework is presented based on the view that the institutional features of particular societies play a mediating role between pervasive pressures such as globalisation and actual patterns of voice, thus cautioning against assuming a simple process of convergence. In analysing employee voice attention must be paid to a range of economic, cultural, and politico-legal variables external to the enterprise and also to organisational-level variables such as management strategies and the power-balance between the parties. The fourth section examines empirical trends in employee voice in comparative terms across the globe in respect of the types of voice mechanisms identified earlier. The final section considers the future of employee voice in the context of globalisation and examines a range of mechanisms by which employee voice may be protected and expressed on a trans-national basis. The major case study is concerned with assessing the effectiveness of the implementation of an International Framework Agreement (IMF) for extending employee voice among workers of a US-based MNC in the Latin American banana industry. Another case study focuses on the extent to which employee voice was accommodated in company restructuring in airlines subject to similar external environmental pressures but based in the UK (a liberal market economy) and Germany (a coordinated market economy). A shorter case study examines the cross-border transfer of employee relations practices in the subsidiaries of US MNCs based in the UK.

Chapter 11, *Employment law* addresses the themes of globalisation, labour market change, cultural variation, EU enlargement and emerging economies, but its main focus is on convergence and divergence. Section 1 explains how and why employment law differs from country to country by examining different legal traditions and how these are manifested in different law regimes. The next two sections focus on dismissal law and the regulation of working time to illustrate the major disputes between regulatory systems in different countries. Section 4 discusses the role of regional convergence through the EU. Section 5 examines the role of the International Labour Organisation (ILO) in promoting greater convergence of employment regimes across the globe. The major case study focuses on wages, social partnership and the roles of the ILO and the EU in the context of the Labour Code in Bulgaria. The smaller case studies address the lack of general protection for US workers who are fired that arises from the doctrine of at-will-employment in the USA, and the impact of regulating for the first time the working time of managers under the French 35-hour working week legislation.

Part 5 Corporate governance, justice and equity

Chapter 12, *Corporate social responsibility and HRM* focuses primarily on the themes of globalisation, cultural change and EU integration and enlargement, and is organised in four broad sections. The opening section addresses the meanings assigned to the term 'corporate social responsibility' (CSR), including the view of the EU that CSR is a voluntary activity beyond minimum legal requirements, that it involves the integration of social and environmental concerns, and that business should see itself as having multiple responsibilities to a range of stakeholders. Further, the authors examine why CSR has become such a prominent issue in the new millennium and the case against the CSR response. The second section turns to examine the links between HRM and CSR, reviewing the relevance of CSR considerations to a wide range of HRM policy and practice areas, with particular reference to pay, working time and employer branding. The third section discusses how CSR can be organised and integrated into the HRM function. Section 4 then turns to the practice of CSR reporting and points to the model of HRM social reporting practice common in continental European countries such as Germany. The major case study focuses on the role of HRM policies in embedding CSR in the context of off-shoring jobs in the Indian subcontinent and in a multinational company operating across developing countries in different continents. The smaller cases focus, respectively, on company CSR reporting practice in a UK-based bank and in relation to human rights in the cocoa industry in Africa.

Chapter 13, *Ethics and organisational justice* places emphasis on the themes of cultural variation, globalisation and convergence and divergence in order to reflect some of the challenges arising from the internationalisation of business, particularly in emerging econo-mies. The authors also touch upon the themes of technological change and the knowledge economy and labour market change. With a focus on secular theories of ethics that are rooted in western moral philosophy, the first section introduces the notion of ethics and identifies the link between ethics and business. Section 2 outlines the major theories of ethics (consequen-tialist, duty and virtue) that underpin business ethics dilemmas and provides examples of how they apply in practice in shaping managerial decisions in cross-cultural situations. Section 3 makes the case for paying greater attention to ethics in HRM practice, in terms of perceived moral decay in the West, declining individualised western economies and emerging competitive collective economies in the Far East, the failure of management education to teach students 'how to manage', and the need for a common good in business and society. The fourth section explores how 'fair' employers, through the actions of HR and line managers, can apply an ethical approach within a framework of organisational justice through its three component parts – distributive justice, procedural justice and interactional justice – and explores the cultural implications of organisational justice. The major case study focuses on the business ethics lessons to be learned from the bankruptcy of Enron. The smaller case studies explore whistleblowing in South Korea in the context of Confucian ethics and collectivism, compare the ethical criteria that govern business people's behaviour in Russia and the USA, and consider the implications of working towards social and organisational justice in sub-Saharan Africa.

Chapter 14, *Employment equality* focuses primarily on the themes of convergence and divergence, cultural variation and labour market change with some reference to the themes of emerging economies and EU enlargement. Section 1 outlines the nature and extent of employment inequalities and the main theories and practice of equality management. In Section 2 national and international legal interventions to address labour market inequalities are identified and explained and the principles underlying them are examined. Section 3 considers a range of equality issues in different parts of the world. Gender equality is discussed in two contexts – firstly in the EU, to show how national differences influence how EU policy may be implemented in different countries; secondly in China, to explore the impact of labour market change in an emerging economy on employment equality, and reflect upon whether the transition towards a market-based economy has been beneficial or detrimental to the relative employment position of women. The issue of racial equality and diversity in Africa is used to show how cultural factors and historical and political legacies have impacted on employment equality. The major case study further develops the theme of labour market change and emerging economies by looking at the issue of gender equality in the transition economies of Eastern Europe. The smaller case studies illustrate cross-national differences between employment law, the different experiences of women in employment in Britain and France, and women's experience of management careers in China.

Chapter 15, *Themes and reflections* summarises the main themes arising from the main chapters and identifies the main HRM challenges of the future.

Employment and human resource management

PART 1

Employment in a global context

CHAPTER 2

Peter Kidger and Matthew Allen

> **CHAPTER OBJECTIVES**
>
> When you have read this chapter you should be able to:
>
> ■ **explain the nature and scope of employment in a global context**
>
> ■ **show how culture and other national differences affect employment management practices**
>
> ■ **define globalisation and evaluate its impact on employment policies and practices**
>
> ■ **list reasons why employment practices may be converging across national boundaries, and reasons why national differences are still important**
>
> ■ **evaluate the choices that multinational companies face in regard to employment policies and practices.**

PURPOSE AND SCOPE

The purpose of this chapter is to examine the global context within which employment occurs and is managed, thus setting the scene for the next chapter on how human resource management (HRM) is shaped and practised across the world. The chapter is structured in relation to the three primary themes that underpin the book: cultural variation, globalisation, and convergence and divergence, from which the other four themes of technological change and the knowledge economy, demographic trends and labour market change, European Union (EU) enlargement and emerging economies emanate. So we focus upon national differences, convergence through globalisation, and the role of multinational companies (MNCs). We begin with an overview of the nature of employment and employment relationships, followed by a discussion of how the context of a world of different nation states impacts on the employment practices that shape HRM strategies and policies. We then move from the national to the global perspective, and discuss why globalisation is tending to promote a convergence of management and employment practices. The role of the multinational company is discussed in relation to the factors that determine the extent to which MNCs promote international employment and HRM policies.

1 THE NATURE OF EMPLOYMENT

Most of the people who work for organisations are directly employed as employees. However, organisations also use the services of individuals who are self-employed, or are provided by an agency, or are employees of a subcontractor. The relationship between employer and employee is generally referred to as the employment relationship, although others who work for an organisation are affected by its employment management processes, especially where they are on the same premises as employees. Employment legislation in the UK sometimes refers to 'workers' rather than 'employees' in recognition that in many instances employers should provide equal treatment for everyone who is contributing to the achievement of their objectives.

Employment relationships concern the formal and informal regulation of the relationship between an employer and those who work for that employer. The formal aspects of the relationship include such things as the terms of employment, including remuneration and reward, disciplinary rules, employee procedures, and collective agreements. The informal aspects include the ways that people actually interact with one another as they seek to agree, define, and implement the terms of the employment relationship. The importance of the formality of employment practice varies between countries, but in all industrialised societies, both formal and informal aspects are present, and the interplay between them is a key factor to understanding the nature of employment relationships and HRM. Regulation implies rules, and the rules governing employment include those that are explicit and those that are based on social understandings.

Except in very small organisations, the 'employer' is an entity rather than an individual. Managers act as agents of the employer, and it is they who interact with employees and shape the nature of the employment relationship and HRM. Employees may be members of a trade union, and in some workplaces the terms of employment are negotiated with unions and set out in a collective agreement. Unions may negotiate with a single employer or with a group of employers who have formed an employers' association and who negotiate with unions through the association. Collective agreements may therefore apply to a single organisation, or they may be regional or national agreements covering an industry sector. Even where unions are not recognised, many aspects of employment in large organisations are collective, in that there are common employment terms and conditions, and communication is with people in work groups. Large organisations with operating units located in different places have to decide whether decisions about employment conditions are made at the level of the organisation or at the level of the workplace.

Influences on employment

Government action, including the use of employment and taxation laws, is an important contextual factor for employment management. Governments are concerned about the economic and social well-being of their citizens, and both of these are affected by the way work is organised and employment is managed through HRM strategies and policies. In modern supply chains, employment decisions may also be influenced by pressure from corporate customers. There are therefore a range of stakeholders and actors whose views and actions determine the terms and conditions under which people are employed within a society.

The employment relationship and the conduct of HRM can be described as having four facets:

Economic
The relationship is about the exchange of financial and other rewards for the time and effort of employees. Employers have to attract, retain and motivate their workers, and individuals seek and make choices about employment on the basis of expected reward (see Chapters 6 and 9).

Political
The relationship involves authority and the exercise of power. In employment, individuals are subject to the authority of the organisation, and their behaviour is controlled in various ways. Management authority is generally accepted, but individuals or groups may contest its limits from time to time. Trade unions developed as a means by which workers could redress the balance of power, and secure both better pay and fairer treatment (see Chapter 10).

Psychological

The relationship contains assumptions about behaviour and mutual obligations that are often referred to as the 'psychological contract' (see also Chapter 3). Behavioural expectations may be explicit, in policies or management statements, or they may be implicit, resting on the norms of the societal culture. There is, however, always a degree of uncertainty about requirements that are implied rather than explicit, and managers and employees may not agree on what is expected on either side. In the UK culture informal understandings are respected but may not be regarded as being as binding as written agreements, particularly when circumstances change.

Social

The relationship is social as well as psychological since both the terms of employment and the relationships between the parties are set in a societal context. Cultural norms determine the attitudes of the parties and their expectations about what is acceptable. Some of these social expectations about workplace behaviour have been translated into employment law, so that society as a whole sets constraints on what may or may not happen at work (see Chapter 11).

At the workplace, conflict and cooperation exist side by side. Managers aim to obtain labour at the best wage, and to control the organisation of work so as to maximise labour performance and generate an economic surplus. Managers recognise, however, that in practice they need a degree of workforce consent to the allocation and organisation of work. Chapter 3 demonstrates how contemporary models of HRM link the achievement of high performance to capability and commitment, and recognise the importance of building a climate of trust at the workplace. Employees have to accept that to a greater or lesser extent they will be exploited at work, but employers equally have to accept that they are more likely to achieve their objectives on a consistent long-term basis if they treat their employees fairly and with respect (see Chapters 12 and 13).

Discussion questions

1   What differences would you expect to find between employment practices and relationships in a small organisation with an owner/manager, and a large organisation with several operating units?

2   Why are governments often interested in employment relations (ER) in the private sector, and what are the ways in which governments try and influence the conduct of ER?

3   Think of an employment situation you have experienced, and list some of the expectations that you and the employer had that could be regarded as part of the psychological contract.

2 NATIONAL DIFFERENCES AND EMPLOYMENT

Nation states

Humankind is a social species. The earliest humans formed into village tribes, which over time linked into larger social units and gradually evolved into the nation states of today. A combination of geographical factors, wars, treaties, colonisation and accidents have defined national boundaries. These boundaries have changed from time to time, and in some places they are still unclear or contested. Within most nation states there are various geographic and social sub-groups, giving many individuals multiple social identities. In the other direction, states work together in a variety of political and economic alliances, including the United Nations (UN), the International Labour Organisation (ILO), the World Trade Organisation (WTO) and the EU.

World politics is largely organised in terms of nation states, and they are important actors in the global economy (Kobrin, 1997; Dicken, 2003). However, countries are not isolated from one another, and few states, if any, have complete economic and political freedom to determine their future destiny without regard to events in the wider world.

Physical and human resources

The development of nation states means that the whole world has been physically divided between different societies. Countries vary in their access to natural resources, and this partly determines the possibilities of wealth creation, and the economic well-being of the population. A country that is able to build its wealth can invest in technology, education and health care, thus creating a more productive labour resource. The economic development of a state depends on its physical and human resources.

Physical resources are relatively fixed by geography, although nations can acquire them through trade and colonisation. The economic value of human resources in a nation resides primarily not in numbers or physical characteristics such as height, but in the skills, knowledge and attitudes that are the result of social norms and education provision. There is variation between states in terms of basic literacy rates, the proportion of the population going into higher education, and the level of technological competence. Societies differ in terms of the kinds of knowledge and skills that are regarded as important, and in attitudes to education, learning and work. Ideally, education ensures not only that there is the skilled population to meet present needs, but also that there is resource capacity and capability to facilitate future growth. It is educational differences that divide the world into developed and underdeveloped labour markets. However, this is not a static situation, and in general terms education levels have changed in countries as they industrialise.

Social and political systems

Differences in the human capital of a country are the result of social systems and values, particularly in education. The distribution of skills reflects differences in the level of investment in basic school education, in vocational training, and in universities. What is deemed to be required knowledge may vary, and in some countries is strongly influenced by the state, sometimes because of political ideology. The predominant learning style influences attitudes. Teaching may be student-centred and democratic, with a strong encouragement to students to participate, to experiment and to innovate. Alternatively, the predominant style may be teacher-centred and directive, in which students are more passive and success is judged on the ability to learn the orthodox views (Tayeb, 2003: 19). Issues such as female participation in the workforce, investment in different levels of education and training, and the learning styles that are adopted, are the consequences of different value systems, and are part of the culture of the social group. These issues are explored more fully in Chapters 7 and 14.

The resources of a state include the systems that have evolved over time to exploit and develop the physical and human resources. The social and political systems of a society govern how people live together, and they include both informal and formal regulation. Socialisation and education create the values, beliefs and customs that shape people's behaviour towards each other, as well as the terms under which they are prepared to accept employment. Social developments and values also affect the political system and distribution of power. Political decisions govern the extent of monopoly, protection from foreign competition, the stability of the economy and workers' rights. Laws, including those governing employment, reflect the balance of power in society, as well as social norms and priorities. National economic policies, based upon interpretations of local and international trends, affect product and labour markets. Wealth, geography, history and education affect the level of available technology, which provides opportunities for, or constraints on, management action, both in relation to task processes and the control of labour.

Employment and the employment practices that shape HRM strategies and policies are affected by these national contextual factors. Because nation states differ in a number of ways, the choices faced by managers in different countries are not identical, even in the same industry sector. Political, economic, social and technological forces impact upon individual organisations, influencing their strategies, structures, systems, and shared values. While it is possible to discuss norms of employment practice, it also has to be recognised that there is uniqueness to employment relationships in all organisations. The context of employment is complex, multilayered, and interwoven.

Although a number of contextual factors affect employment and how it is managed, it can be argued that national culture has to be understood first. Cultural values and assumptions shape the way political and business systems have developed and also impact on aspects of the labour market. If all human behaviour is conceived of as culture-affected, then within the organisation this will include both worker behaviour and management practice. It is important therefore to understand the impact of culture differences on the ways that people behave in organisations. This will be explored in the next section.

Discussion questions

1   Compare the natural and human resources of two different countries with which you are familiar. What might be the economic and social consequences of these differences?

2   How does culture affect the learning of international students studying in a different country?

3   What are the external and internal factors that determine employment relations in a multinational company originating in the UK?

3 A WORLD OF CULTURES

Understanding culture

Culture is widely used to explain differences between human groups, despite the fact that it has no universally agreed definition. It is important to recognise that culture is an attribute of a social group. Hofstede (2001: 2) distinguishes three levels of mental programming in individuals. There is the universal level of *human nature,* the needs and feelings that are found in all human beings. How needs are met and how feelings are expressed are affected by *culture,* which is a characteristic of a group. Finally, there is *personality*, which is specific to an individual. When dealing with intercultural situations, it is important not to confuse personality and culture (Harris *et al*, 2003: 30).

The most obvious way to distinguish social groups from one another is by their observable patterns of behaviour. However, the same behaviour can be used to convey different messages. If a subordinate looks the boss full in the face, is she being open and honest, or is she being aggressive? If a dinner guest eats everything on the plate, does this show he is satisfied with the meal, or that he has not had enough? To understand the observable behaviour, we must know how it is interpreted in the culture. Hofstede (2001) brings this out in his definition of culture as 'the collective programming of the mind which distinguishes the members of one group or category of people from another' (2001: 9).

Schein (1985, 1989) proposed a culture model in three layers:

- artefacts and behaviour
- beliefs and values
- basic assumptions.

Values and basic assumptions are differentiated because the former are open to debate whereas the latter are not. Schein defines culture as 'the assumptions which lie behind the values and which determine the behaviour patterns', or as:

> **'a set of basic assumptions – shared solutions to universal problems of external adaptation (how to survive) and internal integration (how to stay together) – which have evolved over time and are handed down from one generation to the next ... as the correct way to perceive, think about and feel in relation to those problems.'**

A complete definition and understanding of culture has to be broad enough to encompass both what is observable and what is going on in people's minds. Although behaviour cannot be fully understood without reference to the meaning given by underlying beliefs and values, it is equally true that cultural differences only become significant as they are manifest in different behaviour patterns and tangible objects. Underlying assumptions are abstractions until realised in social action. Within a culture the routines of social interaction are taken for granted as people behave in ways they have learned through socialisation, generally without question.

Cultural differences can be understood, then, as the result of different responses to the problems of external adaptation and internal integration. Culture is the consequence of choices. Cultural researchers have therefore conceptualised and measured differences on the basis of dimensions that represent the dilemmas of human existence. The elements of culture have been formed from the way societies have responded to basic questions of how we see ourselves, how we relate to the environment, how we relate to each other, and how we relate to time (Schneider and Barsoux, 2003).

The influence of Hofstede

The studies by Hofstede (2001) have become the best known and most widely quoted work on cultural differences within the management literature, and will feature widely in a number of the subsequent chapters, alongside the work of Schein which is used to explore corporate culture in Chapter 5. Hofstede's original research measured values and beliefs among employees of IBM in more than 40 countries. Through factor analysis of the results of a questionnaire, four independent dimensions were identified which explained the major part of differences between national groups. Each country was given a score on each dimension, based on responses to particular questions in the survey. The dimensions were labelled, and can be described, as follows.

Power distance is the extent to which the less powerful members of organisations and institutions accept and expect that power is distributed unequally. In high power distance countries, such as Malaysia and Panama, there is a tendency towards hierarchical organisations and autocratic leadership. Organisations in low power distance countries – for example, Israel and Austria – generally have flatter structures and more democratic management.

Uncertainty avoidance relates to the extent to which members of a society feel uncomfortable in unstructured situations and try to avoid ambiguity. Organisations in high uncertainty avoidance countries – such as Greece and Portugal – deal with uncertainty through strong bureaucracies, rules, and career stability. Jamaica and Singapore, on the other hand, scored low on the uncertainty avoidance index, and organisations in those cultures are likely to have more flexible structures and encourage a greater diversification of views.

Individualism is the opposite of *collectivism*, and is the degree to which people are expected to look after themselves rather than identify with a larger group such as the extended family. In highly individualist cultures – for example, the USA and Australia – people care primarily for themselves and their immediate family, and the emphasis is on personal achievement. In low individualism countries such as Ecuador and Guatemala, people are integrated into larger cohesive groups that offer long-term continuity based on loyalty and fitting in harmoniously.

Masculinity is the opposite of *femininity*, and refers to the distribution of emotional roles between the genders. It opposes 'tough' masculine virtues of assertiveness and material reward with 'tender' feminine virtues of caring and work–life balance. Japan and Austria had high scores, and Norway and Sweden low scores, on this dimension.

Participants from the same country were not uniform in their beliefs, but the scores represented the overall picture for that society. Each of Hofstede's (2001) dimensions therefore cannot be fully understood in isolation but are more useful when considered in combination (see for example Hoecklin, 1994). Malaysia's high power distance and low uncertainty avoidance scores are thus associated with a highly familial approach within organisation structures and domestic units, and standardised work processes. Sweden's low power distance and low uncertainty avoidance scores are associated with control processes of mutual adjustment that are based on informal communication and clearly specified outcomes.

Subsequently, Hofstede undertook further research in collaboration with Bond, and added a fifth dimension, *long-term orientation/short-term orientation*, in which a high score indicated that value was placed on perseverance, recognition of status and thrift.

Hofstede supported his research findings by demonstrating how his culture dimensions related to the common problems of humanity that have been discussed by anthropologists and cross-cultural psychologists. He postulated causal relationships between cultural values and geography, political structures and heritage, climate and religion. Because culture is deep-rooted in society, Hofstede felt it was a stable phenomenon that would only change slowly, if at all. He related the value dimensions to practice, in terms of organisational structures, management behaviour, and employment practices. His message is that the assumptions underpinning these processes vary between cultures, and so there are no universal solutions to organisation and management problems.

Hofstede's research has been praised and criticised (Sondergaard, 1994; Cray and Mallory, 1998). The concentration of the original research on employees of one multinational meant that factors such as task, technology and corporate culture were controlled, leaving only the difference of nationality. The sample size was impressive. However, a group of IBM employees is not necessarily a representative sample of the population as a whole. Eastern European countries and many less developed nations were not included in the original survey because IBM did not have employees everywhere. The majority of replications of the research support Hofstede's dimensions (Guirdham, 2005: 52), although a common conclusion is that their applicability is affected by the presence of other levels of culture. Overall, despite some doubts about the original method and data, the dimensions seem to appeal both to managers and researchers as a useful way of making sense of national cultural differences. Cultural factors are also important influences on the socialisation of managers and employees, and on the assumptions that shape managerial, employee and customer values, behavioural norms and customs. The relationship between culture and HRM is developed in detail in Chapter 5, and cultural implications are considered in all the book's chapters in relation to a range of HRM activities and issues.

The impact of cultural differences

Anglo-Saxon culture assumes that nature can and should be controlled, tends to value doing over being, and regards human nature as basically sinful. Managers stress their right to manage employment, but employee groups and union representatives also seek control over work organisation and the distribution of the benefits of performance improvement. Managers generally believe that their workers are not to be trusted, and therefore seek to control employees through supervision and the formalisation of workplace discipline. Management-union agreements are written down, and may be regarded as settled and binding only when signed.

An alternative view, found more strongly in some Asian cultures, is to value harmony with nature, to go with the flow of life and adapt to it. Society still seeks improvement, but personal respect is traditionally based more on age and character than on achievement. Relationships are important, and disciplinary action or performance correction at work has to be done so that individuals do not lose face. At home people are part of extended families which are characterised by networking and mutual obligations, and work relationships are treated in the same way. Managing employment in Nigeria reflects many of these facets (Case study 1).

CASE STUDY 1

EMPLOYMENT IN A GLOBAL CONTEXT: MANAGING EMPLOYMENT IN NIGERIA

The more that management practices are meaningful within the Nigerian workers' cultural and environmental contexts, the stronger their identification with the organisation. Nigeria's cultural characteristics suggest that:

1   employees' tendencies reflect a collectivist orientation which entails conformity and identification with an in-group, which includes the organisation, the extended family and other work and non-work affiliations

2   employees' tendencies are consistent with a high power distance culture, and great respect is shown to managers by employees

3   employees expect organisations and managers to be responsible for their welfare, providing nurturing relationships by instituting policies and practices that ensure quality of life

4   employees need guidelines in order to execute job demands.

Almost 300 human resource managers, supervisors or other personnel employed in different organisations in three major cities in Nigeria were surveyed in 2002. The respondents reported that they or their departments perform the following employment management functions: recruitment and selection (67%), training and development (78%), performance appraisal (73%), compensation (50%), termination or firing (57%) and other employment tasks. Additional activities performed by the respondents or their departments include staff welfare services, union and community matters, health and safety, labour relations, consultation, etc.

Specific inquiry into the activities respondents performed on a typical day reveals a wide spectrum, ranging from specifics to general and/or administrative responsibilities, which reflects almost every aspect of managing people. Examples of responses include:

■   manpower planning and selecting the right people, training, developing and motivating employees; formulating manpower policy, managing financial incentives for the organisation, like wages, salary and other fringe benefits

■   checking the manning of various departments; seeing to the proper clothing of staff; attending to the applicants; seeing to the effectiveness of the security departments; passing information from management to all members of staff

■   marking the attendance register daily.

The personnel managers surveyed identified the challenges facing them in their jobs as: skill shortages, bribery and corruption, government regulations, technology, competitive position, nepotism, restructuring, rapid change and legislation. Other challenges were the lack of infrastructure – eg electricity, transportation, road and communication facilities – motivation, poor work attitude, the lack of recognition, and the quota system (regulations to recruit locals). Some of the main challenges identified seem to be job- or company-specific and range from inadequate resources with respect to funds and equipment to the need for autonomy in executing their duties.

Many of the personnel managers surveyed indicated that they took responsibility for employee welfare, which is consistent with the traditional system of organisation in which the organisation should be responsible for the employee's welfare. For example, employees expect from their employers car advances, housing, in some cases subsidised cafeteria and transportation, and salary advances in times of need, vacation pay, a company doctor, a company car, pension and gratuity. Personnel managers also had to monitor employees closely with respect to attendance and dress code.

Source: adapted from Anakwe (2002)

Case study tasks

1. In the African system of work organisation, the head of the group is regarded as the father and is expected to provide for the group members. How does this appear to affect the role of managers in Nigeria?

2. How might bribery, corruption and nepotism affect the recruitment of new employees?

3. What challenges might face the HR function of a MNC intending to set up business in Nigeria which intends to implement its own (western) HR practices?

Cultural values can be seen reflected in the ways that employment practices and institutions have developed in different countries, as well as the ways in which employment is managed within organisations. This can be illustrated by looking at employment relationships in the UK, Germany, France and Sweden, using Hofstede's cultural value dimensions described above.

The UK is low on power distance (egalitarian rather than hierarchical) and uncertainty avoidance (uncertainty is tolerated), and these values are consistent with a long national history of parliamentary sovereignty and the absence of a written constitution. In employment, national institutions have tended to have a weak influence on employment, much of the focus of activity being at the level of the workplace. Informal understandings are as important as formal collective agreements. Individualism is a stronger value than collectivism, and unions often struggle to maintain collective action. The combination of individualism and the residual Christian belief that all people are sinners may explain why managers generally stress the need for workplace control through supervision and disciplinary rules.

Germany shares the values of individualism, relative egalitarianism, and the Protestant Christian ethic. However, German people are higher on Hofstede's uncertainty avoidance dimension. As a result, the formalised aspects of employment relationships are more important in Germany than in the UK. Organisations tend to adhere strictly to rules, including legal duties. Forms of address are more formal than in the UK.

France is higher on power distance than the UK or Germany, and this is reflected in the importance that is placed on hierarchy. There is a high degree of centralisation in government, and unions have been more powerful at national level than might be expected from the size of their active membership.

Sweden is the lowest-ranked country on Hofstede's masculinity dimension, and is also low on power distance. It is therefore not surprising that employment relationships are informal and egalitarian, and that support for women in employment has been stronger for longer than in most European countries. Case studies of IKEA (Grol *et al*, 1998; Jackson, 2002) show how the national and corporate cultures of a Swedish organisation impact on operations in other countries. Problems were encountered in Germany, France and the USA because of differences in cultural values and the 'Swedishness' of organisational practices.

The conclusion that may be drawn from this brief exploration of national differences is that the employment practices of a firm are largely embedded in a national context. However, there are grounds for arguing that cultural and other differences are not preventing at least some cross-national convergence of practice, and we turn to that proposition in the next section.

Discussion questions

1 Think of the first time you visited a particular foreign country. What were the things you noticed that were different?

2 Is the UK culturally nearer to France or the USA? Why?

3 How might the culture dimensions of power distance and uncertainty avoidance affect employment practices and norms?

4 GLOBALISATION AND MANAGEMENT CONVERGENCE

Globalisation and internationalisation

Although we live in a political world of nation states, our societies have always been shaped by interaction with people from other places. However, until fairly recently, relatively few people had direct experience of other cultures, and the absorption of ideas from elsewhere was generally slow. This has changed in the last century, as developments in communications and transport mean that people around the world are more aware of what is happening outside their own country than would have been the case a generation ago. In a sense our perceived world has become larger because technology has made it seem smaller.

The movement towards greater worldwide integration of economic and political activities is referred to as globalisation. Globalisation is a wide-ranging phenomenon that impacts on our lives in a variety of ways. Its underlying theme is our interconnectedness, and the message is that in the global village, events in one part of the planet have ripple effects on the rest of the world.

In relation to the economy, a straightforward definition of globalisation is found in Hill (2005):

'Globalisation refers to the shift towards a more integrated and interdependent world economy. Globalisation has two main components: the globalisation of markets and the globalisation of production.'

The term *internationalisation* is generally taken to refer to the simple extension of economic activities across national boundaries, whereas *globalisation* involves the greater integration of internationally dispersed activities (Dicken, 2003).

A force for good or evil?
Globalisation is an economic phenomenon, but there are social and political consequences of the greater integration of the world economy. Government leaders generally see globalisation as positive, but there is a substantial body of opinion that is not so sure. Since the meeting of the World Trade Association in Seattle in 1999, almost all gatherings of government leaders, or

the inter-governmental agencies that manage the world economy, have been accompanied by protests. In 2005 a consortium of development agencies mounted a campaign in the UK and elsewhere to Make Poverty History. The governments of the richest nations, and the world trade agencies, are accused of managing the world economy in the interests of the developed world, and to the neglect of the poorer nations.

The anti-globalisation protestors frequently see multinationals as part of the problem, and international firms have found themselves under pressure to defend their record on a range of issues that include environmental pollution and employment in third-world countries. In many countries working people are suspicious of the power of multinationals to move jobs to suit corporate rather than local interests.

Economies of scale

De Witt and Meyer (1998) describe the effect of global convergence on MNCs. Partly as a result of worldwide mass communication there is a growing international similarity in product demand that will allow firms to reap global-scale economies through standardisation. Greater standardisation will, in turn, facilitate the international integration of operations and encourage the pursuit of further economies through the centralisation of production at fewer locations. Globalising companies seek global suppliers and are thus both a consequence and a cause of global convergence. Firms operating in such global markets realise that they must be able to coordinate their strategy and activities across nations. The demands of standardisation, centralisation, and strategic alignment are best met by a global firm with a strong centre, rather than by a multidomestic firm with fairly autonomous national subsidiaries.

For some industrial products, markets have become global because the customers are themselves international players who are building supply chains that cross national boundaries. Improvements to transport and communications technology have made such international sourcing both possible and cost-effective. The drive to remove trade barriers is opening markets, increasing competition, and acting as a spur to finding the most efficient ways of working. Many firms are part of a common competitive environment, and, in pursuit of economy, source globally and move production to low-wage labour markets.

Implications for HRM

A key issue in international management is whether the globalisation of markets and supply chains is also facilitating and encouraging a worldwide convergence of management practices and HRM. Competitive pressures for efficiency lead both to improvements in processes and to the worldwide adoption of those methods that are deemed the most effective. There is a growing bank of global information available to the manager as a customer for effective ways of organising the business. Managers in both the developing and industrialised nations have access to knowledge of how others do things, and to current notions of best practice. Knowledge is disseminated in a variety of ways including through books, conferences, the Internet, by management students who have studied in foreign countries, by consultants and, of course, by multinationals.

UK managers have frequently been encouraged to look abroad for inspiration. At different times the models for good employment management practices have been found in the USA, Germany, Sweden and Japan. This is in spite of the undoubted differences that there are between the UK and these other countries in regard to social and business systems. Although the differences are of course recognised, there is a general presumption that management practices are transferable, and that cross-national learning is possible. International benchmarking is therefore another contributor to convergence as managers seek new approaches that will solve problems or bring improved effectiveness.

Regionalisation

One region where there are particular reasons to expect some convergence of employment practices is the EU. The EU is a large single market, but it has had a social dimension since the original Treaty of Rome in 1957, and social policy enacted through EU Directives has grown in importance since the Maastricht Treaty was signed in 1991 (see Chapter 11). This included a social protocol, which set the agenda for employment policy. A crucial change at that time was the introduction of qualified majority voting on certain issues where before measures could be passed only if agreed unanimously by all member states. Employment issues are now divided between those such as health and safety and equal opportunity, which can be introduced through a qualified majority, and those such as the termination of employment and the collective representation of workers, which require unanimity. The enlargement of the EU to 25 member states in 2004 created an expectation that majority voting would have to be extended, although this has not yet happened because of the collapse of the attempt to introduce a new EU Constitutional Treaty.

The European Commission is required to promote dialogue between the social partners – that is, the representatives at the European level of management (employers' associations) and labour (unions). The Social Protocol allows for agreements to be negotiated by the social partners, and the representatives have agreed framework agreements on parental leave and on rights for part-time workers that have been brought into law through EU Directives. The *Work Programme of the European Social Partners 2006–2008*, published in March 2006, continues the process of involving the partners in the development of employment strategy.

The Treaty of Rome provided for the free movement of labour, and the building of the single European market has been accompanied by measures designed to make it a reality. Labour representatives and politicians in some countries have been concerned about the possibility of 'social dumping' by which firms move jobs from high to low labour cost countries. Following the latest EU enlargement in 2004, there is also a concern about the flow of qualified people from the poorer East to the richer West. One measure that has been seen as a counter to the fear of social dumping (Marginson and Sisson, 1998) is the European Works Council Directive. This requires MNCs with at least 1,000 employees and with at least 150 employees in two or more member countries to establish a European Works Council (EWC) if requested by employees, or on the initiative of management. EWCs are still relatively young, and their operation is affected by country of origin, country of location, and other company-specific factors (Hall *et al*, 2003). In some firms EWC agreements are formal and symbolic in nature, but others give the EWC a potentially active role (Carley and Marginson, 2000; O'Hagan, 2002; see also Chapter 10 below).

Social policy has frequently been controversial within the EU, and so the introduction of new measures is often slow. Nevertheless, European organisations now have to be concerned with policy proposals emanating from Brussels, and there is an argument for suggesting that over time the combination of EU social policy and the development of EWCs will promote some convergence of employment practices. However, Case study 2 – which shows that the UK-based subsidiaries of German MNCs adopt very different policies from indigenous UK firms – is a reminder that country-of-origin is a powerful influence that means there is unlikely to be complete convergence in Europe around a common set of practices.

CASE STUDY 2

EMPLOYMENT IN A GLOBAL CONTEXT: SUBSIDIARIES OF GERMAN MNCS IN THE UK

Companies in Germany are subject to a relatively high degree of regulation in the area of employment relations. For instance, legislation allows employees in such companies to ask for a works council to be set up within their establishment. The powers of these works councils depend upon the nature of the decision to be taken. Employment relations in large companies are characterised by a collectivist approach in other ways, too. Many large firms are members of sector-based employers' associations; these associations negotiate with unions over wage rates and general working conditions. The agreements that are reached are legally binding on the member companies of the employers' association. Unions and independent workers' representatives therefore play a more pronounced role in Germany than they do in Anglo-Saxon countries.

It is against this backdrop that researchers have shown considerable interest in the employment relations adopted by German MNCs in more deregulated settings. German MNCs operating in, for instance, the UK may be keen to distance themselves from those collectivist practices that are common in Germany, if those practices are thought to have a detrimental impact on the performance of companies.

At first glance, evidence would appear to suggest that this expectation is correct. For example, in a representative sample that covered both German MNCs operating in the UK and indigenous UK companies it was found that the UK subsidiaries of German MNCs were significantly less likely to adopt a collective approach to employee relations, which relied solely on unions as voice mechanisms, than indigenous UK firms. This may indicate that German MNCs that operate in the UK seek to avoid unions.

Moreover, other evidence from the same survey indicates that UK-based subsidiaries of German MNCs are more likely than indigenous UK companies to use direct involvement mechanisms such as attitude surveys, problem-solving groups, quality circles, newsletters, and team briefings in their management of employee relations. This evidence would therefore appear to support the notion that German MNCs seek to sideline unions where they can.

However, other evidence from the same survey indicates that this is far from the case. UK-based subsidiaries of German MNCs are significantly more likely than indigenous UK companies to adopt a partnership approach to employee relations; that is, such subsidiaries often adopt an approach to employment relations that combines – in a complementary way – collective voice channels, such as unions, with mechanisms that allow employees to voice their concerns directly.

The evidence, therefore, suggests that the UK-based subsidiaries of German MNCs are more likely than indigenous UK firms to adopt a more inclusive approach to employment relations; such an approach is likely to be characterised by a more cooperative and less confrontational attitude towards employees and their (union) representatives. Such an approach to employment relations is, obviously, based on the idea that the skills and knowledge of employees can be an important source of comparative advantage for companies.

Reference: Tüselmann, H.-J., McDonald, F. and Thorpe, R. (2006), 'The emerging approach to employee relations in German overseas affiliates: a role model for international operation?', in *Journal of World Business*, 41 (1): 66–80.

Case study tasks

1   Does the evidence above suggest that employment practices in MNCs are likely to converge?

2   How easily have the employment polices of German companies been transferred to the UK? Would it have been possible for such companies to replicate all of the collectivist employment practices that are common in Germany in the UK?

3   Is the partnership approach adopted by many UK-based subsidiaries of German MNCs in the UK likely to lead to improved establishment performance?

Discussion questions

1   Does convergence of marketing and production practices necessarily mean that there will be convergence of employment practices?

2   Does an MNC need to have a definite ethical policy in relation to the employment of people in the third world?

3   The EU Lisbon strategy aims to turn Europe into 'the most competitive knowledge-based economy in the world, capable of sustainable economic growth, with more and better jobs and greater social cohesion'. How might employment programmes support this strategy?

5 MULTINATIONALS AND EMPLOYMENT

Strategic choice

A simple model of strategic choice for multinationals is to pursue either a multidomestic or a global strategy (Evans and Lorange, 1989; Porter, 1990). In the former, national subsidiaries have a great deal of autonomy to respond to local needs and norms, and so strategies and policies are differentiated. In the latter, strategy and policies are determined globally and are therefore integrated across the worldwide organisation. The approach taken may vary between different functional areas or product divisions, although in general it is to be expected that functional strategies will be internally consistent. In some organisations integration takes place at regional rather than international level. One of the impacts of globalisation has been to encourage established multinationals to move towards greater global harmonisation of strategy and management policies (Kidger, 2002).

Perlmutter (1969) suggested that multinationals go through three stages of relationship with subsidiaries:

1   The first stage is ethnocentric in which management believes that home country practice is generally superior.

2   The second stage is polycentric in which management accepts that practice in subsidiaries should be based on local norms.

3   However, a polycentric relationship often leads to too much differentiation on a country basis, and so in the *geocentric* stage, management in corporate headquarters and local subsidiaries collaborate to establish global best practice in the interest of the whole organisation.

Even if management practice in a multinational evolves towards integration, there is generally a 'country-of-origin' effect since almost all MNCs begin operations in a particular location and have one corporate headquarters. When an MNC enters a new country, it can introduce its own corporate or international employment and HRM policies, or adopt local employment management norms. Many commentators argue that the local or 'host country' effect is stronger than the 'country-of-origin' effect in relation to HRM polices and practices. Empirical evidence has tended to support this in the past, but there are counter-arguments related to globalisation and developments in the EU (O'Hagan *et al*, 2005), which we have looked at in the previous sections. See Chapter 9 for a discussion of this issue in relation to pay and reward.

Strategic influences

What we intend to focus on in this section are the factors that influence the strategy and management of employment polices and practices within MNCs, including the extent to which policy in foreign subsidiaries is likely to be the same as in the home country. In general, companies acquire or start up a foreign subsidiary in order to gain resources, markets, or efficiencies. They bring resources or activities into the organisation structure if this is more reliable or efficient than relying on market transactions. Once started on this track, additional foreign investment generally adds to the scope for efficiencies, provided that the organisation can manage the complexity.

Labour resources in particular may be sought in other countries because of their lower cost or expertise. Historically, labour resources were often acquired by encouraging immigration, but today firms in the developed world are establishing both manufacturing and service subsidiaries in other countries where suitable labour is cheaper.

Efficiency-seekers utilise economies of scale and scope, and manage operations across national boundaries in order to achieve the most productive use of resources. Efficiency is linked to resource-seeking and to the sharing of process know-how within the organisation. Strategic asset-seekers invest in foreign countries in order to secure resources that are of strategic importance, which may include technological or administrative know-how.

Strategic opportunities

As multinationals become established in a number of countries they are able to exploit the resource capabilities of different locations. Management functions or operations can be located where cost or other factors are particularly favourable (Ghosal, 1987), and the ability to shift investment and resources can become an important aspect of multinational capability. Although labour markets are not the only consideration when deciding work location, companies will consider switching both semi-skilled production and certain kinds of professional activities to countries with low labour costs if they can do so without jeopardising required labour quality. There are obvious social consequences of this for developed nations where employers bear a significant part of social security costs, and it is a factor that can make inward investment a double-edged sword. Sugden (1991) argues that firms become multi-nationals in order to dominate labour markets as well as product markets, and it is clear that MNCs use the threat (implied if not actual) of switching production to push through productivity improvements or labour cost reductions (Sisson, 2006).

Labour market considerations include employment laws and institutional frameworks, particularly where these impact on the ease with which change can be implemented. Even if the employment relations climate is not the main reason for choosing a country location, companies are likely to accept the local norms if this is to their advantage. This is illustrated by Case study 3 at the end of this chapter.

Governments compete for foreign investment, and this may affect the way the state regulates labour markets. The UK government, for example, advocates a comparatively light degree of labour market regulation as an incentive to foreign inward investment. Multinationals therefore use their economic power to lobby government in pursuit of favourable employment regulation, and may do this on their own account or by becoming active members of local employers' associations.

Consistency and differentiation

If labour market differences encourage multinationals to adopt a multidomestic approach to employment management, there are other factors that promote a more global approach. The need for consistency in product quality and delivery can lead companies to establish consistent management practices where it is thought that these are necessary to achieving marketing and operational objectives. Many Japanese manufacturers have pursued a global strategy in relation to manufacturing, and so have introduced Japanese work practices in other countries. In support of this, they have often used employment practices that emulate practices in their home operations. Service companies in the fast food and leisure industries want customers to have the same quality experience whatever the country, and standardisation of operating standards may be accompanied by attempted standardisation of employment relations.

Global strategies may also be linked to the presence of a strong corporate culture, under which corporate values and practices are promoted as the 'way we do things round here' (Deal and Kennedy, 1980). Corporate culture (discussed more fully in Chapter 5) may be understood as the espoused values and expectations of the dominant management group (Linstead and Grafton Small, 1992). It is generally in line with the national cultural values of the group, although there are exceptions to this. Sometimes the corporate culture owes much to the influence of a founder or successful chief executive. The IKEA case study (Jackson, 2002) to which we have already referred is a good example of the way these elements link together. As the company internationalised, it adapted its management style to fit the cultural and employment norms of other countries, but was able to do this without losing the IKEA core employment relations values.

Employment management may also be affected by whether a company moves into a foreign country by acquisition or start-up of a new organisation. If a local company has been bought, it is usual that the existing approach to managing employment is retained, at least for an initial period. In a start-up situation management may have more choices, and some multinationals have a definite corporate employment philosophy that they want to impose, subject to any adaptation needed to comply with local employment laws or cultural values.

Finally, it should be noted that companies do not necessarily treat all groups of employees in the same way. In many multinationals there is an international cadre of managers whose employment conditions and development are coordinated globally, whereas the treatment of the majority of staff is determined locally. In some organisations design or research staff are looked upon as a global resource. As we have already suggested, both manufacturing and service companies may ensure cross-national similarity in some aspects of the employment of production workers where this supports the standardisation of operating methods and quality.

Standardisation and differentiation

Standardisation may relate to management style and to employment policies. Management style is an aspect of corporate culture, and as we have seen, there can be problems in taking a management culture developed in the country of origin and applying it elsewhere. Nevertheless, multinationals do promote a global management style where it is a reflection of strong corporate values and is seen as an organisational capability that gives competitive advantage. Similarly, employment policies that relate to the organisation of work and the development of human resources may be standardised as far as possible in the interest of consistent high performance throughout the organisation. Such terms of employment as wage rates, holidays, benefits or hours of work are normally determined locally, although even here there may be some guiding international principles that reflect corporate employment values (see Chapter 9 for a fuller discussion).

Even if the MNC has a differentiated strategy in regard to the determination of rewards and conditions, it does not necessarily mean there is no corporate coordination or influence. Managers of subsidiaries, whether they are locals or expatriates, have to secure corporate agreement for strategic and operational plans, and sometimes for key policies. Corporate managers can influence what happens by their questions and comments, by withholding agreement to local initiatives, and by decisions on resource allocation.

A corporate or regional HR function may coordinate employment relations policies across subsidiaries. Where policy is differentiated, this may be limited to being kept informed about what is going on, with the expectation that the corporate office will only interfere on an exceptional basis. Where policy is integrated, the corporate office is likely to organise regular meetings of HR staff, to use internal benchmarking to facilitate convergence of best practice, and to develop international policies where this is thought to be appropriate.

Discussion questions

1 What are the advantages and disadvantages for a UK-based MNC of locating a call centre in India?

2 How can an MNC use the possibility of switching operations to another country as a way of putting pressure on employees and national governments?

3 What would be the main priorities for an international employment relations manager in an MNC with a strategy of global integration?

CONCLUSIONS AND FUTURE ISSUES

The development of employment management around the world has been affected by a range of national contextual factors. Within organisations there are a variety of formal and informal aspects to the relationship between employer and workpeople. It is important to business success that the employment relationship is managed well, since the commitment of workers to the organisation may be lost if they feel they are being exploited and treated badly.

In general, the regulation of employment still takes place at national level, although there is some international regulation, especially within the EU. However, there are changes occurring through globalisation and worldwide communication that are encouraging convergence in management practice. We can expect this trend to progress, but not necessarily to impact uniformly on the ways in which managers deal with employees and trade unions. The range of national differences will probably ensure that the way in which people are managed across the world will never be completely uniform, but it is likely that we will see a growing willingness by management to learn from the experiences of others in different cultures and situations.

Multinational companies are at the centre of these developments, and the challenge for them is to develop and maintain a clear strategy that will enable them to succeed within the complex and changing world of international employment and employment relationships.

CASE STUDY 3

EMPLOYMENT IN A GLOBAL CONTEXT: SUBSIDIARIES OF US MNCS IN GERMANY

Employment relations in the USA are often characterised by entrenched anti-unionism, generally weak trade unions, and sophisticated employment policies, associated with best practice in the literature on human resource management, which are designed to gain the commitment of employees to the company's goals. In short, US companies have tended to prefer to implement their own employment policies that are free from outside interference – whether in the form of government regulation or unions. Many US companies therefore believe that there is no need for such interference, because managers should implement employment policies that ensure their employees' well-being.

The ways in which US MNCs have to adapt to employment relations in other countries have been of interest to researchers. This interest is even keener when US MNCs operate in relatively highly regulated business systems, such as Germany. Given US companies' predilection for operating in a union-free environment in which managers prefer to communicate directly with workers, it can be expected that US MNCs are likely to be reluctant to see strong forms of independent employee representation and involvement established. This reluctance is even likely to come to the fore in countries such as Germany that have laws allowing works councils – which are a strong form of employee participation – to be set up in most companies. This is, indeed, the case. As a senior HR manager in a US company producing consumer goods in Germany noted (Muller-Camen *et al*, 2004: 19):

'**Our corporate position is that we believe it's better for the company and better for employees to be able to deal directly [with one another].**'

This view has been echoed by managers in other US MNCs with subsidiaries in Germany. For instance, a HR manager in a German-based subsidiary of a US MNC (cited in Muller-Camen *et al*, 2004: 19) argued that:

'We have [']best place to work['] initiatives. We strive to be an employer who is attractive [so] that consultants want to join us and stay with us. And that is more than any works council could offer. When the company, all the HR people and all the senior managers are daily putting a lot of effort into finding ways to make this an attractive place to work, then they are doing exactly the same as what a works council would do.'

This quotation also highlights a point made above: US managers, even those in subsidiaries abroad, are likely to see the establishment of strong forms of independent employee representation as superfluous, because managers should be pursuing policies that make the company an attractive place to work. This sentiment was echoed in the comment by a senior HR manager at the headquarters of a company that manufactured consumer and professional products. However, in that company, local traditions were also respected (cited in Muller-Camen *et al*, 2004: 19):

'Our corporate position is that we believe it's better for the company and better for employees to be able to deal directly. So you take that as an overall position. Given that, we recognise that in a lot of countries in the world the tradition is to have some other sort of representation for employees.'

However, some managers in German-based subsidiaries of US MNCs saw the establishment of works councils as a failure of their own policies. In the words of a member of a works council in a US company in Germany (cited in Muller-Camen *et al*, 2004: 19), the initial view of management was that 'if a works council [was] set up, then management had failed in the eyes of the Americans – failed, meaning that was the end of your career'. Similarly, a HR manager in the German subsidiary of a US logistics company (cited in Muller-Camen *et al*, 2004: 20) noted that:

'Works councils are set up if employees want them, if they hope for some advantages by having a works council. If communication between management and employees is good, which is fundamental, there are usually no advantages. Normally, the reason why employees want to set up works councils is because of management mistakes. If a works council is set up, we must ask ourselves what we have done wrong. We can't prevent them. But it is better to be aware of problems

before things get that far and to try to solve them through communication.'

Despite these initial views of works councils amongst managers in subsidiaries of US MNCs in Germany, some of these managers have adapted to the institutional constraints on them, and the presence of a works council is no longer seen as a signal to management that their policies have failed. Indeed, some managers in the German subsidiaries of US MNCs now view works councils as a means by which to improve firm performance. As one member of the works council in the German subsidiary of a US logistics company noted (Muller-Camen *et al*, 2004: 20):

'[The company] has now realised the advantages of having a works council, at least in our case. In the past, the attitude was that anyone who criticised [the company] was inherently bad. Now they have realised that criticism can be positive and that people are willing to contribute.'

In short, although the traditions of employee relations in the USA may make managers of US MNCs who operate in a more highly regulated setting reluctant to see the establishment of independent employee representation mechanisms, some of these managers have been able to adapt to these more highly regulated settings and have learned how to use such mechanisms to the company's advantage.

Reference: Muller-Camen, M., Tempel, A., Almond, P., Edwards, A., Ferner, A., Peters, R. and Wächter, H. (2004), *Human Resource Management of US Multinationals in Germany and the UK*, Report for the Anglo-German Foundation for the Study of Industrial Society, London: AGF, available at: http://www.agf.org.uk/pubs/pdfs/1292web.pdf, accessed 25 January 2006.

Case study tasks

1   Would US MNCs that operate in Germany have been able to resist the establishment of works councils?

2   Once a works council has been established within a workplace, should managers seek to sideline it by communicating directly with employees?

3   What advantages might a works council have over forms of direct voice?

REFERENCES

Anakwe U. P. (2002) 'Human resource management practices in Nigeria: challenges and insights', *International Journal of Human Resource Management*, Vol. 13, No. 7: 1042–59.

Carley M. and Marginson P. (2000) *Negotiating European Works Councils*. Dublin: European Foundation for the Improvement of Living and Working Conditions.

Cray D. and Mallory G. R. (1998) *Making Sense of Managing Culture*. London: International Thomson.

Deal T. and Kennedy A. cf. 29 (1980) *Corporate Cultures: The rites and rituals of corporate life*. London: Penguin.

De Wit B. and Meyer R. cf. 24 (1998) *Strategy: Process, content, context* (3rd edition). London: Thomson.

Dicken P. (2003) *Global Shift* (4th edition). London: Sage.

Evans P. and Lorange P. (1989) 'The two logics behind human resource management', in Evans P., Doz Y. and Laurent A. (eds) *Human Resource Management in International Firms*. London: Macmillan.

Ghosal S. (1987) 'Global strategy: an organising framework', *Strategic Management Journal*, vol. 8: 425–40.

Grol P., Schoch C. and the Centre de Perfectionnement aux Affaires, Paris (1998) 'IKEA: managing cultural diversity', in Oddou G. and Mendenhall M. (eds) *Cases in International Organisational Behaviour*. Oxford: Blackwell.

Guirdham M. (2005) *Communicating across Cultures at Work*. Basingstoke: Palgrave.

Hall M., Hoffman A., Marginson P. and Muller T. (2003) 'National influences on European Works Councils in UK- and US-based companies', *Human Resource Management Journal*, Vol. 13 No. 4: 75–92.

Hancké B. (2000) 'European Works Councils and the motor industry', *European Journal of Industrial Relations*, 6 (1): 35–60.

Harris H., Brewster C. and Sparrow P. (2003) *International Human Resource Management*. London: CIPD.

Hill C. W. L. (2005) *International Business: Competing in the global marketplace* (5th edition). London: McGraw-Hill.

Hoecklin L. (1994) *Managing Cultural Differences*. Harlow: Addison-Wesley Longman.

Hofstede G. (2001) *Culture's Consequences* (2nd edition). London: Sage.

International Confederation of Free Trade Unions (ICFTU) (2000) *A Trade Union Guide to Globalisation*, www.icftu.org

Jackson T. (2002) *International HRM: A cross-cultural approach*. London: Sage.

Kidger P. J. (2002) 'Human resource management responses to global strategy in multinational enterprises', in Debrah Y. A. and Smith I. G. (eds) *Globalisation, Employment and the Workplace*. London: Routledge.

Kobrin S. J. (1997) 'The architecture of globalization: state sovereignty in a networked global economy', in Dunning J. H. (ed) *Governments, Globalisation and International Business*. Oxford: Oxford University Press.

Linstead S. L. and Grafton Small R. G. (1992) 'On reading organisational culture', *Organization Studies*, Vol. 13, No. 3: 331–55.

Marginson P. and Sisson K. (1998) 'European collective bargaining: a virtual prospect?', *Journal of Common Market Studies*, vol. 36, No. 4: 508–28.

Muller-Camen M., Tempel A., Almond P., Edwards A., Ferner A., Peters R. and Wächter H. (2004), *Human Resource Management of US Multinationals in Germany and the UK*, Report for the Anglo-German Foundation for the Study of Industrial Society, London: AGF, available at http://www.agf.org.uk/pubs/pdfs/1292web.pdf, [accessed 25 January 2006].

O'Hagan E. (2002) *Employee Relations in the Periphery of Europe*. Basingstoke: Palgrave Macmillan.

O'Hagan E., Gunnigle P. and Morley M. J. (2005) 'Issues in the management of industrial relations in international firms', in Scullion H. and Linehan M. (eds) *International Human Resource Management: A critical text*. Basingstoke: Palgrave Macmillan.

Perlmutter H. V. (1969) 'The tortuous evolution of the multinational corporation', *Columbia Journal of World Business*, Vol. 4, No. 1: 9–18.

Porter M. E., (1990) *The Competitive Advantage of Nations*. Basingstoke: Macmillan.

Schein E. H. (1985) *Organisational Culture and Leadership*. San Francisco: Jossey Bass.

Schein E. H. (1989) 'Organisational culture: what it is and how to change it', in Evans P., Doz Y. and Laurent A. (eds) *Human Resource Management in International Firms*. London: Macmillan.

Schneider S. and Barsoux J. (2003) *Managing Across Cultures* (2nd edition). Harlow: FT/Prentice Hall.

Sisson, K. (1993) 'In search of HRM', *British Journal of Industrial Relations*, Vol. 31 No. 2: 201–10.

Sisson K. (2006) 'International employee representation – a case of industrial relations systems following the market?', in Edwards T. and Rees C. (eds) *International Human Resource Management*. Harlow: FT/Prentice Hall.

Sondergaard, M. (1994) 'Hofstede's consequences: a study of reviews, citations, and replications', *Organization Studies*, Vol. 15, No. 6: 447–56.

Sugden R. (1991) 'The importance of distributional considerations', in Pitelis C. N. and Sugden R. (eds) *The Nature of the Transnational Firm*. London: Routledge.

Tayeb M. (2003) *International Management: Theories and practices*. Harlow: FT/Prentice Hall.

Tüselmann H.-J., McDonald F. and Thorpe R. (2006), 'The emerging approach to employee relations in German overseas affiliates: a role model for international operation?', in *Journal of World Business*, Vol. 41, No. 1: 66–80.

Human resource management

CHAPTER 3

Rosemary Lucas and Susan Curtis

CHAPTER OBJECTIVES

When you have read this chapter you should be able to:

■ explain the nature and scope of the HR function

■ evaluate and differentiate theoretical approaches to HRM

■ conceptualise comparative and international approaches to HRM and appreciate how they impact upon how HRM is delivered

■ evaluate the status and roles of HR specialists and line managers in different countries.

PURPOSE AND SCOPE

In the context of the themes and concepts introduced in Chapter 2, the purpose of this chapter is to detail how employment is managed through human resource management (HRM). We move beyond western perspectives of strategic HRM and address HRM in comparative and international contexts, thereby setting the scene for the more detailed discussion of individual topics in subsequent chapters. We begin with an overview of the nature and scope of HRM and introduce the concept of strategic HRM. Next we journey through a critical discussion of comparative HRM, beginning with western perspectives of HRM rooted predominantly in American and Anglo-Saxon thought, which includes brief reference to key HRM models. We then discuss in some detail how variations in national HRM practices can be modelled and better understood. In the subsequent section we consider how far the concepts of international and global HRM are meaningful, suggesting that cross-vergent HRM emerges from the interaction of convergent and divergent HRM. We conclude with the management of HRM, looking at the factors that influence the status of the HR function in organisations internationally, the problems and benefits of devolving the function to line managers, the role of information technology (IT) in HRM, and how HR departments function in different countries.

1 THE NATURE AND SCOPE OF HRM

Introducing HRM

'Human resource management is the basis of all management activity, but it is not the basis of all business activity. ... The basis of management is always the same: getting the people

> **of the business to make things happen in a productive way, so that the business prospers and the people thrive.'**
>
> Torrington *et al* (2005: 4)

Taking this a step further, Delery and Shaw (2001) note general agreement that:

■ human capital can be a source of competitive advantage

■ HR practices have the most direct influence on the human capital of the firm

■ the complex nature of HRM systems or practices can enhance the inimitability of the firm.

The importance and controversies of HRM not only surround its possibilities as an internal management tool for achieving better organisational effectiveness and efficiency but also how its potential contribution can be identified and linked to sustainable and improved organisational performance in a wider competitive environment. What the organisation is trying to make happen will be embodied in its vision, mission, values and business strategy. An example of how the people dimension underpins the strategic goals of the P&O Group is shown in the box below.

P&O GROUP: BUSINESS STRATEGY AND THE HUMAN DIMENSION

Business strategy

P&O is a global transport operator. It is one of the world's foremost port companies and one of the UK's leading ferry operators. With the widely recognised house flag and brand name, P&O's businesses are focused on achieving world-class operational and financial performance and on delivering a first-class service to customers.

P&O is committed to focusing its capital on those businesses where it is a market leader and which offer strong growth and value creation opportunities.

Human dimension

Social responsibility ... our activities should be conducted in a way which is economically, environmentally and socially sustainable.

Workplace ... creating and maintaining a working environment in which the capabilities of all employees are developed are core values within P&O ... committed to achieving the highest standards in safety ... senior management are leading this approach ... our global Sharesave Plan offers all eligible employees the opportunity to participate in the values we are creating.

Community ... we have contributed to society through the creation of jobs ... we continue to give priority to requests for help with educational and environmental projects.

Source: P&O Group (2005)

Pinpointing HRM activity

HRM, formerly labelled 'personnel management' or 'personnel administration', is a specialist managerial function, like finance or marketing, and a profession backed by formal qualifications (for examples see the box below). It is also an integral part of the work of any manager that has direct responsibility for one or more employees or workers (human resources). The HR or personnel function thus signifies either an activity such as recruitment or training and/or a departmental presence.

INTERNATIONAL HR SOCIETIES AND ASSOCIATIONS

The World Federation of Personnel Management Associations was founded in 1976 to aid the development and improve the effectiveness of professional people management (www.wfpma.com).

The Arabian Society for Human Resource Management, founded in 1991, is dedicated to the management and development of human resources and the exchange of information and expertise (www.ashrm.com).

The Bulgarian HRM and Development Association was established in 2000 to support and develop HR professionals (www.bhrmda.orbitel.bg).

The Chartered Institute of Personnel and Development started life in the UK in 1913 as the Welfare Workers' Association (www.cipd.co.uk).

In 1980, the two professional bodies created in India during the 1950s after Independence merged to form the National Institute of Personnel Management (www20.brinkster.com/nipm).

The term 'human resources' can be viewed in two contrasting ways. Placing emphasis on the word *human* implies that an organisation's assets are valuable human beings with feelings and aspirations that should be respected and nurtured. Highlighting the word *resource* may have the effect of devaluing the human element by relegating people to a mere resource that is to be deployed as effectively and efficiently as possible, like a piece of machinery. These variations have been embodied as 'soft' and 'hard' HRM (Storey, 1992). 'Soft' HRM is often associated with quality-enhancing and value-adding measures, whereas 'hard' HRM is linked to cost-cutting and cost-minimisation strategies (Schuler and Jackson, 1987). These variations are developed further in Chapters 4, 5 and 7.

Traditionally HRM in Britain has centred on five broad areas of activity: *resourcing* the organisation, ensuring that the human resources *perform* effectively and efficiently, *developing* human resources, regulating the *employment relations* between management and workforce, and *paying and rewarding* the workforce (Torrington *et al*, 2005). Some of the key areas of activity are:

- resourcing – strategic aspects, formulating contracts, use of contractors and consultants, recruitment, selection, retention, ending the contract, interactive skill (selection interviewing)

- performance – strategic aspects, organisational performance, individual performance, team performance, leadership and motivation, diversity and equality (legal and business cases), interactive skill (appraisal interviewing)

- learning and development – strategic aspects, competencies and national vocational qualifications (NVQs), learning and development, career development, interactive skill (presentation and teaching)

- employment relations – strategic aspects, trade union recognition and consultation, employee voice, health, safety and welfare, grievance and discipline, interactive skill (grievance and disciplinary interviewing)

- pay and reward – strategic aspects, job evaluation, pay structures, incentives, pensions and fringe benefits, interactive skill (negotiation).

Although Torrington *et al*'s (2005) view of the scope of HRM provides an adequate description of the key activities relating to the management of human resources, it does not locate them in a broader context that pays sufficient regard to contextual factors such as cultural and country variation, social norms, economic and political developments and legal frameworks. Nor does it wholly embrace ethical considerations and notions of justice and fairness that underpin employment relationships. As we shall see throughout the book, these are fundamental to any discussion of HRM in a comparative or international context.

A strategic framework for HRM

Given the emphasis on the importance of HRM as a strategic activity, it becomes important to appreciate why the notion of strategy is not straightforward and remains controversial. Four broad schools of thought (Whittington, 2001) have evolved in the western world, primarily from North America.

In the *classical approach* strategic HRM is a rational, analytical, long-term planning process undertaken by the senior management team and implemented by line managers in pursuit of profit maximisation (Porter, 1980, 1985). Alternatively, if one accepts that market unpredictability militates against heavy investment in strategic plans, HRM strategy is an *evolutionary approach* and the firms that survive are the fittest and most efficient (see Friedman, 1953; Einhorn and Hogarth, 1988). In the *processual approach* HRM strategy emerges from the day-to-day activities of the firm, rather than being a function of the market, and is a continuous, formative and adaptive process (adaptive rationality) or a pragmatic response to events that may only be identifiable in hindsight (Mintzberg and Waters, 1985). Finally, a s*ystemic approach* suggests that organisations can plan ahead, but strategic HRM goals and processes are shaped by social and economic systems and factors such as culture (for example, Granovetter, 1985; Whitley, 1999). It thus acknowledges a range of contextual factors beyond those observed in the Anglo-Saxon cultures of the United States of America and the United Kingdom, including the role and strength of financial institutions and different political regimes.

The issue for HRM is how far each of these approaches may be discrete or whether we can identify elements of more than one approach within particular HRM strategies. Intuitively, the latter appears to be more realistic, as Boxall and Purcell (2003: 50) clearly imply in their list of key characteristics of an HR strategy:

- critical goals and means for managing labour

- inevitably affects performance

- made by whole management structure

- partly planned and partly emergent

- different goal/means for different groups

- easiest to define at business level
- more complex in multidivisional firms
- more complex in international firms.

Discussion questions

1. Why are people so important to organisations?

2. How far are the terms 'human' and 'resource' incompatible in the context of managing people effectively and efficiently?

3. Should HRM be strategic? If it should, why is this important?

2 COMPARATIVE MODELS OF HRM

Western perspectives

Strauss (2001: 874) identifies five broad definitions or models of HRM in the western economies: two that typify HRM in the USA and three that are more akin to HRM in Britain, Australia and New Zealand.

The USA

- *Traditional personnel work*, including recruitment and selection, training, health and safety, pay and benefits – In this approach personnel specialists simply react to line managers' requests for assistance by providing prescriptive solutions and a largely administrative service.

- *More integrated and sophisticated personnel* involves some strategic planning because personnel activities are intended to have a relationship with each other, which is often referred to as 'internal fit'. For instance, appraisal outcomes are linked to training and development needs and pay and benefits strategies.

Britain, Australia and New Zealand

- *A much wider range of people-oriented practices*, including job design, organisational culture and reward systems that encompass traditional personnel, organisational behaviour and employment relations.

- *All people-oriented practices* must be *internally consistent and consistent with* – and determined by – *the organisation's competitive strategy*. HRM practices must thus not only be internally coherent but they must also be consistent with the organisation's business strategy – for example, low cost or high innovation (see *Organisation context* below) – which is often referred to as 'external fit'. Hence HRM is seen as highly strategic, may be a configuration of HRM practices that are deemed appropriate to the firm's internal and external needs, and is contingent in that the practices will differ according to the nature of the firm's competitive strategy. This HRM strategy is often known as 'best fit', and may tend towards hard HRM and efficiency.

■ *A set of 'best practices'*, such as extensive training, semi-autonomous work groups and lifetime employment, designed to build employee motivation and commitment to the organisation. Strategic HRM is concerned with long-term asset-building, based on 'one best way' or a universalistic set, configuration or bundle of HRM practices that are consistent with soft HRM, effectiveness and high-performance or high-commitment work systems.

Strategic HRM is most clearly articulated in the 'best fit' and 'best practice' models in that HRM is intended to contribute to improving firms' performance and overall business success. In the case of 'best fit' models, the impact of HR practices depends on the contextual variables – a point we develop in more detail in the next section.

There are two variations to 'best practice' HRM. The universalistic model posits that some HR practices are appropriate for *all* firms, whereas the configurational model is premised on particular combinations or 'bundles' of mutually reinforcing HR policies. Simple adoption of these practices may make a more important contribution to firm performance than seeking internal or external fit (Huselid, 1995). Combining high-skill jobs and high job discretion may lead to better performance outcomes than using either one in isolation (MacDuffie, 1995). Conversely, the combination of teamwork with a payments system of individual incentives would be inappropriate. In response to the lack of agreement about which 'bundles' of practices characterise high-performance or high-commitment work systems, Guest *et al* (2004) suggest that priority should be given to teamwork, job design, training and development, performance appraisal, employee involvement, equal opportunities and information provision. Other non-significant practices may still be needed for legal reasons.

Other western perspectives on strategic HRM

According to the *resource-based view* (RBV) HRM is valued not only for its role in implementing a particular strategic choice, such as cost leadership, but also in its role for being a base of strategic capability itself (Barney, 1991). In short, the source of competitive advantage comes from the human capital within the firm, not in relation to the firm's position relative to its competitors. It is based upon the presence of HR practices that are valuable (efficient and effective), rare (not widely available), inimitable (not easily replicated by competitors), non-substitutable (other resources cannot fulfil the same function) and non-transferable (cannot be purchased in the resource market) (Barney, 1991). Whereas a major strength of the RBV lies in its focus on the implementation of HR strategy, a substantial weakness lies in practising the RBV in highly dynamic environments that demand more flexible and cost-sensitive modes of HRM.

Kaplan and Norton's *balanced scorecard* (1996, 2001) has sought to overcome the major difficulties not only of linking the cause and effect of HR practices to particular performance outcomes but also in measuring their effects, particularly the difficulties of relating critical, non-financial HR factors to demonstrably financial outcomes. Successful implementation stems from satisfying the requirements of three key stakeholders – investors, customers and employees. A key weakness of the balanced scorecard approach is the failure to address the role of managers and the need to develop high-quality managerial capability to formulate and deliver strategy (Boxall and Purcell, 2003: 41).

The re-emergence of *HR accounting* within the strategic HRM literature highlights the importance of attempting to measure the value of human resources both to reinforce their strategic and competitive importance and to embed the credibility of HRM (Toulson and Dewe,

2004). Premised on reporting people as organisational resources in financial and managerial accounting terms, more recent approaches also incorporate non-financial approaches.

The need to incorporate quantitative and qualitative evidence also underpins *human capital management* (HCM), which is related to the RBV (see also Chapter 6). Organisations must develop internal (CIPD, 2005) and external measures of human capital issues 'to demonstrate their effectiveness in sourcing, managing and retaining vital human capital they need for business success' (CIPD, 2003). Taking an HCM perspective, Scarbrough and Elias (2002) argue that it is the activity of measuring, not the measures themselves, that contribute to our understanding of human capital in particular contexts. Swedish companies have led the way by publishing statements in their annual reports about human resources in addition to financial circumstances, and this is now a legal requirement in large British companies.

A more recent perspective on the role of the customer as a stakeholder in HRM can be found in Korczynski's (2002) analysis of the direct impact of customer interaction within the employment relationship in *service work* (see also Lucas, 2004), an issue considered in more detail in Chapter 5. The customer is integral to the labour process because management's key objective is to ensure that HRM policies and practices promote 'the dual, efficient and customer-oriented behaviour that is required from workers [and] seeks to cope with the ensuing tensions' (Korczynski, 2002: 196), based on the creation of a (fragile) social order that can generate profit. In short, management's key task is to ensure that workers have the ways and means (are empowered) to cope with customers, particularly awkward ones, in the conduct of their work. If workers develop coping strategies that are not in the customers' or management's best interests, such as being rude to customers or engaging in petty theft, these practices will alienate customers, cost the organisation time and money, jeopardise market share and impact negatively on sustaining and improving business performance.

The concept of *the psychological contract* has been found useful as a method for capturing the employment relationship. The psychological contract consists of the perceptions of both parties – the employee and the employer – of the reciprocal promises and obligations implied in the relationship (Guest and Conway, 2002). If one of the parties perceives that the other has failed to fulfil the promised obligations, then feelings of psychological contract violation may occur. Guest's surveys on the psychological contract in the UK have found it to be in a good state generally (for example, Guest *et al*, 1996; Guest and Conway, 2001). It may be that there are international differences in the perception of the psychological contract. Cassar's (2001) study of Maltese employees found that reporting of violations was lower than that reported in other contexts. Also, Westwood *et al*'s (2001) study of Hong Kong managers found that cultural values influence the promise-obligation exchange in contracts and that the sense of duty and obligation in Chinese cultures meant that employees see their own obligations to the organisation as greater than the organisation's obligations to them. The psychological contract proves useful in highlighting these international differences and similarities in the employment relationship.

Limitations of western models

These predominantly Anglo-Saxon approaches, which feature widely in the HRM literature, may no more than describe the experiences of western economies (Weinstein and Obloj, 2002). They do not necessarily resonate to the more dynamic world of international business and the globalisation of world markets, where international firms and multinational companies (MNCs) have to design and implement HRM policies and practices in the context of wide-ranging cross-national differences. We next suggest how organisations can better understand these differences, and how we can move beyond western-centric HRM.

Cross-national HRM

The significance of contextual constraints on firms' HRM policies and practices is highlighted in Brewster's (1995) European model of HRM. Four levels of constraints are identified: international (European Union), national (culture and legislation), organisational (patterns of ownership) and HRM (trade union involvement and consultation). He also differentiates 'outside' and 'internal' constraints on HRM. Outside constraints include the legal framework, vocational education and training programmes, social security arrangements, and public or private ownership. Internal constraints include trade union influence and employee involvement arrangements. This model is also useful for analysing HRM at national level.

Budhwar and Debrah's (2001: 505) model of national HRM policies and practices is a function of two broad sets of contextual influences – national (outer context) and organisation (inner context). This model can be used as the basis for cross-national or cross-cultural comparisons, and provides greater insights into particular HRM issues in different countries outside Europe.

National context

Culture
National culture has been detailed in Chapter 2, using Hofstede's (2001) five dimensions of culture: power distance, uncertainty avoidance, individualism, masculinity and long-term orientation/short-term orientation, which are better understood in combination. For example, Japan is high on uncertainty avoidance, masculinity and long-term orientation and middling on power distance and individualism. While national differences in HRM are largely embedded in national contexts, this does not prevent cross-national convergence. Schein's (1985, 1989) three-layered model of artefacts and behaviour, beliefs and values and basic assumptions was also outlined, and will inform the exploration of corporate culture in Chapter 5.

Institutions
These include national labour laws, the degree to which employment is highly regulated or deregulated (see Chapters 11 and 14), and the respective role and strengths of employers' federations and associations, and trade unions (see Chapter 10). Britain, France and the USA have experienced a significant decline in trade union membership and influence, whereas in India the trade unions and other pressure groups exert strong pressure on HRM (Budhwar and Khatri, 2001). The role of professional bodies, education and training systems and labour market dynamics constitute other systemic influences. Unique characteristics of the labour market in India are based on social relations, political contacts, caste, religion and economic power (Budhwar and Khatri, 2001).

Dynamic business environment
Competitive pressures may drive productivity, quality and labour cost measures, including more focus on total customer satisfaction. These pressures may lead to new business alliances and forms of corporate governance (see Chapter 13). Demographic change and developments in information technology are significant influences on employment practices and work organisation (see Chapter 4). Managers in emerging or transformational economies such as Poland (Egorov, 1996), Slovakia (Lucas *et al*, 2004a) and Bulgaria (Lucas *et al*, 2004b) have found it hard to make the 'psychological transformations' that are necessary to manage HRM in the newly developing service sector (see Case study 4). Workforces are similarly inert, suggesting that demographic and labour market conditions may militate against strategic HRM changes required to deploy the 'right attitude' in customer-service work (Lucas *et al*, 2004a, b). Organisational restructuring may lead to the transfer of work across a new international

division of labour – for example, the outsourcing of UK clothing manufacture to Eastern Europe and the Far East. It may also result from the transfer of convergent best practice, such as the Japanisation of production systems.

CASE STUDY 4

HRM IN TRANSITION IN CENTRAL AND EASTERN EUROPE

Until 1989 countries such as Bulgaria and Czechoslovakia were governed under a Communist regime. After four years of post-socialist development, Czechoslovakia split into the Czech Republic and Slovakia. The shift to a market economy has led to an expansion of the service sector in these countries, including a tourist sector geared to competitive international markets rather than to a closed, national market.

The ideology of central planning and the Communist Party's political orientation shaped the role played by the personnel function. ... Independent decision-making was neither required nor encouraged. ... Strategic changes were initiated and approved at a higher level by the central authorities and enterprises were only supposed to implement them. ... The role of Director of Personnel was to direct, not to manage, people. ... These departments had to play a primary political and social role, upon which all personnel activities were dependent.

Orientation to a market economy urged managers into new roles requiring increased autonomy of decision-making and responsibility. ... Changes were made in a short time ... Managers were concerned with their survival. ... Adoption of the HRM rhetoric was seen as proof of their competence. ... Managers preferred to be selective rather than applying a coherent model. ... Barriers to the adoption of modern HRM activities include the socialist legacy of command-and-control management style.

Over a decade later, managers in Bulgaria have not yet achieved the state of 'psychological transformation' that is necessary to implement more sophisticated HRM policies and practices in tourism-related activities. In Slovakia there has been a move away from the rigid socialist type of personnel management. ... The emergent 'model' is a hybrid of traditional western HRM and basic HRM activities, alongside which some legacies of the socialist personnel function still exist.

Sources: Anastassova and Purcell, 1995; Koubek and Brewster, 1995; Egorov, 1996; Weinstein and Obloj, 2002; Lucas *et al*, 2004a, b.

Case study tasks

1   What new management challenges have arisen from the need to manage HRM in a service context?

2   What are the implications of these changes for management education and training?

3   What is meant by 'psychological transformation', and how would you recognise that it has occurred?

Industrial sector

The main influences on HRM policies and practices include regulations and standards, common developments in business operations and cross-sector cooperative arrangements. Privatisation of the Norwegian energy industry has caused a shift in focus from engineering and technical issues towards customer service, operational costs and productivity, and a shift from job-based to people-based HR performance management systems, including the need to introduce performance-related pay (PRP) (Mikkelsen *et al*, 2002) (see Chapters 8 and 9). Additional factors included the need for sector-specific knowledge, and sector-specific labour markets or skill requirements.

Organisation context

Organisational contingencies

Contingent variables internal to the organisation that affect HRM policies and practices relate to its size (number of employees), age, level of technology, life-cycle stage, type of ownership, the presence of HRM as a department or at board level, and union status. Take the example of recruitment in small and medium-sized enterprises (SMEs) that grow in size and enter a new developmental stage. During start-up recruitment will be a function of the owners' personal and social networks, whereas in the growth phase the firm's business networks will become the primary source of searching for new talent (Tansky and Heneman, 2003) (see Chapter 6).

Organisational strategies and policies

Miles and Snow (1984) identify three types of business strategy that drive HRM policies and practices. 'Defenders' have limited and stable product lines and aim to grow through penetration and compete on the basis of strong efficiencies. HRM emphasis is placed on processes for the development of existing employees. 'Prospectors' have changing product lines, and secure growth through innovation and new developments, which dictate the buying in of new skills and results-oriented reward policies. 'Analysers'' competitive strategies and HRM policies are a mix of those pursued by defenders and prospectors.

Schuler and Jackson's (1987) adaptation of Porter's (1985) three competitive strategies – cost leadership (lowest unit costs), product differentiation (superior quality or service) and market focus (a niche player in cost or differentiation) – is even more influential because it develops more fully the link between strategy, HR practices and employee behaviours. For example, cost-reduction will be based on short-term relationships, the design of repetitive jobs, minimal staff numbers, perfunctory training and development and the reward of high-output or predictable behaviour. By contrast, achieving differentiation through superior service quality would entail the identification and assessment of particular employee and job attributes in recruitment and selection, customer-focused training, the design of autonomous and empowering jobs, and more sophisticated performance and reward systems.

The implications of contextual constraints are addressed in Case study 5.

CASE STUDY 5

HRM IN TRANSITION IN MULTINATIONAL BANKING COMPANIES IN PAKISTAN

The banking industry in Pakistan was once monopolised by public sector enterprises and known for poor HRM practices. It has been invigorated since the deregulation of the economy in the early 1990s. Owing to constrained training facilities and limited job opportunities, Pakistan – like other developing countries – has been encouraging the growth of international corporations in order to benefit from their technical and management know-how. Multinationals are seen as tools for providing employment, bringing in new technology and work practices from their parent companies, as well as providing training grounds for the local workforce. In an environment with low creativity and innovation, multinationals are expected to act as 'agents of change'. Disappointment with the existing traditional HRM practices of the public sector in Pakistan increases openness to influences of modern HRM techniques. Multinationals are not really expected to adopt local practices.

However, in five multinational banking companies studied in Pakistan, it was found that not all HRM practices were implemented in line with the multinational's country of origin. A process of HRM change is taking place in three of the banks studied. In these organisations, HR managers are currently involved in bringing HRM to the level of other business functions and changing long-held traditional views about little or no involvement of HR departments in conducting business. They have introduced practices like management by objectives, open performance appraisals and needs-led training programmes. The other two banks studied have not yet applied integrated and consistent new HRM practices. Their HR departments are involved only in administrative tasks such as arranging for training (without considering it a function that responds to organisational and individual employee needs), salary disbursal and tax deductions.

While new policies at all organisations incorporated similar concepts of employee empowerment and employee involvement, the outcome was not the same. A gap between policy and practice was observed, especially in two of the banks who were undergoing HRM change. Although policies were formulated in the HR departments, the implementation was dependent upon line managers. Used to being in a high power distance culture, some of them are referred to as 'old dinosaurs'. For example, feedback-oriented performance appraisals that called for greater employee involvement were introduced at one bank undergoing HRM change. According to the policy, line managers are required to hold individual meetings with their employees during which they are asked mutually to discuss strengths and weaknesses. It is clear that employees are given the freedom to express themselves and input feedback. In the case that they disagree with their managers, an impartial arbitrator is to be appointed by the HR department to make final recommendations. However, in practice, some line managers do not follow the guidelines but conduct individual meetings solely for the purpose of communicating their own decisions to the employees – and when an employee does not agree, he is ignored. Eventually, this leaves the employee frustrated and angry. Despite differences of opinion with their managers, most employees sign off their appraisals, either not knowing they had the right to disagree or not sure if it would do any good.

The problem is that these organisations have preserved core cultural characteristics by retaining a formal and hierarchical structure. Consequently, HRM is centralised. Policies are formulated at head offices in isolation and then cascaded down to each office or division in an attempt to attain a uniformity of objectives and culture. Employees cannot approach their HR departments directly. Going through the proper channels is almost always stressed. Employees are given little autonomy and they are not encouraged to provide feedback in the process of policy formulation or implementation. The social set-up requires surrendering to authority – employees generally therefore accept authority unquestioningly.

Source: adapted from Khilji (2002)

Case study tasks

1   To what extent are high power distance and a culture which encourages the unquestioning acceptance of authority affecting the implementation of HRM practices in multinational banks in Pakistan?

2   How could new HRM practices be implemented with greater effectiveness in these organisations?

3   What is the role of the line manager in the implementation of HRM practices?

Discussion questions

1   Do you consider that some aspects of national context are more important influences on HRM policies and practices than others? If so, which are those aspects, and why are they more important?

2   Are organisational contingencies more helpful than organisational strategies and policies in understanding how and why HRM polices and practices may differ between organisations?

3   Taking a country with which you are familiar, is national context more important to HRM policies and practices than organisational context?

3 INTERNATIONAL AND GLOBAL HRM

Is there a difference?

A distinction between globalisation and internationalisation has already been made in Chapter 2, but specifically within HRM Sparrow *et al* (2004) differentiate these terms in a similar way:

- *international HRM* is managing an international workforce including expatriates, frequent commuters, cross-cultural team members and specialists involved in international knowledge transfer

- *global HRM* is managing international HRM activities through the application of global rule-sets.

Although we accept that these distinctions can be made, like many others – for example, Von Glinow *et al* (2002) – for the purposes of this chapter we use these terms synonymously as international HRM (IHRM), which can be conceptualised as combining both activities, with particular emphasis on the management of HRM activities. While our global understanding is increasing, we shall expose some major regional and country gaps where more research from an international HRM perspective is needed. Indeed, if western firms are contemplating investing in other countries, they need to know what is happening.

Given the potential contextual variations that have been considered, the notions of international and global HRM seem somewhat problematical. As noted in Chapter 2, if they are to be found at all, we have to look to MNCs, where the HR practices of the parent company may be more widely applied globally in a variety of countries. MNCs are key players in the transfer of western ideas, but the cultural context is vitally important when translating principles into practice. In contrast, HR practices within the small firms that predominate in most economies are more likely to be culturally specific to particular countries, sectors or their owners. The key question becomes to what extent we can expect HRM policies and practices to converge towards a common set of macro western universals, to remain divergent at the micro level because they are culturally determined (Budhwar and Khatri, 2001), to occur simultaneously (Khilji, 2002), or to cross-verge from the interaction between economic ideology and national culture to produce a unique value system that is neither one nor the other (Anakwe, 2002).

The degree to which HR practices may converge or diverge across ten countries is addressed in the Best Practices Project reported by Von Glinow et al (2002), who use the terms 'etic' to denote HR practices of universal generalisation, and 'emic' to signify HR practices in a particular culture. By comparing the HR practices of the USA (emic a) that are applied to another country – for example, Australia (imposed emic) – HR practices in Australia's culture (emic b) can be identified. A derived etic would be where any overlap in HR practices is found. The findings do reveal the existence of IHRM best practices, but they are not as universal as expected, so a unifying theory of IHRM cannot be suggested. In short, there remains considerable regional or country-cluster and country-specific divergence in HR practices. While this research takes a selective view of HRM, because it only addresses compensation, selection, appraisal, training and development and strategic orientation, some interesting observations are nevertheless made, an example of which is shown in Table 1.

Table 1 IHRM practices in strategic orientation across ten countries

HR practice	Universal practices	Regional or country clusters	Country-specific
Relation to business strategy	**Training and development and performance appraisal are the HR practices most closely related to organisational capability in most countries**	**Low cost and differentiation strategies are linked with HR practices in Asian countries**	**Organisational capability is not linked to HR practices in Mexico Organisational capability is linked weakly to HR practices in Japan and Taiwan**

Source: Derived from Von Glinow et al (2002: 135)

Another 'best practice' study examined the HR practices of US, Japanese, German and French companies in UK companies they had acquired (Faulkner et al, 2002). Some convergence was illustrated by the application of PRP and increased training in the new subsidiaries, although a distinct difference in other HR practices within these subsidiaries was influenced by country practices of the parent company (see Chapters 2 and 10).

The case for some adaptation or modification of HRM policies and practices is therefore persuasive. Although a parent company may seek consistency in HR practices across nations in the interests of fairness or to promote a single corporate culture, particular practices may convey different and unintended meanings in another culture (Geary and Roche, 2001). Country or regional norms may prevail, regardless of whether the industrial relations system is weak, as in Ireland, or strong, as in Germany. Alternatively, the emergence of company-based systems among the individual MNCs has been observed (Marginson and Sisson, 1994). The HR practices of Ford in Germany, Belgium and the UK have come increasingly to resemble one another, and may in turn create increasingly different patterns of country or sectoral employment relations (Ferner and Hyman, 1998). Indeed, competitive pressures on European MNCs in Germany, France, and Italy are forcing them to emulate the global coordination of activities that are more characteristic of American and British MNCs. In short, there is some 'Anglo-Saxonisation' within existing host country business systems.

While western MNCs are likely to invest in some of the most lucrative emerging markets, such as Mexico, Brazil, Argentina, South Africa and China, sub-Saharan Africa lacks these countries' appeal of rich resources, expanded infrastructure and economic growth. Unlike many former Communist regimes, large swathes of the subcontinent are not emerging or in transition from a centrally planned economy. They are also characterised by other entrenched problems rooted in a colonial past, political instability, volatile leadership, strong tribal culture, and widespread corruption. Kamoche (2002) further suggests that MNCs have engaged in unethical practices, work exploitation and the destruction of the environment (see Chapters 12 and 13).

Discussion questions

1   With reference to Sparrow *et al*'s distinction between international and global HRM, can HRM ever be truly global? If it can, how would we recognise it?

2   Which strategic IHRM orientation do you think McDonald's adopts?

3   Do you agree with Geary and Roche (2001) that HR practices may convey different meanings in another culture?

4 THE MANAGEMENT OF HRM

The status of the HR function

The status of the HRM function varies across countries and is high in Australia and low in Indonesia (Von Glinow *et al*, 2002). It may well be that HR departments in Australia are viewed as the preservers of the egalitarian value system, ensuring that HR practices like selection, rewards, and performance appraisal are fair to all employees (Bowen *et al*, 2002). In many countries with low-status HRM, the barriers to implementation of the HRM framework can be attributed to the following factors:

■   The lack of credibility of the HR function – This derives from the lower status of the HR function and the widespread view in the public opinion 'that managing people is something anyone can do as long as he/she acquires some practical experience and uses common sense' (Cabral-Cardoso, 2001).

■   The size, ownership and structure of the organisation, a barrier that is thus structural in nature – Many economies comprise mainly SMEs, often family-run businesses, with no distinct personnel function (Cabral-Cardoso, 2001, quoted in Cabral-Cardoso, 2004).

■   The power of the function within the organisation – US companies rarely have their HR executive on the board of directors. The top department in terms of power is finance, followed by marketing, production, planning or strategy and HR. The only department rated lower than HR is research and development (Jacoby *et al*, 2005).

According to Jacoby *et al* (2005), in both Japan and the USA high relative HR power is associated with:

- stronger internal labour markets for managers
- greater centralisation of operating decisions
- greater influence over executive career decisions
- budgetary allocations
- strategic business decisions.

One of the results of a powerful finance function in America (and elsewhere, such as the UK) is a focus on flexibility and on treating employees as costs to be minimised (Jacoby *et al*, 2005) (see Chapter 4).

Bowen *et al* (2002) caution that countries embroiled in political turmoil, or that are lower on the industrialisation or globalisation chain, or those that are moving from centrally planned towards more market-driven economies, are all subject to dramatic shifts influencing the role and status of HR departments.

The changing nature of the HR function

France and Portugal are the European countries in which the HR function is carried out by personnel specialists and is not devolved to line managers (Mesner Andolsek and Stebe, 2005; Cabral-Cardoso, 2004). The formation of a devolution process is strongly influenced by contextual factors (Budhwar, 2000). For example, devolution is low in the UK due to the increasing amount of employment legislation, resulting in numerous lawsuits relating to unfair employee dismissals (Harris *et al*, 2002). Mesner Andolsek and Stebe's (2005) survey of European countries found that a written HR policy was the factor that contributed most to the extent of the process of devolution of the HR function in the organisations. Devolution is sometimes not a goal of defined HR policy but a result of underrating HRM and leaving it as a function of line management (as in Spain). Devolution is most common in the area of responsibility for increasing or decreasing the number of employees and then in the area of staffing. HR specialists remain very important in the area of managing employment relationships (see Chapters 2 and 10) and selection of staff (see Chapter 7).

Renwick (2003) on 60 indicated that leaving too much responsibility for HR work to the line manager runs the risk that HR issues are not handled either properly or professionally, do not receive sufficient priority, are inconsistent, and lack specialist expertise. On the other hand, retaining too many personnel specialists runs the risk that problems will not be owned by line managers, that they will lack a business focus and that they will be ignored. Completely dispensing with the HR department can lead to the adoption of a hard resource-based approach to the management of people, without any systematic integration of HR policies and strategy (Thornhill and Saunders, 1998).

According to Stanton and Coovert (2004) IT currently plays a role in all three of the broad, interlocking functional areas of human resources:

- finance – HR professionals research, recommend, and manage the organisation's use of monetary rewards and perquisites for personnel.

- administration – HR professionals ensure and maintain the organisation's compliance with organisational, union, local and government regulations as they pertain to traditional personnel actions (eg recruiting, hiring, appraisal, dismissal).

- performance – HR professionals develop, deploy, and maintain the programmes in the organisation that allow individuals, teams, and larger groups of workers to create value with the available 'human capital' (eg assessment, training performance management, talent management).

The first two functions can be outsourced, regardless of whether the outsourcing is to headquarters, a consulting firm in another city, or even an overseas service provider. The third function is less likely to be supplanted by information systems (Stanton and Coovert, 2004). Problems of outsourcing have included:

- a sense of ambiguity prior to going ahead with the outsource, as to whether it was going to happen or not

- an annual minimum charge paid irrespective of volume, which meant that the firm was paying a higher price per individual recruited than it originally envisioned

- resistance to change by the HR staff.

Benefits included (Pollitt, 2004a, b):

- HR specialists freed up to do more strategic work

- implementation of a training programme for the retained HR organisation that focused on issues such as internal consulting skills, change management skills and project management skills

- employees with continuous web-enabled access to information such as their benefits

- bringing HR processes into alignment across different sites and countries.

The role of HR departments in different countries

Nohria and Ghoshal (1994) distinguish between firms that make a strategic decision to develop 'differentiated fit' with distinctive local conditions and those that promote global 'shared values' across the company. Taylor *et al* (1996) identify three generic strategic IHRM (SIHRM) orientations in MNCs: adaptive, exportive and integrative.

- An adaptive SIHRM orientation is one in which top management of the MNC attempts to create HRM systems for affiliates that reflect the local environment. The MNC generally copies the HRM systems that are being used locally by hiring competent human resource specialists or managers who have knowledge of local practices.

- An exportive SIHRM orientation is one in which top management of the MNC prefers a wholesale transfer of the parent firm's HRM system to its overseas affiliates.

- MNCs with an integrative SIHRM orientation attempt to take 'the best' approaches and use them throughout the organisation in the creation of a worldwide system. According to the SIHRM orientation, the focus is on substantial global integration with an allowance for some local differentiation.

However, the notion of being able to export or integrate HRM systems has been questioned.

Khan and Ackers (2004) argue that the external environment has to be taken into consideration and that HR practices implemented in different cultures will often be ineffective. They cite the case of the Gambian Ports Authority, which after having made workers redundant found the same workers still employed in the organisation. The western practice of redundancy did not fit with their practice of recruitment, which is for individuals to apply to their religious or family leader for employment. The individual's need of employment takes priority over the organisation's objectives. The inability to export HRM practices applies also to western countries, as Geary and Roche (2001) found in (mostly American) multinationals in Ireland. Brewster and Suutari (2005) comment that the wider convergence-divergence debate tends to assume that the HRM system as a whole converges or remains divergent, rather than considering whether some parts of the overall HR system might be converging, in some regions or geographies, while other parts might be diverging. Moreover, even within a single HR function there might be convergence at one level but divergence at another. Gamble (2003) points out that globalisation will increasingly affect the internal operation of companies. He cites a Chinese company that has a joint venture with a British do-it-yourself (DIY) retailer. The Chinese chief executive has lived and worked in North America and various staff had been educated and trained in countries other than China. Employees had previously worked in state-owned enterprises, collective firms, private firms and various types of foreign investment enterprises, including Taiwanese, Japanese, Hong Kong, German, French, Thai, Malaysian and American-invested firms.

Discussion questions

1   To what extent do you think that managers take the attitude that 'managing people is something anyone can do'?

2   Do you agree with Gamble that globalisation will increasingly affect the internal operation of companies?

3   What effect might devolution have on the HR function in the long run?

CONCLUSIONS AND FUTURE ISSUES

HRM has possibilities as an internal management tool for achieving better organisational effectiveness and efficiency, but how this can be realised remains a moot point. The key activities relating to HRM must be located in a broad context that pays sufficient regard to contextual factors such as cultural and country variation, social norms, economic and political developments and legal frameworks, and that embraces ethical considerations and notions of justice and fairness that underpin employment relationships. If it is to be taken seriously, HRM is important as a strategic activity and it may be that different approaches to strategic HRM can be combined depending upon prevailing circumstances. Western perspectives on HRM vary between traditional reactive personnel work and the more proactive approach in which 'best practices' are implemented in order to achieve high performance and high commitment from the workforce, but there is no consensus on which type of HRM approach suits particular organisations. However, western perspectives do not necessarily resonate to the more dynamic world of international business, where international firms have to design and implement HRM policies and practices in the context of wide-ranging cross-national differences. Cultural differences arise from the way societies have responded to basic questions of how we see ourselves, how we relate to the environment, how we relate to each other, and how we relate to time, and we have yet to see the development of credible alternative models in many countries, such as sub-Saharan Africa. IHRM is managing an international workforce including expatriates, frequent commuters, cross-cultural team members and specialists involved in international knowledge transfer. This differs from global HRM, which is managing IHRM activities through the application of global rule-sets. Whether HR practices may converge (be applied internationally) or diverge (local differences remain evident) has been the subject of research, and it would appear that often cultural differences are sufficiently great to inhibit the introduction of HR practices from, for example, a parent MNC. Some multinationals are more determined than others to secure convergence.

The status of the HR function varies between countries and depends upon the credibility of the function, structural factors and the power of the function within the organisation. The function is changing and is frequently devolved to line managers or outsourced. International companies may attempt to adapt to local conditions by hiring HR specialists who have knowledge of local practices, or they may attempt to export their practices to overseas affiliates, or finally they may adopt an integrative approach and attempt to combine the best approaches from all countries with which they deal. Increasingly, globalisation will affect individuals as more people travel to gain work experience abroad or to be educated abroad, and the staff of many organisations will become international themselves.

CASE STUDY 6

MANAGING *GUANXI* IN A SWISS–CHINESE JOINT VENTURE

Swissotel Hotels and Resorts is a global hotel management company owned by Raffles International Hotels and Resorts. It is one of the largest hotel chains in the world. It owns hotels in 31 destinations, including Asia, Australia, Europe, North and South America. In order to open a hotel in China, the company started the process of entering into a joint venture with Chinese partners in the late 1980s. Almost 10 years later, in 1998, a joint venture between Swissotel and Dalian Emporium Bloc came to fruition, and a new hotel – Swissotel Hotel Dalian – was opened. This is a luxurious five-star hotel with more than 600 employees, and enjoys a reputation as the most famous accommodation-provider in Dalian.

Despite the fact that the Chinese and Swiss are in business together, there are strong cultural differences which affect the running of the hotel. Joint ventures are fairly common in China because there is a need for western management expertise. The Swiss partners found that operating in China meant that management practices that they had previously taken for granted had now to be established. The Swiss general manager commented that 'A big problem with Chinese partners is their lack of understanding of how modern hotels work. They agreed to follow our practices initially, but since then we have experienced a lot of opposition from the staff.' The Swiss resident manager said that he had found attitudes to be very different between the two countries: 'What I have found is a lack of initiative among many people here. I have to tell them exactly what they ought to be doing. The older Chinese managers have problems in understanding and absorbing foreign management ideas, such as the need for clear performance measures. This can lead to disagreements and the feeling of "them" and "us" in the hotel.'

In China, business dealings rely more on individual relationships and are fairly informal. In the West, doing business is based upon legal requirements, which in turn are based on concepts such as justice and equity. In China, a personalised and close business relationship is called *guanxi*, and it plays a paramount role in business. *Guanxi* involves relationships among individuals that create obligations for the continued exchange of favours. For organisations, *guanxi* serves as a strategic tool, especially for those without strong government ties. At the individual level, managers may establish and use *guanxi* to carry out business. It can be used to gain access to new customers, keep existing clients, facilitate daily business operations, or even avoid government investigations. One of the Swiss managers at the hotel said: 'Relationships in Switzerland are often focused at the level of the firm, but in China *guanxi* is focused on the individual level. In Switzerland, relationships will form after a deal is accomplished, but in China, *guanxi* has to be established before a deal starts. Chinese people make friends first, build up *guanxi*, and then do business later.'

The Swiss public relations manager considers that good *guanxi* with the staff is important because it enhances the working environment, creates a good atmosphere in which to work and the mutual trust built up enables staff to accomplish tasks smoothly. Harmony is the highest goal of action and thought in Confucianism, and in order to maintain it, everyone wants to seek compromise, not confrontation. Managers may lose their good *guanxi* if they treat staff badly in public: good *guanxi* is maintained by treating everyone with respect.

Also, good *guanxi* with local government officials, local customs and local tax office officials is considered a potential strategic resource because the relationship can be exploited to the joint venture's advantage. The Chinese purchasing manager and the Swiss general manager often have dinner with the officials of the Dalian Customs Department. The general manager learnt through bitter experience that this is the best way to conduct relations. When he began working in China he could not understand why it took so long for the customs officials to check new supplies for the hotel when they were being transported from another Chinese city. He has now learnt that by building up *guanxi* with the officials, whenever new supplies are expected, a phone call to the officials of the Customs Department will ensure that the goods are checked very quickly. Also, good *guanxi* with suppliers is essential because the hotel needs substantial amounts of fresh high-quality food and beverages every day, especially when banquets are organised on the spur of the moment. Good *guanxi* with the suppliers ensures that they will deliver food and drinks whenever needed.

However, the Swiss restaurant manager considers that the establishment of *guanxi* is very expensive for the hotel. He commented that 'Relationships start with friendship; then there are little gifts here and there. The surprise to me was how much food and drink and entertaining is involved in building up the relationship. They tend to drink Mao Tai (an expensive wine in China) – it's a good opportunity to have it! In Switzerland it's acceptable to go for a sandwich together, but here you have to spend a lot of time and effort to get to know each other. In China, people in a hurry don't succeed. We frequently treat government officials to fine dining and present them with gifts such as a full set of golf clubs worth $10,000 – these are normal social activities.'

The Chinese personnel manager also was unhappy with *guanxi* because it means that often the better qualified candidates for jobs are not hired. The recruitment process at the hotel is still based on *guanxi*. The personnel manager has said that this means that when she receives applications for a position on the hotel staff, there is sometimes attached to the application form a note from a senior government official which says 'Could you pay special attention to this person?'; or a note from a Chinese department manager in the hotel saying 'Take care of this person.' She says that recommendations from important officials have to be acted upon because of the importance of the relationship. 'You cannot refuse their requests because there would be trouble. If I didn't get these notes, I probably wouldn't employ these people. When I am recruiting, I have to consider each applicant's position in society. If they have no skills, I just give them a very easy job.'

The Chinese front-of-house manager said that he well remembered a young woman whose father was a good friend of a senior manager at the hotel. Without knowing about that, he employed her to clean the toilets in the lobby. The senior manger objected strongly to this and continually insisted on better positions for her. She was promoted to a good position in housekeeping, although no extra staff were needed in that department at the time.

At the hotel, new graduates were frustrated to find their educational qualifications treated with little respect by the management. When a group of graduates started their graduate training at the hotel, a non-graduate was among the group. One of the graduates commented: 'We all had better qualifications than the non-graduate, yet he was given first choice of position, and he chose the computing department in the front office. He obtained a position that was interesting and easy because he had *guanxi* with a senior manager. Although I have a degree, I had no *guanxi*, and went into the housekeeping department. My work was much harder than his and involved doing morning, evening and night shifts.' The promotion of those with *guanxi* rather than ability is still the norm, and the result is that unqualified personnel occupy decision-making posts, and the hotel experiences poor management, low productivity and further nepotism which negatively influences performance.

Due to the importance of *guanxi* for business in China, most of the management posts in the hotel in Personnel, Purchasing and Sales are taken by Chinese staff. The expatriate Swiss managers occupy the positions which do not depend upon *guanxi* in order to function effectively – general manager, resident manager and restaurant manager. Although there are disadvantages to *guanxi*, it enables businesses to run smoothly in China, and the lack of contacts for foreign managers, coupled with the length of time it takes to build up contacts, means that it is very difficult for them to manage in China without foreign partners.

Source: Du (2004)

Case study tasks

1   Are notions of fairness and justice which underpin the employment relationship in China different from those in western societies?

2   To what extent is the HR strategy partly planned and partly emergent in the hotel?

3   The western perspective of a firm may be that it is a business set up in order to make a profit. How might *guanxi* represent a different view of the firm?

REFERENCES

Anakwe U. P. (2002) 'Human resource management practices in Nigeria: challenges and insights', *International Journal of Human Resource Management*, Vol. 13, No. 7: 1042–59.

Anastassova L. and Purcell K. (1995) 'Human resource management in the Bulgarian hotel industry: from command to empowerment?', *International Journal of Hospitality Management*, Vol. 14, No. 2: 171–85.

Barney J. (1991) 'Firm resources and sustained competitive advantage', *Journal of Management*, Vol. 17: 99–120.

Bowen D. E., Galang C. and Pillai R. (2002) 'The role of human resource management: an exploratory study of cross-country variance', *Human Resource Management*, Vol. 41, No. 1: 103–22.

Boxall P. and Purcell J. (2003) *Strategy and Human Resource Management.* Basing-stoke: Palgrave Macmillan.

Brewster C. (1995) 'Towards a European model of human resource management', *Journal of International Business*, Vol. 26: 1–22.

Brewster C. and Suutari V. (2005) 'Global HRM: aspects of a research agenda', *Personnel Review*, Vol. 34, No. 1: 5–21.

Budhwar P. S. (2000) 'Evaluating levels of strategic integration and devolvement of human resource management in the UK', *Personnel Review*, Vol. 29, No. 2: 141–61.

Budhwar P. S. and Debrah Y. (2001) 'Rethinking comparative and cross-national human resource management research' *International Journal of Human Resource Management*, Vol. 12, No. 3: 497–515.

Budhwar P. S. and Khatri N. (2001) 'A comparative study of HR practices in Britain and India', *International Journal of Human Resource Management*, Vol. 12, No. 5: 800–26.

Cabral-Cardoso C. (2001) 'The European HRM debate revisited: a Southwestern perspective', paper presented at the Founding Conference of the European Academy of Management, Barcelona, 18–21 April.

Cabral-Cardoso C. (2004) 'The evolving Portuguese model of HRM', *International Journal of Human Resource Management*, Vol. 15, No. 6: pp. 959–77.

Cassar V. (2001) 'Violating psychological contract terms amongst Maltese public service employees: occurrence and relationships', *Journal of Managerial Psychology*, Vol. 16, No. 3: 194–208.

CIPD (2003) *Human Capital, External Reporting Framework: The change agenda.* London: CIPD (www.cipd.co.uk).

CIPD (2005) *Human Capital, Reporting an Internal Perspective: A guide.* London: CIPD (www.cipd.co.uk).

Delery J. E. and Shaw J. D. (2001) 'The strategic management of people in work organisations: review, synthesis and extension', *Research in Personnel and Human Resources Management*, Vol. 20: 165–97.

Du Y.-Y. (2004) *'Managing guanxi in a Swiss/Chinese joint venture',* unpublished MSc dissertation, Manchester Metropolitan University.

Egorov V. (1996) 'Privatisation and labour relations in the countries of Central and Eastern Europe', *Industrial Relations Journal*, Vol. 27, No. 1: 89–101.

Einhorn H. J. and Hogarth R. M. (1988) 'Behavioural decision theory: process of judgement and choice', in D. E. Bell, H. Raiffa and A. Tversky (eds) *Decision-making: Descriptive, normative and prescriptive interactions.* Cambridge: Cambridge University Press.

Faulkner D., Pitkethly R. and Child J. (2002) 'International mergers and acquisitions in the UK 1985–94: a comparison of national HRM practices', *International Journal of Human Resource Management*, Vol. 13, No. 1: 106–22.

Ferner A. and Hyman R. (1998) 'Introduction: towards European industrial relations?', in A. Ferner and R. Hyman (eds) *Changing Industrial Relations in Europe.* Oxford: Blackwell.

Friedman M. (1953) 'The methodology of positive economics', in M. Friedman, *Essays in Positive Economics.* Chicago: University of Chicago Press.

Gamble J. (2003) 'Transferring human resource practices from the United Kingdom to China: the limits and potential for convergence', *International Journal of Human Resource Management*, Vol. 14, No. 3: 369–87.

Geary J. F. and Roche W. K. (2001) 'Multinationals and human resource practices in Ireland: a rejection of the "new conformance thesis" ', *International Journal of Human Resource Management*, Vol. 12, No. 1: 109–27.

Granovetter M. (1985) 'Economic action and social structure: the problem of embedded-ness', *American Journal of Sociology*, Vol. 91, No. 3: 481–510.

Guest D. E. and Conway N. (2001) *Organisational Change and the Psychological Contract.* London: CIPD.

Guest D. and Conway N. (2002) 'Communicating the psychological contract: an employer perspective', *Human Resource Management Journal*, Vol. 12, No. 2: 22–38.

Guest D., Conway N. and Dewe P. (2004) 'Using sequential tree analysis to search for "bundles" of HR practices', *Human Resource Management Journal*, Vol. 14, No. 1: 79–96.

Guest D. E., Conway N., Briner R. and Dickman M. (1996) *The State of the Psychological Contract in Employment.* London: CIPD.

Henderson B. D. (1989) 'The origins of strategy', *Harvard Business Review*, November-December: 111–19.

Hofstede G. (2001) *Culture's Consequences* (2nd edition). London: Sage.

Huselid M. A. (1995) 'The impact of human resource management on turnover, productivity, and corporate financial performance', *Academy of Management Journal*, Vol. 38: 635–72.

Jacoby S. M., Nason E. M. and Saguchi K. (2005) 'The role of the senior HR executive in Japan and the United States: employment relations, corporate governance and values', *Industrial Relations*, Vol. 44, No. 2: 207–41.

Kamoche K. (2002) 'Introduction: human resource management in Africa', *International Journal of Human Resource Management*, Vol. 13, No. 7: 993–87.

Kaplan R. and Norton D. (1996) *The Balanced Scorecard: Translating strategy into action.* Boston, MA: Harvard Business School Press.

Kaplan R. and Norton D. (2001) *The Strategy-Focused Organization.* Boston, MA: Harvard Business School Press.

Khan A. S. and Ackers P. (2004) 'Neo-pluralism as a theoretical framework for understanding HRM in sub-Saharan Africa', *International Journal of Human Resource Management*, Vol. 15, No. 7: 1330–53.

Khilji S. E. (2002) 'Modes of convergence and divergence: an integrative view of multinational practices in Pakistan', *International Journal of Human Resource Management*, Vol. 13, No. 2: 232–53.

Korczynski M. (2002) *Human Resource Management in Service Work.* Basingstoke: Macmillan.

Koubek J. and Brewster C. (1995) 'Human resource management in turbulent times: HRM in the Czech Republic', *The International Journal of Human Resource Management*, Vol. 6, No. 2: 223–47.

Lucas R. E. (2004) *Employment Relations in the Hospitality and Tourism Industries.* London: Routledge.

Lucas R. E., Marinova M., Kucerova J. and Vetrokova M. (2004a) 'HRM practice in emerging economies: a long way to go in the Slovak hotel industry?', *International Journal of Human Resource Management*, Vol. 15, No. 7: 1049–66.

Lucas R. E., Marinova M. and Vodenska M. (2004b) 'HRM in Bulgarian hotels: looking far enough ahead?', paper presented at Management, Work and Organisation in Postsocialist Societies, 19th ERJ Conference, Cardiff University, September.

MacDuffie J. P. (1995) 'Human resource bundles and manufacturing performance: organisational logic and flexible production systems in the world auto industry', *Industrial and Labor Relations Review*, Vol. 48, No. 2: 197–221.

Marginson P. and Sisson K. (1994) 'The structure of transnational capital in Europe: the emerging Euro-company and its implications for industrial relations', in R. Hyman and A. Ferner (eds) *New Frontiers in European Industrial Relations.* Oxford: Blackwell.

Mesner Andolsek D. and Stebe J. (2005) 'Devolution or (de)centralization of HRM function in European organisations', *International Journal of Human Resource Management*, Vol. 16, No. 3: 311–29.

Mikkelsen A., Nybo G., and Grönhaug K. (2002) 'Exploring the impact of deregulation on HRM: the case of the Norwegian energy sector', *International Journal of Human Resource Management*, Vol. 13, No. 6: 942–57.

Miles R. E. and Snow S. S. (1984) 'Designing strategic human resources systems', *Organization Dynamics*, Vol. 13: 36–52.

Mintzberg H. and Waters J. A. (1985) 'Of strategies, deliberate and emergent', *Strategic Management Journal*, Vol. 6: 257–72.

Nohria N. and Ghoshal S. (1994) 'Differentiated fit and shared values: alternatives for managing headquarters-subsidiary relations', *Strategic Management Journal*, Vol. 15: 491–502.

P&O Group (2005) *Annual Review and Summary Financial Statement 2004.*

Pollitt D. (2004a) 'Outsourcing HR: the contrasting experiences of Amex and DuPont', *Human Resource Management International Digest*, Vol. 12, No. 6: 8–10.

Pollitt D. (2004b) 'Cable and Wireless rings the changes', *Human Resource Management International Digest*, Vol. 12, No. 5: 29–32.

Porter M. E. (1980) *Competitive Strategy: Techniques for analysing industries and firms.* New York: The Free Press.

Porter M. E. (1985) *Competitive Advantage: Creating and sustaining superior performance.* New York: The Free Press.

Renwick R. (2003) 'Line manager involvement in HRM: an inside view', *Employee Relations.* Vol. 25, No. 3: 262–80.

Scarbrough H. and Elias J. (2002) *Evaluating Human Capital.* CIPD Research Report. London: CIPD.

Schein E. H. (1985) *Organizational Culture and Leadership.* San Francisco: Jossey Bass.

Schein E. H. (1989) 'Organizational culture: what it is and how to change it', in Evans P., Doz Y. and Laurent A. (eds) *Human Resource Management in International Firms.* London: Macmillan.

Schuler R. S. and Jackson S. E. (1987) 'Organisational strategy and organisational level as determinants of human resource management practices', *Human Resource Planning*: Vol. 10: 125–41.

Sparrow P., Brewster C. and Harris H. (2004) *Globalising Human Resource Management.* London: Routledge.

Stanton J. M. and Coovert M. D. (2004) 'Guest editors' note: turbulent waters: the intersection of information technology and human resources', *Human Resource Management*, Vol. 43, Nos 2 and 3: 121–5.

Storey J. (1992) *Developments in the Management of Human Resources.* Oxford: Blackwell.

Strauss G. (2001) 'HRM in the USA: correcting some British impressions', *International Journal of Human Resource Management*, Vol. 12, No. 6: 873–97.

Tansky J. W. and Heneman R. (2003) 'Introduction to the special issue on human resource management in SMEs: a call for more research', *Human Resource Management*, Vol. 42, No. 4: 299–302.

Taylor S., Beechler S. and Napier N. (1996) 'Toward an integrative model of strategic human resource management', *Academy of Management Review*, Vol. 21, No. 4: 959–85.

Thornhill A. and Saunders M. N. K. (1998) 'What if line managers don't realize they're responsible for HR?', *Personnel Review*, Vol. 27, No. 6: 460–76.

Torrington D., Hall L. and Taylor S. (2005) *Human Resource Management* (6th edition). Harlow: Pearson Education.

Toulson P. K. and Dewe P. (2004) 'HR accounting as a management tool', *Human Resource Management Journal*, Vol. 14, No. 2: 75–90.

Von Glinow M. A., Drost E. A. and Teagarden M. B. (2002) 'Converging on IHRM best practices: lessons learned from a globally distributed consortium on theory and practice', *Human Resource Management*, Vol. 4⁻, No. 1: 123–40.

Weinstein M. and Obloj K. (2002) 'Strategic and environmental determinants of HRM innovations in post-socialist Poland', *International Journal of Human Resource Management*, Vol. 13, No. 4: 642–59.

Westwood R., Sparrow P. and Leung A. (2001) 'Challenges to the psychological contract in Hong Kong', *International Journal of Human Resource Management*, Vol. 12, No. 4: 621–51.

Whitley R. D. (1999) 'The social construction of business systems in East Asia', *Organization Studies*, Vol. 12, No. 1: 1–28.

Whittington R. (2001) *What is Strategy – and Does it Matter?* (2nd edition). London: Thomson.

Work organisation, flexibility and culture

Work organisation and flexibility

CHAPTER 4

Carol Atkinson and Laura Hall

CHAPTER OBJECTIVES

When you have read this chapter you should be able to:

- analyse the major influences on work organisation in the twenty-first century

- understand the drivers for flexibility in the employment relationship from the perspective of both employer and employee

- explain the policy framework within which flexibility is implemented in the UK, and compare and contrast it with other policy frameworks

- outline the nature of employer-driven flexible working practices and the implications of these for the employment relationship

- outline the nature of employee-driven flexible working practices and the implications of these for the employment relationship.

PURPOSE AND SCOPE

In this chapter we consider the nature of work organisation and flexibility, presenting both employer and employee perspectives. We integrate many of the book's themes, the most prominent being consideration of globalisation and technological change/the knowledge economy and their impact on employer-driven flexibility, together with demographic trends and labour market change and their impact on employee-driven flexibility. We further consider the extent to which the UK is similar to/differs from other economies (convergence/divergence) and the impact of emerging economies on work organisation – for example, the offshoring of work in India, and the perspectives on work flexibility in transition economies such as Poland. Finally, we consider cultural variation through the lens of male/female employment patterns and acknowledge the impact of EU enlargement through issues such as the impact of the influx of Eastern European labour into the UK. We conclude that the UK's liberal deregulated approach has privileged employer needs over employee needs. This has driven greater numerical flexibility at the expense of promoting greater work–life integration (WLI), which may be at odds with the need to foster a cadre of highly skilled knowledge workers required to compete more successfully in a global economy. In summary, we argue that both employer- and employee-driven flexibility are important, and that in establishing a successful employment relationship, there is a need to reconcile the competing demands of each.

1 AN OVERVIEW OF WORK ORGANISATION AND FLEXIBILITY

Work organisation and flexibility considers how employers design jobs and working patterns in order to meet both their own and their employees' need for flexibility. It is central to the whole employment relationship, given its impact on the working conditions of employees and the implications it has both for organisational performance and for working life as it is experienced by employees.

Employer-driven flexibility has dominated the flexibility debate from the mid-1980s until relatively recently, many employees experiencing significant change to traditional working patterns. Models such as that proposed by Atkinson (1984) have been used to explain employer behaviour in terms of work organisation and flexibility. Supply-side pressures have, however, in the past few years created a position whereby in order to recruit and retain scarce labour, employers have increasingly been obliged to consider the employee requirement for working-time flexibility. While less conceptually developed than demand-side flexibility, there is nevertheless an emerging body of literature that considers employee-driven flexibility, often termed 'work–life balance' or 'work–life integration' (WLI). As we demonstrate in what follows, although many of the influences on both employer- and employee-driven flexibility apply internationally, their impact on the employment relationship is mediated by differing policy frameworks applied by governments in various countries. We consider the UK's position and provide comparative information from a range of countries that demonstrates both similarities and differences in approach to work organisation and flexibility.

2 THE MAJOR INFLUENCES ON WORK ORGANISATION AND FLEXIBILITY

In this section, we consider the factors influencing the increased flexibility of labour, in terms of both its demand and its supply. From the end of World War II to the 1970s saw the broad adoption of a 'standard working-time model' (Allan and Brosnan, 1998) in which most employees worked an approximately 8-hour day in daylight hours from Monday to Friday. Since the 1980s, however, there has been a dramatic move away from this standard working-time model to one in which far more flexible working hours are inherent. We outline below the major drivers of this increased working-time flexibility.

Demand factors

The overriding employer driver of such flexibility has been the globalisation of markets that has led to ever greater product market competition and an increased need to seek means of competitive advantage (Williams, 2000). Striving for this competitive advantage has induced firms to employ more 'flexible' workers and to provide less secure jobs in order to keep costs down and to retain or increase market share (Burchell et al, 1999).

Technology has also had a key role in driving flexibility from an employer perspective (Williams, 2000), enabling a greater control of workflow (Burchell et al, 1999) and requiring flexible working hours to facilitate extending capital utilisation (Allan and Brosnan, 1998). General changes, such as the move from the industrial to the post-industrial knowledge-based economy, have also impacted on working hours in both industrial and emerging economies, such as China. For example, jobs in a knowledge-based economy tend to be more flexible than industrial jobs, with more varied working hours (Bishop, 2004). These changes have been accompanied, at least in many western economies, by a shift to a focus of employment in the service sector and, in the UK, relaxation of certain trading practices. For example, Sunday trading has increased demand for labour at non-standard times (Williams, 2000). Although the shift to a knowledge-based economy has been the received wisdom of the past 20 years, more recent evidence suggests that it has been more limited than is generally accepted, and that, in the UK at least, the increasing importance of the service sector has been the most significant recent sectoral change (Nolan and Wood, 2003).

While the drivers outlined above have, to a great extent, impacted on working-time flexibility internationally, the role of the state as a facilitator of such flexibility has been fundamental to the outcomes of such influences. In the UK, for example, the government has adopted a liberal approach, promoting deregulation in respect of economic policies and rights of labour (Burchell *et al*, 1999). This stands in contrast both to other Western European countries, such as France and Germany, and certain transition economies such as Hungary and Slovenia (Tang and Cousins, 2005). The UK's approach has, perhaps unsurprisingly, led to a growth of non-standard employment contracts and atypical working hours (den Dulk *et al*, 2004) driving a flexibilised and casualised labour market.

Supply factors

The changes in the demand for labour in the UK outlined above have coincided with labour market changes that have occasioned a greater supply of labour at non-standard times. Increasing labour force participation of women, particularly women in the child-bearing years, has been accompanied by an increasing need for childcare and flexible working arrangements (Fagnani *et al*, 2004). There has been a shift away from the traditional 'nuclear' family and associated male-oriented employment, with a marked increase in single-parent families and dual-career couples. An increasing proportion of the workforce thus has to deal with both work and non-work commitments, leading to an enhanced supply of labour at non-standard times – notably nights and weekends (Williams, 2000). Such changes have also been accompanied by the overall ageing of the population, which impacts in two ways. Flexibility is increasingly required as workers have to deal not just with childcare but also elder care. Additionally, the supply of older workers is becoming increasingly important to employers who face shortages of skilled labour in Europe and North America (Strachan and Burgess, 1998). For possible financial reasons in terms of pension provision, older workers also may wish to make flexible choices in terms of their labour supply, and this applies in economies beyond the UK (Tang and Cousins, 2005).

Working-time flexibility and work intensification

Although we present above a coincidence in drivers of working-time flexibility in terms of both labour supply and demand, we support the argument that employer-driven approaches to renegotiating working time have predominated in UK organisations (Beynon *et al*, 2002). Allan and Brosnan (1998) suggest that this has also been the case in France, Belgium and the Netherlands, Australia and New Zealand (see Case study 7) and in transition economies such as Poland (Stenning and Hardy, 2005). This has not been so evident, however, in Germany and Sweden, where employee-oriented policies have continued to predominate, or in similarly highly regulated transition economies such as the Czech Republic and Hungary (Tang and Cousins, 2005). Allan and Brosnan (1998) further suggest that the debate about working time has not been so intense in the USA and Japan because these countries have had less regulation of working time and employers already possess considerable flexibility. The policy frameworks surrounding work organisation and flexibility will be explored further in the next section.

The outcomes of a shift away from the standard working-time model for employees have been significant, those most widely reported being the growth of work intensification (Worral and Cooper, 1999; Stenning and Hardy, 2005) and job insecurity (den Dulk *et al*, 2004). These trends have been particularly evident in, but are not confined to, the UK where average working hours among full-time workers are the longest in Western Europe (Bishop, 2004). In transition economies, work intensification more typically arises from low wages and the struggle to earn enough to achieve an acceptable standard of living (Stenning and Hardy, 2005).

Green (2001) challenges the work intensification alleged to have taken place in manufacturing in the 1980s and in the public services in the 1990s in the UK, arguing that there has been a reduction in average weekly working hours from the early post-war years. He argues that it is increasing work pressure, as opposed to length of working hours, that is driving perceptions of intensification. Whatever the specific causes of work intensification in the UK, there is a general trend for employees to wish to reduce working time, as compared to countries such as the USA, Canada and Germany. In these countries, underemployment – that is, working fewer hours than desired – is typically considered to be more of an issue (Boheme and Taylor, 2004).

CASE STUDY 7

WORKING TIME AND DEREGULATION IN AUSTRALIA AND NEW ZEALAND

After World War II, Australia and New Zealand – in common with many other industrialised countries – adopted a 'standard working-time model' based on a typical 8-hour working day, during daylight hours, Monday to Friday, for a total of 40 hours a week. In the 1970s, flexible working-time arrangements in these countries were taken to mean providing employees with greater control over their own hours and periods of work. In the 1980s and 1990s, however, the debate about the nature of working time changed, driven largely by employer demands for greater control over the timing of work. Working time has thus become contested terrain between employers and trade unions, with the competing pressures of employee- and employer-driven flexibility.

In response to employer pressure for greater labour market flexibility, governments in Australia and New Zealand adopted markedly different approaches to decentralising industrial relations. New Zealand adopted a dramatic programme of deregulation, abolishing the arbitral system of industrial relations and replacing it with a voluntary system. Decentralisation in Australia, however, occurred more gradually, providing a moderate pace of liberalisation and retaining a relatively centralised arbitral model. By 1995, therefore, the two countries were operating very different systems, the study reported here investigating whether the deregulated New Zealand system provided employers with more working-time flexibility than the modified system in Australia.

The study demonstrated that substantial changes to the standard working-time model had taken place in both countries, a significant proportion of workplaces (although a lower proportion of employees) working non-standard hours in both countries. Such non-standard hours included early starts, late finishes, and night and weekend working. In both countries, employer-driven flexible practices predominated over employee-driven practices.

One of the striking findings of the study was that there were only minor differences in working hours between the two countries, suggesting that deregulation is not a major factor in determining whether employers adopt flexible working-time arrangements. The study suggests that production or service delivery requirements necessitated that firms operated at given times and working time was scheduled accordingly. The distribution of working time was thus primarily driven by product market demand patterns and the nature of technology. This challenges the conventional thinking of those who suggest that stronger regulation will prevent excesses of employer-driven working time flexibility by proposing that such regulation may not be very effective.

Source: Allan and Brosnan (1998)

Case study tasks

1 How does the experience of Australia and New Zealand compare to that in the UK or another country with which you are familiar?

2 Thinking about your own organisation or one with which you are familiar, to what extent has flexibility increased in work organisation?

3 What have been the major drivers of these increases in flexibility?

In this section, we have considered influences on both employer- and employee-driven flexibility. Case study 7 presents an insight into what the dominant employer drivers are, and indicates that they are usually privileged over employee drivers. One, perhaps contentious, suggestion in this case study is that levels of regulation have little impact on work organisation and flexibility. We go on now to consider the UK policy framework and contrast its outcomes to the approaches and outcomes of other countries in order to explore this issue further.

Discussion questions

1 What are the implications of changes in labour supply for work organisation and flexibility in the UK (or another country with which you are familiar)?

2 How are these implications manifested in your organisation (or one with which you are familiar)?

3 Why have changes in labour demand prevailed in importance over changes in labour supply?

3 POLICY FRAMEWORKS IN RESPECT OF WORK ORGANISATION AND FLEXIBILITY

Regulation of employer-driven flexibility

As noted above, the past two decades have seen deregulation and the application of liberal policies to the employment relationship in the UK. In this section, we consider the implications of this policy approach to working time in the UK, overviewing the implications of the legislation that is in place (the details of the provisions of such legislation are provided in Chapter 11). We compare the UK's approach to that of other countries in the EU and elsewhere and consider the implications of different policy approaches.

Voluntarism
The UK has historically adopted a voluntarist approach to the employment relationship, relying upon social regulation through means of trade unions. Thus, prior to the Working-Time Regulations (WTR, 1998) there was no comprehensive regulation of working time in the UK. The light-touch application of these regulations – the 48-hour maximum working week being subject to an opt-out which is widely applied (Boheme and Taylor, 2004) – has meant that there has been little reduction in overall working hours since its introduction (Smithson and Stokoe, 2005). Indeed, the UK has recently successfully argued to retain this opt-out, in the face of EU pressure to abolish it (Anon, 2005).

Social partnership

The UK's approach stands in contrast to that of much of the rest of Europe, which adopts a more socially democratic approach to regulation of the employment relationship requiring co-determination through the 'social partners' – the state, employers and employees (or their representatives). Such strong institutional arrangements in France, Denmark and Sweden have seen much less erosion of the standard working-time model than in the UK (Bishop, 2004). Indeed, in Germany, the outcome of social regulation is that working-time flexibility still centres to a great extent on the needs of employees (Singe and Croucher, 2003). Transition economies have had a similarly varied approach, countries such as Bulgaria and Romania applying a deregulated approach and adopting a 'forced flexibility' model in the face of economic crisis (Wallace, 2002), as opposed to the Czech Republic and Hungary, which have retained greater regulation and adopted a 'regulated anti-flexibility' approach (Tang and Cousins, 2005). Limited regulation has also seen dramatic increases in flexibility in Central America (International Labour Organisation, 2005), and Wong (2001) presents further evidence of the marked increases in flexibilisation that have occurred in Hong Kong in respect of contingent workers who are not protected by employment legislation.

The outcome of the UK's approach is that working hours are unstandardised when compared to other EU member states (Kodz, 2003), and the above studies suggest that regulation may serve to limit employer-driven flexibility, which stands somewhat at odds with the findings of the previous case study (7). It seems that this is an area that would benefit from further investigation.

In the following case study we discuss France's regulatory experiment with reducing working time and introducing greater working-time flexibility, considering the benefits and disadvantages experienced. (This experiment, approached from a different angle, also forms the basis of Case study 33, in Chapter 11.)

CASE STUDY 8

THE 35-HOUR WEEK IN FRANCE

France stood out in the general deregulation of the 1980s and 1990s because it maintained an interventionist state, the climax of such intervention being the passing of the Aubry laws (1998 and 2000) which introduced a 35-hour working week. The question of working time in the French debate is linked with the question of unemployment and the collective reduction in hours of work, the main objective of the law being to prompt companies to reduce individuals' working hours in order to employ more staff. The legislation was, however, imposed by the government on a generally hostile management.

By the end of 2000, 50% of employees worked 35 hours or less, compared to 7% in 1998. These reductions in working time were financed by the state (via financial support), by companies (via productivity gains linked to reorganisations) and by employees (who accepted increased levels of flexibility and wage freezes or small increases). While driven by legislation, such working-time flexibility was implemented by collective bargaining at local level, thereby maintaining the central role of the traditionally influential French trade unions. Early outcomes of the legislation suggested that the reduction in working hours apparently contributed 30% of the new jobs created in 2000, and the legislation was thus hailed as successful (Alis, 2003).

Fagnani and Letablier (2004), however, argue that a secondary objective of the Aubry legislation was to improve work–life integration for French employees. Fagnani and Letablier's study considers the extent to which this has been achieved, revealing inequalities between those employed in sheltered economic sectors and family-friendly companies and those who have to accept unsocial or flexible hours of work in exchange for a reduction in their working time. They argue that the 35-hour working week, in pratice annualised to 1,600 hours per year, has widened the gap between these two groups irrespective of gender and professional status, and that the annualisation of working hours has, in fact, led to work intensification with particular periods of long working hours for certain employees.

The above two studies provide contrasting evidence as to the success of the 35-hour legislation. More recently it has been reported that France is beginning to dismantle its experiment with the 35-hour working week as a result of rising unemployment and increased competition from Asia and Eastern Europe (Evans-Pritchard, 2005). While unemployment fell to the year 2000, it then started to rise, and by 2004 stood at 10%, the cost of financing the legislation being reported to have cost the state £10 billion (Czemy, 2004). Such problems have led to challenges to the legislation – employers have won the right to ask employees to work up to 5 extra hours per week in return for extra pay – although such changes may be gradual because many companies are locked into agreements with unions (Evans-Pritchard, 2005). It seems, then, that the French 'experiment' with working-time legislation may have achieved mixed results in terms of achieving its objectives.

Sources: Derived from Alis (2003), Czemy (2004),
Evans-Pritchard (2005) and Fagnani and Letablier (2004)

Case study tasks

1 To what extent do you think the twin objectives of the Aubry laws – tackling unemployment and improving work–life integration – are compatible?

2 Why did the French adopt the mechanism of collective bargaining as a means for implementing this legislation?

3 How does France's attempts to reduce working time compare to working-time trends elsewhere in Europe or elsewhere in the world?

Regulation of employee-driven flexibility

Having thus considered the UK's liberal policy approach to employer-driven flexibility, we now turn to consider the policy framework in respect of employee-driven flexibility. In order to give clarity to the distinction between employer- and employee-driven flexible working practices, we adopt in this section 'work–life integration' (WLI) as the term in use within the academic community.

Public policy in the UK

The Labour Government's policy approach to WLI has been incremental rather than radical. While the reconciliation of paid work and family has had a higher profile since 1997, this has been through limited policy changes and a high-profile 'work–life integration' campaign, the government regarding its role as limited to engendering a 'family-friendly culture' in business via the provision of voluntary measures which are underpinned by a fairly basic statutory framework (Harker and Lewis, 2001). For example, the government has adopted a minimal approach to parental leave and has afforded the right to request, rather than to have, flexible working.

Although minimalist in nature, the enhancing of such rights has often led to employer opposition in the UK, usually on the grounds of the cost to the business, especially for small firms who are argued to be ill able to afford the extra financial burden imposed upon them (Morrison, 2005). While the Government has tried to promote a 'business case' argument for adopting WLI policies (see *Employee-driven mechanisms of flexibility* below), there has nevertheless been argued to be a possible backlash from those without families and a negative impact on the recruitment of females. The business case approach is not, therefore, necessarily self-evident (White *et al*, 2003).

Comparative public policy approaches
The policy objective of reconciliation of employment and family life moving gradually on to the political agenda in the UK has been reflected across many other countries, different welfare regimes having strong implications for how much different countries place the onus for reconciling employment and family life on public policy and how much on individuals, families and employers (Pierson, 2001). As noted above, the UK has adopted a liberal approach to this, the responsibility remaining firmly with the individual and family. Public policy arguments such as social justice and the need to encourage female labour into the market to enhance national competitiveness in the face of skills shortages have, however, led other countries to adopt a variety of approaches (den Dulk *et al*, 2004). Norway, for example, stands in strong contrast to the UK in adopting a social democratic approach in which the welfare state is a strong actor and the labour market is highly regulated (Pierson, 2001): more details on this are presented in Case study 9.

Employment patterns
A variety of public policy approaches and their implications for employment patterns are presented below in Table 2. (These are also explored in Chapter 14 in the context of employment equality.)

Table 2 Comparative public policy approaches to work–life integration

Country	Employment patterns	Public policy approach
NORWAY, SWEDEN 'Egalitarian model'	Long part-time or full-time jobs. Short parental leave (one year)	Extensive use of public schemes supporting working parents (subsidised childcare arrangements, paid parental leave, flexible working hours ...)
FRANCE 'Dual earner' model	Long part-time or full-time jobs. Long parental leave (three years)	Extensive use of public schemes supporting working parents (subsidised childcare arrangements, paid parental leave, flexible working hours ...)
UK NETHERLANDS 'Modified male breadwinner' model	Short part-time jobs for women (as long as children are under school age); full-time jobs for men (often long hours)	Reduction of working time Kin/private childcare Flexibility at workplace level

PORTUGAL 'Dual earner' model	Full-time jobs. Long working hours for both partners	Kin/private childcare
SLOVENIA 'Dual earner' model	Full-time jobs. Long working hours for both partners	Use of public schemes supporting working parents (subsidised childcare over 3)
BULGARIA 'Dual earner' model	Full-time jobs for both partners	Long parental leave for mothers

Source: Adapted from Fagnani *et al* (2004: 172)

The above data reflect full-and part-time working patterns across a range of economies, although there is no internationally recognised definition of the hours that constitute 'part-time' working, each country applying its own definition (ILO, 2005). The outcomes of the UK's liberal approach to WLI are presented as being high levels of part-time work among women with 1½-earner households, in which there is a polarisation of long full-time versus short part-time hours (Bishop, 2004). This contrasts with the social democratic approach in Norway, Sweden and France in which a more egalitarian or dual-earner model drives long part-time or dual full-time working in couples. It should be noted that full-time working is usually argued to be beneficial, given that part-time roles (at least those created for the benefit of the employer) are often in low-status, low-waged and marginal roles (Fagan, 2001) that thus disadvantage those holding them, usually women. Liberal policy approaches could therefore be argued to have a negative affect on women's employment prospects as compared to more socially democratic approaches.

The Netherlands is characterised in the above table as sharing a similar approach to the UK whereby WLI has been considered to be a private problem to be solved within the family, and a high proportion of Dutch women (especially mothers) work part-time. Remery *et al*'s (2003) study, however, considers a shift in public policy, and increased WLI legislation – via albeit basic statutory schemes – in the Netherlands has provided a framework for employers and unions to negotiate family-friendly arrangements at company or industry level. The Dutch Government has expressly opted to leave employers and employees to extend (or not) the schemes in their negotiations – for example, parental leave is unpaid – and the WLI debate is still largely reliant upon a business case. Remery *et al* (2003) express little confidence in the success of such measures in improving WLI in the Netherlands.

Such doubts are echoed by commentators considering the progress of WLI in other countries adopting liberal policy approaches. For example, the business case approach dominates in Australia where legislative rights to protect workers with families do not apply to casual workers and arguably limited progress towards WLI for these workers has been made (Strachan and Burgess, 1998). Further, Doherty (2004) argues that WLI only works in tight labour markets and that without such pressures on recruitment and retention, a strong floor of statutory rights is required to induce employers to offer flexibility that is beneficial to employees. Public policy approaches in transition countries have seen a diminution in state provision of childcare with associated increases in work intensification for, largely, female workers (Stenning and Hardy, 2005).

In this section, we have presented the UK's liberal policy approach to both employer and employee-driven flexibility, contrasting this to policy approaches taken in other countries. Although there is some conflicting evidence, it appears that liberal policy approaches privilege employer mechanisms of flexibility over employee needs and that progress towards WLI may be impeded by such liberal approaches. We move now to consider in more detail both employer and employee mechanisms of flexibility.

Discussion questions

1   To what extent do you think the Working-Time Regulations (1998) have impacted on working-time trends in the UK and elsewhere in the EU?

2   Discuss how the varying policy approaches outlined above have contributed to the differing working-time patterns of males and females in European countries.

3   What are the advantages and disadvantages of relying on a 'business case' approach to achieving work–life integration?

4 EMPLOYER-DRIVEN FLEXIBLE WORKING PRACTICES

In this section we present practices that we consider to be employer-driven in terms of creating flexibility in working time, arising often from a strategic approach to HRM that demands the alignment of employee effort to strategic objectives. While we note above that there can be coincidence of employer and employee need in flexible working practices, we draw on the arguments of Bishop (2002) and Harris (2003) who suggest that there are inevitably tensions between employer and employee need and that what employers characterise as beneficial to employees often is not. We further adopt the argument that whether a practice is employer- or employee-driven depends on whether the employee has access to a contract of choice (Rosendaal, 2003), and present in this section practices that are typically adopted for the benefit of employers, those being beneficial for employees being presented in the following section.

Employers are argued to be able to avail themselves of a number of mechanisms that increase working-time flexibility, one of the best known models being presented by Atkinson (1984) who characterised flexibility as being numerical, temporal and functional in nature, and being applied in varying ways to employees dependent on the core–periphery divide.

Core employees

Core employees are permanent, often full-time, and form part of an internal labour market with good career prospects and are usually well rewarded financially. It is through such employees that organisations achieve *functional flexibility*, adopting mechanisms such as teamwork and multi-skilling, enabling the organisation to deploy human resources more effectively as employees can cover for each other and there is no downtime. Arguably, however, functional flexibility affords greater responsibility to the employee, which may contribute to the intensification of work discussed above. It has been suggested that UK organisations have been less successful at developing functional flexibility than elsewhere in Europe, often as a result of resistance or lack of training (Torrington *et al*, 2005). Indeed, a high degree of functional flexibility may be incompatible with the *numerical flexibility* that prevails in the UK as a result of its deregulated labour market (Tuselmann, 1996), a pattern that also prevails in many transition economies (Stenning and Hardy, 2005). In contrast, Germany, with its high levels of regulation, has a focus on functional flexibility, and numerical flexibility is more limited (Singe and Croucher, 2003).

Periphery employees

Periphery employees divide into two types. One type comprises those who are skilled but whose skills are either not in short supply or not specific to the firm – eg secretarial skills. For these employees, employers typically rely on the external labour market, offering limited career prospects and a range of employment contracts. The second group of periphery employees are those who are low-skilled and are typically offered little employment security, through a variety of insecure employment contracts – for example, cleaners and other manual workers. It is these groups of peripheral employees who provide an employer with *numerical flexibility*, enabling the employer to reduce or expand the workforce quickly and cheaply through the use of part-time, temporary or fixed-term contracts and agency working. As noted above, this type of flexibility is common in the UK and has increased in recent years with the use of outsourcing of work or indeed 'offshoring' – the transfer of work to other parts of the world where labour costs are typically lower than in the UK. This has happened to a significant degree in the past five years in the UK, during which period many thousands of jobs in call centres have been transferred to India. Both outsourcing and offshoring are typically associated with negative outcomes for employees.

Temporal flexibility

Temporal flexibility, the move away from a standard working-time model noted above (Allan and Brosnan, 1998), is achieved by varying hours worked and can be applied to either core or periphery employees. Working hours are made more flexible by use of mechanisms such as annual hours contracts, part-time working, job share and a variety of non-standard contracts or shifts. As noted above, the need for temporal flexibility has significantly increased with the shift to service work and a '24/7' culture in which consumers expect to be able to access retail and other services over extended periods.

Trends in flexibility

Although there are criticisms of Atkinson's model – Legge (1995) arguing, for example, that flexibility is not used strategically but in a pragmatic way to meet employer need – it has been generally accepted that work organisation has changed and that flexibility has increased over the past two decades. Rosendaal (2003), for example, notes the steady increase in part-time work across Europe in this period. Findings from the ESRC-funded 'Future of Work Programme' in the UK have, however, called into question the extent to which working patterns are changing. Nolan and Wood (2003), for example, argue that their empirical results do not support much of the 'grand narrative' (p.165) of changing work organisation. They suggest that full-time permanent employment remains dominant, applying to around 90% of employees, and that small, and indeed declining, numbers of employees are engaged on temporary or fixed-term contracts. This is, however, at odds with other empirical data from other countries. Singe and Croucher (2003), for example, suggest that while the extent of non-standard systems in Germany is uncertain, only 15% of Germans work a 35–40-hour week from Monday to Friday with no variations. Rosendaal (2003) additionally suggests that 37% of employees in the Netherlands work part-time, while increasing flexibilisation is noted in many transition economies (Tang and Croucher, 2005). It seems again that further empirical work is needed to inform the debate over the extent to which flexibility prevails.

Flexibility and HRM

One theme within the flexibility debate is the extent to which it is compatible with 'best practice' human resource management (HRM) (Guest, 2001) and its relation to 'soft' or 'hard' approaches to HRM (see Chapter 3). Research on organisational flexibility highlights the critical role of HRM practices in enabling organisations to respond quickly to developments in technology and to greater uncertainty and competition in product markets as well as increasing workforce diversity (Knox and Walsh, 2005). Kalleberg (2003) presents two approaches to this – the 'high road' (soft HRM) versus the 'low road' (hard HRM) to flexibility, the 'high road' adopting high-commitment HRM practices and promoting functional flexibility through a bundle of practices such as flexible job design, cross-training, use of teams and work groups and job rotation and enlargement (Knox and Walsh, 2005). The 'low road', however, is reliant upon cost-cutting measures and the utilisation of disposable or contingent labour. Such numerical flexibility thus often equates with insecurity, creating an inevitable tension with the commitment that best practice HRM seeks to create among employees. Knox and Walsh's (2005) study of working-time flexibility in Australian hotels suggests that such workplaces tend to be associated with high levels of numerical and temporal flexibility and informal HR practices. Lepak and Snell (1999) argue that the high- and low-road approaches may not be mutually exclusive and that the ability to manage different employment modes simultaneously may become a 'core capability' that other organisations may not be able to imitate – one that relies upon clear, consistent HRM policies. Again, the complexity in the application of flexibility is apparent.

Implications of part-time working

Given that much of the focus of working-time flexibilisation has been in creating part-time employment (Rosendaal, 2003), we consider the implications of part-time working in more detail in this section. We again note the lack of an agreed definition of part-time working, each country determining what constitutes part-time working for its own purposes. While part-time working is often employer-driven, employers nevertheless argue that such employment has benefits for employees – for example, that it meets the needs of women, students and men at retirement (Fagan, 2001) and contributes to better WLI. Nevertheless, despite the reported positive effect of shorter working time on task performance, employers have been reluctant to provide such opportunities unless it is specifically in response to their own needs, expressing concerns over overhead costs and levels of commitment when requested by employees (Rosendaal, 2003). Part-time working has, therefore, in the main been created in response to employer need as a cost-reduction strategy. This has meant that many part-time employees have fallen within the periphery rather than in the core of the organisation and that employers have provided jobs that are often low-skilled and marginalised rather than affording employees flexibility on their own terms (Fagan, 2001). Thus, as was suggested in the section on policy approaches, part-time working is often disadvantageous for employees, especially women.

Do employees lose out?

There is empirical data available internationally to demonstrate that part-time working as a benefit to employers, often at employees' expense, is not a phenomenon confined to the UK. For example, Thom and Blum (1998) in their survey of the flexibilisation of Swiss working hours demonstrate that while 70% of organisations use flexible working hours, most practices are primarily designed to meet employers' requirements and employees gain no significant additional control over their working time. Further, Wong (2001) considers the use of contingent labour, arguing that most research has focused on western developed economies in the past two decades, and provides case study findings from the Hong Kong retail sector in the wake of the Asian financial crisis of 1997. She reports that one third of Hong Kong companies resorted to using contingent labour while restructuring or downsizing, and that part-time employment doubled (although only to 4%). The use of such contingent labour was made easier by the supply of unemployed and under-employed labour and, given the extent to which it enabled employers to drive down wages levels, can hardly be characterised as beneficial to employees.

A similar situation has been reported in Poland (Stenning and Hardy, 2005). Such data supports the argument that most of the growth in part-time employment is involuntary and leads to lower job satisfaction (Allan, 2000).

As noted above, numerical flexibility has been somewhat limited in Germany as a result of high levels of employment regulation. We present in Case study 9 below the German response to the need for flexibility, which increasingly focuses on temporal flexibility, characterising it as an approach beneficial to employees.

CASE STUDY 9

TRUST-BASED WORKING TIME IN GERMANY

A cooperative management–works council innovation, trust-based working time (TBWT) is part of the German 'high road' to flexibility adopted from the late 1980s. TBWT is absent from many economies, yet as a small and still new development it is relatively common in Germany. It has generated an innovative way to manage working time, partly as a response to its highly regulated economy in which employee-driven mechanisms of flexibility have dominated. This employee focus arises from the 35-hour working week and the requirement for co-determination of the employment relationship among the social partners which has constrained employer mechanisms of flexibility.

TBWT ends formal management attempts to check and record employees' working time. Individuals and teams become primarily responsible for fulfilling tasks and meeting targets, and time becomes a secondary consideration. It is part of broader trend to de-hierarchisation and indirect management of which teamworking is a characteristic indicator, the crucial feature being a shift from a time to a results orientation. The following are inherent in TBWT:

- Employees are themselves responsible, in cooperation with work teams, for organising times in accordance with the law and sectoral agreements.
- Employees participate in keeping to and updating standards (eg service levels, quality, keeping of deadlines, required staffing levels).
- The employer does not check working time.

TBWT is part of attempts to maximise productivity and reduce costs that demand internalised employee commitment rather than a crude measure of time spent at work. While there is no comprehensive data on the existence of TBWT, it is suggested to exist in around 40% of German firms, being more common in private than in public sector and in larger firms. According to the German system of co-determination, TBWT requires the agreement of works councils but appears to be congruent with collective agreements and is often used by organisations as a path-breaker in working-time innovation.

Much of the emergent stream of literature on TBWT is produced by government or management protagonists seeking ways to increase national economic performance. They argue that its benefits include a reduction in administrative costs and overtime, that it is a driver of reorganisation, that it increases motivation and that it is an appropriate reaction to broader societal developments including the dissolution of boundaries between employer and employee. Union-oriented writers have developed more critical perspectives casting doubt upon the mutual gains scenario, arguing that there is a fundamental ambiguity between organisational requirements for flexibility and employee needs. For employees it promises increased autonomy, but also threatens to further blur the demarcation between work and life beyond work. As managers devolve responsibility for monitoring working time, workers – especially those who are highly qualified – may find their exceeding the maximum 10 hours per day is overlooked, leading to what Germans have begun to call 'arbeit ohne ende' (work without end). Further problems may arise from the high levels of trust and appropriate management styles required, and a legitimate system to deal with work overload would seem to be needed. While its incidence is predicted to increase, the authors argue that understanding of the phenomenon is at an early stage and that more research is required.

Source: Singe and Croucher (2003)

Case study tasks

1   What role has regulation played in limiting work flexibility in Germany?

2   Compare and contrast TBWT to more traditional approaches to work organisation.

3   To what extent do you believe that TBWT is likely to be beneficial to employees?

In this section we have presented mechanisms for flexibility typically associated with creating benefits for the employer. We have noted the general trend towards the adoption of such mechanisms, and that there is some challenge to this development. While various types of flexibility apply, it is suggested that the new labour market is structured around four groups: core, experienced or skilled contingent, low-skilled contingent and external workers (Noyelle, 1990). We have also suggested that despite employers characterising such practices as beneficial to employees, there are often, in fact, negative outcomes for them. We move now to consider mechanisms for flexibility from which employees typically derive benefit.

Discussion questions

1   To what extent are functional, numerical and temporal flexibility evident in your organisation (or one with which you are familiar)?

2   Outline what you consider the tensions to be between working-time flexibility and employee commitment.

3   Why is part time employment characterised as disadvantageous to employees – and is that inevitable?

5 EMPLOYEE-DRIVEN FLEXIBLE WORKING PRACTICES

In this section of the chapter, we present flexible working practices we consider to be employee-driven, often termed 'work–life balance' or 'work–life integration' practices (Smithson and Stokoe, 2005). This term is intended to denote that WLI practices are applicable to the whole spectrum of employees for a broad range of issues that extend beyond family concerns. As noted above, we adopt in this chapter WLI as a term in use within the academic community, although we have argued elsewhere that this term continues to create gendered perceptions and that a more gender-neutral approach is required (Atkinson and Hall, 2005). Despite attempts at positioning WLI as relevant to all employees, as the data we present below reflects, the dominant perception remains that it is a 'women's issue'.

The 'business case' as a policy approach

While employers have traditionally driven most of the bargaining on flexible working time, there is growing evidence of employee demand for increased autonomy to meet their demands for WLI (Thornthwaite, 2004). The UK's approach, adopted in other countries such as Australia and the Netherlands, is to consider WLI issues to be a private individual issue, family obligations being defined in respect of the nuclear family of spouses and children (Millar and Warman, 1996). As noted above, the UK has typically adopted a 'business case' approach to WLI, promoted through the Labour Government's 'Work–Life Balance' campaign in which the Government attempts to persuade employers, through largely voluntary measures, of the benefits of implementing WLI policies (White *et al*, 2003).

The business case presented suggests that WLI policies will not threaten the economic success of either party and may in fact enhance it, being predicated upon employer benefits such as improved recruitment and retention and reduced sickness absence (Hall and Atkinson, 2005a). This business case has been widely evidenced. For example, Boheme and Taylor (2004) demonstrate that working hours constraints are significant factors within labour turnover and that rigidities in the labour market exist which impair the welfare of employees. It is also suggested that employers introduce flexible working policies beneficial to employees to enhance their job satisfaction (Green, 2001), although this is often in response to a tight labour market (Remery *et al*, 2003).

In an earlier section we discussed alternative public policy approaches to WLI, and later in the final case study of this chapter we present Norway's approach to WLI, predicated as it is upon social democracy and egalitarian principles, in contrast to the UK's business case. It is interesting to note that approaches such as that adopted by Norway do not necessarily reduce perceptions of work–life conflict. Levels of such conflict are noted as being perceived to be high in Sweden, despite the country's adopting a similar public policy approach to Norway, and much lower in countries such as Romania and Bulgaria, which have seen the erosion of formerly high levels of state support for working parents (Tang and Cousins, 2005). It is argued that this relates to employee aspirations in such countries, those in Sweden prioritising issues of work–life integration, those in Romania and Bulgaria prioritising the provision of basic necessities for their families and not having the 'luxury' of worrying about work–life integration.

Types of WLI policy

Policies often introduced to improve WLI include part-time working, flexitime, a compressed working week, annual hours, term-time working, job share, self-rostering, shift-swapping, unpaid leave, sabbaticals and working from home (Thornthwaite and Sheldon, 2004; Torrington *et al*, 2005). Strachan and Burgess (1998), however, adopt a broader approach, suggesting that WLI is about more than just leave and working-time arrangements shown in the box below.

TYPES OF WLI POLICY AND THEIR IMPLICATIONS

TYPE OF ARRANGEMENT	IMPLICATIONS
Income security	Achieving minimum pay rates; having a regular and predictable income
Employment security	Predictable hours and ongoing employment; ability to take career breaks, ability to undertake financial commitments
Access to care arrangements	Childcare, in some cases elderly/disabled care; subsidisation, employer provision, complementary to working-time arrangements
Access to flexible leave arrangements	Access to standard leave entitlements; ability to switch between different types of leave; access to paid and unpaid maternity and paternity and family leave
Flexible working time arrangements	Ability to vary hours around family commitments; split shifts, flexitime; job sharing
Access to training and career paths	Generating income and employment security; enhancing ability to qualify for benefits
Innovative work arrangements	Study leave; home work; telecommuting; arrangements that allow for the flexible deployment of time

Source: Strachan and Burgess (1998: 252)
Reproduced with permission, Emerald Publishing

Thus they argue that appropriate policies on income and job security are also important. Employment that does not generate enough income to support a family cannot be described as 'family-friendly', and casual employees – who often remain outside the organisation's internal labour market – may be denied WLI benefits.

Whereas it may not be unexpected that employer policies adopted as a 'low road' to flexibility will create tensions for employee WLI, it is also argued that there is conflict between high-performance management practices and work–life balance policies (White *et al*, 2003). For example, best practice HRM seeks to obtain 'discretionary effort' from employees – that is, to imply that they should go beyond the requirements of the employment contract, with potentially negative impacts on WLI. Indeed, White *et al* (2003) suggest that the biggest influences on 'work to home negative spillover' are long working hours and high-performance HRM practices such as appraisal, team-based working and individual incentives. We consider here emerging literature on two practices which may be considered to be beneficial to employees' flexibility: teleworking and self-rostering.

Teleworking
Teleworking allows employees to work remotely from the workplace, often at home, and thus to better balance work and outside commitments, which is usually characterised as beneficial to

employees (Strachan and Burgess, 1998). It is argued, however, that this depends whether working from home is a choice or a requirement, and that this will determine employee perceptions of the practice. Harris (2003), for example, presents a case study in which employees were compelled to move from an office to a home-based working arrangement and notes the erosion of trust that lack of support for employees generated. Felstead *et al* (2002), on the other hand, present teleworking as an employee strategy that enhances WLI if employees can be afforded considerable autonomy. They go on to note that there is little evidence on how to manage home workers and that high levels of trust are required, leading often to its being reserved as a privilege rather than an opportunity for all. Indeed, the findings from the Future of Work Programme suggest that teleworking tends to be reserved for those in managerial or professional positions (Nolan and Wood, 2003).

Self-rostering

Self-rostering allows employees to determine their own work patterns within certain para-meters and thus tailor working hours to maximise their compatibility with domestic responsibili-ties and other interests. Thornthwaite and Sheldon (2004) argue that if they are implemented with WLI intent, self-rostering systems enable employees to generate autonomy over working hours that enhances their control over the boundaries and relationships between work and non-work spheres. While it is not a new concept, such working-time models with a high degree of flexibility are typically used only in individual cases for those with a high degree of autonomy (Thom and Blum, 1998). Thornthwaite and Sheldon's (2004) case study, however, derives from the manufacturing sector and demonstrates that it is possible to achieve self-rostering in repetitive, low-skilled production environments.

What emerges from the above is the theme of autonomy and its role in creating working-time flexibility. We have argued, as a result of our research investigating flexible working in the NHS, that the degree of control exercised over working time is as important as access to the flexible working practices outlined above (Hall and Atkinson, 2005b). This notion of 'time sovereignty' (Fagan 2001; Sheridan 2004) is gaining momentum within the WLI literature, White *et al* (2003), for example, arguing that flexible hours systems and personal discretion over starting and finishing times tend to reduce the problem of 'work to home negative spillover'. While such time sovereignty is currently limited to particular groups in the UK, both Case study 9 above and Thornthwaite and Sheldon's (2004) study demonstrate that opportunities exist to grant autonomy to employees on a wider basis. It would seem that this is a key area of development within the WLI arena.

Implementation of WLI policy

We turn now, however, to consider take-up of the formal WLI policies outlined above, noting that provision of such policies is generally better in the public than in the private sector (Hogarth *et al*, 2001). Research indicates that even where such policies exist, there is a 'take-up gap' (Kodz *et al*, 2002), a term used to describe those who would like to but do not take up flexible working options. Although issues such as limited policies and procedures and line manager resistance have been reported as barriers to uptake (Torrington *et al*, 2005), we focus here on what we have argued elsewhere to be an under-explored barrier to take-up of flexible working options: gender (Atkinson and Hall, 2005).

Gender barriers

We draw on the work of writers such as Smithson and Stokoe (2005) and Sheridan (2004) who argue that cultural gender roles in the UK which reinforce a 'caring' role for women and a 'breadwinner' role for men render WLI a 'women's issue'. This creates a position where long working hours for men create a barrier to the transformation of household division of labour (Green, 2001) and flexible working options are accessed, in the main, by women with either childcare or elder care responsibilities. We suggest that in the UK changes in terminology from 'family-friendly' to WLI have done little to render these issues gender-neutral, and that the situation of flexible working policies within a diversity agenda (see Chapter 14 for a discussion of this term) in an attempt to demonstrate their applicability to a wide range of employees (Doherty, 2004) has been largely unsuccessful. Opportunities to work part-time, especially where such roles are low-paid and -skilled, entrench women in a caring role and leave the male norm unchallenged (Strachan and Burgess, 1998). There is also low usage of practices such as parental leave by males, often because of the reduced income or damage to careers that results (Sheridan, 2004). In summary, WLI practices remain a highly gendered issue, a situation which we suggests creates a significant barrier to their uptake by a high proportion of the working population.

Rhetoric or reality?

While there are a number of high-profile examples in the HR press of the implementation of flexible working practices that benefit the employee, we turn now to consider the extent to which such practices are genuinely embedded in the employment relationship. Evidence suggests that working parents' preferences are largely unmet and that working-time schedules remain a critical source of work–family conflict (Thornthwaite and Sheldon, 2004). Despite the WLI rhetoric, employers continue to drive flexibility, responding to new conditions by simply allocating labour in more profitable ways without considering family needs (Legge, 1995).

Strachan and Burgess (1998) suggest that the Australian experience demonstrates that WLI has more to do with cost reduction and improved temporal flexibility than it has to do with genuine WLI arrangements. They further suggest that flexible working policies are usually poorly defined and need to be negotiated with the employer, leading to a position which is dependent upon bargaining power and in which business need may override individual need if the employee is low in the firm's hierarchy. Indeed, they further suggest that in Australia, at least, employee choice is decreasing and management prerogative is increasing.

The minimal implementation of WLI policies is also demonstrated in the Netherlands (Remery *et al*, 2003) and in the UK (Nolan and Wood, 2003). The latter draw on the findings of the Future of Work Programme to demonstrate that the long hours of UK workers mean that dissatisfaction with WLI has increased from 1992 to 2000. Further, most UK companies are doing no more than the legal minimum to meet needs of employees (Nolan and Wood, 2003). Thus the evidence suggests that WLI policies are little more than an aspiration for the majority of British employers (White *et al*, 2003).

In conclusion, we argue that the UK's business case approach to the achievement of WLI is meeting with limited success. WLI is likely to be successful only when drivers such as tight labour markets exist and thus requires a floor of statutory rights (Doherty, 2004). Studies show that it is easier to use WLI policies when they are formulated as a universal right for all parents (like parental leave) rather than when they demand negotiations with employers (Brandth and Kvande, 2001). We suggest that the business case for WLI is not self-evident (White *et al*, 2003), and in the Case study 10 below we present details on the social democratic public policy approach in Norway, which stands in stark contrast to that adopted in the UK.

In summary, we have in this section presented information on WLI practices in the UK and suggested that the UK's 'business approach' to WLI means that despite the benefits that are argued to accrue to employers, the implementation of such practices by many employers is very limited. We present evidence that indicates that autonomy over working time may be as important as WLI practices in enabling employees to manage work and other responsibilities. We further suggest that cultural gender norms and the public policy approach that reinforces them create a position whereby WLI continues to be perceived to be as a women's issue. We also present the outcomes of Norway's socially democratic public policy approach and argue that stronger mechanisms are required in the UK to support the genuine development of WLI.

Discussion questions

1   Outline the 'business case' that encourages firms to adopt policies that promote WLI.

2   To what extent do you consider high-performance management practices and those promoting WLI to be compatible?

3   How successful are WLI practices in your organisation (or in one with which you are familiar)?

CONCLUSIONS AND FUTURE ISSUES

In this chapter we have discussed the drivers for changing work organisation and increasing flexibility from both an employer and employee perspective. We have presented the UK's approach to such flexibility, reliant as it is on a relatively liberal, deregulated approach to employment. The UK adopts a particular perspective on work organisation and flexibility and, to highlight this, we have contrasted it with alternative policy approaches in other countries. We have presented evidence to underpin our argument that the UK's liberal approach has privileged employer needs over employee needs, and that despite increasing public policy interest and tight labour markets, relatively little progress has been made in the UK towards adopting mechanisms that successfully promote WLI for employees. This is set against a background in which increases in numerical flexibility are accepted by most to have occurred to a significant extent, the increase in part-time opportunities being created largely to meet employer demand and engendering jobs in the predominantly low-wage, low-skilled sector. It seems to us that if, as is widely suggested, the UK has to compete in the international economy utilising a cadre of highly skilled knowledge workers, much remains to be done in terms of work organisation and flexibility to achieve this position.

CASE STUDY 10

WLI IN NORWAY

We seek to demonstrate in this case study an alternative approach to that of the UK in terms of institutional systems and cultural background for WLI, exploring Norway's social democratic approach. The underlying principle of the Norwegian welfare state model is universalistic: Norwegian society is characterised by social homogeneity and strong egalitarian traditions. Egalitarian values provide widespread support for public policy that promotes gender equality, both in the labour market and in the family. The welfare state continues to be a major actor and the institutions of the welfare state have been strengthened in respect of the labour market, gender equality and especially family policies.

The notion of equal opportunities for both males and females to combine paid work and parenthood only started to develop in Norway in the 1990s, the male-breadwinner/ female-housewife model being dominant prior to this. From this point, however, policies have been developed to support a symmetric 'dual-earner/dual carer' family model. The state is seen as a responsible agent for offering support in care of dependants and combining parenthood and employment, and its interference in these matters is widely accepted. Indeed, the focus of social policy is more flexible arrangements between work and family for both mothers and fathers, and a ministry exists the sole purpose of which is to develop policies to offer families with young children a wider set of choices in balancing their work and family lives.

Although the share of GDP devoted to social protection systems is similar in Norway and the UK, the level of expenditure devoted to family and children is more generous in Norway. Indeed, in Norway, family obligations in respect of childcare are considered to be minimal and there is generous state provision. As noted earlier, employment patterns are characterised by long part-time or full-time jobs, and in combining work and unpaid work Norwegians make extensive use of public schemes supporting working parents (subsidised childcare arrangements, paid parental leave, flexible working hours).

Subsidised daycare is available for pre-school children, although this only started in the early 1990s, prior to which policies supported women in traditional roles as full-time housewives. Despite this, 66% of 1–5-year-olds are now in such daycare centres and this was forecast to reach 80% in 2005, the state aiming to offer a place in a state-subsidised childcare centre for anyone who wants one. Alternatively, parents can take state subsidy to fund themselves while they stay at home to care for children, and 20% of mothers and 5% of fathers have used this 'cash for care' to reduce their working hours.

Norwegian policies are also positive in terms of allowances for leave and absence from work following the birth of a child, contrasting with the less supportive political and social attitudes and policies in the UK. This leave is, however, characterised as parental rather than maternity leave, much of the leave entitlement being available to either parent. Such parental leave is either 42 weeks at full pay or 52 weeks at 80% pay, four weeks of which is the father's quota and cannot be transferred to the mother, being forfeited if not used. Prior to the implementation of this policy, only 2% of fathers took parental leave, whereas the figure now stands at over 80%. Up to two further years leave unpaid (one year per parent) is available and is supported by a 'time account' system in which parents can take portions of paid leave in combination with part-time work and thus work shorter hours without a reduction in income until the child is two or three years old. There are also generous paid carer leave policies to look after sick children under the age of 12 of up to 10–15 days per parent, depending on number of children.

Such policies have encouraged a convergence in employment patterns, Norway having an unusually high rate of female labour force participation. 76.4% of all Norwegian women aged 15–64 participate in the labour market and Norwegian mothers with children 0–6 years of age increased their employment rates significantly during the 1990s. The rate for mothers with children below three years of age rose from 66% in 1991 to 74% in 2000. The rate for mothers with children between the ages of three and six rose from 73% to 82% in the same period. Fathers with young children have meanwhile reduced their actual working hours throughout the 1990s. The gender gap in labour market behaviour among Norwegian parents has, therefore, diminished in the

1990s and more full-time work among mothers and shorter working hours among fathers has resulted in more similar contractual working.

It can thus be argued that women's employment in Norway has been facilitated by the public take-over of the provision of education, health and welfare services such as daycare for children and services for the elderly. Despite this, a fully egalitarian system does not prevail and work–family balance is still a 'feminine dilemma' even in Norway. There remains segregation in the Norwegian labour market where almost 50% of women work part-time and in lower-paying occupations, and part-time rates remain high among mothers and rare among fathers. The public sector appears to accommodate the greatest flexibility in its workforce and also offers better economic compensations to its employees. However, the 'worker-carer' model seems to conflict with structures and cultures in the private sector, and Norwegian workers are not exempt from the demands of new jobs that require 'flexibility', leading to problems of overtime and difficulties in boundary-setting – problems for those with families.

Source: Fagnani *et al* (2004)

Case study tasks

1   How does the role of the welfare state in Norway differ from that in the UK (or a country with which you are familiar)?

2   To what extent do you think that Norway's public policy approach accounts for the difference between working-time patterns in Norway and the UK (or a country with which you are familiar)?

3   To what extent is Norway's public policy approach likely to be able to offset the pressures of increasing employer-driven flexibility?

REFERENCES

Alis D. (2003) 'The 35-hour week in France: the French exception?', *Personnel Review*, Vol. 32, No. 4: 510–25.

Allan C. (2000) 'The hidden organisational costs of using non-standard employment', *Personnel Review*, Vol. 29, No. 3: 34–48.

Allan C. and Brosnan P. (1998) 'Non-standard working-time arrangements in Australia and New Zealand', *International Journal of Manpower*, Vol. 19, No. 4: 234–49.

Anon (2005) 'UK's working time opt out remains intact … for now', *Personnel Today*, 7 June, p.1.

Atkinson C. and Hall L. (2005) 'Improving working lives: the role of gender in flexible working', paper presented to the Gender, Work and Organisation Conference, Keele University, July 2005.

Atkinson J. (1984) 'Manpower strategies for flexible organisations', *Personnel Management*, August.

Beynon P, Grimshaw D., Rubery J. and Ward K. (2002) *Managing Employment Change*. Oxford: Oxford University Press.

Bishop K. (2004) 'Working time patterns in the UK, France, Denmark and Sweden', www.statistics.gov.uk/articles/labour_market_trends_/working_time_patterns.pdf

Boheme R. and Taylor M. (2004) 'Actual and preferred working hours', *British Journal of Industrial Relations*, Vol. 42, No. 1: 149–66.

Brandth B. and Kvande E. (2001) 'Flexible work and flexible fathers', *Work, Employment and Society*, Vol. 15, No. 2: 251–67.

Burchell B. J., Day D., Hudson M., Ladipo D., Mankelow R., Nolan J., Reed H., Wichert I. and Wilkinson F. (1999) *Job Insecurity and Work Intensification: Flexibility and the changing boundaries of work*. London: Joseph Rowntree Foundation.

Czemy A. (2004) 'France's 35-hour week "has failed" ', *People Management*, 3 June.

den Dulk L., Peper B. and van Doorne-Huiskes, A. (2004) 'Gender, parenthood and the changing European workplace', Transitions Research Report # 2: Literature Review for the EU Framework 5 funded study. Printed by Manchester Metropolitan University: Research Institute for Health and Social Change.

Doherty L. (2004) 'Work–life balance initiatives: implications for women', *Employee Relations*, Vol. 26, No. 4: 433–52.

Evans-Pritchard A. (2005) 'France to abandon the 35-hour week', *Daily Telegraph*, 24 March, p.38.

Fagan C. (2001) 'Time, money and gender order: work orientations and working-time preferences in Britain', *Gender, Work and Organization*, Vol. 8, No. 3: 239–66.

Fagnani J. and Letablier M.-T. (2004) 'Work and family life balance: the impact of the 35-hours law in France', *Work, Employment and Society*, Vol. 18, No. 3: 551–72.

Fagnani J., Houriet-Ségard G. and Bédouin S. (2004) 'Gender, parenthood and the changing European workplace', Transitions Research Report # 1: Context Mapping Report for the EU Framework 5 funded study. Printed by Manchester Metropolitan University: Research Institute for Health and Social Change.

Felstead A., Jewson N. and Walters S. (2003) 'Managerial control of employees working at home', *British Journal of Industrial Relations*, Vol. 42, No. 2: 241–64.

Green F. (2001) 'It's been a hard day's night: the concentration and intensification of work in late twentieth-century Britain', *British Journal of Industrial Relations*, Vol. 39, No. 1: 53–80.

Guest D. (2001) 'Human resource management: when research confronts theory', *International Journal of Human Resource Management*, Vol. 12, No. 7: 1092–1106.

Hall L. and Atkinson C. (2005a) 'The impact of flexible working on organisational performance', paper presented to the Performance and Reward Conference, Manchester Metropolitan University, April 2005.

Hall L. and Atkinson C. (2005b) 'The role of control in flexible working', paper presented to the CIPD Professional Standards Conference, Keele University, June 2005.

Harker L. and Lewis S. (2001) 'Work–life policies: where should the government go next?', in Birkett, N. (ed.) *A Life's Work: Achieving full and fulfilling employment*. London: Institute of Public Policy Research.

Harris L. (2003) 'Home-based teleworking and the employment relationship', *Personnel Review*, Vol. 32, No. 4: 422–37.

Hogarth T., Hasluck C. P., Winterbotham M. and Vivian D. (2001) *Work–Life Balance 2000: Results from the baseline study*, Research Report 249. London: DfEE.

Hollinshead G., Nicholls P. and Tailby S. (2003) *Employee Relations* (2nd edition). Harlow: FT/Prentice Hall.

Kalleberg A. L. (2003) 'Flexible firms and labour market segmentation', *Work and Occupations*, Vol. 30, No. 2: 154–75.

Knox A. and Walsh J. (2005) 'Organisational flexibility and HRM in the hotel industry: evidence from Australia', *Human Resource Management Journal*, Vol. 15, No. 1: 57–75.

Kodz J. (2003) *Working Long Hours: A review of evidence*, Vol. 1. Employment Relations Research Series, No. 16.

Kodz J., Harper H. and Dench S. (2002) 'How to ... improve the work–life balance in your organisation', *The Guide to Work–Life Balance*. London: CIPD

Legge K. (1995) *Human Resource Management: Rhetoric and realities*. Basingstoke: Macmillan.

Legge K. (1998) 'Flexibility: the gift-wrapping of employment degradation?', in Sparrow P. and Marchington M. (eds) *Human Resource Management: The new agenda*. Harlow: FT/Prentice Hall.

Lepak D. P. and Snell S. A. (1999) 'The human resource architect: toward a theory of human capital allocation and development', *Academy of Management Review*, Vol. 24, No. 1: 31–48.

Marlow S. (2002) 'Regulating labour management in small firms', *Human Resource Management Journal*, Vol. 12, No. 3: 25–43.

Millar J. and Warman A. (1996) *Family Obligations in Europe*. London: Family Policy Studies Centre.

Morrison D. (2005) 'Costly delivery for company profits: burden placed on smaller firms by new "family friendly" laws', *Daily Telegraph*, 7 June, p.24.

Nolan P. and Wood S. (2003) 'Mapping the future of work', *British Journal of Industrial Relations*, Vol. 41, No. 2: 165–74.

Noyelle T. (1990) 'Toward a new labour market segmentation', in Noyelle T. (ed.) *Skills, Wages and Productivity in the Service Economy*. San Francisco, Westview.

Pierson P. (2001) *The New Politics of the Welfare State*. Oxford: Oxford University Press.

Remery C., van Doorne-Huiskes A. and Schippers J. (2003) 'Family friendly policies in the Netherlands', *Personnel Review*, Vol. 32, No. 4: 456–73.

Rosendaal B. W. (2003) 'Dealing with part-time work', *Personnel Review*, Vol. 32, No. 4: 474–91.

Sheridan A. (2004) 'Chronic presenteeism: the multiple dimensions to men's absence from part-time work', *Gender, Work and Organization*, Vol. 11, No. 2: 207–25.

Singe I. and Croucher R. (2003) 'The management of trust-based working time in Germany', *Personnel Review*, Vol. 32, No. 4: 492–509.

Smithson J. and Stokoe E. H. (2005) 'Discourses of work–life balance: negotiating "genderblind" terms in organizations', *Gender, Work and Organization*, Vol. 12, No. 2: 147–68.

Stenning A.and Hardy J. (2005) 'Public sector reform and women's work in Poland: "working for juice, coffee and cheap cosmetics" ', *Gender, Work and Organization*, Vol. 12, No. 6: 503–26.

Strachan G. and Burgess J. (1998) 'The "family friendly" workplace', *International Journal of Manpower*, Vol. 19, No. 4: 250–65.

Tang N. and Cousins C. (2005) 'Working time, gender and family: an East–West comparison', *Gender, Work and Organization*, Vol. 12, No. 6: 527–50.

Thom N. and Blum A. (1998) 'The structure of working hours in Swiss companies', *Human Resource Management Journal*, Vol 8., No. 3: 77–84.

Thornthwaite L. and Sheldon P. (2004) 'Employee self-rostering for work–family balance: leading examples in Austria', *Employee Relations*, Vol. 26, No. 3: 238–54.

Torrington D., Hall L. and Taylor S. (2005) *Human Resource Management*. Harlow: FT/Prentice Hall.

Tuselmann H. (1996) 'The path towards greater labour flexibility in Germany: hampered by past success?', *Employee Relations*, Vol. 18, No. 6: 26–47.

Wallace C. (2002) HWF Research Report 1: *Critical Review of Literature and Discourses about Flexibility*, pp.5–26. Vienna: Research Consortium, Institute for Advanced Studies. Available online at http://www.hwf.at.

White M., Hill S., McGovern P., Mills C. and Smeaton D. (2003) 'High-performance management practices, working hours and work–life balance', *British Journal of Industrial Relations*, Vol. 41, No. 2: 175–95.

Williams R. D. (2000) 'An introduction to the UK Time Use Survey from a labour market perspective', www.statistics.gov.uk/articles/labour_market_trends/time_use_survey.pdf

Wong M. (2001) 'The strategic used of contingent workers in Hong Kong's economic upheaval', *Human Resource Management Journal*, Vol. 11, No. 4: 22–37.

Worral L. and Cooper C. L. (1999) 'Working patterns and working hours: their impact on UK managers', *Leadership and Organization Development Journal*, Vol. 20, No. 1: 6–10.

www.ilo.org/public/english/employment/strat/analysis/lmpo/publ.htm

Culture change management

CHAPTER 5

Paul Brook and Elke Pioch

CHAPTER OBJECTIVES

When you have read this chapter you should be able to:

- understand the place and importance of managing corporate culture within HRM and related service management approaches

- evaluate the principal theoretical debates on the nature, form and dynamics of organisational culture

- critically assess the extent to which it is possible for companies to manage their corporate culture within and across international borders

- appreciate the reasons for the high importance given to managing culture in service settings

- critically examine employees' experience of corporate culture management in the delivery of customer service.

PURPOSE AND SCOPE

The purpose of this chapter is to provide an overview of the range of debates on – and empirical evidence within HRM and services management for – culture change management as a central plank in the strategic management of employees. To date, theoretical and empirical contributions to the culture management debate have, with rare exception, emanated from the USA and the UK (Harris and Metallinos, 2002). As markets internationalise apace and competition becomes fiercer, the corporate search for competitive advantage has increasingly focused on developing employees with 'enterprising' attributes via culture change programmes. Here the primary objective is to create a sensitivity to markets and customers which suffuses day-to-day organisational life, thereby shaping employee beliefs and behaviours. Indeed, for many international companies there is a desire to create a corporate culture that can be replicated across borders. We therefore focus on the themes of cultural variation, globalisation and convergence and divergence. We conclude that culture management interventions may increase customer orientation among employees but do not necessarily remove an underlying relationship of conflicting interests between management and workers. Further, multinational companies' attempts at cross-border replication may only be partly successful because local cultural pressures produce variable and hybrid cultures, whereas industries may possess macro-cultures that reproduce internationally.

1 INTRODUCING CULTURE CHANGE MANAGEMENT

The notion that it is feasible to manipulate an organisation to create a strategically oriented single culture raises a range of questions:

- What is organisational culture?

- Do organisations possess a single culture, or are there many?

- Who has ownership and control of organisational culture?

- What are the dynamics of cultural stability and change?

- How much cultural power and influence rests with managers as opposed to employees or even customers?

- Can cultures be replicated, or are they always unique products of their own organisational/territorial 'eco-system'?

- Do indigenous cultures constrain the creation of international corporate cultures?

These questions mean that the possibility of effectively managing corporate culture is highly problematic, not least when it is attempted by companies on an international basis. Not surprisingly, there is a long-running and wide-ranging debate about its feasibility. We shall provide an accessible tour of these arguments.

The success or otherwise of corporate culture change boils down to the experience and reaction of the employees, which are all too often taken for granted in normative HRM and service management approaches. The chapter will therefore also explore arguments about corporate culture that start with the experience of the employee, providing a critical analysis 'from below'.

Given the often greater emphasis on culture management in large service companies, much of this more critical work has drawn on the experience of customer service workers. There is ample evidence of a complex interplay between employee consent, compliance and resistance to management attempts to shape customer service interactions. In particular, there is a focus on the management of emotional labour and its effects on the service worker. Over-arching these cultural facets of service work is the constant pressure on front-line workers to deliver a service that marries corporate demands of efficiency and conformity with the fickle, individual expectations of customers. This tension possesses the potential to cause confrontation between workers and employers.

2 WHAT IS CULTURE?

There is no widely accepted definition of 'culture'; consequently, there is a plethora of academic definitions and complex debates over its precise nature and dynamics (see Harris and Ogbonna, 1998a, 1998b; Martin, 2002; Legge, 1994, 2005). Nevertheless, within the range of definitions it is possible to identify a set of three core elements that ought to be shared by a given social group: behaviours, values and beliefs. There is also broad agreement that a culture comprises observable behaviours (tangible manifestations) peculiar to that social group, and unobservable (intangible) dimensions – that is, the values and assumptions shared by group members.

These broadly agreed dimensions are illustrated by Schein's (1984: 9) definition:

> '... a pattern of basic assumptions – invented, discovered or developed by a given group as it learns to cope with its problems of external adaptation and internal integration – that has worked well enough to be considered valid, and therefore

> **to be taught to new members as the correct way to perceive, think, and feel in relation to those problems.'**

Although Schein's definition is underpinned by the three elements of behaviours, values and beliefs, it appears to assume that culture is a neatly bounded phenomenon which has a single set of basic assumptions that are 'invented, discovered or developed' exclusively within the social group. Furthermore, he states that these are taught to new members as 'the correct way' to feel, think and act in what seems to be a one-way cultural production-line.

For most academic writers this is too one-dimensional (see Legge, 2005) and understates the complexity and dynamism of cultures which they perceive as fuelled by multiple influences – internal and external events and people, outgoing and incoming members. Thus, a definition of culture has to be both holistic – encompassing the notion of a social group sharing behaviours, values and beliefs – and pluralistic in that it captures the complex array of contributions to, and influences on, a culture. An example of just such a definition is offered by Ogbonna and Harris (2002a: 34) who suggest that the 'collective sum of beliefs' are not necessarily entirely the internal product of social group members and furthermore that they only 'help to shape' the responses of the group rather than wholly determine them:

> **'the collective sum of beliefs, values, meanings, assumptions that are shared by a social group and that help to shape the ways in which they respond to each other and to their external environment.'**

The debate about defining culture is much more than a semantic exercise. What is at stake is the theoretical belief that it is feasible to manage organisational culture in the same way as other HR elements such as job design. Schein's definition suggests that culture is a relatively tightly bounded and internally regulated phenomenon that would appear to lend itself to management – whereas Ogbonna and Harris offer a definition that suggests a more fluid, complex and dynamic set of social interactions that would be less amenable to control by management.

Discussion questions

1   What are the three core elements shared by definitions of culture?

2   In addition to the three core elements, what other assumptions does Schein make about the nature of culture?

3   In what assumptions does Ogbonna and Harris's definition vary from that of Schein's?

3 CULTURE AND HUMAN RESOURCE MANAGEMENT

Why manage culture?

By the 1990s many organisations sought to build a more 'enterprising' and 'customer-oriented' workforce. A key tool in this search for competitive advantage, certainly amongst US- and

UK-based companies, is culture management as an integral element of human resource management systems that seek a strategic 'fit' in the context of implementing high-performance work systems (Boxall, 2003; Ogbonna and Whipp, 1999; see also the discussion in Chapter 3).

Why, then, is culture management so popular amongst practitioners? Four principal reasons are prevalent (Ogbonna and Harris, 2002a):

- Much management theory assumes that an organisation's culture is discrete and unitary. It is therefore possible for it to be controlled by senior management.

- If it is possible to control culture, to fail to do so is to miss an opportunity to harness an organisation's human resources.

- Managing culture to create a unifying set of values in tune with the interests of senior managers produces a corresponding improvement in business performance.

- An organisation's unique culture, as a source of competitive advantage, is extremely difficult for competitors to replicate.

Culture in HRM theory

Contemporary enthusiasm for culture management emerged in the late 1970s and early 1980s principally through the popular proselytising works of US culture management gurus, most notably Peters and Waterman (1982) and Deal and Kennedy (1982). Pioneering conceptual and empirical foundations were laid by Hofstede (1980, 1991) in his study of IBM's corporate culture in over 40 countries. He argued that variations in IBM's culture were not due primarily to management inconsistencies from country to country but rather to what he identified as national differences in work-related values (see Chapter 2 for a more detailed discussion).

In the UK, Guest's (1987, 1990) normative model of 'soft' HRM has done much to establish the prominence of culture management in academic debates. Guest argues that for an organisation to successfully implement HRM it is necessary to build and manage four dimensions holistically:

1   *strategic integration* (of human resources)

2   *commitment* (of employees to organisational goals)

3   *quality* (of staff and performance)

4   *flexibility* (of skills and organisational structures).

In order to meld all four into a fully functioning managerial system it is necessary to forge an organisational culture with a set of common core values and practices that facilitate and require commitment, enterprise and adaptability from its members.

With cultural change offering the prize of commitment there also rides the belief that labour performance will improve qualitatively. This is because committed employees will not just work flexibly but rather endeavour to succeed by '"going the extra mile" in pursuit of customer service and organisational goals' (Storey, 2001: 8). Superficially, at least, this sounds a plausible business goal.

The assumption that it is possible to manipulate a culture to generate employees' commitment thereby improving organisational performance continues to underpin many of the recent debates and developments in HRM, such as high-performance and high-commitment work systems (Legge, 2001). Indeed, Storey (2001: 8) claims that the aspiration to manage culture has become so central (in Anglo-Saxon contexts) in recent decades that 'the twin ideas of "managing culture change" and moving towards HRM have often appeared to coincide and become one and the same project.' This is despite the fact that it is not clear that strong corporate cultures are sufficiently flexible to respond quickly and as required in highly competitive markets and volatile economic conditions (Legge, 2005; Clegg et al, 2005).

Culture management is more associated with 'softer' variants of HRM (see Chapter 3), such as Guest's model (above). This is because softer models emphasise the development of resourceful humans through policies of treating employees as valuable assets via winning their commitment and trust, building their skills and adaptability, and facilitating their empowerment to enable a creative, proactive contribution. 'Harder' models seek competitive advantage by stressing the management of the human 'resource' as a calculative rather than a developmental endeavour thereby optimising its contribution to 'bottom-line' profits. Essentially, it is 'headcount' management to ensure that there are enough employees with the right skills, in the right place, at the right time, and at the right price (see Legge, 2005; Lucas, 2004).

All HRM models and practice, however, comprise soft and hard dimensions (Storey, 2001). Every HR strategy seeks varying degrees and mixes of employees' internal self-control through empowerment and commitment as well as external control through direct supervision and standardisation. The degree to which one dimension is pursued more than the other is principally contingent upon the extent to which a product and/or service is low-value, mass-volume and uniform or high-value, differentiated and high-quality (Lucas, 2004). Culture management must therefore be understood as on a continuum where it is pursued to a greater or lesser degree depending on the specific mix of hard or soft dimensions within the overall HR strategy (Bowen and Lawler, 1995; Wilkinson et al, 1998). In practice, companies pursue a variety of culture change programmes with differing goals, ranging between employee commitment and behavioural compliance, depending on the needs of the business (Pioch, 2003).

Customer orientation and the New Service Management School

Many of the most high-profile culture change programmes are found in service companies where customer service is a core feature of the 'product', such as retailers, airlines, call centres, financial services and hospitality (Brook, 2004). Here, companies are engaged in a continuous effort to establish competitive advantage by instilling an ethos of customer orientation amongst front-line workers and to a lesser extent support staff. In response, a specific HRM for front-line service workers has developed, alongside generic HRM, which has come to be referred to as the New Service Management School (NSMS) (Korczynski, 2002).

The NSMS writers explicitly seek to provide service managers with the HR ideas and tools to produce a consistent and improving level of service quality from front-line workers that delivers customer satisfaction (Gabbott and Hogg, 1998). These requirements focus very heavily on the behavioural and emotional role of the front-line worker and, in doing so, necessitate the strategic development of a culture of service quality through customer-orientation programmes (Lucas, 2004).

In responding to the challenge to provide a 'services HRM' that creates a customer-focused front-line workforce there emerged a consensus amongst NSMS writers. This has taken the form of the 'customer satisfaction/workforce satisfaction mirror' or for short, the 'mirror of satisfaction' (see Schneider and Bowen, 1995; Zeithaml and Bitner, 1996):

More specifically, Snape *et al* (1998: 857) in their comparative study of the practice of and attitudes to performance appraisals in Hong Kong and Britain found that:

> **'The judgemental, less participative approach reported by Hong Kong respondents is to some extent reflected in their views about what appraisal should be like ... The suggestion is ... that the practice of appraisal has been adapted to suit the cultural characteristics of the society. ...'**

They conclude by arguing (p.857) for a contingency approach where Anglo-Saxon management practices, 'while operating under individualist or low power distance cultural assumptions in their societies of origin, need not necessarily operate under quite the same assumptions when transplanted to a different culture'. Contingency approaches are not uncommon in cross-border mergers and acquisitions. Frequently, human resource managers have to adapt practices and values to balance the needs of the parent's 'strategic fit' with the demands of the new national context (Aguilera and Dencker, 2004).

We return to these issues later in the chapter in Case study 14, which presents an example of a cross-border acquisition by a foreign, global retailer of a leading British chain. It explores the process and effects of the parent company's efforts to transfer its highly distinctive corporate culture into its new foreign subsidiary.

Discussion questions

1   In your opinion, why do international retail companies seek to project a 'family' image as part of their corporate culture?

2   Make a list of three possible local cultural obstacles to a company with Anglo-Saxon origins wholly integrating its corporate culture into new national contexts.

3   List the main advantages and disadvantages for a company in the creation of a single international corporate culture spanning a variety of countries.

5 EVALUATING CULTURE CHANGE PROGRAMMES

Empirical evidence on culture change

Prescriptive HRM writers and their NSMS counterparts make the assumption that organisational culture is a discrete variable that can be manipulated to produce the requisite values and beliefs. On this basis, how is the effectiveness of culture change programmes to be evaluated? One common measure is Schein's (2004) model of culture that posits the existence within an organisation of three internal levels of cultural manifestation:

SCHEIN'S MODEL OF CULTURAL LEVELS

LEVEL 1

Visible artefacts (behaviours) – easily identifiable physical manifestations of culture

LEVEL 2

Values – those ideas that govern behaviour and explain the behaviour of a group

LEVEL 3

Basic assumptions (beliefs) – preconscious, 'taken for granted' assumptions that are the essence of culture

Source: adapted from Schein (2004)

According to Schein (2004), only when a prescribed company culture has been assimilated at the deepest level of basic assumptions amongst the workforce is it safe to claim that a culture management programme has been successful. This is because it is only at the level of basic assumptions that an organisational member can be said to be committed to the same objectives espoused in the formal corporate culture. Whether this is an adequate definition of successful culture change is debatable, as is revealed by the evidence from empirical research examined below. Schein's model does, however, suggest that organisational culture is not a singular entity but one that is variegated and fluid thereby posing difficulties in evaluating culture change.

Much empirical analysis of culture change programmes has found little evidence of successful employee acculturation at the equivalent of Schein's (2004) Level 3 (see Ogbonna, 1992; Martin, 1992; Rosenthal *et al*, 1997; Frenkel *et al*, 1999; Ogbonna and Harris, 2002b). Nevertheless, research into a range of service companies' – retailing, hospitality and call centres – culture change programmes aimed at securing customer orientation among employees does reveal varying degrees of success in shifting attitudes and behaviour towards valuing the importance of customer service. However, many front-line workers possessing a strong customer orientation do not demonstrate a similar level of attachment and commitment to their employers and their objectives. Indeed, they frequently employ informal individual and collective strategies to pursue their own more personalised version of 'excellent' customer service often in opposition to a cost-conscious and uniform model imposed by senior management (Rosenthal *et al*, 1997; Harris and Ogbonna, 1998b; Korczynski, 2001, 2002; Taylor and Bain, 2003). Culture change programmes can therefore be double-edged swords.

There is also evidence of other unintended and unpredictable outcomes. Payne *et al*'s (2002) study of a US community bank revealed that three years into a major culture change programme there was evidence of widespread cultural divergence and contested interpretation rather than the intended cohesion. And Ng and Tung's (1998) study of a Canadian bank found that it was the culturally heterogeneous branches that outperformed homogeneous branches in terms of absenteeism, productivity and financial performance, despite lower levels of job satisfaction and organisational commitment amongst staff.

Even in those companies with well-established and celebrated corporate cultures, where commitment to customer service and even a love of the product (see below) is the norm among staff, this does not guarantee that management can rely on employees' internalised commitment alone to achieve its performance targets. It is still necessary to enforce behavioural compliance on a day-to-day basis with a strict regime of incentives, targets and punishments as in the case of UK hi-fi separates retailer Richer Sounds (Wilkinson *et al*, 1998: 173):

> **'Being a "fun" employer, however, does not mean easy work for staff. On the contrary, staff acknowledge the hard work and, both the company and staff agree, this is not a culture to everyone's liking. Beneath the fun and gimmicks is a tough managerial style with little time for people who are unable to perform in this environment.'**

If it is so difficult for management to achieve profound and consistently experienced cultural change at the level of taken-for-granted assumptions, is this then an appropriate measure of successful 'transformation'? Should not a more contingent assessment be made of each culture management intervention within the specific context of a company's industry and market? This is the conclusion reached by Ogbonna and Harris (2002a: 40–1) in their study of culture management in two hotel and two restaurant-wine bar chains in the UK:

> **'The level at which a company targets its culture change intervention is related to the conduciveness of critical industry characteristics. This suggests that certain industry-specific factors may reduce the probability of achieving cultural change at the deepest levels of basic underlying assumptions across the organisation. Interviewees in all four companies alluded to various aspects of working conditions and terms of employment in the hospitality industry that imposed significant barriers to achieving deeper-level cultural transformation.'**

Ogbonna and Harris (2002a) argue that as a consequence of an unstable and largely dissatisfied workforce, managers appear to recognise that the prospect of cultural change at the level of basic assumptions is unlikely and that their response is a more realistic assessment about the level at which change should be targeted and the type of success that can be achieved.

This argument for a contingent evaluation of the effectiveness of culture management is also taken up by Harris and Metallinos (2002) in their study of culture change in a medium-sized Greek food retailer. Here they consider the extent to which generic culture change programmes – in this case deriving from UK and US food retailing – can be transposed across national borders (Case study 11).

CASE STUDY 11

MANAGING CULTURE IN A MEDIUM-SIZED GREEK FOOD RETAILER

The company

Established in 1965, operating out of 17 outlets by the end of the 1990s, with a turnover of £10 million and nearly 500 full-time staff (significantly more in the summer months to meet demand), capturing just over a quarter of its regional market.

The culture change programme and its consequences

Responding to perceived increased competitive pressures within the Greek retailing industry, partly due to the growth in foreign competitors, top managers initiated a culture change programme, which was rapidly implemented. Modelled partly on reported success stories of change initiatives in the UK and the USA, a rolling programme to alter operations, alter the use of technology and alter the underlying philosophy of the organisation was implemented.

Employees perceived these changes according to their place within the organisation. Top management and the majority of head office staff regarded compliance with the new measures – considered to promote the common good of the company – as rational. In contrast, half the store managers, who had to act as change agents in their stores, experienced increased levels of workload, stress and a concomitant disillusionment with the process. The majority of shopfloor workers, although accepting the rationale for the change, considered it as an unwelcome evil.

Feelings of an erosion of their power base disaffected a number of store managers and shopfloor workers experienced deskilling, demotivation and reduced job satisfaction:

> **'Now I feel that what I am doing can be done by anyone in the world – and this doesn't really make me happy ... my responsibilities are very limited, since the machines are doing everything.'**

> Shopfloor worker, 35, eight years of service

Disdain was expressed with the company's copying of foreign practices, which resulted in mere behavioural compliance rather than deep-rooted change:

> **'I am sure top management understand that changes cannot be copied so simply. ... I mean, I cannot have the same attitude as a Tesco worker. We're so different in many ways.'**

> Shopfloor worker, 24, four years of service

> **'I have been told to smile at the customers at all times. I do not**

99

> **really want to behave in this way. I cannot see what I can gain from this. But if this is how the company want me to behave, then I guess I will have to do it.'**
>
> Shopfloor worker, 27, five years of service
>
> Following an extensive period of attempting to motivate shopfloor staff through rewards and recognition for complying with expected behaviours, some impact on their attitude was reported. Unexpectedly, despite some high-profile resignations at store management level, staff turnover during the 12 months change period decreased by 20% and sales increased considerably.
>
> Source: extracted from Harris and Metallinos (2002)
>
> ## Case study tasks
>
> 1. Considering the evidence from the Greek food retailer, how feasible do you suppose it is to transpose cultural ideas from one cultural zone (here Anglo-American) to another (here Mediterranean)?
>
> 2. At which of Schein's cultural levels do you assume the change to take hold?
>
> 3. In your opinion, which role did the culture change programme play in increasing sales and reducing staff turnover? How feasible might it be to sustain this early success?

Harris and Metallinos' (2002) analysis shows that a naïve acceptance of the power of culture change programmes reported as successful in other national contexts may not meet with the same success in different (national) circumstances. In addition, their research powerfully demonstrates that the level of acceptance of senior management's cultural beliefs and values varies between different hierarchical levels in the organisation (see Section 6 below).

By contrast, Peccei and Rosenthal's (2000) study of a customer orientation (CO) programme in a UK food retailer suggests it is possible for widescale cultural transformation at deeper levels of basic assumptions. They identified 46% of employees as being 'committed' – exhibiting positive customer service attitudes and behaviours – and a further 32% as possessing a degree of internalised pro-service values and beliefs. They conclude, therefore, that management's horizons, even in low-paid and high-labour-turnover service work, should not be limited to mere behavioural compliance as argued by Ogbonna and Harris (2002a). However, even this evidence does not demonstrate a wholesale cultural transformation across an organisation but rather a shift of employees' cultural-discourse terrain towards the desired customer service attributes.

'Love of product'

A 'love of product' on the part of employees, Peters and Waterman (1982: 76) claimed, would be one of the results of a successfully managed culture, thereby strengthening their bonds with the organisation and the customer. Some products, however, are more lovable than others. Retailers, for example, selling computers, music systems, fashion clothing and outdoor pursuits equipment can expect to recruit sales staff with at the very least enthusiasm for the product, if not a passion. Whereas companies selling less exciting products – such as supermarkets – cannot rely on recruiting 'foodies' to sell coffee and rice. Evidently, those companies that are able to recruit staff who are already interested in the product and who can relate to customers with shared interests appear to be at an advantage when seeking their commitment and a customer-oriented perspective (Wilkinson *et al*, 1998).

Case study 12 presents an example of a specialist UK retailer where the employees not only possess a love of product but are also enthusiastic participants in the leisure culture associated with the product. These twin dimensions can also be found in service and production workers in a range of fields including computers, cars, cuisine, sport, music, gardening, reading and the arts. In these organisations there is likely to be a shared enthusiasm between senior management and employees for their product and a passion for its associated cultural activities. However, is it possible to assume that a love of product automatically translates into shared basic assumptions amongst senior management and employees?

CASE STUDY 12

UP FRONT'S 'LOVE OF PRODUCT' CULTURE

UP FRONT is a small outdoor leisure retailer situated in the English Peak District and North Wales. In 1987, Bill, the owner-manager, opened the first store in a village near a popular climbing destination with the aim of attracting climbers and 'real outdoor users', such as serious walkers, together with passing Sunday and holiday trade.

UP FRONT specialises in climbing hardware and prides itself in having the best hardware counter in Britain and possibly Europe. It employs 25 full-time and an equal number of casual members of staff. All employees are expected to be active participants in outdoor activities.

Owner-manager Bill contends that although the business side of UP FRONT is very important, it is not everything, and giving climbers a 'good deal' is just as important. One sales assistant claimed that he wants to make British climbers better by educating them in how to use equipment properly. There is thus a consensus between the MD and most UP FRONT employees that customers should not be pushed or persuaded to buy anything that is unsuitable, even if it means not making a sale.

The dedication to provide genuine support for the outdoor fraternity is supported by UP FRONT's service ethos. Bill wants employees to 'be in people's faces' – meaning a relatively aggressive approach to customers. At one level this refers to the way in which the specialists give advice on the best suitable gear, and at another it relates to the interaction between shopfloor workers and customers. Sales assistants are encouraged to 'cut through customers' smokescreens' and are not expected to accept inappropriate behaviour for the sake of a sale. In return, they are required to treat shoppers with the same respect that they would demand.

Employees are aware that it is very much Bill's company – his possession – expressing his vision, no matter how much they may enjoy working at UP FRONT. This was brought home to them when Bill took the unilateral decision to refuse staff an annual pay rise one year when the annual accounts did not balance.

Source: adapted from Pioch and Brook (2000)

Case study tasks

1   Assess the extent to which the congruence between employees' leisure pursuits and the products they sell encourages organisational uniformity at Schein's third Level of culture.

2   To what extent does 'love of product' at UP FRONT hinder or improve customer orientation?

3   What impact could owner-manager Bill's unilateral decisions have on staff commitment to the business goals?

Discussion questions

1   Summarise Ogbonna and Harris's argument as to why a contingent approach to culture management is more realistic and appropriate.

2   Why do Peccei and Rosenthal argue that it is feasible to pursue cultural transformation at the level of taken-for-granted assumptions?

3   List five examples of different companies in your own country where workers are recruited for their 'love of product'.

6 IS MANAGING CULTURE FEASIBLE?

Smircich's analytic foundations

The debate on the feasibility of managing culture is based largely on Smircich's (1983) exploration of the two principal competing paradigms on organisational culture – the functionalist (unitarist) and the interpretive (pluralist).

The functionalist paradigm is instrumental in that it is concerned with what a culture can be and ought to be – usually seen as a variable an organisation *has* in the possession of management, which is amenable to manipulation. This paradigm, as discussed above, tends to be favoured by prescriptive writers who are concerned to argue that it is feasible to manage organisational culture at the level of basic beliefs and assumptions. It implies it is possible for a sub-culture's beliefs and values – in this case senior management's – to override other sub-cultures' beliefs and values amongst employees, across work groups and within localities. Schein's (1984) definition of culture, with its implied bounded, unitary set of values and its one-way hierarchical process of inculcating cultural belief and behaviours, fits this perspective.

The interpretative conception of culture is essentially explanatory rather than instrumental. Here, culture is something an organisation *is* – that is, a product of continuous review and negotiated continuity and/or amendment involving all organisational members acting as either individuals or sub-groups. Culture is then conceived as pluralistic in nature and highly dynamic in practice. The result is that it cannot be objectively mapped for the purposes of manipulation by any particular individual or sub-group such as senior management. The potential for culture management is therefore limited except during periods of organisational upheaval when the old ways of doing things frequently weaken or dissolve because they are no longer applicable, permitted or feasible (Martin and Meyerson, 1988). Examples of these types of events would include the takeover of one company by another, particularly in a cross-border acquisition (see Case study 14), or the occurrence of large-scale job losses.

Martin's three-perspective framework

The underpinnings of much of the prescriptive and critical culture research have also been challenged by Martin (1992, 2002). She argues that at any given time an organisation comprises three broad perspectives of its culture: integration, differentiation and fragmentation.

- The *integration* perspective assumes that culture has the potential to be discrete, consistent and consensual across an organisation and is, therefore, manageable.

- The *differentiation* perspective stresses the existence within an organisation of sub-cultures between which there is the potential for competition and conflict. These sub-cultures can be delineated along a horizontal–functional axis (eg departments) or a vertical–hierarchical axis (eg managers and staff), or are context-specific, 'based on networks of personal contacts, friendships and demographic identities' (Martin, 2002: 103). The assumption is that consensus exists within a sub-culture but that competing sub-cultures possess conflicting ideas.

- The *fragmentation* perspective views culture as unstable, dynamic, complex and context-specific. The fragmentation perspective therefore perceives culture as largely unmanageable at the organisational level.

Harris and Ogbonna (1998a) and Ogbonna and Harris (2002a) develop Martin's initial conceptual framework further, following the studies of three UK retailers and four hospitality companies respectively. They found that the prevalence of each perspective amongst an organisation's members is directly related to their hierarchical position and function. Managers required to think strategically prefer the *integration* perspective, whereas those managers who have to bridge differing elements of an organisation, such as local branches and head office, view the *differentiation* perspective more favourably. Front-line and shopfloor workers with limited understanding and exposure to the organisation as a whole, and who tend to feel remote from the source of major decisions, are most likely to experience culture from the *fragmentation* perspective.

Martin (2002) stresses that the three perspectives should not simply be viewed as three levels of analysis congruent respectively with organisational levels – company-wide, social group and individual. Rather, 'at any point in time all three perspectives are relevant' (p.148) and there is no such thing as an *integrated*, *differentiated* or *fragmented* culture, but that the same culture can be viewed from contrasting perspectives by different members simultaneously. Any interpretation of organisational culture that is limited to only one of these three perspectives does not do justice to the complexity in organisations and as such fails to deliver a comprehensive understanding. Harris and Ogbonna (1998a) and Ogbonna and Harris (2002a) suggest that there are practical managerial implications that flow from the three-perspective analysis, in particular that differing culture change programmes should be directed at different levels of the organisational hierarchy. This, they argue, has two further implications for the content of culture management interventions (1998a: 120):

'First, it would appear that head office managements should direct more attention to appreciating differing perspectives (for example, the design of training and change programmes must reflect not only the cultural perceptions and assumptions of head office managers but also those of store [branch]-level employees including managers). Second, during cultural change it may be the case that behavioural consistency is the best that could be hoped for in respect of shopfloor staff whose cultural perspective is highly fragmented.'

Martin's three-perspective framework challenges the prescriptive HRM and NSMS approaches preoccupation with the integration perspective and highlights the plurality of ideas, sectional interests and expectations residing within an organisation at any given time irrespective of culture change interventions.

Discussion questions

1   Who are the members of an organisation most likely to possess the integration perspective on corporate culture? Explain why.

2   Who are the members of an organisation most likely to possess the differentiation perspective on corporate culture? Explain why.

3   Who are the members of an organisation most likely to possess the fragmentation perspective on corporate culture? Explain why.

7 CULTURE: A CONTESTED TERRAIN?

So far culture has been discussed in terms of its content and of whether it is feasible to manage its change so as to generate employee commitment to corporate goals. The discussion on the feasibility of managing culture did not ask the question whether the nature of the relationship between an employer and employee is of itself a structural barrier to the assimilation by workers of a senior management's desired set of values and beliefs. Nor has the question been asked why the successful infusion of customer service values amongst staff does not automatically translate into an acceptance of management's prescribed version of customer service. This next section of the discussion addresses these questions directly by assessing two analyses in which the terrain of organisational culture and customer service is contested to varying degrees by managers, front-line workers and customers.

Customer service in the customer-oriented bureaucracy

The characterisation of contemporary service organisations as customer-oriented bureaucracies (COBs) emerged out of a major study of call centres in Australia and Japan (Frenkel *et al*, 1999). The premise of the argument is that in western consumer societies the ideology of the authority of the consumer is now so embedded that it becomes increasingly difficult to challenge the idea and language of 'customer sovereignty'. However, the challenge to meet consumer expectations of authority continually clashes with the bureaucratic and cost-sensitive realities of manufacturing service. The production of customer service in contemporary service organisations therefore necessitates dual and opposing objectives:

'… the requirement for the organisation to be both formally rational, to respond to competitive pressures to appeal to customers' wishes for efficiency, and to be formally irrational, to enchant, responding to the customers' desire for pleasure, particularly through the perpetuation of the enchanting myth of customer sovereignty.'

Korczynski (2002: 64)

The existence of a dual logic is a source of constant tension for front-line workers. They have to perform a continuous juggling act between processing the requisite quantity of customers within a prescribed format and at the same time relating to each one as an individual, with varying desires. The result is that the more 'customer-oriented' front-line workers are, the more likely they are to experience discomfort and frustration:

> **'I'm damned if I do, damned if I don't. You just can't win. Either [the boss] is mad at me, or the customer is. If I don't get my work done, [the boss] is going to yell at me. But if I don't help the customers, they get pissed at me.'**
>
> Weatherly and Tansik (1992: 5), quoted in Korczynski (2002: 76)

According to COB theory, the distress caused by performing customer service is made all the more painful because the work is a potential source of pleasure and job satisfaction for front-line workers by virtue of the promise of meaningful social interaction with the individual customer. In this way, the dual logic is experienced as both pleasure and pain by workers. Consequently, they constantly strive to enhance the pleasurable side of customer service by seeking to personalise the encounter which is often under pressure from, or at variance with, the more bureaucratised and impersonal approach demanded by organisational systems and performance targets. What results is a contest over the terms of what constitutes 'excellent' customer service and as such a challenge to the legitimacy of the espoused values, beliefs and behaviours in the official corporate culture:

> **'What type of customer is being projected as the source of authority? Is it the disembodied "average" customer that management appears to prioritise, or is it the socially embedded specific individual customers with whom service workers have empathy?'**
>
> Korczynski (2003: 61)

The COB theory's argument that the very system of producing customer service generates a mix of pleasure and pain for workers, and underlying tension with management, clearly questions the feasibility of creating a single and unifying corporate culture. Moreover, the COB has been criticised for exaggerating the degree of potential and real pleasure front-line workers either expect or experience. Taylor and Bain's evidence of work in Indian (2005) and UK call centres (2001) leads them to argue that the COB adherents overplay the impact of the customer-orientation logic within organisations as the source of potential and real satisfaction. Their findings lead them to argue that labour is performed more commonly at the bureaucratic end of the spectrum where front-line workers experience managerial intervention and control as oppressive much more than is acknowledged by COB proponents.

Emotional labour: the commercialisation of feeling

We now turn to the issue of the individual effects on the front-line worker of performing customer service work, involving a display of emotions. This issue is a major source of controversy in what has come to be known as the 'emotional labour' debate (see Korczynski, 2002; Bolton, 2005). The debate was pioneered by Hochschild (1983) following her seminal study of emotional labour amongst flight attendants and debt collectors in the United States, *The Managed Heart*.

Hochschild's analysis rests on a distinction between what she refers to as 'emotion work' and 'emotional labour'. Emotion work is the process of managing and presenting our emotions in the private sphere of our lives. Emotional labour, by contrast, is 'the management of feeling to create a publicly observable facial and bodily display' (Hochschild, 1983: 7) by front-line service workers. In the 'public sphere' of emotional labour – customer service – front-line workers' feelings are commercialised through a 'transmutation' of private-sphere feelings into a package of emotions 'consumed' by the customer as a commodified service interaction. Workers' feelings are transformed into a commodity that is bought and sold entirely for the purposes of commercial gain. This process has the effect of alienating front-line workers by wresting ownership and control from them of the form, timing, giving and withdrawal of emotional feelings, moods and their display:

> '... when the product – the thing to be engineered, mass-produced, and subjected to speed-up and slowdown – is a smile, a mood, a feeling, or a relationship, it comes more to belong to the organisation and less to the self.'
>
> Hochschild (1983: 198)

This alienation is compounded by two other aspects of the front-line worker's emotional labour. First, in the commercial sphere there is an unequal relationship with the customer – 'the customer is always right!' In our private lives we tend to experience a much greater level of equality in our emotional interactions:

> 'In private life we are free to question the going rate of exchange and free to negotiate a new one. If we are not satisfied, we can leave. ... But in the public world of work, it is often part of an individual's job to accept uneven exchanges, to be treated with disrespect or anger by a client, all the while closeting into fantasy the anger one would like to respond with. Where the customer is king, unequal exchanges are normal ...'
>
> Hochschild (1983: 85–6)

Second, management, in order to maximise the potential for delivering the requisite quality of customer service, impose and enforce systematic 'feeling rules' on front-line workers. These rules dictate the form, content and appropriateness of workers' emotional displays to customers.

Hochschild argues that the feeling rules imposed by management often go further than demanding behavioural compliance – what she calls 'surface acting'. Management go on to strive for front-line workers' internalisation of the feelings they are required to display (culture change!). Not only does this enhance the 'quality' of the emotional display but it also diminishes the likelihood of 'emotive dissonance' caused by the strain of continuously bridging what is really felt with what has to be feigned over long periods. Hochschild argues that the response by many emotional labourers is 'to try to pull the two closer together either by changing what we feel or by changing what we feign' (1983: 90). She calls this internalisation process 'deep acting'.

Deep acting is the result of workers' seeking a more comfortable space for their 'self' through the fusion of its real and acted dimensions. It is a deeply contradictory condition and therefore an unstable one. Fusion does not alleviate the fundamental alienation of the front-line worker. This is because emotional labourers still experience as 'normal' the undermining of their 'real self' through the commodification of their emotions, an unequal relationship with customers, and management's imposition of feeling rules. When this is combined with management's unrelenting drive for greater effort and service quality there is the potential for emotional labourers to question and challenge in whose interests they are performing:

> **'Often the test comes when a company speed-up makes personal service impossible to deliver because the individual's personal self is too thinly parcelled out to meet the demands made on it. ... The worker wonders whether her smile and the emotional labour that keeps it sincere are really hers.'**
>
> Hochschild (1983: 133)

One such example is the Cathay Pacific Airlines flight attendants' 1993 strike famously captured by the evocative phrase 'the perfumed picket line' (Linstead, 1995) (Case study 13).

CASE STUDY 13

CATHAY PACIFIC AIRLINES – THE PERFUMED PICKET LINE

In 1993 Cathay Pacific Airways flight attendants went on strike following the sacking of three colleagues for refusing to work flights as 'down-graded' junior flight attendants due to staff shortages. The strike lasted for 16 days. After the dispute both the union and airline management agreed that there was a lot of conciliatory work necessary to rebuild the Cathay Pacific culture.

The advertising imagery of Cathay Pacific flight attendants:

Cathay Pacific like most Asian airlines features in its advertisements beautiful, demure and sensual stewardesses, whose only apparent wish is to serve – typically smiling but averting their gaze in respectful submission …

What the *South China Sunday Morning Post* said:

In the advertisements, the Cathay girls fix sultry smiles then avert their faces with Asian humility … this servile image has been smashed by the perfumed picket line which has shown itself to be tough, resilient and well orchestrated.

What the striking flight attendants said:

They are always telling us that we are pretty and intelligent and that we are a very important part of the company – and then they treat us as if we clean the toilets … AND no matter what happens we must always SMILE.

The flight [to Taipei] *takes 55 minutes, an hour at the most, and there are more and more of these fights all the time. In that time we have to do a full meal service. Drinks, dinner, coffee, tea, everything! The aircraft flies to Taipei – we run there.*

What the Cathay Pacific management said:

We have to reserve the right to discipline our employees … to take disciplinary action against those who have acted against the interests of the company. This dispute remains, as it has from the beginning, about a company's right to manage its affairs in the interests of all parties – our customers, our staff, and our shareholders.

Source: adapted from Linstead (1995)

Case study tasks

1 Outline the type of emotional labour flight attendants in general and Cathay Pacific Airways stewardesses in particular have to perform.

2 What were the key reasons for the breakdown in relations between Cathay Pacific Airways management and flight attendants?

3 To what extent does management's assumed right to 'manage its affairs' affect flight attendants' emotional labour?

Hochschild is criticised for her 'absolutism' in only identifying the harmful, alienating effects of emotional labour rather than recognising that it contains both pleasure and pain (Wouters, 1989; Tolich, 1993). Bolton (2005) meanwhile urges a qualitative shift beyond Hochschild's concept of emotional labour. She argues that in the workplace there is enough emotional space for workers to keep in touch with their comfortable 'self' through 'having a laugh', misbehaviour and resistance to rules, emotion gift exchange with co-workers and chosen customers, bonding with co-workers, and building self-identity.

Despite critical reactions to Hochschild's thesis, it continues to pose profound questions regarding the politics and ethics of commodifying human emotions as customer service (issues that you may find it useful to consider in the context of the discussion in Chapters 12 and 13 on ethics and corporate social responsibility). It also raises awkward questions about how 'real' and robust organisational culture change is at the level of workers' assumptions and values. This is because Hochschild's analysis treats as pivotal the front-line workers' daily experience of emotional subordination to managers' rules and targets and customers' varying moods and desires. As a deeply structured inequality, emotional labour poses a constant source of potential front-line resistance to the norms of corporate culture and managerial legitimacy.

Discussion questions

1   What is a customer-oriented bureaucracy, and in what way does it imply a dual logic?

2   What is the difference for Hochschild between 'emotion work' and 'emotional labour'?

3   What is surface acting, and how does it differ from deep acting?

CONCLUSIONS AND FUTURE ISSUES

With the intensifying pressures of global competition, companies' search for competitive advantage has increasingly settled on the need to secure optimum employee contribution via an 'enterprising' corporate culture. This movement towards the strategic centrality of culture management has emanated from the experience and prescriptions of primarily US and UK managers and academics – not least via the HR strategies of these countries' ever-expanding MNCs.

What then of the feasibility of culture management? The debate on whether or not an organisation's culture can be managed in the same way as, for example, job design will continue apace. It is likely to remain dominated by the two broad perspectives of neo-unitarism and pluralism that understand organisational culture as, respectively, either a discrete element amenable to manipulation or a dynamic and fluid phenomenon escaping managerial capture.

How then to identify successful corporate acculturation? Here the question of whether or not it is necessary to achieve a transformation in employees' basic assumptions as the essential measure of success has become central. Yet there is mounting evidence that it is neither a relevant nor a practicable measure for many companies, especially labour-intensive, low-value service companies (eg Ogbonna and Harris, 2002a). Equally, there is also evidence that culture management interventions in the form of 'customer-orientation' programmes can achieve a degree of success in generating customer focused discourse and behaviour amongst employees (eg Peccei and Rosenthal, 2000). Significantly, customer orientation amongst employees does not equate to a concomitant commitment automatically to the company and its objectives but rather to the individual customer.

As for the 'export' of corporate cultures by MNCs, a plethora of empirical evidence reveals that attempts at cross-border replication are only partly successful. Local cultures continue to assert themselves in opposition to generic corporate cultures (isomorphism), producing variable and hybrid cultures from location to location. Moreover, there is now evidence that industries possess macro-cultures that reproduce internationally (Gordon, 1991). These may be more significant than national cultures (Dastmalchian et al, 2000) and will provide fertile territory for future research and practice.

More critical sociological studies (eg Korczynski, 2002; Hochschild, 1983) which delve into the employees' emotional experience of culture management interventions provide an important perspective 'from below'. Here there is frequently a concern to interpret workers' experience in the context of wider social and organisational tensions, resulting in an underlying relationship of conflicting interests between management and workers. Thus, there is an implicit rejection of the notion that a single, unifying corporate culture is feasible, or desirable. Instead, they interpret organisational life as a contested terrain with the potential for resistance by workers – often via trade unions – to the imposition of managerial cultural beliefs and behaviours. In this wider sociological field there is considerable focus on the emotional experience of work, especially service work. With it is coming a rich picture of organisational emotional life and, *de facto*, a deeper understanding of the impact of culture change management.

CASE STUDY 14

WHEN LET'S-SHOP MET VALUE-PLUS

In the late 1990s, Let's-Shop (UK) was acquired by Value-Plus, one of the world's leading retailers, to form Let's-Shop-Plus. In previous years Let's-Shop had already modelled many of its business practices on the new parent company and thus appeared a good match with regard not only to shop formats and merchandise but also to company cultures.

At the outset, both companies had similar – but separate – mission statements that emphasised a value proposition, excellent customer service and community involvement. This was to be achieved through valued and committed employees, who were accordingly called 'colleagues' regardless of their status within the organisations.

At first the training provision for shopfloor staff was altered. Whereas Let's-Shop traditionally offered courses that were externally recognised, Let's-Shop-Plus increasingly shifted towards in-house training, which reinforced the parent company's corporate values. While some shopfloor colleagues embraced the new opportunities, others were worried about the implications of losing external accreditation.

Next, pay reward and recognition arrangements were addressed. Both companies had used various schemes to instil and maintain colleagues' commitment to company values. They included bonus payments based on company performance and share option schemes, together with individual financial and non-financial incentives based on performance. These remained largely untouched and their roll-out across all organisational levels was welcomed.

However, the introduction of a new pay scheme that eroded enhanced payments for overtime, shift, Sunday and Bank Holiday work for hourly-paid colleagues caused a great deal of anguish and dissatisfaction. Here, management tried to persuade employees by using language congruent with Let's-Shop-Plus's organisational culture, such as 'top earners' and 'new world system'. This was more accepted by new employees and younger workers, although established staff tended to perceive such phrases as 'a clever ploy' to reduce overall pay levels and flexibility despite a higher hourly rate, and refused to be transferred onto the new system.

While incentive schemes that result in redeemable cash vouchers are valued by shopfloor workers, recognition systems that reward via a series of 'badges' muster little respect. This goes hand in hand with reluctance by longer-serving staff to accept the concept of 'key colleagues'. These are shopfloor workers who take on more responsibility without an increase in pay. Newer members of staff, especially younger ones, however, see this role as a potential to gain experience and progress in Let's-Shop-Plus.

A further way of binding employees into the organisation and its culture is a company-based legal scheme that can be joined for a minimal subscription. This is taken up at all levels of the organisation, but some more cynical older members of staff see it as a way of undermining trade union membership. Trade unions have been – and still seem to remain – relatively strong in Let's-Shop, although Value-Plus operates an aggressive union-free business in its home country. There is no obvious or overt anti-union policy in Let's-Shop-Plus but workers also have a voice via (non-union) company representatives and colleague circles.

All company policies, schemes and culture management initiatives are underpinned by an increasingly formalised communications system. Let's-Shop-Plus views communication as a two-way process by which information is cascaded down from the top to all of its nearly 300 stores and distribution centres, and percolates up from the bottom, ideally facilitating a lively exchange between management and shop floor. The previous more informal channels at Let's-Shop have been progressively replaced by formalised systems along Value-Plus's systems. An array of participatory tools are in operation, such as a colleague suggestion scheme, colleague circles, communication zones in store corridors, regular videos and frequent staff meetings. All of these are used either to disseminate company information, ideas and directives or to pass on staff suggestions.

The objective to instil a uniform Let's-Shop-Plus culture is supported at intervals through 'culture conferences' at head office. Mainly management representatives from each store participate in one- to two-day activities that spell out the values of the organisation and how colleagues are encouraged to put them into practice with a view to achieving the organisational goals.

At store level, buy-in to the cultural changes varies depending on how they are perceived to impact on working conditions. Additionally, the further away colleagues are from decision-making processes, such as night shift workers, the more there is a sense of disconnectedness from company values and culture, and a strong sub-culture pervades. Younger employees, those having joined the company after acquisition and employees with ambition to progress in Let's-Shop-Plus are more willing to embrace cultural values introduced from above.

Last but not least, especially among long-serving store employees, there is a sense of pride in doing a good job and serving the customer as they would want to be served themselves. Changes which support that goal and do not subvert working conditions are embraced and supported; others are viewed with scepticism and reluctantly adhered to or circumvented.

Source: adapted from Pioch (2003)

Case study tasks

1   Why did Let's-Shop-Plus introduce change in a staged approach?

2   What do you think are the potential difficulties the parent company may encounter when trying to mould the subsidiary in its own image?

3   What do you think is the reason for the difference between long-serving and new members of staff in their attitude to and acceptance of the culture change programme?

REFERENCES

Aguilera R. V. and Dencker J. C. (2004) 'The role of human resource management in cross-border mergers and acquisitions', *International Journal of Human Resource Management*, Vol. 15, No. 8: 1355–70.

Arnold S., Kozinets R. and Handelman J. (2001) 'Hometown ideology and retailer legitimation: the institutional semiotics of Wal*Mart flyers', *Journal of Retailing*, No. 77: 243–71.

Bolton S. (2005) *Emotion Management in the Workplace*. Basingstoke: Palgrave-Macmillan.

Bowen D. E. and Lawler E. E. (1995) 'Empowering service employees', *Sloan Management Review*, Summer: 73–84.

Boxall P. (2003) 'HR strategy and competitive advantage in the service sector', *Human Resource Management Journal*, Vol. 13, No. 3: 5–20.

Brook P. (2004) 'Customer-oriented militants? A critical assessment of the "customer-oriented bureaucracy" on front-line service worker trade unionism', paper at Work, Employment and Society Conference, UMIST, Manchester.

Clegg S., Kornberger M. and Pitsis T. (2005) *Managing and Organizations: An introduction to theory and practice*. London: Sage.

Dastmalchian A., Lee S. and Ng I. (2000) 'The interplay between organisational and national cultures: a comparison of organisational practices in Canada and South Korea using the Competing Values Framework', *International Journal of Human Resource Management*, Vol. 11, No. 2: 388–412.

Deal T. E. and Kennedy A. A. (1982) *Corporate Cultures: The rites and rituals of corporate life*. Reading: Addison-Wesley.

Ferner A. and Quintanilla J. (1998) 'Multinationals, national business systems and HRM: the enduring influence of national identity or a process of "Anglo-Saxonisation"?', *International Journal of Human Resource Management*, Vol. 9, No. 4: 710–31.

Frenkel S. J., Korczynski M., Shire K. A. and Tam M. (1999) *On the Front Line: Organization of work in the information economy*. Ithaca/London: Cornell University Press.

Gabbott M. and Hogg G. (1998) *Consumers and Services*. Chichester: Wiley.

Gamble J. (2003) 'Transferring human resource practices from the United Kingdom to China: the limits and potential for convergence', *International Journal of Human Resource Management*, Vol. 14, No. 3: 369–87.

Gap Inc. [online] (visited 20 January 2003 and 7 July 2005). Available from http://www.gapinc.com.

Gordon G. G. (1991) 'Industry determinants of organisational culture', *Academy of Management Review*, Vol. 16, No. 2: 396–415.

Guest D. (1987) 'Human resource management and industrial relations', *Journal of Management Studies*, Vol. 24, No. 5: 503–21.

Guest D. (1990) 'Human resource management and the American dream', *Journal of Management Studies*, Vol. 27, No 4: 378–97.

Harris L. C. and Metallinos G. (2002) 'The fact and fantasy of organisational culture management: a case study of Greek retailing', *Journal of Retailing and Consumer Services*, Vol. 9: 201–13.

Harris L. C. and Ogbonna E. (1998a) 'A three-perspective approach to understanding culture in retail organisations', *Personnel Review*, Vol. 27, No. 1/2: 104–23.

Harris L. C. and Ogbonna E. (1998b) 'Employee responses to culture change efforts', *Human Resource Management Journal*, Vol. 8, No. 2: 78–92.

Hochschild A. R. (1983) *The Managed Heart: Commercialisation of human feeling*. Berkeley: University of California Press.

Hofstede G. (1980) *Culture's Consequences*. London: Sage.

Hofstede G. (1991) *Cultures and Organisations: Software of the mind*. Maidenhead: McGraw-Hill.

IKEA [online] (visited 20 January 2003). Available from http://www.ikea.com.

Korczynski M. (2001) 'The contradictions of service work: call centre as customer-oriented bureaucracy', in A. Sturdy, I. Grugulis and H. Willmott (eds) *Customer Service: Empowerment and entrapment*. London: Palgrave Macmillan.

Korczynski M. (2002) *Human Resource Management in Service Work*. Basingstoke: Palgrave.

Korczynski M. (2003) 'Consumer capitalism and industrial relations', in P. Ackers and A. Wilkinson (eds) *Understanding Work and Employment*. Oxford: Oxford University Press.

Legge K. (1994) 'Managing culture: fact or fiction?', in K. Sisson (ed.) *Personnel Management: A comprehensive guide to theory and practice*. Oxford: Blackwell.

Legge K. (2001) 'Silver bullet or spent round? Assessing the meaning of the "high-commitment management"/-performance relationship', in J. Storey (ed.) *Human Resource Management: A critical text*. London: Thomson.

Legge K. (2005). *Human Resource Management: Rhetorics and realities*. Basingstoke: Palgrave-Macmillan.

Linstead S. (1995) 'Averting the gaze: gender and power on the perfumed picket line', *Gender, Work and Organization*, Vol. 2, No. 4: 192–206.

Lucas R. (2004) *Employment Relations in the Hospitality and Tourism Industries*. London: Routledge.

Martin J. (1992). *Cultures in Organisations: Three perspectives*. New York: Oxford University Press Inc.

Martin J. (2002). *Organisational Culture. Mapping the Terrain*. London: Sage.

Martin J. and Meyerson D. (1988) 'Organisational culture and the denial, channelling and acknowledgement of ambiguity', in L. Pondy, R. Boland and H. Thomas (eds) *Managing Ambiguity and Change*. New York: Wiley.

Ng E. S. W. and Tung R. L. (1998) 'Ethno-cultural diversity and organisational effectiveness: a field study', *International Journal of Human Resource Management*, Vol. 9, No. 6: 980–95.

Ogbonna E. (1992) 'Organisation culture and human resource management: dilemmas and contradictions', in P. Blyton and P. Turnbull (eds) *Reassessing Human Resource Management*. London: Sage.

Ogbonna E. and Harris L. C. (2002a) 'Managing organisational culture: insights from the hospitality industry', *Human Resource Management Journal*, Vol. 12, No. 1: 33–53.

Ogbonna E. and Harris L. C. (2002b) 'Organisational culture: a ten-year two-phase study of change in the UK food retailing sector', *Journal of Management Studies*, Vol. 39, No. 5: 673–705.

Ogbonna E. and Whipp R. (1999) 'Strategy, culture and HRM: evidence from the UK food retailing sector', *Human Resource Management Journal*, Vol. 9, No. 4: 75–90.

Payne B. M., Nielsen J. F. and Tyran K. L. (2002) 'An investigation of cultural cohesion in a community bank', *International Journal of Human Resource Management*, Vol. 13, No. 4: 677–96.

Peccei R. and Rosenthal P. (2000) 'Front-line responses to customer orientation programmes: a theoretical and empirical analysis', *Journal of Human Resource Management*, Vol. 11, No. 3: 562–90.

Peters T. J. and Waterman R. H. (1982) *In Search of Excellence: Lessons from America's best run companies*. New York: Harper & Row.

Pioch E. (2003) 'Business as usual? Retail employee perceptions of organisational life after takeover', paper at EAERCD International Conference, Paris.

Pioch E. and Brook P. (2000) 'Staying alive: the case of UP-FRONT, an outdoor leisure retailer', paper at Retail Case Study Conference, Manchester.

Rosenthal P., Hill S. and Peccei R. (1997) 'Checking out service: evaluating excellence, HRM and TQM in retailing', *Work, Employment and Society*, Vol. 11, No. 3: 481–503.

Schein E. H. (1984) 'Coming to a new awareness of organisational culture', *Sloan Management Review*, Winter: 3–16.

Schein E. H. (2004) *Organisational Culture and Leadership*. San Francisco: Jossey Bass.

Schneider B. and Bowen D. E. (1995) *Winning the Service Game*. Boston, MA: Harvard Business School Press.

Smircich L. (1983) 'Concepts of culture and organisational analysis', *Administrative Science Quarterly*, Vol. 28, No. 3: 339–58.

Snape E., Thompson D., Ka-Ching Yan F. and Redman T. (1998) 'Performance appraisal and culture: practice and attitudes in Hong Kong and Great Britain', *International Journal of Human Resource Management*, Vol. 9, No. 5: 841–61.

Storey J. (2001) 'Human resource management today: an assessment', in J. Storey (ed.) *Human Resource Management: A critical text*. London: Thomson.

Taylor P. and Bain P. (2001) 'Trade unions, workers' rights and the frontier of control in UK call centres', *Economic and Industrial Democracy*, Vol. 22, No. 1: 39–66.

Taylor P. and Bain P. (2003) 'Call centre organising in adversity: from Excell to Vertex', in G. Gall (ed.) *Union Organizing: Campaigning for trade union recognition*. London: Routledge.

Taylor P. and Bain P. (2005) 'India calling to the far away towns: the call centre labour process and globalisation', *Work, Employment and Society*, Vol. 19, No. 2: 261–82.

Tolich M. B. (1993) 'Alienating and liberating emotions at work', *Journal of Contemporary Ethnography*, Vol. 22, No. 3: 361–81.

Toys "R" US [online] (visited 20 January 2003). Available from http://www9.toysrus.com.

Weatherly, K. and Tansik, D. (1992) 'Tactics used by customer-contact workers: Effects of role stress, boundary spanning and control', *International Journal of Service Industry Management*, Vol. 4, No. 3: 4–17.

Wilkinson A., Redman T., Snape E. and Marchington M. (1998) *Managing with Total Quality Management: Theory and practice*. London: Macmillan.

Wouters C. (1989) 'The sociology of emotions and flight attendants', *Theory, Culture and Society*, No. 6: 95–123.

Zeithaml V. and Bitner M. (1996) *Services Marketing*. New York: McGraw-Hill.

Recruiting, managing and developing people

Recruitment and selection

CHAPTER 6

Sue Shaw and Maryam Herin

CHAPTER OBJECTIVES

When you have read this chapter you should be able to:

- explain the role of recruitment and selection in developing human capital advantage in organisations

- understand the external and internal context of organisational recruitment and selection

- understand the nature of the processes associated with recruitment and selection

- explain the role of technology in recruitment and selection

- understand the nature of the recruitment and selection of international staff

- critically examine the role of recruitment and selection in organisations operating in a global environment in the twenty-first century.

PURPOSE AND SCOPE

This chapter critically explores organisational recruitment and selection in an international context. In doing so, the chapter addresses a number of the themes of the book: globalisation, cultural variation, technological change and the knowledge economy, and demographic trends and labour market change. We begin with a consideration of recruitment and selection's importance in developing human capital advantage and its conceptualisation within various models of HR strategy. Factors such as the ongoing search for competitiveness, the development of the knowledge-based economy and skills shortages make recruitment and selection one of the most important human resource activities in contemporary organisations. The recruitment of a talented workforce is consistent with the resource-based view of HR strategy in which human capital is the key to sustained competitive advantage and organisational success, and it is also an important aspect of best fit and best practice models.

We move next to a consideration of the external and internal context in which recruitment and selection operates, and the factors explored here provide support for the best-fit models of HR strategy. In looking at the external context it is important to see how differences in countries' labour markets, in their economic, education, training and employment law policies and in their cultures might impact on practice. We also examine the internal context of the organisation, and the ways organisational culture, business strategy, attitude to labour market and type of jobs influence recruitment and selection. We then move on to analyse the various stages in the process, making the distinction between recruitment strategies and processes and selection methods. We explore the ways in which recruitment and selection activities are changing to meet current and future demands and argue for the relevance of the best-practice model in the adoption of generic selection practices. The ways in which developments in technology are shaping recruitment and selection processes are examined in some detail before we go on to explore the recruitment and selection of international staff, arguing that recruitment and selection practices are more complex when they are taken into an international arena. We close by summarising the key themes of the chapter and consider future issues that will impact on recruitment and selection.

1 CONCEPTUAL OVERVIEW

The importance now placed on the role of human resources in developing sustained competitive advantage ensures that recruitment and selection is regarded as a core element of an organisation's resourcing activity and part of a much wider strategic approach to staffing (Chew and Horwitz, 2004). Recruiting highly skilled and talented staff is the first step in the development of human capital advantage within organisations. Taylor and Collins (2000) suggest that recruitment must be seen as one of, if not *the*, most important human resource system not only because it acts as a kind of 'gatekeeper' determining in effect whether applicants have the opportunity or desire to engage further with the organisation and its other human resource systems but also because it shapes applicants' perceptions about these other human resource systems by providing direct information and signals about them.

The notion of 'contribution' or 'payback' is another important consideration. Whereas human capital theory emphasises people's asset value (Armstrong and Baron, 2002), it is important to reflect on the potential size of the investment, which in addition to the actual cost of recruitment and annual salary costs and pension contributions could include bonuses and annual salary increases for what might be five or ten years' employment.

Furthermore, the context in which recruitment and selection is being undertaken is changing. The increasing globalisation of business, rise in cross-border mergers and acquisitions and developments such as EU enlargement have led not only to the convergence of practice but also to an increasing internationalisation of the workforce as organisations find more and more of their employees are located in other countries and employ increasing numbers of foreign nationals in their home country as well. The traditional approach to recruitment and selection has emphasised a systematic approach but increasing internationalisation and the rate and pace of change raises questions about the relevance of a systematic model that is essentially ethnocentric and backward-looking.

The HRM approach to resourcing has shifted the focus away from simple replication of past practice and behaviour to one in which organisations seek to acquire people with the skills and competencies to enhance their future strategic capability, while the international dimension has introduced issues such as the transfer of practice and recruiting to trans-national and international teams. Chew and Horwitz's (2004) study of MNCs in Singapore found that their main priorities were staffing for global operations with the appropriate mix of core industry-specific and outsourced competencies, ensuring an appropriate people/organisation cultural fit and enhancing multicultural diversity.

Recruitment and selection and HR strategy

The debate in the HRM literature between universalism or best practice and contingency theory or best fit (detailed in Chapter 3) is relevant to any examination of recruitment and selection. The idea of strategic fit is central to the notion of strategic HRM, and 'fit' either as a set of ideal HR practices, a set of HR practices contingent on organisational circumstances or as a bundle or particular configuration of HR practices has implications for how recruitment is conceptualised within the different models of HRM.

Best practice

Best-practice models or high-commitment models (see, for example, Beer et al, 1984, and more recently Pfeffer, 1998) emphasise, among other things, the importance of selective hiring of people with the critical skills and attributes needed to achieve a high-commitment high-performing organisation. Armstrong and Baron (2002) argue that there is a need to distinguish between those characteristics that predict performance and the likelihood of staying and that must be present at recruitment, such as attitudes, values and cultural fit, and those that can be developed subsequently. Best-practice models have been challenged because they fail to take account of national variations in culture, management style and law (Marchington and Grugulis, 2000) and these factors will impact on recruitment and selection. At the same time, as will be argued later, such critiques do not preclude the adoption of good practice at the level of selection technique (Boxall and Purcell, 2003).

Best fit

The models covered by the 'best fit' school suggest that recruitment and selection strategies (among others) should be integrated with the organisation's stage of development (Kochan and Barocci, 1985; Baird and Meshoulam, 1988) or its particular business or competitive strategy (Schuler and Jackson, 1937; Miles and Snow, 1978). At the start-up and growth stages in Kochan and Barocci's life-cycle model, organisational emphasis might be on attracting the best technical and professional skills at the outset and ensuring the right numerical and skill mix subsequently through a mixture of external and internal labour market recruitment. This is in comparison to the situation where an organisation has reached maturity or even decline, where there is less emphasis on recruitment and even workforce contraction. According to Miles and Snow's model different approaches to product lines and growth strategies would lead to very different staffing strategies, such that organisations with a limited stable product line and planning growth through market penetration would put emphasis on an internal labour market development-driven approach, and organisations with changing product lines and planned growth through innovation and market development would emphasise external recruitment. In Schuler and Jackson's (1987) model – which is based on Porter's typology of competitive strategies – generic strategies of innovation, quality enhancement and cost minimisation require different kinds of employee behaviour. This in turn has implications for the kinds of skills sets needed and consequently for an organisation's recruitment strategy and practice. For example, creativity and risk-oriented behaviours delivered through highly skilled individuals would be most appropriate in a competitive policy of differentiation whereas repetitive behaviours delivered through tightly defined job descriptions would be more appropriate where there is a strategy of cost minimisation.

Models which align HR strategy with competitive strategy have been criticised for their over-simplification of organisational reality and over-reliance on one dominant external variable. Configurational approaches which focus on unique bundles of HR practices are an attempt to address this criticism and additionally provide a degree of coherence and internal fit (MacDuffie, 1995; Delery and Doty, 1996). Internal coherence in recruitment and selection means ensuring that selection systems are consistent, avoid duplication and add value rather than being over-designed or unnecessarily burdensome to candidates (Delery and Doty, 1996). It is also about ensuring that recruitment and selection systems complement and support rather than run counter to other human resource systems (Baron and Kreps, 1999).

The resource-based view (RBV)

The resource-based view that looks at how resources and competences internal to the firm can be a source of competitive advantage provides an appropriate conceptual framework for understanding recruitment effectiveness at the macro level. Taylor and Collins (2000) contend that recruitment is a source of competitive advantage and go on to show how it satisfies Barney (1991) and Barney and Wright's (1998) five criteria of value, rarity, imitability, substitutability and organisation. Recruitment has the potential to create value by reducing staff costs and by impacting positively on applicants' perceptions of the recruitment experience. Cost-effectiveness is achieved through efficient and effective recruitment systems character-ised by targeted channels, speedy processes and high-quality job information. Value is also created by specifically targeting and attracting people who can enhance organisational differentiation of their product or service, and who by their presence in the organisation might enhance the employer brand. Moreover, it is the quality and effectiveness of the recruitment practices that can lead to the attraction and retention of this scarce or rare and highly sought-after talent. Finally, it is the way in which an organisation invests in, develops, configures, customises, implements and horizontally integrates a particular set of what are in effect universally available recruitment and selection practices and techniques that ensures that such practices are capable of being neither imitated nor substituted and make a sustained and coherent contribution to the achievement of competitive advantage.

Recruitment and selection is an important element in the development of an organisation's strategic human resource capability, and the above exploration of how recruitment and selection is conceptualised within strategic HRM has suggested that 'both general principles and specific contexts' must be taken into account (Boxall and Purcell, 2003: 70). Recruitment and selection does not occur in a vacuum: it is undertaken in a complex organisational and country context – and it is to a consideration of these influences that we now turn.

Discussion questions

1 What key arguments would you use to persuade your Chief Executive of the importance of recruitment and selection to your organisation?

2 What changes have occurred in the recruitment and selection context in recent years, and what implications does this have in practice?

3 How does knowledge of the different theories and models of HRM help in the understanding and delivery of recruitment and selection practice?

2 THE CONTEXT FOR RECRUITMENT AND SELECTION

Recruitment and selection strategies and practices are influenced by both the external and internal environment, and recruiters must recognise the diversity that exists (Zanko, 2003). The major sources of environmental influence are economic, legal, political, socio-cultural and technological, and internal influences include the organisation's stage of internationalisation, its culture and structure, and its attitude to external and internal labour markets.

The external context

Recruiters must understand the nature of the labour market in which they operate and the way it is changing. That labour market may be local, regional, national and international, depending on the job and skill level and the nature of the organisation's business and level of internationalisation. For instance, continuing globalisation of the free market economy facili-tates the migration of international workers particularly in areas of acute shortage, so that workforces in developed countries are becoming increasingly reliant on well-educated workers from developing and transition economies (Harvey *et al*, 2003). Indeed, confining the source of recruits to a local marketplace 'may be an outdated recruitment strategy' (Choi *et al*, 2000: 61). Moreover, the practice of 'offshoring' certain operations can quickly transform a workforce profile and clearly has recruitment and selection implications, particularly when the operation is not outsourced (Simms, 2004).

Labour market characteristics

Labour markets around the world vary in size, age profile, skill set and gender and ethnic breakdown. They are related to a country's level of economic, industrial and technological advancement, its attitude to and levels of unemployment, its economic, social and education policies, and its general education levels and vocational training systems. In general, techno-logical developments and the growth of knowledge economies in developed nations have led to a demand for high-calibre and high-skilled recruits (Whicker and Andrews, 2004). The highly skilled labour force found in most developed western countries may be under threat or simply not exist in less developed countries. Venezuela's worsening economic situation and the resultant exodus of qualified professionals is forecast to have serious consequences for future recruitment (Gomez-Samper and Monteferrante, 2005), and the HIV/AIDS pandemic in much of Africa has devastated workforces and resulted in severe skills shortages, particularly in younger age-groups (WorldLink, 2005).

Many aspects of recruitment and selection in China have proved particularly challenging since the early 1990s. The country currently faces an acute shortage of experienced managers to put into leadership positions because the Cultural Revolution led to a shortage of professional managers and a skills mismatch in the existing managerial stock as the older generation were deskilled and the cadre followed a technical 'career route' (Shaw, 2005). Moreover, the south-east of the country also faces shortages of migrant factory workers because the one-child policy implemented since 1979 impacts on the numbers of people in the 15–20 age-bracket, and rising expectations have meant that that kind of work environment has become less attractive (Larkin, 2005).

Employment regulation

All countries regulate employment to some degree, many socialist countries going as far as explicitly to incorporate labour provisions within their national constitution (Tayeb, 1996). Legislation can be an important influence on an organisation's recruitment and selection process – for example, in the area of equal opportunities (see Chapter 14 for a detailed discussion). Additionally, regional rules and regulations may add a further layer of influence. The European Union is a prominent example of this in the way that a series of European Directives establishes a common framework across all member states in respect of discrimi-nation on the grounds of sex, race, sexual orientation, religion or belief, disability and age. Government policy and the political context may directly influence an organisation's recruitment strategy. Zhu and Dowling's (2002) review of Chinese staffing practices found that many of the senior managers – particularly those working in state-owned enterprises – are still government appointees.

Cultural factors

Country culture is another important consideration. Home-country culture impacts on all organisations, but foreign culture impacts according to the extent of the organisation's internationalisation and/or the degree of diversity of its workforce. As noted in Chapter 2, cultural characteristics have been shown to exhibit a high degree of difference between countries (Hofstede and Bond, 1988; Hofstede, 2001), with important consequences for how individuals view and engage with the various aspects of the recruitment and selection process, as we shall see later in the chapter.

The organisational context

Factors within organisations also impact on recruitment and selection practices. As well as the business strategy/recruitment and selection relationship discussed above, the firm's international strategy and its stage of internationalisation are also important considerations.

International orientation

Multinational firms may have different international orientations which in turn influence their international staffing strategy and recruitment and selection practices within subsidiaries (Dowling *et al*, 1999). Four approaches are generally identified (see Chapter 2): ethnocentric, where all key posts are filled by parent-country nationals (PCNs); polycentric, where all key posts are filled by host-country nationals (HCNs); geocentric, where all key posts are filled by the best person for the job including individuals from a third country (TCNs); and regiocentric, where all key posts within a region – for example, within Asia-Pacific – are filled by individuals whether PCNs, HCNs or TCNs (Perlmutter,1969; Heenan and Perlmutter, 1979).

Firm-specific factors

Other internal factors are important. Recruitment and selection can be a very costly exercise and the state of a firm's finances or the extent to which it will commit resources to the process is therefore important in determining what recruitment and selection methods are adopted. The industrial sector and nature of the business, together with aspects of organisation culture and structure such as the degree of centralisation, formalisation, standardisation and specialisation which to some degree are related to size, will also have an impact. Large organisations, for instance, may have a centralised and highly professionalised HR function with well-defined recruitment and selection procedures (Zhu *et al*, 2005), whereas small organisations may rely on ad hoc, informal methods (Di Milia, 2004; Zanko, 2003). Another important consideration is the company's approach to internal and external labour markets. Organisations that rely heavily on an internal labour market that is enhanced through training and development will have a very different approach to recruitment and selection from one which chooses to fill its key vacancies predominantly from the external labour market.

Standardisation/differentiation of practices

The extent to which any MNE can standardise the same recruitment processes across multinational subsidiaries or differentiate to suit local needs is a well-debated issue. Studies of Chinese recruitment and selection practices suggest that a number of factors are involved, including institutional and country culture and firm practices (Gamble 2003), the business environment and the role of the HR function (Zhu *et al*, 2005), and the parent firm's economic considerations, venture structure and HRM conditions (Farley *et al*, 2005). Studies on the convergence of practice reveal a complex and constantly shifting picture, particularly in rapidly developing economies such as China (Warner, 2000; Bamber *et al*, 2000; Rowley and Benson, 2004). Warner's study (2002) of the Asia-Pacific economies suggests that the sheer variation in geography, population, economies, labour markets and HRM/IR systems in for instance China, Hong Kong, Japan, Singapore, Vietnam, Indonesia, South Korea and Taiwan make it difficult to talk about any form of convergence of practice beyond 'soft' convergence.

It is clear from the above discussion that a complex set of external and internal contextual factors impact on recruitment and selection strategies and processes, and these strategies and processes are explored in the next section.

Discussion questions

1   Why is an understanding of the context in which recruitment and selection takes place an important prerequisite of the recruitment and selection activity?

2   In what ways might the recruitment context in China be different from that in the United States?

3   Would an MNC expect to adopt the same recruitment and selection practices and procedures in all of its centres of operation around the world?

CASE STUDY 15

HOSPICE AFRICA UGANDA

Hospice as an organisation was first established in Zimbabwe 25 years ago, and spread quickly to South Africa. In the past 15 years it has spread in varying degrees to other parts of Africa. The HIV/AIDS pandemic has increased the urgency for palliative care.

The development of Hospice Africa Uganda (HAU), an NGO, over the past 12 years illustrates the impact of external and internal contexts on an organisation's recruitment and selection practices. From a staff base of three, HAU now employs 103 staff in three locations – Kampala, Mbarara and Hoima – and an army of volunteers who assist in a variety of ways from caring for patients to organising fund-raising activities. Although the organisation employs general administrative and support staff at various levels – drivers and general assistants – the core staff are health professionals, predominantly doctors and nurses.

A shortage of skilled labour and government regulation continues to affect HAU's recruitment and selection practices. Hospice requires its nurses to be skilled in palliative care and part of their job is administering oral morphine. However, when Hospice was set up, Uganda – like most other African countries – had no tradition of palliative care. Although there was a plentiful supply of qualified Ugandan nurses, they lacked appropriate palliative care skills – and this continues to be a problem as HAU expands. Moreover, government health regulations stipulate that oral morphine is administered by doctors or state-registered nurses (SRNs). Hospice's response has therefore been to recruit SRNs and then to train them in the necessary palliative care skills during the first nine months of their employment before they begin productive work.

HAU's internal structure and culture are also important determinants of recruitment and selection practice. Over the years Hospice has expanded as the number of patients treated has grown, and it now has an HR manager and formalised HR practices. Informal recruitment and selection practices (such as word of mouth and personal referrals) have now been replaced by a more systematic process that has included the adoption of clearly defined job descriptions and employee specifications, the placement of a job advertisement, screening and selection interview, and sometimes a selection test. The selection process also reflects HAU's culture. Hospice is linked with Christian religious denominations as well as having an underlying philosophy encapsulated as 'the Hospice spirit'. Willingness to subscribe to and ability to adopt 'the Hospice spirit' in the work context are essential selection criteria which pervade all aspects of the process from employee specification to interview documentation.

Case study tasks

1   What other recruitment and selection strategies might HAU have employed to overcome its skills shortages?

2   Identify the issues a newly appointed HR professional may face when introducing formal recruitment and selection practices into an organisation for the first time.

3   What specific issues are created in the recruitment and selection of volunteers?

3 RECRUITMENT AND SELECTION STRATEGIES AND PROCESSES

The importance of a systematic approach to recruitment and selection has already been highlighted. Recruitment activities typically start with a definition of what is needed followed by the identification and adoption of appropriate recruitment channels designed to attract applicants. Organisations are faced with choices at each stage, and there is an increasing recognition of the strategic nature of the recruitment process in that an organisation's particular recruitment strategy is determined by its power in the labour market and the capacity of its internal structures and resources to develop appropriate labour market strategies (Windolf, 1986). The changed nature of work referred to earlier has impacted on the kinds of knowledge and skills needed to undertake particular job roles (O'Leary et al, 2002). Developments which create a high demand for knowledge professionals at one end of the skill continuum and for operators used to heavily automated work at the other, underline the importance of the definition stage of the recruitment process and recognition that the simple replication of past practice is no longer adequate.

Job and role analysis

Traditionally the starting point has been the development of a detailed job description from which an employee specification can be devised (IRS, 2003). However, the dynamic nature of many of today's jobs has shifted the focus from a job-based approach to an approach oriented towards the person and the qualities needed to do the job (IRS, 1999) and even the person–organisation fit (Chew and Horwitz, 2004) or the person–group fit (Werbel and Johnson, 2001). A competency approach which identifies the personal attributes, knowledge, experience, abilities, skills and values required to perform a job role within a wider organisational context represents one such response (Boam and Sparrow, 1992). Country culture and values may be a mediating factor in the determination of an employee specification. For example, Vietnam's protracted experience of war has led companies to value commitment, which along with discipline – defined as deference to authority, dependability and punctuality – are seen as the most important selection criteria (Quang and Thang, 2004).

Recruitment

Attracting candidates is the second stage, and traditional recruitment channels such as advertising, commercial recruitment consultants and executive search, employment agencies, recruitment fairs, noticeboards and word of mouth or personal referral have been complemented in recent years by technologically based methods. A number of organisational factors including the nature and level of the job, the organisation's human resource systems, policies and resources, budgetary constraints and the size of the firm determine the choice of recruitment channel. There are cultural differences as well. Country cultures that place importance on relationships, as happens in many South-East Asian and Latin American countries, privilege more personalised channels such as networking and word of mouth over more formal procedures (Braun and Warner, 2002; Leung, 2003; Rodriguez et al, 2005). The state of the labour market is another important consideration, and employers are increasingly finding that established channels are no longer adequate in today's 'highly competitive and sophisticated marketplace' (Taylor and Collins, 2000: 305). The existence of tight labour markets for certain jobs in most developed and some developing countries leads organisations to look for ways to reach 'better' pools of candidates and to attempt to sell the organisation to them. Consequently, strategies in the USA, in South-East Asia and even in developing countries have included casting a wider net to hire applicants, extending recruitment channels to include technology-based sources offering financial and non-financial inducements such as internal talent development, and finally promoting the organisation as a good place to work (Collins, 2000; Horwitz et al, 2003; Huo et al, 2002).

Selection

Whereas recruitment is concerned with generating a candidate pool, selection is about evaluating and deciding on an individual's suitability for a particular job. The selection process involves a number of stages, and the key issue is about accurate prediction of job performance. Much of the literature on selection is about improving the effectiveness of the process. Consequently, models of best practice do have some relevance here (Boxall and Purcell, 2003). Screening applications against predetermined selection criteria derived from the employee specification is usually the first step, and developments such as the use of biodata, self-selection questionnaires on company websites and software packages have sought to make the process more streamlined and more effective (Buckley et al, 2004; Van Rooy et al, 2003). Interviews, tests, assessment centres, work sampling and references including new forms of these such as video simulations and virtual reality tests, are the most commonly used selection methods, whereas tools such as graphology remain controversial and not widely adopted (CIPD, 2005; Salgado et al, 2001).

Validity of selection methods
Although a number of factors influence the choice of selection technique – including the nature and level of the vacancy, cost, ease of implementation and the likelihood of adverse impact on different ethnic or gender groups – the overriding consideration is the extent to which it accurately predicts job performance (Ryan and Tippins, 2004). Numerous studies over the past 30 years have explored the validity and reliability of different selection methods (see Salgado et al, 2001, for a comprehensive summary of predictive validity). Many of these have focused on the interview, for which meta-analyses have reported higher validity when a structured approach is adopted (Rynes et al, 2000; Klehe and Latham, 2005). Psychometric tests are another well-researched area: while early studies suggested they had low predictive validity, more recent studies using the 'Big Five' personality traits – emotional stability, extroversion, openness to experience, agreeableness and conscientiousness, around which there is greater consensus – have shown that they have better psychometric qualities and relationship with job performance (Salgado, 2003; Ones and Viswesvaran, 2001). Although much of the research into the reliability and validity of selection methods is western and predominantly US in origin, a number of recent studies suggest that the five-factor model can be transferred across cultures (Salgado et al, 2001; McCrae and Allik, 2002; Robie et al, 2005). At the same time it is

worth emphasising that good practice in the use of both interviews and psychometric tests is far from universally adopted, as Arias-Galicia's (2005) study of practices in Mexico shows.

Cultural differences in selection

Recently, research has begun to explore the similarities and differences between practices in different countries (Yuen and Kee, 1993; Huo *et al*, 2002). These studies show that politics, demographic characteristics, culture, geographic proximity and evolution of HR practice account for observed differences in selection practices. For example, in Chinese state-owned enterprises weight is still given to political background (Zhu and Dowling, 2002); a candidate's race, clan or religion is important in Malaysia or Papua New Guinea (Manshor *et al*, 2003; Hess and Imbun, 2003); family connection is important in Mexico (Gomez and Sanchez, 2005) and non-technical criteria are important in Taiwan and Japan due to people's concern for harmonious relationships (Huo *et al*, 2002). At the same time there is evidence for the convergence of practice in that technical competence to do the job and a personal interview are deemed to be of high importance both currently and in the future for many developed and developing countries (Huo *et al*, 2002).

Employee perspectives

To date the discussion has focused on the employer perspective. However, recruitment and selection is increasingly seen as a two-way process, particularly within the context of the human capital debate (Lievens *et al*, 2003). Indeed, Breaugh and Starke (2000) suggest that process variables such as applicant attention and self-insight mediate the relationship between recruitment activities and recruitment outcomes. Candidates' experience of the process, their treatment and the subsequent relationship play an important part in their decision to continue to engage with the process, their perception of its fairness and their ultimate acceptance of any job offer (Phillips and Gully, 2002). Moreover, recruiters must understand that value systems and cultural differences have been shown to influence applicants' reactions to various types of selection methods (Ryan and Tippins, 2004). For instance, differences in power distance and collectivism amongst job applicants in Singapore and the United States causes the former to accept selection methods however unfavourable and the latter to accept methods demonstrating their individual skills and proficiency (Phillips and Gully, 2002). At the same time, there are consistencies across a number of developed countries such that assessees from the USA, France, Germany Portugal, Spain and South Africa rate personality tests in the middle range in a scale of preferences of perceptions (Steiner and Gilliland, 2001).

Evaluation

The overall objective of the selection process is to gather enough information about each individual to make a decision, and good practice suggests that each candidate should be assessed against the selection criteria (Torrington *et al*, 2005). The final stage is an evaluation of the process in terms of effectiveness, fairness and efficiency. Although there is now a substantial body of knowledge about the effectiveness of different methods in relation to retention and performance, lack of time, lack of resources and the inaccessibility and overly theoretical nature of some of the studies have meant that this has not transferred across to practice: for example, HR managers remain unaware of which methods lead to higher turnover (Taylor and Collins, 2000; Ryan and Tippins, 2004; Rynes *et al*, 2002). Recruiters must also be concerned with how recruitment and selection methods impact on workforce diversity, and it may be that certain effective strategies such as employee referrals adversely affect organisational diversity thereby creating additional challenges (McManus and Ferguson, 2003). Finally, recruitment and selection should be administratively efficient both in terms of cost and time. Developments in technology have had an important impact here, and the role of technology in recruitment and selection is now explored.

Discussion questions

1   What factors should an organisation take into account when determining the recruitment method(s) it is going to use for a particular position?

2   In what ways might recruitment be said to be strategic?

3   To what extent is it possible to talk about a universal good practice selection model?

CASE STUDY 16

THE RECRUITMENT AND SELECTION OF HOTEL STAFF IN MALI, WEST AFRICA

The case study is a hotel-restaurant based in Bamako, in Mali, West Africa. Mali has approximately 12 million inhabitants; the average number of children per family is 6.58, and the average life expectancy is 46. This is still an environment where the minority 'white' people have the riches and the means to do business but the indigenous people do not. Many Malians are employed by the white population as domestic workers.

The hotel's owner-manager has many years of business experience in both Africa and France. Established 20 years ago, the business has expanded in recent years, resulting in the need to recruit new staff with a variety of different skills. Recruitment is both an interesting and a difficult process incorporating a mix of western and local practices.

When a vacancy arises, the core requirement of the job is clear and reflected in the job title, such as Chef or Housekeeper. However, documentation to support the recruitment process such as job advertisement, job description and person specification is non-existent. Recruitment is predominantly by word of mouth. The owner usually asks existing employees and friends if they know of anyone who might be suitable. Jobs are so scarce that as soon as the vacancy becomes public knowledge, there can be a huge number of names coming forward and the owner selects those that merit an interview. The interview and selection criteria are usually based around previous experience and a character reference from people the owner knows and has confidence in. This is to ensure there is a 'fit' between the owner and the team, and it provides the owner with a form of referencing and validation of the candidate. Successful candidates are provided with a contract of employment in the same way as in Europe, in an attempt to provide some job security and to build the basis of a good relationship between the employer/ employee. An official start date is agreed after a trial period.

Case study tasks

1   Evaluate the recruitment and selection practices described here against those discussed in the wider chapter.

2   What do you see as the main contextual factors impacting on the recruitment and selection practices in the hotel?

> 3   What suggestions might you make to the proprietor in order to improve the recruitment and selection activity?

4 THE ROLE OF TECHNOLOGY IN THE RECRUITMENT AND SELECTION OF STAFF

Technological developments have had a profound impact on organisations' recruitment and selection practices and also changed the way job-seekers think about the process. A study of the Global 500 companies' adoption of e-recruitment via corporate websites shows a growth from 29% in 1998 to 91% in 2002 (www.JobsDB.com), and the CIPD's annual survey of UK organisations' recruitment, retention and turnover practices reports placing vacancies on the organisation's website as the third most frequently used method of attracting candidates, below local press and recruitment agencies (CIPD, 2005).

Technology impacts on each stage of the process starting with the job description and concluding with the incorporation of the successful candidate's personal information into the organisation's human resource information system. Job analysis is being automated and large-scale databases are able to link the characteristics of a job with the knowledge, skills, abilities and psychological traits needed by the jobholder to produce an employee specification. Web-based search methods now challenge traditional recruitment channels, and personal computer (PC) and Internet-based delivery of selection instruments including cognitive ability tests, personality tests, situational judgement tests and realistic job previews together with telephone- and video-conferencing-based assessment procedures are replacing traditional models (Anderson, 2003). Furthermore, administration at all stages of the process – including initial vacancy enquiries, pre-screening methods such as recruitment shortlisting and communication – can be automated and electronic using PC or web-based and interactive voice response (IVR) employee selection systems.

Recruitment and selection and the Internet

E-recruitment
The Internet has dramatically changed how both employers and job-hunters approach recruitment, and Cappelli (2001) argues that e-recruitment has created a true labour market which is neither constrained geographically nor controlled by individual companies, and in which each day thousands of job-seekers post their details on online hiring sites. Used initially predominantly in the IT industry, e-recruitment is now a fast-growing global activity extending to other professional, graduate and many mid-level staffing positions (Chapman and Webster, 2003). In the United States, for instance, it has been reported that more than 75% of HR professionals use Internet job boards alongside traditional recruitment methods, and over 18 million people each year put their curriculum vitae on Monster.com (Feldman and Klaas, 2002). Indeed, Snell (2002) in his survey of Global 500 companies' Internet site recruiting activities concluded that Internet recruiting strategies were approaching complete saturation, utilisation reaching 95% in North America, 92% in Europe and 90% in Asia-Pacific.

E-recruitment usually refers to the process whereby organisations either undertake activities directly using their own company website or use the services of an e-recruitment service such as an online job board or job portal (Tong and Sivanand, 2005). It can also refer to a media site where electronic advertisements appear simultaneously with traditional printed versions (Galanaki, 2002). E-recruitment service providers may be international such as Monster.com or regional such as JoblinkAsia.com, but notwithstanding the rapid numerical growth of such providers, profitability remains an issue even for the large international firms (Tong and Sivanand, 2005).

E-selection

Computer technology has also changed the way selection methods such as interviews and tests are implemented. As the Internet opens up a global market for recruitment it is likely that video-based interviews and telephone interviews will become more common. However, research into their comparability with face-to-face interviews to date is limited, and one of the few studies undertaken so far signals caution because differences in questioning techniques and absence of verbal cues may affect the way interviewers interpret candidate responses and impact ultimately on the decision-making process (Silvester and Anderson, 2003). Computerised testing has increased significantly, and multimedia, web-based, computer-adaptive and video testing are now being incorporated into organisational selection systems, developments including new instruments or new versions of existing tests and questionnaires. Studies have generally provided support for equivalence between computerised and pen-and-paper versions without loss of psychometric properties (Lievens and Harris, 2003; Konradt *et al*, 2003; Salgado and Moscoso, 2003).

Advantages and disadvantages in e-recruitment and selection

A number of benefits of introducing technology-based systems into the recruitment and selection process have been identified. Cost savings such as cheaper advertising, elimination of placement fees, more economic test administration and reduced mailings are seen as one of the major benefits (Galanaki, 2002). However, the technology requires an investment of resources, expertise and time which if not forthcoming leads to candidate dissatisfaction (Feldman and Klaas, 2002). Access to a global labour market and the conveyance of a positive brand image are other reported benefits (Galanaki, 2002; Jattuso and Sinar, 2003), although not all studies support the view that more equals better (Boehle, 2000; Chapman and Webster, 2003). It is also argued that the new technology has the potential to reduce adverse impact on under-represented groups within the workforce by removing the human element and the effect of rater bias at the selection stage (Chapman and Webster, 2003). However, this must be set against the present existence of a 'digital divide' which, while likely to close in time (McManus and Ferguson, 2003), currently impacts adversely at the recruitment stage as a result of differences between minorities of Internet access (Anderson, 2003).

Improved efficiency through increased automation, standardisation of entire selection systems and shorter recruitment cycles which free up HR professionals' time for more strategic issues is a further reported benefit (Buckley *et al*, 2004). However, the effectiveness of the medium depends not on the source but on the quality of the process in general and its implementation, and organisations need the necessary resources, expertise and time to achieve this (Galanaki, 2002).

The impact of Internet recruitment and selection

The effect of the technology on individuals and their perceptions of it are important not just because of the equal opportunities issues identified above but also because of the wider human capital arguments. Web technology has the potential to provide potential applicants with customised information thereby enhancing the organisation–person fit and the employer brand (Dineen *et al*, 2002). Research into candidates' reaction to corporate websites is in its infancy (Anderson, 2003). However, if employers want to maximise the number of job-seekers engaging with their website, they must not only better understand how individuals undertake job-related searching and consequently design their sites more appropriately in terms of language and terms (Jansen *et al*, 2005) but also make website navigation more user-friendly and consider links to generic sites (Feldman and Klaas, 2002). The nature of the corporate recruitment site has been shown to be an important determinant of organisational attraction in terms of system speed, efficiency and user-friendliness as well as website content and style (Sinar *et al*, 2003; Cober *et al*, 2003).

Researchers have also explored differences between applicants' reactions to computerised testing and traditional tests. Although the reactions to computer-based tests are somewhat mixed, those to web-based tests are as positive as – and in some cases more positive than – traditional forms (Anderson, 2003; Salgado and Moscoso, 2003). However, it has been suggested that these reactions may be moderated by individual differences such as test-taking self-efficacy, level of computer skill and computer anxiety as well as selection outcome, and recruiters ought to take account of this (Weichmann and Ryan, 2003). While it may be that the technology can benefit the individual through realistic job preview, convenience and speed (Bartram, 2001), there is also evidence to suggest that relational issues are an important part of the job choice decision (Boswell *et al*, 2003). Consequently, employers must ensure that the kind of relationship that is built up during conventional recruitment and selection processes is not lost when the processes become more technologically based.

Summary

Although technology is undoubtedly playing a more important part in recruitment and selection than in the past, and notwithstanding the benefits associated with it, there is evidence to suggest that organisations still use a mix of traditional and technological methods in their recruitment activities (Chapman and Webster, 2003). Moreover, for many job-seekers the Internet is not the first option, candidates perceiving networks or personal contacts and executive search as more effective (Feldman and Klaas, 2002) and finding the most jobs when they search using a mix of traditional and web-based methods (Van Rooy *et al*, 2003). It is likely, however, that HR technologies will continue to grow in importance, particularly in the context of international recruitment and selection, which is the focus of the next section.

Discussion questions

1   In what ways has technology transformed an organisation's approach to recruitment and selection?

2   What arguments would you use to persuade your CEO of the need to introduce technologically based systems into your organisation's recruitment and selection processes and procedures?

3   How might technology-based recruitment and selection impact on candidates, and what implications does this have for the organisation's recruitment and selection strategies and processes?

CASE STUDY 17

JOBSDB.COM

JobsDB.com, founded in 1998, is now one of the leading online recruitment networks in Asia-Pacific, employing 540 staff. With headquarters in Hong Kong, it now operates also in Australia, China, India, Indonesia, Korea, Malaysia, the Philippines, Singapore,

Taiwan, Thailand and the USA. Although operating through a regional network, JobsDB is firmly committed to a local service and localised content to meet needs in specific countries. It has built up a very large database in the region encompassing over 4.6 million job-seeker members and over 150,000 corporate clients: an estimated 350,000 job-seekers visit its websites daily.

Job-seekers have access to constantly updated employment opportunities both locally and across the region either as registered members or as visitors. Through MyjobsDB they receive a personalised, confidential and comprehensive service which enables them to search and apply for jobs online, to input text and video resumés together with covering letter, to track their application history and advertise their availability through Talent Market, to use a clipboard for managing applications and to approve or reject resumé requests from employers, and to operate a resumé request filter. In addition, job-seekers have access to a range of other facilities such as careers guidance and employment-related seminars.

For employers, services include a geographically extensive interactive recruitment network and a comprehensive recruitment management system, JobsDB Dimension. Through the interactive recruitment network employers can utilise job-posting and resumé management systems, undertake candidate searches, set up automatic candidate alerts and access the Talent Market, as well as link directly to their corporate website to give candidates more information about the company. JobsDB Dimension is a flexible e-recruitment solution which provides applicant tracking and a total recruitment management system. It enables employers to build a private and permanent resumé bank, to screen and shortlist candidates easily and accurately, to support multi-entries and adopt a multilingual approach to build their own career website in line with company image and identity, and to post directly to it, and it provides a means of monitoring and evaluating the process through data analysis.

Source: http://www.JobsDB.com

Case study tasks

1 What arguments would you use to persuade your CEO that your organisation should register with JobsDB.com for recruiting staff for its operations in Australia?

2 Take any of the jobs advertised on the Global List on JobsDB.com's home page and from the information supplied critically analyse the advertisement for content and effectiveness. Are there other recruitment channels which might be used for the job you have selected?

3 Look at the websites of an international e-recruitment service such as Monster.com and a regional one such as JobsDB.com and evaluate each of them in terms of its service to employers and its service to job-seekers.

5 THE RECRUITMENT AND SELECTION OF INTERNATIONAL STAFF

In a knowledge-based economy, international assignments play a 'critical strategic role in a firm's internationalisation' particularly for senior staff (Bonache and Fernandez, 1999: 179). Yet many companies fail to adopt a strategic approach to international recruitment and selection, assignments tending to be short-term and ad hoc (Brewster and Scullion, 1997). International recruitment and selection must be seen within the context of an organisation's international staffing strategy (Torbiorn, 2005), and the extent to which this is ethnocentric, polycentric, regiocentric or geocentric will influence the organisation's international recruitment and selection practices and offer different advantages and disadvantages (Harzing, 2004; Shen and Edwards, 2004).

Recruiting and selecting expatriates

Much of the literature on the recruitment and selection of international staff relates to expatriates (Harzing, 2004). Dowling *et al* (1999) argue that the selection of expatriates is more complex than that of domestic employees because predicting performance in a foreign environment adds an additional level of uncertainty. (See Chapters 8 and 9 for discussion on the issues around rewarding expatriates and managing their performance.) Research has focused not only on the criteria MNEs use when assessing candidates for global assignments but also selection methods and barriers to international mobility (Bonache and Fernandez, 1999). Much of the expatriate selection literature prescribes best practice yet arguably a contingency approach is more appropriate – not only because parent-country and company culture may affect practice (Shen and Edwards, 2004) but also because the focus for the role may vary between control and coordination, knowledge transfer and management develop-ment (Harzing, 2001; Baron and Kreps, 1999). Such role differences involve the parent organisation in different selection choices and require different types of knowledge, skills and abilities on the part of the jobholder (Bonache and Fernandez, 1999).

During the selection process the MNC is faced with a number of strategic choices about, *inter alia*, whether the appointment should be internal or external, the relative importance of technical qualifications vis-à-vis other selection criteria and the role of psychological testing and the involvement of family in the selection process (Bonache and Fernandez, 1999). Research suggests that most multinationals rely almost exclusively on internal recruitment for foreign management positions (Scullion, 1994) and that the positions they seek to fill are predominantly at senior management level (Harzing, 2001b).

Selection criteria for expatriates

Developing appropriate selection criteria is important not only because of the complexity of the expatriate role but also because expatriate failure has been given a high profile in the literature for almost two decades (Tung, 1982; Brewster, 1988; Dowling and Welch, 1988). Although the nature and level of failure and the reasons for it have been challenged (Harzing, 1995; Forster, 1997; Brewster and Scullion, 1997; Anderson, 2005), early repatriation or under-performance during the assignment nevertheless represents a selection error which organisations seek to address through their selection criteria and methods. However, establishing criteria for the selection of expatriates is problematic.

Writers have identified a number of factors that are important in expatriate selection and are in general agreement that selection criteria should include technical ability as well as a range of other factors such as cross-cultural suitability, resilience, adaptability, relational skills and family situation (Tung, 1981; Arthur and Bennett, 1995; Dowling *et al*, 1999). Harris *et al* (2002) are critical of the research to date not only because it is prescriptive and predominantly North American but also because there is a gap between theory and practice. A further issue is the relative importance of the criteria. Writers suggest that some skills such as leadership, emotional stability, initiative and motivation are important in all international assignments, whereas others such as cultural sensitivity, technical skill and flexibility are related to functional specialism and are assignment-specific (Baumgarten, 1995) or related to the strategic role the expatriate is expected to play (Bonache and Fernandez, 1999).

Notwithstanding these arguments and the evidence that multiple factors are responsible for successful expatriate job performance, research suggests that MNCs appear to rely heavily on technical competence and a successful track record at home when making a selection decision (Anderson, 2005) either because it is relatively easy to identify or is a low-risk strategy (Harzing, 2004). Country of origin may also influence practice – for example, in the Chinese multinationals in Shen and Edwards' study (2004), no attention was paid to cross-cultural characteristics, initiative and creativity, emotional stability and maturity, or domestic situation.

A further issue relates to how non-technical skills are assessed. Cultural differences in the definition and evaluation of personality traits, reticence to use and the cultural boundedness of some tests creates problems with using psychometric tests as predictors of cultural adjustment (Dowling et al, 1999). One attempt to overcome this links four dimensions – self-orientation, others' orientation, perceptual and cultural toughness – and proposes that these dimensions should guide the selection process (Mendenhall and Oddou, 1985).

Issues in expatriate selection
There is evidence that actual selection decisions are made in advance of the formal interview. The existence of closed informal systems which privilege personal recommendation from either line managers or specialist HR staff turns the interview into a formality and a forum for negotiating the expatriate package rather than determining the suitability of the candidate against an ideal criteria profile (Harzing, 2004; Harris and Brewster, 1999).

The selection of expatriates is compounded by two further problems: the time pressures associated with international assignments, which often work against a lengthy screening process (Dowling et al, 1999), and the potential rejection of the job assignment by the candidate (Selmer, 2001). This latter point may vary across cultures. Because Chinese multinationals use work meetings to appoint assignees to expatriate postings, which are seen as honourable and beneficial, it is very difficult for individuals to decline an assignment (Shen and Edwards, 2004). Notwithstanding possible cultural variations, expatriate availability will become increasingly important in the future – and we consider future issues in recruitment and selection issues in the concluding section of the chapter.

Discussion questions

1   What advice would you give an organisation wishing to improve the effectiveness of the recruitment and selection of its international staff?

2   In what ways is the recruitment and selection of international staff different from that of domestic staff?

3   How might knowledge of Hofstede's five dimensions assist a recruitment manager of an MNC to develop a recruitment and selection strategy for its operations in Central and South America?

CONCLUSIONS AND FUTURE ISSUES

The role of human capital in sustained competitive advantage will ensure that the recruitment and selection of staff remains of strategic importance for firms and a core activity within human resource management. It is likely that a number of issues will become increasingly important in the future.

Recruitment and selection of staff for a knowledge-based economy will continue to be a priority, and pressure to identify and attract high-calibre talent that can contribute to the organisation both now and in the future will be one of the major challenges for HR practitioners. It will require them to partner with external providers of knowledge (Whicker and Andrews, 2004) and pay careful attention to employer branding, particularly in a global context where it is important that messages are consistent, realistic and meaningful to all audiences (IDS, 2003). In addition to making wider use of their own talent pools, recruiters in certain areas such as the newly enlarged European Union will recognise the need to tap into wider markets, including migrant workers (Davison, 2005). Talent, particularly managerial talent, will be perceived globally, and this will impact on future recruitment policies and processes which will become increasingly geocentric (Johnson, 2003). Moreover, the competence of these future global managers will shift from technical and functional considerations to an ability to manage diverse and complex cross-border operations, and this will have implications for selection methods (Harvey et al, 2003).

The two-way nature of the process will continue to be important. The ongoing technological transformation of recruitment and selection and increasing use of Internet-based selection systems will further highlight issues of fairness and privacy (Chapman and Webster, 2003). Until experience shapes applicants' perceptions of the fairness of, for example, automated screening systems, organisations must ensure that such systems are consistent and fully informative, and build in a human element (Dineen et al, 2004). Moreover, organisations operating in a global context must be aware of the legislative, societal and cultural differences in the approach to privacy, and more research is needed into applicants' perceptions of privacy in relation to Internet-based selection systems and how they impact on application behaviour across different country contexts (Harris et al, 2003).

There will be increasing emphasis on making the candidate experience more personal and more positive, and the technology if used strategically has the potential to build a meaningful customer relationship (Kent, 2005). Consequently, research into applicant reactions and decision-making processes will assume greater importance in the future as the increasing importance of attracting as well as selecting people to work for the organisation is acknowledged (Anderson et al, 2001; Boswell et al, 2003).

CASE STUDY 18

THE RECRUITMENT AND SELECTION OF SENIOR STAFF IN AN INTERNATIONAL CONTEXT – THE CASE OF ESTONIA

Bob Gallienne is the CEO of the water and waste-water utility company AS Tallinna Vesi in Estonia, where United Utilities (UU) are the majority shareholder in a 15-year contract to manage water and waste-water operations for the capital Tallinn, serving over 400,000 people. Bob is responsible for 350 staff, including three expatriate staff. He has held the post for three and a half years and prior to this spent two years in Bulgaria and three years in the Philippines. This case draws on his experience in these different countries and particularly Estonia. It illustrates the power of the majority shareholder in determining recruitment and selection practices.

As part of meeting the business plan, Bob has to ensure that he has the right people in the right place at the right time. He oversees all senior appointments to ensure that the right skills, expertise and experience are brought in at this level. Cultural fit is also important, and to date it has mainly been UU people who have been appointed to these senior vacancies – a practice local staff have accepted because the appointments are seen to enhance the organisation's strategic human resource capability This is because UU is a strong FTSE-100 organisation with solid experience and an impressive long-term record. Senior management must have the expertise and track record to be credible with local Estonians as well as be able to transfer their skills to local managers. Bob's recruitment and selection record is good, people staying in post on average for two to three years.

Overseas recruitment and selection at all levels follows UU best-practice guidelines. A number of recruitment methods may be used. For the majority of vacancies internal recruitment is the main method, and positions are advertised on the intranet. Where necessary, vacancies are also advertised externally in order to attract the best pool of candidates. With senior positions, a recruitment agency is sometimes engaged as part of the search and selection process and in parallel with an internal search. Bob also uses more informal methods, recognising that networking is an effective way to recruit for overseas posts, particularly specialist ones. Selection is usually by interview against the criteria detailed in the job and person specifications. Bob does not currently use psychometric tests. The terms and conditions of the job offer will be flexible depending on the individual, and will take account of what personal/family needs have been disclosed at interview.

Bob believes expatriate senior post-holders need resilience and self-sufficiency – qualities that are not necessarily required of local candidates, for, as he puts it: 'Working at arm's length from your home nation, there is a different support structure in place. It is not the same and it works differently and it affects people differently.' Consequently, interviewers must identify this resilience in the individual. For example, in the case presented here, an individual would have to understand Estonia, its culture and how it works, apply his or her own skills and knowledge to any particular situation and then understand how the context might make it different. Bob also feels that individuals must demonstrate that they can learn and acclimatise themselves to their environment, and he recognises that this takes time. He also looks for previous overseas experience as well as taking a close look at domestic circumstances in the UK in order to understand the nature of an applicant's family commitments in terms of children and aged parents. He rates the importance of good listening and understanding skills, change management skills and interpersonal skills, the latter because he defines success as achieving results through others. A large part of the job of any senior manager in the company at this point in time is about transforming the organisation and culture and taking out the bureaucracy, but at a pace that is sustainable and successful over time and that enables the redeployment of local management back into the more senior positions.

Bob has recently overseen the recruitment and selection of a chief finance officer. The first stage following post approval was the production of job and person specifications. The post was advertised on LU's intranet and placed with a recruitment agency. Applications were by curriculum vitae together with a covering letter explaining why applicants believed they would be suitable for the job. Bob also had detailed discussions about the post requirements with the recruitment agency, including his expectations of expatriate applicants. The process followed that described above and an internal candidate from UU was appointed. The process took three months, which Bob estimated to be half the time that an external appointment might have taken.

This case study illustrates how recruitment and selection processes might work in a joint venture in an emerging economy. The situation described above has been in place for the last four years, since the partnership with UU was formed. Above all, what UU has provided is a more formal procedure. It has introduced the following concepts: technology-enabled recruitment, internal competition, strategic alliances with recruitment agencies and the ensuing increased business for them, and an increasing amount of openness and trust between employees and employer. One of the reasons for its success and ability to influence is related to the balance of the shareholding in the joint venture and the fact that the processes were driven in Tallinn by the majority shareholder, UU, and in the context of a country and company willing to learn and change in a climate of cooperation and trust.

Case study tasks

1   Evaluate the approaches used in the case study for the recruitment and selection of international staff against those described in this chapter.

2   What argument would you put forward in support of and against the organisation's perceived preferred strategy of using internal recruitment in situations such as those described here?

3   To what extent to you agree with Bob's assessment of the selection criteria needed for expatriates?

REFERENCES

Anderson B. (2005) 'Expatriate selection: good management or good luck?', *International Journal of Human Resource Management*, Vol. 16, No. 4: 567–83.

Anderson N. (2003) 'Applicant and recruiter reactions to new technology in selection: a critical review and agenda for future research', *International Journal of Selection and Assessment*, Vol.11, No. 2/3: 121–36.

Anderson N., Born M. and Cunningham-Snell N. (2001) 'Recruitment and selection: applicant perspectives and outcomes', in N. Anderson, D. S. Ones, H. K. Sinangil and C. Viswesvaran (eds) *Handbook of Industrial Work and Organisational Psychology*, Vol. 1. Thousand Oaks, CA: Sage.

Arias-Galicia F. (2005) 'Human resource management in Mexico', in M. M. Elvira and A. Davila (eds) *Managing Human Resources in Latin America*. Oxford: Routledge.

Armstrong M. and Baron A. (2002) *Strategic HRM: The key to improved business performance*. London: CIPD.

Arthur W. and Bennett W. (1995) 'The international assignee: the relative importance of factors perceived to contribute to success', *Personnel Psychology*, Vol. 48: 99–114.

Baird L. and Meshoulam I. (1988) 'Managing two fits of strategic human resource management', *Academy of Management Review*, Vol. 13, No. 1: 116–28.

Bamber G., Park F., Lee C., Ross P. K. and Broadbent K. (2000) *Employment Relations in the Asia-Pacific: Changing approaches*. London: M. E. Sharpe.

Barney J. (1991) 'Firm resources and sustained competitive advantage', *Journal of Management*, Vol. 17, No. 1: 99–120.

Barney J. and Wright P. (1998) 'On becoming a strategic partner: the role of human resources in gaining competitive advantage', *Human Resource Management*, Vol. 37, No. 1: 31–46.

Baron J. and Kreps D. (1999) 'Consistent human resource practices', *California Management Review*, Vol. 41, No. 3: 29–53.

Bartram D. (2001) 'Internet recruitment and selection: kissing frogs to find princes', *International Journal of Selection and Assessment*, Vol. 8, No. 4: 261–74.

Baumgarten K. E. E. (1995) 'Training and development of international staff', in A.-W. K. Harzing and J. Ruysseveldt (eds) *International Human Resource Management*. London: Sage.

Beer M., Spector B., Lawrence P., Quinn Mills D. and Walton R. (1984) *Managing Human Assets*. New York: Free Press.

Boam R. and Sparrow P. (1992) *Designing and Achieving Competency: A competency-based approach to managing people and organisations*. London: McGraw-Hill.

Boehle S. (2000) 'Online recruiting gets sneaky', *Training*, Vol. 37, No. 5: 66–74.

Bonache J. and Fernandez Z. (1999) 'Strategic staffing in multinational companies', in C. Brewster and H. Harris (eds) *International HRM: Contemporary Issues in Europe*. London: Sage.

Boswell W. R., Roeling M. V., Lepine M. A. and Moynihan L. M. (2003) 'Individual job-choice decisions and the impact of job attributes and recruitment practices: a longitudinal field study', *Human Resource Management*, Vol. 42, No. 1: 23–37.

Boxall P. and Purcell J. (2003) *Strategy and Human Resource Management*. Basingstoke: Palgrave Macmillan.

Braun W. H. and Warner M. (2002) 'Strategic human resource management in western multinationals in China', *Personnel Review*, Vol. 31, No. 5: 553–79.

Breaugh J. A. and Starke M. (2000) 'Research on employee recruitment; so many studies, so many remaining questions', *Journal of Management*, Vol. 26, No 3: 405–34.

Brewster C. (1988) *The Management of Expatriates*, Human Resource Centre Monograph No. 2. Cranfield: Cranfield Institute of Technology.

Brewster C. (2003) 'In the line of fire', *People Management*, 20 March: 23.

Brewster C. and Scullion H. (1997) 'Expatriate HRM: a review and an agenda', *Human Resource Management Journal* Vol. 7, No. 3: 32–41.

Buckley P., Minette K., Joy D. and Michaels J. (2004) 'The use of an automated employment recruiting and screening system for temporary professional employees: a case study', *Human Resource Management*, Vol. 43, No. 2/3: 233–41.

Cappelli P. (2001) 'Making the most of on-line recruiting', *Harvard Business Review*, Vol. 79, No. 3: 139–46.

Chapman D. S. and Webster J. (2003) 'The use of technologies in the recruiting, screening, and selection processes for job candidates', *International Journal of Selection and Assessment*, Vol. 11, No. 2/3: 113–20.

Chew I. K. H. and Horwitz F. M. (2004) 'Human resource management strategies in practice: case study findings in multinational firms', *Asia Pacific Journal of Human Resources*, Vol. 42, No. 1: 32–56.

Choi J.-G., Woods R. H. and Murrmann S. K. (2000) 'International labor markets and the migration of labor forces as an alternative solution for labor shortages in the hospitality industry', *International Journal of Contemporary Hospitality Management*, Vol. 12, No. 1: 61–7.

www.cipd.co.uk/subjects/recruitment/

CIPD (2005) *Recruitment, Retention and Turnover*. Annual survey report. Available on http://www.cipd.co.uk/download/recruit_ survey2005.pdf.

Cober R. T., Levy P. E., Brown D. J., Cober A. B. and Keeping L. M. (2003) 'Organisational web sites: web site content and style as determinant of organisational attraction', *International Journal of Selection and Assessment*, Vol.11, No.2/3: 158–69.

Davison L. (2005) 'How to recruit migrant workers', *People Management*, 1 September: 50–1.

Delery J. and Doty D. (1996) 'Modes of theorizing in strategic human resource management: tests of universalistic, contingency and configurational performance predictions', *Academy of Management Journal*, Vol. 39, No. 4: 802–35.

Di Milia L. (2004) 'Australian management selection practices: closing the gap between research findings and practice', *Asia Pacific Journal of Human Resources*, Vol. 42, No. 2: 214–28.

Dineen B. R., Ash S. R., and Noe R. A. (2002) 'A web of applicant attraction: person-organisation fit in the context of web-based recruitment', *Journal of Applied Psychology*, Vol. 87, No. 4: 723–34.

Dineen B. R., Noe R. A. and Wang C. (2004) 'Perceived fairness of web-based applicant screening procedures: weighing the roles of justice and the roles of individual differences', *Human Resource Management*, Vol. 43, No. 2/3: 127–45.

Dowling P. J. and Welch D. (1988) 'International human resource management: an Australian perspective', *Asia-Pacific Journal of Management*, Vol. 6, No. 1: 39–65.

Dowling P. J., Welch D. E. and Schuler R. S. (1999) *International Human Resource Management: Managing people in an international context* (3rd edition). Cincinnati, OH: South-Western College Publishing.

Evers A., Anderson N. and Voskuijl O. (eds) (2005) *The Blackwell Handbook of Personnel Selection*. Oxford: Blackwell Publishing.

Farley J. U., Hoenig S. and Yang J. Z. (2005) 'Key features influencing HRM practices of overseas subsidiaries in China's transition economy', in M. Warner (ed.) *Human Resource Management in China Revisited*. Abingdon: Routledge.

Feldman D. C. and Klaas B. S. (2002) 'Internet job hunting: a field study of applicant experiences with on-line recruiting', *Human Resource Management*, Vol. 41, No. 2: 175–92.

Forster N. (1997) 'The persistent myth of high expatriate failure rates', *International Journal of Human Resource Management*, Vol. 8, No. 4: 414–33.

Galanaki E. (2002) 'The decision to recruit online: a descriptive study', *Career Development International*, Vol. 7, No. 4: 243–51.

Gamble J. (2003) 'Transferring human resource practices from the United Kingdom to China: the limits and potential for convergence', *International Journal of Human Resource Management*, Vol. 14, No. 3: 369–87.

Gomez C. and Sanchez J. I. (2005) 'Managing HR to build social capital in Latin America within MNCs', in M. M. Elvira and A. Davila, *Managing Human Resources in Latin America*. Oxford: Routledge

Gomez-Samper H. and Monteferrante P. (2005) 'Human resource management in Venezuela', in M. M. Elvira and A. Davila, *Managing Human Resources in Latin America*. Oxford: Routledge.

Harris H. and Brewster C. (1999) 'The coffee-machine system – how international selection really works', *International Journal of Human Resource Management*, Vol. 10, No. 3: 488–500.

Harris H., Brewster C. and Sparrow P. (2002) *Globalising HR*. London: CIPD.

Harris M. M., Van Hoye G. and Lievens F. (2003) 'Privacy and attitudes towards Internet-based selection systems: a cross-cultural comparison', *International Journal of Selection and Assessment*, Vol. 11, No. 2/3: 230–6.

Harvey M., Kiessling T. S. and Novicevic M. (2003), 'Staffing marketing positions during global hyper-competitiveness: a market-based perspective', *International Journal of Human Resource Management*, Vol. 14, No. 2: 223–45.

Harzing, A. W. K. (1995) 'The persistent myth of high expatriate management failure rates', *International Journal of Human Resource Management*, Vol. 6, No. 2: 457–75.

Harzing A. W. K. (2001a) 'Of bears, bumble-bees and spiders: the role of expatriates in controlling foreign subsidiaries' *Journal of World Business*, Vol. 36, No. 4: 366–79.

Harzing A. W. K. (2001b) 'An analysis of the functions of international transfer of managers in MNCs', *Employee Relations*, Vol. 23, No. 6: 581–98.

Harzing A. W. K. (2004) 'Composing an international staff', in A. W. K. Harzing and J. V. Ruysseveldt (eds) *International Human Resource Management*. London: Sage.

Heenan D. A. and Perlmutter H. V. (1979) *Multinational Organisation Development*. Reading, MA: Addison-Wesley Longman.

Hess M. and Imbun B. Y. (2003) 'Papua New Guinea', in M. Zanko and M. Ngui, *The Handbook of Human Resource Management Policies and Practices in Asia-Pacific Economies*, Vol. 2. Cheltenham: Edward Elgar.

Hofstede G. (2001) *Culture's Consequences* (2nd edition). London: Sage.

Hofstede G. and Bond M. (1988) 'The Confucian connection from cultural roots to economic growth', *Organisational Dynamics*, Vol. 16, No. 4: 4–21.

Horwitz F. M., Heng C. T. and Quazi H. A. (2003) 'Finders keepers? Attracting, motivating and retaining knowledge workers', *Human Resource Management Journal*, Vol. 13, No. 4: 23–44.

Huo Y. P., Huang H. J. and Napier N. K. (2002) 'Divergence or convergence: a cross-national comparison of personnel selection practices', *Human Resource Management*, Vol. 41, No. 1: 31–44.

IDS (2003) *Recruitment Practices*. IDS Study No. 751, June: 1–6.

IRS (1999) *The Business of Selection: An IRS survey*. Employee Development Bulletin No. 117: 5–16.

IRS (2003) *Recruitment and Retention*. IRS Employment Review No. 776, 23 May: 41–8.

Jansen B. J., Jansen K. J. and Spink A. (2005) 'Using the web to look for work', *Internet Research*, Vol. 15, No. 5: 49–66.

Jattuso M. L. and Sinar E. F. (2003) 'Source effects in Internet-based screening procedures', *International Journal of Selection and Assessment*, Vol. 11, No. 2/3: 137–40.

www:JobsDB.com. JobsDBDimension: Global Market Trend of e-recruitment

Johnson R. (2003) 'Final destination', *People Management*, 23 January: 40–3.

Kent S. (2005) 'Get on board', *People Management*, 28 July: 38–40.

Klehe U.-C. and Latham G. P. (2005) 'The predictive and incremental validity of the situational and patterned behaviour description interviews for team-playing behaviour', *International Journal of Selection and Assessment*, Vol. 13, No. 2: 108–15.

Kochan T. A. and Barocci T. A. (1985) *Human Resource Management and Industrial Relations: Text, readings and cases*. Boston: Little Brown.

Konradt U., Hertel G. and Joder K. (2003) 'Web-based assessment of call center agents: development and validation of a computerized instrument', *International Journal of Selection and Assessment*, Vol. 11, No. 2/3: 184–93.

Larkin L. (2005) 'Skills crisis puts Chinese dragon on the back foot', *Personnel Today*, 5 July: 10.

Leung A. (2003) 'Different ties for different needs: recruitment practices of entrepreneurial firms at different developmental phases', *Human Resource Management*, Vol. 42, No. 4: 303–20.

Lievens F. and Harris M. M. (2003) 'Research on Internet recruitment and testing: current status and future directions', in C. L. Cooper and I. T. Robertson (eds) *International Review of Industrial and Organisational Psychology*, Vol. 18. Chichester: John Wiley & Sons.

Lievens F., de Corte W. and Brysse K. (2003) 'Applicant perceptions of selection procedures: the role of selection information, belief in tests, and comparative anxiety', *International Journal of Selection and Assessment*, Vol. 11, No.1: 67–77.

McCrae R. R. and Allik J. (2002) *The Five-Factor Model of Personality Across Cultures*. New York: Kluwer.

MacDuffie J. P. (1995) 'Human resource bundles and manufacturing performance: organisational logic and flexible production systems in the world auto industry', *Industrial and Labor Relations Review*, Vol. 48, No. 2: 197–221.

McManus M. A. and Ferguson M. W. (2003) 'Biodata, personality, and demographic differences of recruits from three sources', *International Journal of Selection and Assessment*, Vol. 11, No. 2/3: 175–83.

Manshor A. T., Mazuki J. and Simun M. (2003) 'Diversity factors and preferential treatments in selecting employees', *Journal of Management Development*, Vol. 22, No. 7: 643–56.

Marchington M. and Grugulis I. (2000) '"Best practice" human resource management: perfect opportunity or dangerous illusion', *International Journal of Human Resource Management*, Vol. 11, No. 6: 1104–24.

Mendenhall M. and Oddou G. (1985) 'The dimensions of expatriate acculturation: a review', *Academy of Management Review*, Vol. 10, No. 1: 39–47.

Miles R. and Snow C. (1978) *Organisation Strategy, Structure and Process*. New York: McGraw-Hill.

O' Leary B. S., Lindholm M. L., Whitford R. A. and Freeman S. E. (2002) 'Selecting the best and brightest: leveraging human capital', *Human Resource Management*, Vol. 41, No. 3: 325–40.

Ones D. S. and Viswesvaran C. (2001) 'Integrity tests and other criterion-focused occupational personality scales (COPS) used in personnel selection', *International Journal of Selection and Assessment*, Vol. 9, No. 1/2: 31–9.

Perlmutter H. V. (1969) 'The tortuous evolution of the multinational corporation', *Columbia Journal of World Business*, Vol. 4, No. 1: 9–18.

Pfeffer G. (1998) *The Human Equation: Building profits by putting people first*. Boston, MA: Harvard Business School Press.

Phillips J. M. and Gully S. M. (2002) 'Fairness reactions to personnel selection in Singapore and the United States', *International Journal of Human Resource Management*, Vol. 13, No. 8: 1186–1205.

Quang T. and Thang L. C. (2004) 'HRM in Vietnam', in P. S. Budwar (ed.) *Managing Human Resources in Asia-Pacific*. London: Routledge.

Roberts G. (2005) *Recruitment and Selection*. London: CIPD.

Robie C., Brown D. J. and Bly P. R. (2005) 'The big five in the USA and Japan', *Journal of Management Development*, Vol. 24, No. 8: 720–37.

Rodriguez D., Rios R., De Solminihac E. and Rosene F. (2005) 'Human resource management in Chile', in M. M. Elvira and A. Davila, *Managing Human Resources in Latin America*. London: Routledge.

Rowley C. and Benson J. (eds) (2004) *The Management of Human Resources in the Asia-Pacific Region: Convergence reconsidered*. London: Frank Cass.

Ryan A. M. and Ployhart R. E. (2000) 'Applicants' perceptions of selection procedures and decisions: a critical review and agenda for the future', *Journal of Management*, Vol. 26, No. 3: 565–606.

Ryan A. M and Tippins N. T. (2004) 'Attracting and selecting: what psychological research tells us', *Human Resource Management*, Vol. 43, No. 4: 305–18.

Rynes S. L., Barber A. E. and Varma G. H. (2000) 'Research on the employment interview: usefulness for practice and recommendations for future research', in C. L. Cooper and E. A. Locke, *Industrial and Organisational Psychology: Linking Theory with Practice*. Oxford: Blackwell.

Rynes S. L., Colbert A. E. and Brown K. G. (2002) 'HR professionals' beliefs about effective human resource management practices: research findings versus practitioner beliefs', *Human Resource Management*, Vol. 41, No. 2: 149–74

Salgado J. F. (2003) 'Predicting job performance using FFM and non-FFM personality measures', *Journal of Occupational and Organisational Psychology*, Vol. 76, No. 3: 323–46.

Salgado, J. F. and Moscoso, S. (2003) 'Internet-based personality testing: equivalence of measure and assessees' perceptions and reactions', *International Journal of Selection and Assessment*, Vol. 11, No. 2/3: 194–205.

Salgado J. F., Viswesvaran C. and Ones D. S. (2001) 'Predictors used for personnel selection: an overview of constructs, methods and techniques', in N. Anderson, D. S. Ones, H. K. Sinangil and C. Viswesvaran (eds) *Handbook of Industrial Work and Organisational Psychology*, Vol. 1. Thousand Oaks, CA: Sage.

Schuler R. and Jackson S. (1987) 'Linking competitive strategies and human resource management practices', *Academy of Management Executive*, Vol. 1, No. 3: 207–19.

Scullion H. (1994) 'Staffing policies and strategic control in British multinationals', *International Studies of Management and Organisation*, Vol. 24, No. 3: 86–104.

Searle R. H. (2003) *Selection and Recruitment: A critical text*. Milton Keynes: Palgrave Macmillan.

Selmer J. (2001) 'Expatriate selection: back to basics?', *International Journal of Human Resource Management*, Vol. 12, No. 8: 1219–33.

Shaw S. R. (2005) 'The corporate university: global or local phenomenon', *Journal of European Industrial Training*, Vol. 29, No. 1: 21–39.

Shen J. and Edwards V. (2004) 'Recruitment and selection in Chinese MNEs', *International Journal of Human Resource Management*, Vol. 15, No. 5: 814–35.

Silvester J. and Anderson N. (2003) 'Technology and discourse: a comparison of face-to-face and telephone employment interviews', *International Journal of Selection and Assessment*, Vol. 11, No. 2/3: 206–14.

Simms J. (2004) 'Home or away?', *People Management*, 3 June: 35–6, 38–9.

Sinar E. F., Reynolds D. H. and Paquet S. L. (2003) 'Nothing but' Net? Corporate image and web-based testing', *International Journal of Selection and Assessment*, Vol. 11, No. 2/3: 150–7.

Snell A. (2002) *Global 500 Internet Site Recruiting: 2002 survey*. San Francisco, CA: iLogos research/recruitmentsoft.com

Steiner D. D. and Gilliland S. W. (2001) 'Procedural justice in personnel selection: international and cross-cultural perspectives', *International Journal of Selection and Assessment*, Vol. 9, No. 1&2: 124–37.

Tayeb, M. (1996) *The Management of a Multicultural Workforce*. Chichester, John Wiley & Sons.

Taylor S. T. and Collins C. J. (2000) 'Organizational recruitment: enhancing the intersection of research and practice', in C. L. Cooper and E. A. Locke, *Industrial and Organisational Psychology: Linking theory with practice*. Oxford: Blackwell.

Tong D. Y. K. and Sivanand C. N. (2005) 'E-recruitment service providers review: International and Malaysian', *Employee Relations*, Vol. 27, No. 1: 103–17.

Torbiorn I. (2005) 'Staffing policies and practices in European MNCs: strategic sophistication, culture-bound policies or *ad-hoc* reactivity?', in H. Scullion and M. Linehan, *International HRM: A critical text*. Basingstoke: Palgrave Macmillan.

Torrington D., Hall L. and Taylor S. (2005) *Human Resource Management* (6th edition). Harlow: Pearson Education.

Tung R. L. (1981) 'Selection and training of personnel for overseas assignments', *Columbia Journal of World Business*, Vol. 16, No. 1: 68–78.

Tung R. L. (1982) 'Selection and training procedures of US, European and Japanese multinationals', *California Management Review*, Vol. 25, No. 1: 57–71.

Van Rooy D. L., Alonso A. and Fairchild Z. (2003) 'In with the new, out with the old: has the technological revolution eliminated the traditional job search process?', *International Journal of Selection and Assessment*, Vol. 11, No. 2/3: 170–4.

Warner M. (2000) 'Introduction the Asia-Pacific HRM model revisited', *International Journal of Human Resource Management*, Vol. 11, No. 2: 171–82.

Weichmann D. and Ryan A. M. (2003) 'Reactions to computerized testing in selection contexts', *International Journal of Selection and Assessment*, Vol. 11, No. 2/3: 215–29.

Werbel J. D. and Johnson D. J. (2001) 'The use of person-group fit for employment selection: a missing link in person-environment fit', *Human Resource Management*, Vol. 40, No. 3: 227–40.

Whicker L. M. and Andrews K. M. (2004) 'HRM in the knowledge economy: realising the potential', *Asia Pacific Journal of Human Relations*, Vol. 42, No. 2: 156–65.

Windolf P. (1986) 'Recruitment, selection, and internal labour markets in Britain and Germany', *Organisation Studies*, Vol. 7, No. 3: 235–54.

Worldlink (2005) 'Africa focuses on triple bottom line', *WorldLink*, Vol. 15, No. 2: 1.

Yuen E. C.and Kee H. T. (1993) 'Headquarters, host-culture and organisational influences on HRM policies and practices', *Management International Review*, Vol. 33, No. 4: 361–83.

Zanko M. (ed.) (2002) *The Handbook of Human Resource Management Policies and Practices in Asia-Pacific Economies*, Vols 1 and 2. Cheltenham: Edward Elgar. (For information specifically on Asia-Pacific countries; for other country-specific information see the Routledge Global Human Resource Management series edited R. S. Schuler, S. E. Jackson, P. Sparrow and M. Poole (www.routledge.com.))

Zanko M. (2003) 'Change and diversity: HRM issues and trends in the Asia-Pacific region', *Asia Pacific Journal of Human Resources*, Vol. 41, No. 1: 75–87.

Zhu C. J. and Dowling P. J. (2002) 'Staffing practices in transition: some empirical evidence from China', *International Journal of Human Resource Management*, Vol. 13, No. 4: 569–97.

Zhu C. J., Cooper B., De Cieri H. and Dowling P. J. (2005) 'A problematic transition to a strategic role; human resource management in industrial enterprises in China', *International Journal of Human Resource Management*, Vol. 16, No. 4: 513–31.

Learning and development

7

Andrew Rowe and Carol N. Scutt

When you have read this chapter you should be able to:

■ use the insight you have gained into the different forms of learning in terms of learning as acquisition of skills as well as participating together, involving the different cultural influences important for international human resource management (IHRM)

■ describe the evolution of 'learning and development' (L&D) from 'training and development' and the challenges faced in implementing a strategic position for L&D in an international context

■ describe the important role of HR practitioners as 'thinking performers' and 'learning architects' and the significance of that role for IHRM

■ describe the various types of development activities available to HR practitioners as well as to general managers.

PURPOSE AND SCOPE

This chapter investigates how L&D frameworks can help to provide tools that support organisations and their members in the context of the diverse cultural settings in which HRM is practised. This is important because HR practitioners have increasingly to become 'thinking performers' and 'learning architects' designing effective L&D policies across the organisation – which increasingly transcends national boundaries. Consequently, a number of the main themes in this book are addressed, revolving around the impact of globalisation and the increased significance of working in a knowledge-driven economy.

Traditionally, learning has been seen as the *acquisition* of knowledge and skills by individual learners, or collectives of individual learners (Elkjaer, 2004: 419). By facilitating learning (through individually focused learning-styles approaches or group team/learning methodologies), heightened organisational capabilities arise – potentially resulting in a learning organisation (Senge, 1992). However, this is only one way to understand L&D. As anyone who can remember their first day at school or in a new job, learning is as much a question of being able to *participate* within an unfamiliar (and perhaps intimidating) context, appreciating the socio-cultural dimension of learning (Gherardi, 1999). This chapter uses both the 'participation' as well as 'acquisition' metaphors, highlighting the integration of formal training interventions (ie off-the-job training) with less formal activities. There is no either/or, but each perspective reveals a different piece of the jigsaw puzzle that is learning – not only beneficial for the individual employee but also providing a vital source (ultimately the only one, according to Arie de Geuss) for organisational competitive advantage.

This chapter will cover the broad themes relating to L&D. The first ('why') section provides an overview of the impact of the IHRM context upon L&D issues. Secondly, the 'what' section defines what is meant by L&D and reveals how it has evolved from the more traditional conceptualisations of 'training and development'. Thirdly, the 'who' section discusses the role of various stakeholders in L&D looking beyond the organisation to include governmental and non-governmental agencies. Fourthly, the 'how' looks at the various activities available – the panoply of activities both formal as well as informal and their application.

1 THE 'WHY': L&D IN AN IHRM CONTEXT

The increased concern surrounding the theory and practice of HRM reflects the changing shape of organisations and the ways in which they transcend traditional geographical boundaries.

Globalisation in places has resulted in increased flexibility through crude 'low-road' HR practices – cost-cutting using disposable or contingent labour. However, there are many instances where firms have benefited through 'high-road' practices, in which investment in the L&D of employees is central in the design of human resource architecture that facilitates organisational capabilities (Lepak and Snell, 1999).

It has been noted in Chapter 2 that organisations take different organisational orientations towards internationalisation, from the ethnocentric to the polycentric and to the geocentric (Heenan and Perlmutter, 1979). The different organisational orientations affect individuals: who is involved and their L&D needs. For example, an organisation with an ethnocentric orientation favours the extensive use of expatriates in the host country – who are familiar with corporate procedures but are unfamiliar with both the technical/legal and the cultural *mores* that can prevent effective working. On the other hand, a more decentralised, polycentric orientation involves reliance upon locally recruited key workers, who are familiar with indigenous working policies and practices, yet these individuals may be unable to interface with expatriate staff and struggle to cope with the working requirements of corporate headquarters.

The key message from this chapter is that although there are key differences in orientation, increasingly it can be seen that similar L&D challenges face all internationally focused organisations. They have to address the learning needs of key workers to cope with the demands of working in a multinational company (MNC). The knowledge required cannot simply be transferred through formalised activities typical of traditional 'training and development' policies. Although the ideal of a geocentric orientation is disputed, whereby staffing decisions are not made on nationality grounds, clearly, cultural issues are still important. As Sparrow *et al* (1994) point out in their defining of successful IHRM, there is a need for both knowledge and skills that integrate employees dispersed around the world (convergence) alongside knowledge and skills that take account of local variations in culture and policy (divergence).

In addition, at an individual level, the impact of globalisation has influenced the nature of employee career paths. The rise of the 'global manager' is the most obvious (Black *et al*, 1991), although this label is disputed, partly because of the simplistic idea that one generic model fits all. However, there are common aspects that all managers have to deal with when working in any context: changing political, economic, social, technological and legal conditions that are magnified in an international situation.

2 DEFINING L&D

It is important to emphasise that the term 'L&D' has emerged from a number of streams – from HRM, human resource development (HRD), organisational development, and from management development. As part of the essential background, these streams provide the practitioner with many practical solutions ... and many practical problems.

Defining learning

The long-running debate over what constitutes 'learning' – between the behaviourist school (focusing upon stimulus – response changes) and the cognitive school (which looks inside the 'black box' to reveal thought processes when people make decisions or understanding the world around them (Langfield-Smith, 1992). However, moving out of the laboratory and into the workplace, the boundaries become more blurred. Buchanan and Huczynski (2004: 110) use a compromise definition of 'learning' as being [emphasis added]:

> **'The *process* of *acquiring knowledge through experience* which leads to an *enduring change* in behaviour.'**

Note the italicised words: learning is ongoing, knowledge (whether formal knowledge or tacit knowledge) is gained through experiences that result in permanent change – not a reflex action, but significant development in how the learner performs in the workplace.

It is important to refine existing strategies to efficiently meet current goals – to engage in instrumental or 'single-loop' learning (Argyris, 1999). However, massive changes in markets, technologies, etc, mean that this is insufficient, because the theories underpinning the individual (or organisational) world view become obsolete. This is even more important in the globalised world of the twenty-first century. Instead, higher-level 'double-loop' learning is needed: existing goals need reassessment, along with the underlying assumptions. Successful learners are able to use both this higher- and lower-level learning to understand how to 'learn how to learn'. This includes both formal training and informal learning from the daily experiences of managers and staff. This is vital for learning at the individual and organisational level.

Learning from experience, from classroom or workplace, requires learners to reappraise their current skills. The traditional view of learning uses the metaphor of 'acquisition' – of particular critical thinking skills – but recent views of learning additionally draw upon the metaphor of 'participation': the capabilities of individuals to work and learn together in a particular context.

Also, if an organisation is to reap the benefits of the learning of its staff, it has to be sensitive to the differing needs of non-managerial staff as well as general and line managers. HR practitioners therefore take up an even more central role: integrating the needs and potential of the individual – for example, taking account of gender issues (Marshall, 1995; Vinnicombe and Singh, 2003) – with the demands of the organisation, with its current strategic context.

What is meant by 'L&D' in the twenty-first century?

As Harrison (2004) notes, L&D is replacing what used to be called HRD. The main purpose is the development of knowledge to achieve goals for both individual and organisation. This necessitates that L&D is stimulated and facilitated – ensuring effective working relationships that make the most of and respect workforce diversity.

This new term emphasises firstly that knowledge development involves both explicit knowledge – codified in manuals, information systems and handbooks – and the tacit knowledge held in individuals' minds (Nonaka, 1991). Consequently, ideas have emerged which emphasise how people use their tacit knowledge in 'communities of practice', for example (Brown and Duguid,

1991). Secondly, it refers to the achievement of goals, both at the individual and the organisational level. Thirdly, it emphasises a collaborative approach, reflecting the importance of *all key stakeholders*: governmental, organisational and individual working together to provide opportunities, as well as to identify further needs, for L&D.

This necessitates the need for effective *strategic* design for L&D – going beyond ad hoc implementation of various training and development-related interventions. Here, future L&D needs are addressed within the organisation in such a way that the members themselves are able to re-evaluate changes to the design and its components. It requires genuine commitment by all organisational members towards Continuous Professional Development (CPD). However, this does not fit easily with the traditional practices of learning outside of Anglo-American countries.

Learning as acquisition: effective information processing

The learning as 'acquisition' metaphor favours an information-processing view of organisational learning (Elkjaer, 2004). Higher-level 'double-loop' learning involves change in individual 'world views' (cognitive maps) about how to perform particular tasks more effectively (the behavioural dimension). At an organisational level, these changes need then to be institutionalised, embedded into repositories (systems, standard operating procedures, etc), forming resources through which an organisation is able to leverage improved performance. These may be tangible resources (eg a database of customers) but intangible resources are also important (eg good relationships with customers). For instance, it is not just having a database of international customers – it is how this information is used to maintain links with them, to maintain a valued and professional relationship with them, which really gives a competitive advantage. Consequently, there is a clear focus upon a firm's gaining competitive advantage from its capability to acquire and accumulate invisible assets (goodwill) because these are not easily copied by competitors (Luoma, 2000). This forms an organisational resource that has to be updated through the recruitment of new staff, the secondment of existing staff on projects, working alongside team members from outside the organisation or from different departments, etc.

However, this does *not* mean that HR practitioners are merely information processors for the organisation. Firstly, not all knowledge can be made explicit – codified into procedures and systems – as some will always remain tacitly held within the minds of staff members (Nonaka, 1991). Staff know more than they can ever articulate in documentary form. Secondly, not all changes in individual cognition or behaviour results in an organisational response. For example, senior management in a Canadian logging company (Zietsma *et al*, 2002) when faced with a complex and changing environment, refused to reconsider their institutionalised knowledge: they stuck to established procedures – what *they thought* were the best solutions. Many managers and staff outside of the senior management 'strategic apex' could see that there was a desperate need to change, but their ideas were perceived as irrelevant and threatening. The company fell foul of a 'legitimacy trap', whereby alternative ideas and approaches were ignored. Previous learning was actually preventing future learning. L&D is thus linked with the power relations within organisations, of which HR practitioners must be aware.

Research suggests a direct link between L&D and a firm's competitive advantage (Pucik, 1998), provided that it is appropriately planned and executed. HRM plays a potentially vital role, because of the importance placed upon the invisible assets of the organisation – namely, the knowledge contained within its staff. From this *resource-based view* (see Chapters 3 and 6) IHRM practitioners can provide a number of key processes:

- recruiting staff with the necessary skills and knowledge to augment the current knowledge base

- reviewing and evaluating existing staff – identifying learning opportunities to expand their capabilities

- retaining staff by ensuring that key workers are rewarded for their contribution to the organisation's capabilities

- removing staff whose performance is inadequate (but only after reviewing their development potential).

In addition, the tools through which the organisation's memory is stored and updated – intranets, 'best practice' information, standard operating procedures, etc – are often the domain of the HR function in many organisations … again revealing the importance of HRM. However, it is important to note that the complexities of multinational operations place greater demands upon the capabilities of HR practitioners to be able to maintain and align HR functions. Notwithstanding the technical complexities, there are often key cultural factors to grapple with. For example, in 'high context' cultures (such as Russia) information tends to be tied to individuals – information being shared through informal, unofficial channels rather than strictly following established pathways and procedures (Engelhard and Nagele, 2003). The 'learning as acquisition' metaphor therefore only goes so far.

There are three key points to draw from the above:

1   Learning takes place at various levels: knowledge acquired by individuals and teams in practice can be (potentially) incorporated into organisational capabilities.

2   It also suggests that the cultural aspect of learning is vital – we need to understand how informal knowledge is passed around within communities, although not all are able to participate in this process.

3   Hence, it is important that consideration is given not only to the content but also to how learning is facilitated. Both formalised learning-focused activities (Type 3 – ie classroom-based courses: Mumford, 1987) as well as informal learning task-focused activities (Type 1 – ie derived from secondments) are important. Ideally, both Types could be combined to give Type 2 learning (see Figure 1 below).

The importance of L&D at all levels

L&D has emerged from the earlier emphasis upon 'training', which used to be the province of training and personnel departments – towards a twenty-first-century view of HRD. However, some are sceptical. Russ Vince suggests that not much has changed at all, that there is an over-simplified view of development at the individual level alone, with too often mechanistic learning based upon a limited range of models (Vince, 2003: 559). Vince warns that diverse L&D needs of staff are often ignored and that staff are discouraged from transferring their learning to the organisation.

This reflects the traditional view of L&D as focused upon 'training' being 'done to' passive learners. This view is being replaced by broader notions associated with developing not only technical skills but also interpersonal skills – and especially conceptual understanding through critical thinking.

L&D occurs at different levels, in practice overlapping – but note how the major focus has moved from the individual level towards the collective, both the group/team and organisational and increasingly the inter-organisational – through the rise of international joint ventures, for example.

Individual learning: learning styles in an international context

The experiential school – which sees learning in terms of an ongoing process of action and reflection on action – has influenced management thinking for many years. The rise of self-development in the 1970s through the likes of Mike Pedler (2004) has been useful in describing how different learning styles must be understood through approaches such as action learning – which encourage learning by individuals as mature learners in the workplace, rather than as passive absorbers of 'knowledge' provided by teachers.

At the heart of self-development is the importance of 'learning to learn'. This necessitates that the adult learner understands how he or she learns from practice. The experiential learning 'loop', drawing from the work of David Kolb and others, shows how learning follows an iterative cycle of concrete experience; drawing observations and reflections from these experiences; making abstract conceptualisations (generalising and linking experience to theory); and finally implementation. Kolb says that most people 'naturally' take to one or two phases of this cycle: some are naturally more reflective, whereas others prefer to experiment instead.

The significance for the L&D practitioner is to understand that individual learners respond to different ways of learning. The Learning Styles Inventory has been developed from this cycle into an effective tool to analyse the needs of individual learners (Kolb, 1984). This has informed other frameworks. For example, the Learning Styles Questionnaire of Honey and Mumford (1996), which defines four categories: activist, reflector, theorist and pragmatist–, suggests that it is possible to develop one's less preferred styles to become a more effective learner.

The key to engaging in higher-level learning is the ability to apply 'critical thinking'. Proponents note that this should apply widely, from education through to politics and religion (Paul and Elder, 2001). They add a second level of thinking to the prejudices of ordinary (first-order) thinking. Through reflection, the learner can progress through stages in order to develop as a critical thinker, from an 'uncritical learner' (unaware of significant problems in his/her thinking) through to a 'master thinker' for whom skilled and insightful thinking become second nature (Paul and Elder, 2001: 22).

However, the IHR practitioner must be aware that these models describe experiential learning from a partial western perspective. Jackson (1995, 1996) has investigated a variety of international cultures in order to reformulate Kolb's model. He notes that learning styles vary in terms of *receptivity* towards either practical or theoretical learning, as well as *perception*– whether learners prefer a rational sequential or a more intuitive bias towards filtering and judging information. Thirdly, Jackson highlights a *cognitive* modality; here, learners prefer either a logical, scientific approach to making 'objective' factual decisions, or a more subjective method. Finally, Jackson uses a *behaviour* modality – the extent to which learners prefer an instructor-centred approach or favour self-directed learning without such a sharp distinction between instructor and student.

The implications are significant for the appropriate choice of L&D activity to match learning styles in different cultures. For example, whereas French learners are at home with theoretical stimuli, Polish and British students place greater emphasis upon learning by doing through practical experience. Similarly, whereas Taiwanese and British prefer to learn in groups, their

French counterparts prefer to learn alone. The delivery of activities will have to be different, because whereas British learners may feel at home with a more action-learning perspective – wherein learner and facilitator are learning together – this may not translate to French or Taiwanese cultures that prefer a more traditional student/teacher relationship. Similarly, the investigation of emotions and personal beliefs in less didactic L&D approaches could provide a challenge to the logical bias of German learners. As Hofstede's (1991) seminal work points out, some cultures are at home with uncertainty while others prefer to avoid uncertainty. Consequently, L&D activities must take account of these cultural preferences.

CASE STUDY 19

L&D ACROSS CULTURES

Most of the standard texts on L&D have emerged from Anglo-American culture. The critical thinking regarded as central to higher-level learning involves challenging cultural norms – both organisational as well as wider cultural values. Examples from recent research noted many instances in which exasperated Anglo-American expatriate managers experienced severe problems trying to work with Russian staff, the latter being (in the eyes of their bosses) capable of collating and calculating key business measures, yet seemingly incapable (or unwilling) to critically reflect upon the implications of the figures produced. This proved to be a cultural clash that was both irritating and unhelpful to all concerned (Engelhard and Nagele, 2003).

This higher-level learning involves the questioning of deeply held beliefs – which may certainly cause problems because it can threaten the individual's own sense of security. This is a challenge in specific cultural contexts where it is even more traumatic. Chinese education is traditionally based upon the one-way translation of knowledge (from master to pupil), emphasising conformity and deference to authority figures (Chan, 1991) – far removed from an Anglo-American view of learning. Elsewhere, in a Bangladesh commercial bank (Cundale, 2005) western consultants found that L&D involved 'students' sitting silently in classrooms listening to 'teachers' imparting explicit knowledge, which gave little or no opportunity for staff members to engage with critical thinking about what constituted 'good practice': such as the removal of unnecessarily bureaucratic processes and the mismanagement of bank funds.

Case study tasks

1   In your organisation, or one which you are familiar with, to what extent is higher-level thinking encouraged?

2   What factors enable/inhibit this?

3   Think of any instances (at work, in college, etc) in which you have worked/studied with those from other cultures. What issues in relation to learning have arisen?

Learning at the group/team level

Research has found that the success of many Asian firms, for example, has been built upon the ability (based upon their collectivist cultural orientation) to develop and share both explicit and tacit knowledge in groups and teams (Nonaka, 1991). Key to the rise of interest in collective learning has been methodologies such as dialogue (Isaacs, 1993). The essence of these methodologies is that critical thinking can raise the *defensive routines* of members – questioning deeply held assumptions can be threatening to the individual emotionally. The key point is that it is important to understand that questioning these mental models is not addressed to the *person* but to the *idea* (see Senge, 1992).

However, the impact of hierarchical relationships, competing departmental agendas, etc, has led some to question their applicability (Rowe, 2001). Again, there are cultural problems of translating western ideas of surfacing difficulties – they may be 'undiscussable' in cultures where the preservation of 'face' is prominent and where there is a high power distance such that inequality is accepted and it can be more difficult for different levels to 'dialogue' openly, as in India (Hofstede, 1991). Nevertheless, as Senge (1992) notes, teams form 'the rubber on the road' for organisations, because increasingly work is team-based and increasingly these teams are cross-organisational.

Learning at the organisational level: the rise of the learning organisation

The learning organisation in the USA (Senge, 1992) or the learning company in the UK (Pedler *et al*, 1989) moves beyond individual learning to understand how learning collectively can result in improved performance. Both forms emphasise the need to facilitate learning at the organisational level through transforming the learning capabilities of individuals and teams – hence the importance of the team learning methodologies mentioned above.

These are generic labels for unique entities. Although no two learning organisations/companies can ever be the same, they share commonalities such as the use of information-processing systems that enable higher-level learning. There is a need for a partnership between HR practitioners and general managers. That learning organisations/companies emphasise the importance of transferring what individuals learn from their experiences into organisational memory has been fundamental to the traditional 'learning as acquisition' approach. Jaw and Liu (2003) have highlighted the importance of organisational learning and self-renewal in Taiwanese firms, who for decades have withstood major economic and social upheavals. Although the concept of the learning organisation/company has been questioned for its practicality, the evidence is there that successful organisations have had to manage their L&D and develop capabilities that allow them to survive changes in the international marketplace.

Looking beyond the learning organisation

Whereas the 'learning organisation' was radical in the 1990s, inter-organisational learning is the theme of the early twenty-first century. This is because of the changing shape of the organisation – from the traditional bureaucracy, with its many levels covering the key functions, towards more flexible designs of organisations. These de-layered, team-based firms are more reliant upon working and learning with their supply chain.

Small and medium-sized enterprises (SMEs) are particularly reliant upon learning across their supply chain (European Commission, 2004; Macpherson and Wilson, 2003). Learning occurs not just in the organisation but as part of its stakeholder environment, through the network environment (Gibb, 1997) in SME 'clusters' (European Commission, 2004). Similarly, research into large-scale Public Private Partnership projects can bring together many organisations from differing organisational cultures in their network of teams and parent organisations (Tranfield *et al*, 2004). The use of science parks across Asia and Europe attracts small start-up companies as well as major global firms (Kermani and Gittins, 2004). There are parallels with communities of practice (Brown and Duguid, 1991): by providing the facilities and the culture of learning and innovation, it is possible to encourage informal as well as formal learning. Hence there is still a key role for L&D practitioners to manage human resources more effectively (eg Evans and Keogh, 2004).

Significantly, these learning connections can extend beyond national boundaries. This gives rise to many opportunities to learn from other cultures, but also can lead to many problems. The impact of cultural differences has been covered by many, building upon the pioneering work of Hofstede (1991). These issues will be increasingly important to globalised industries for their employees – host nationals or home-country expatriates – to appreciate how to work together in practice: to learn how to participate in communities of practice (Brown and Duguid, 1991).

Learning as participation: how to perform together

The ideas contained in the above sections indicate the need to understand learning at various levels – individual and collective. A key weakness from an IHRM perspective of learning styles or learning organisations is their ethnocentric view of the world. They reflect their Anglo-American cultural assumptions (see Case study 19 above). A key point is that L&D is a cultural – as much as an individual – phenomenon. Recently, greater attention has been given to understanding learning in practice – for example, in communities of practice wherein learning, innovation and working are combined and which transcend formal boundaries (Brown and Duguid, 1991).

CASE STUDY 20

LEARNING AS PARTICIPATION: GETTING ON IN THE COMMUNITY

This movement towards understanding learning as a social/cultural practice is particularly significant for IHRM. The 'learning as participating' perspective is increasingly regarded as vital for improved organisational performance, yet can be seen as very different from many people's experiences (often bad) of learning at school or in training for occupations, where the emphasis was upon acquiring technical skills or abstract knowledge often in order to reproduce in a written or oral exam.

However, the learning as participation idea is entirely pertinent for all. Think of your first day at school/work – feeling insecure, not knowing what to say or do, worried in case a member of the teaching staff shouted at you or, even worse, in case you looked 'uncool' in front of your new classmates. Over time, you began to understand how to perform in class, no longer the peripheral kid at the back of the class. In social learning theory, this progression from 'outsider' to 'part of the community' is referred to as legitimate peripheral participation (Wenger, 1998). Much has been written recently about learning in 'communities of practice': the most famous examples include 'skunk works' such as McDonnell Douglas' massive establishment in the Everglades, but there are relatively mundane office departments as well (Wenger, 1998).

But remember that although communities of practice can facilitate working, learning and innovation across boundaries, they can also *inhibit* learning. Going back to the school example, informal gangs can disrupt the smooth running of a class or even a whole school through their attempts to go against the formal organisation. Etienne Wenger's website has some useful information on the theory and practicalities of the communities of practice idea (http://www.ewenger.com/research/index.htm).

Case study tasks

1   Can you think how this idea of 'communities of practice' applies in your organisation (or one you are familiar with)?

2   How do these 'communities' enable/inhibit learning?

3   How might an understanding of the idea of 'communities of practice' be useful to managers in organisations?

Discussion questions

1   What are the differences between learning from a cognitivist and learning from a behavioural perspective?

2   How can conceptualising learning as 'participation' and/or as 'acquisition' help us to understand learning in the workplace?

3   How does 'learning and development' differ from more traditional ideas of 'training'?

3 THE 'WHO': THE KEY PLAYERS IN L&D

Who is responsible for L&D? – the macro-level view

One vision of L&D is of a collaborative approach between government, organisations and individuals (see Harrison, 2004). Yet history suggests that governments are loath to spend money on L&D, and there have been recent moves towards a market-based approach to the provision of L&D opportunities. For example, in the UK, the post-war era saw the disputed impact of Industrial Training Boards (ITBs). However, there is evidence across the world that governments are beginning to invest in L&D (ie lifelong learning). The important influence of supra-national bodies upon IHRM policies is increasing. For example, in European Union countries the Social Chapter enshrines the rights of workers to have vocational training. In addition, the International Labour Organisation (ILO) has attempted to establish international convergence on and support for vocational training.

Attitudes towards the provision of L&D in different countries differ considerably. For example, in the United States expenditure upon L&D must clearly add value to the 'bottom line'. The criticisms of the lack of practical relevance of American business education have seen a rise in the prevalence of corporate provision of formal development – for instance, through the use of corporate universities (Thomson *et al*, 2001). In contrast, the Japanese model has traditionally focused upon the organisational provision of on-the-job training, rather than the use of higher education, Japanese managers traditionally having to study abroad for MBAs, while receiving intensive development through informal experiential learning by placements. Similarly, the French have prided themselves on the generalist education provided by their *Grandes Écoles*, as opposed to MBAs and other vocationally oriented education, in contrast to for instance the German apprenticeship system. Whatever the cultural variations, Thomson *et al* (2001) note a common trend away from the state's accepting the responsibilities of development provision, and towards a more market-driven approach. This means that increasingly, organisations have to focus more upon their own provision of L&D (whether bought-in or in-house) and how this expenditure is justified in an increasingly global marketplace, where external job opportunities for the highly skilled employee entices them away before the organisation reaps the benefits.

Other stakeholders have also played a changing role over the years. The 1960s and 1970s saw a high-profile role for unions – through their participation in ITBs, for example. More recently, UK and EU policies have, to an extent, encouraged their input into the L&D movement. In 2002 the Employment Act gave paid time off for union learning representatives, while the Trades Union Congress (TUC) is beginning to support learning actively.

The role of HR practitioners in L&D: learning architects and thinking performers

The increasing attention given to organisations to facilitate their learning potential has resulted in what could be a vital role for HR practitioners. This increased status for HR professionals has not been mirrored – as yet – in certain cultures. However, by working alongside general managers, there is a strong argument for the vital role of HR professionals as learning architects and thinking performers – and for the need to encourage general managers to *perform similar functions*.

The next subsection describes the increasingly important role given to HR practitioners for facilitating L&D, which has been summarised in recent ideas such as 'learning architects' and 'thinking performers' (Harrison, 2004). In this, HR practitioners perform a vital role facilitating and enabling others. The subsection thereafter explores the implications of the L&D agenda for other key players. General managers have to take more responsibility, and are in a particularly opportune position, to oversee the L&D of their subordinates. The leaders of the future have been portrayed as 'global managers'. In MNCs it is important for all employees to possess particular technical skills (ie multilingualism), but increasingly MNCs rely upon key managers as 'global explorers' (Black *et al*, 1999). Indeed, who are these leaders of the future? There is a danger of assuming that we rely on the stereotype of the white middle-class male leader, which has influenced so many of the earlier classic texts on leadership.

Learning architect: a tough role for IHRM
It must be remembered that 'learning' can take place without any formal intervention: arguably, it happens 'naturally' whenever people engage with their work and colleagues. Consequently, whereas the training and personnel officer was someone who 'did' training, now the learning architect facilitates the natural learning.

Calveley (2005) has explored the competencies required by IHR managers. She breaks this down into organisational knowledge. This includes an understanding not only of the organisation's functioning but of the macro-level economic, political and legal frameworks that impact upon the organisation. She also notes the importance of practical skills – reflected in an understanding of the implementation of HR activities within the local/national/trans-national context (for instance, where EU legislation defines the rights of employees to vocational training). However, she also points to the importance of interpersonal and communication skills to ensure that company HR policies are communicated effectively and are aligned with a variety of national contexts. These are similar to the requirements of HR practitioners generally, but made even more complex when working across geographical boundaries. For instance, in terms of interpersonal and communication skills, not only is multilingualism important in dealing with managers and staff but cultural sensitivity is vital when engaging in employee relations in countries that are highly unionised.

The HR practitioner as 'learning architect' must be able to address the *relations* within an organisation to ensure that innovations in processes and procedures and the challenging of existing mental models are facilitated. This requires 'unlearning' – the deliberate removal of the accepted assumptions through double-loop learning. What is also required is to understand how learning takes place through the participation of staff.

Experimentation and risk-taking is also important to develop knowledge. But can L&D practitioners do this without a partnership with management? Edmondson's (1999) study of manufacturing workers revealed the negative learning impact of unsupportive management responses that diminish both risk-taking behaviour and open discussion to evaluate mistakes – important for critical thinking. It is therefore vital to work with leaders and managers to develop a conducive workplace culture – perhaps by the use of local champions, not only HR but other 'influential' managers.

Recently, HR practitioners have been identified as, potentially, learning architects. The UK's Chartered Institute of Personnel and Development (CIPD) is keen to point out that all personnel development practitioners are 'thinking performers' – involving not only technical knowledge of L&D but also conceptual skills – that they are critically reflective about the L&D performance.

UNPACKING THE LEARNING ARCHITECT ROLE

Learning architects are highlighted as providing a number of key services to facilitate L&D:

- They play a strategic role in raising awareness of the need to encourage knowledge productivity. They sensitively oversee workplace learning.

- They concentrate on *re-learning* (transferring old learning to new contexts), but not learning the same old things again (new situations require different approaches), so *unlearning* is vital as well.

- They use multiple methods to encourage critical thinking (external learning sources, facilitating communities of practice along with formal methods).

- They promote a culture of challenge and creativity. (Again the *relationship* between HRD and management is vital.)

- They ensure that 'customary players' do not dominate the learning environment.

- They use local champions – not only HRD but 'influential' managers – in partnerships that can be knowledge-productive.

Source: adapted from Harrison (2004)

An architect not only designs and configures the materials that constitute buildings. He or she also gives *space* for others to live/grow and has to consider the future needs for an increasingly diverse workforce. Learning is *not* just something that can be programmed in or done by specialist units. Informal learning gained from daily experience is as important as formal learning drawn from classes. The role of the learning architect involves ensuring that the 'customary players' do not predominate. This means that learning architects are politicians as well.

Taking into account the internationalisation of companies requires HR practitioners (in their 'learning architect' role) to face other sets of questions. Which HR practices are to be designed centrally or locally (and who designs them)? Consistency between HR policies is a key issue – whether local practices take precedence over the global organisation, for example – influenced by the orientation of the organisation (ie polycentric or ethnocentric). The movement of personnel between countries and continents places a greater emphasis upon ensuring not only that staff acquire the appropriate explicit knowledge (about products, for example) but that they are able to develop more tacit understandings of the cultures in which they have to live and work.

CASE STUDY 21

L&D AT ACCENTURE, IN INDIA

India has for some time been an important location for business processing outsourcing (BPO) for the management consultancy and technology company Accenture. Accenture Technology Infrastructure Services (ATIS) is a wholly-owned Accenture subsidiary. ATIS has helpdesk support services (HDS) contact centres in Dublin, Ottawa, Bangalore and China (concentrating on Asian languages) to serve the needs of Europe, North America, the Middle East and Africa and Asia-Pacific regions. These centres are known as 'captive centres' – they serve almost exclusively Accenture employees.

The HDS centre in Bangalore has 125 employees, some 50 of them in support activities – technology support, training voice and accents, process and infrastructure work, and in supervisory and management roles. The other 75 are the technicians. These are the people who receive the calls from Accenture consultants who need help on immediate IT problems. The 75 technicians are mainly in their mid-twenties and some 40% are women. It is considered an attractive job. Corporate support has some advantages over third-party contact; in an IT helpdesk technicians are given technical training and obtain mastery of technical processes – an evident transferable skill.

On commencement all new hires receive five weeks off-the-job training in technical processes, the Accenture culture, and voice and accent. There is then a four-week 'incubation' period with a buddy. The challenge is to customise training in order to sensitise staff to the client's requirements. For example, a lot of emphasis is placed on conversational styles. US callers are chattier than Europeans, so fillers are needed. However, the US callers also display greater urgency in their requests.

There are plans for expansion and up to 50 new hires could be recruited each month. All new hires are graduates and it is essential that they have had prior experience on a technical helpdesk. Recruitment takes place initially through agencies. There is a technical test on Microsoft products, followed by assessment with a voice and accent coach. Gautum Lahiri, one of the centre managers, envisages no difficulty in obtaining recruits of the necessary culture. At some stage applicants may come from further afield but 'Bangalore is the place to be'.

Case study tasks

1   In what ways does the L&D approach taken at ATIS reflect learning as 'acquisition of skills' or 'learning to participate'?

2   In what ways does the national and organisational culture impact upon the provision of L&D at ATIS?

3   What key issues arise here for the role of the HR practitioner as 'learning architect'?

Thinking performers: helping to develop the (global) leaders of the future
According to the CIPD (CIPD Professional Standards, 2001), there is a key need for HR and general managers to become 'thinking performers' who must:

- show knowledge and competence in their various fields
- be able to critique organisational policies and procedures
- provide advice on how L&D capabilities can be nurtured in the future.

Managers must be able not only to focus upon the acquisition of appropriate cognitive skills, but also to emphasise 'inclusive' learning that is multicultural, incorporating opposing viewpoints and religious implications, varying organisational 'learning' stances – across continents.

Along with the 'learning architect' idea, this connects with the socio-cultural view of how learning is moving away from focusing upon the individual out of context, and how learning is increasingly and significantly a collective activity. It is a view that is becoming more important, given that there is still considerable debate surrounding the supposed rise of the 'global manager'. Whether the global manager is understood as an expatriate manager or as someone who works across borders (Baruch, 2005), MNCs will require those who can manage beyond national boundaries.

Recent management development emphasises the importance of transformational leadership and specific competencies. Diversity research has attacked the lack of understanding of alternative approaches to leadership and management. The gender issue has not been addressed sufficiently well. Vinnicombe and Singh (2003) critique MBA students and their 'macho' learning culture at a top international business school, suggesting that (the small minority of) female students were heavily disadvantaged in their dealings with male peers – having to learn how to adapt to the individualistic, competitive environment or become marginalised. The impact of this is that the next generation of managers are being socialised into performing in particular ways – neglecting the potential benefits of a more feminine approach to learn (with a greater focus upon the emotional dimension of learning, along with a more collaborative learning style). Similarly, ignoring cultural differences in working and learning can have a major problem in performing together in the workplace. Consequently, part of the formal training programme run by the Union Bank of Switzerland is deliberately to send expatriate managers out to work in the voluntary sector (Mendenhall *et al*, 2003), in order for the managers to challenge their own perspectives before they head out into a different national culture. Also, when a German bank was taken over by a larger British competitor, there followed a whole series of formal workshops that used lectures and role-plays to help managers from each nation understand more about the working practices of the other.

Discussion questions

1   What responsibilities do governments, organisations and HR practitioners have in facilitating L&D?

2   What challenges are faced by HR practitioners in establishing L&D in organisations?

3   How can HR practitioners and managers become 'learning architects'? Can you identify anyone who performs this role in an organisation with which you are familiar?

4 THE 'HOW': APPROACHES FOR L&D

This section discusses the various options available for encouraging L&D. Interventions can be described as having two significant dimensions. Firstly, is the *focus* upon the individual (aimed at development on an individual basis, with only indirect benefits for the organisation itself), or is it focused upon improving the performance of the organisation, or both? Secondly, is the *purpose* of the intervention behavioural – are particular new behaviours being encouraged/ existing ones discouraged? On the other hand, is the intervention aimed at preparing the staff member for the next step in his or her career progression?

Also, it is important to evaluate the practical implications for any intervention. This investigation has to take into account the individual, his/her organisation, and the requirements for the HR practitioners.

KEY QUESTIONS TO EVALUATE L&D INTERVENTIONS

Individual development

- immediate impact, or future?
- further learning: when? how?
- priorities: technical/interpersonal skills?

For the organisation

Organisational strategy

- consolidation/expansion into new markets
- centralisation/decentralisation of HRM

Resourcing considerations

- balance (ie of interventions that address differing developmental needs)?
- trends and fads in management development (can this intervention demonstrate added value)?
- resource availability/return on investment?

HR and training function

- roles (supporting/leading)?
- changes (is there a need to augment HR capabilities through recruitment/ outsourcing)?
- future strategic role (medium-/long-term impact upon organisation)?

Not all interventions can be used on all occasions, but their potentials can be evaluated through the questions in the box above. Overall, development approaches can be understood as being any of four different types. Firstly, there is perhaps what might be traditionally associated with training and development – for instance, formal development activities such as

MBAs for senior and high-fliers. Here there has generally been little concern for the tasks themselves (eg writing essays) but a high concern for the learning drawn from these activities. This has been termed 'Type 3' learning (Mumford, 1987). Secondly, in contrast, there are those development activities in which the performing of particular tasks is paramount (eg being mentored or coached, as well as being involved in a new project or solving unfamiliar problems), although the participant has little awareness of the learning involved. This can be designated Type 1 learning.

These two types reflect lost opportunities to integrate both task and potential learning results. However, the following sections demonstrate that there are moves to attempt to rectify the lack of practical applicability of tasks performed in formal educational contexts (Type 3), alongside the higher profile given to the learning stemming from informal (Type 1) methods. In doing so, it is argued that successful integration of both task and learning outcomes in the minds of learners will enable a third type of learning (Type 2). Failure to achieve this integration can lead to a complete lack of interest in the tasks involved and in the potential learning as well (Type X).

Figure 1 Four development types

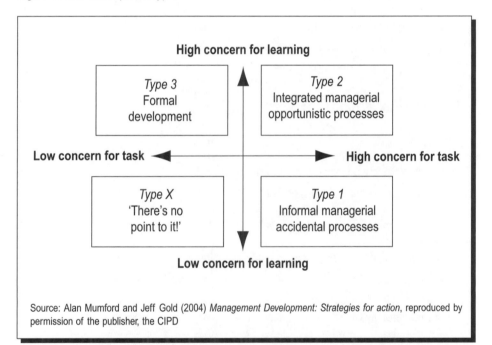

Source: Alan Mumford and Jeff Gold (2004) *Management Development: Strategies for action*, reproduced by permission of the publisher, the CIPD

Mumford's 'four types' framework reveals that learning can take place not only through the transfer of explicit knowledge in the classroom but through the transfer of tacit knowledge informally in the workplace. The types are examined in turn.

Type 3: formal L&D activities and the role of higher education

This particular type of L&D can be characterised in a number of ways:

- formal, planned approaches, often off-the job
- either real or detached approaches
- usually developed by particular providers (in-house/external)

■   reviewed through a formalised approach.

Examples of these have been discussed at length elsewhere (see Mumford and Gold, 2004). Such approaches range from traditional education provision to more fashionable approaches towards management development. For example, arts-based courses (Gibb, 2004) may use theatre as a metaphor and an experiential tool for developing insights into leadership or problem-solving (eg at The Praxis Centre, at Cranfield University). These interventions are intended to provide alternative ways of helping participants acquire new skills (team-building, communication, for example) and learn how to participate within a particular context.

It is advisable to note the lack of empirical evidence for the benefits of some of these interventions. For example, the ever-popular staple of management development, the Outward-Bound courses (Shivers-Blackwell, 2004), are claimed to develop self-awareness and confidence. But there is little hard evidence to reinforce the anecdotal evidence that improved performance comes about through forcing (sometimes unwilling) participants along rivers and over deep valleys, translating the political environment from the office (Ibbetson and Newell, 1999). Similarly, are arts-based courses merely 'infotainment' – being used to 'spice up' boring management development courses with little emphasis upon the transferability of skills learned to the workplace?

Clearly, these interventions at least provide novel ways of challenging mental models, and therefore enable learning to take place. However, a number of issues must be borne in mind with these Type 3 approaches. Firstly, there is the relevance of learning from courses in which the content may not accurately reflect the contemporary workplace.

The relationship between educational institutions and the workplace has been re-examined. Many are concerned at current trends in the provision of L&D. Of particular concern is the rise of the MBA as a panacea for management education despite criticism that it ignores both practical relevance and critical conceptual skills (Currie and Knights, 2003). The increase in international MBAs – such as Henley and Open University Management Schools cooperating in New Zealand and China (Anonymous, 2002) – does seem to suggest that the cultural dimension of learning is being addressed.

A second related issue is whether these interventions do actually equip employees with the critical skills that help them to learn how to learn. The Master's in HRM course at Manchester Metropolitan University advocates a self-development approach. Students throughout the course put together a learning portfolio which contains evidence of learning, incorporating learning logs, CPD plans and reports assessed by staff and fellow students. This is demanding for students already busy with coursework and exams – but it does allow students to examine and revisit their own learning history. This is important for enabling students to develop the learning-to-learn skills, which they use in their work life. The CIPD (2001) has been working to spread the gospel of CPD, as has the Chartered Management Institute, in order to ensure that managers move through an ongoing cycle of assessing and reflecting upon their L&D needs – drawing upon the experiential learning loop.

There is more concern now surrounding the practical relevance of knowledge generated by academic research institutions. The debate surrounds the need for Mode II 'knowledge into action' alongside traditional Mode I (academic knowledge 'produced for its own sake') approaches (van Aken, 2005). The Advanced Institute of Management in the UK has tried to strengthen the link between academia and the workplace.

Of course, the cost implications of sending key workers on courses to external providers or the in-house provision of training programmes have to be considered. Indeed, one of the benefits of more Type 1 approaches, such as informal coaching, is that they appear to provide cheap opportunities for learning. However, the benefits of any approach must be calculated in terms of whether they are immediate or longer-term. For example, sending an inexperienced staff member on a course could provide him or her with practical skills for an upcoming first international assignment – or it could help him or her to develop skills that might turn out to be essential through a series of foreign postings.

Type 1: informal approaches

There are so many examples of informal learning opportunities, from coaching/mentoring (although either can use a highly formalised Type 3 approach) through to covering for a colleague while he or she is on holiday – provided that the learner is prepared to engage in critical reflection. Working in MNCs affords many opportunities to learn informally from participating in unfamiliar contexts – whether from expatriates on assignment abroad or from the calling of host nationals to headquarters. Indeed, assignments have been seen as inducing more efficient learning than formal training programmes because of the exposure to new technical and cultural knowledge (Brewster and Suutari, 2005).

These less formal approaches are *not* a replacement for Type 3 approaches. Indeed, they are not a panacea either for development needs. Mumford and Gold (2004) have three concerns over this naïve supposition. They warn of *idealisation* (assuming that those behaviours demonstrated in previous experiences are taken for granted as correct), of *narrowness* (often the learner only draws upon a limited set of experiences – for example, restricted to the one organisation/ function) and of *obsolescence* – whereby past experiences are superseded by rapidly changing circumstances, which can lead to informal learning's actually inhibiting performance. In an IHRM context this is particularly significant. Expatriates sent abroad with little support (for themselves or their families) find it difficult to reflect on their experiences. Thus, as is detailed elsewhere (Brewster and Suutari, 2005), there is a significant role for both formal and informal support mechanisms – such as forums or periodic returns to the classroom – which can help the employee to overcome problems both while on assignment and after repatriation.

Type X and Type 2: the best and the worst of L&D

Simply implementing coaching/mentoring or sending managers off on courses is no guarantee that this will translate into learning either at the individual or the organisational level. There are many examples of expatriate workers who have been sent overseas with no consideration of what they can learn from this experience, or mentors who do not have either the training or the inclination to perform their roles effectively. Similarly, many have been sent on courses which (in the eyes of the attendees) have little or no relevance to their current jobs or to their future personal development. Mumford sums this situation up as 'Type X' development: here there is little concern for carrying out the associated tasks or for the learning that can arise (whether formal or informal learning).

Conversely, the ideal approach to development ensures that all participants are able to relate to the tasks they perform during the learning activity, and they can grasp the significance of the learning gained from the activity. This means that tasks and learning are integrated (Type 2), which benefits both individual and organisation. Not all approaches attain this level of integration. However, formalised education and training increasingly accents practical experience, while informal approaches increasingly focus upon drawing reflective learning from coaching sessions. Mumford suggests on the other hand that often there is a clear emphasis in development towards either completing tasks (Type 1) or upon the learning content of the activity (Type 3).

Action learning

Action learning (AL) can be seen as an example of Type 2 learning because it specifically engages with both the completion of the task and the learning that can be drawn from it. It constitutes a good exemplar of the need to engage with both 'learning as skill acquisition' as well as 'learning as participation' (Elkjaer, 2004), and for many years Reg Revans (1980) and his followers have grappled with the implications for participants. Revans first introduced the world to *action learning* and devised the formula:

$$L = P + Q$$

in which L stands for learning, P for programmed learning (ie current knowledge, material already known, what is in books, etc) and Q for insight-seeking questioning (Pedler, 2004).

The classical principles emerged through his writings that spanned some 50 years, and include personal and organisational learning from reflection upon action and working with problems where there are no right answers, through learners working in peer 'sets' (or groups) to support and challenge each other (Pedler *et al* in Pedler, 2005: 58–9).

One of the authors has experience with multicultural, multiethnic groups of managers and professionals following a course of study in a college or university, utilising a form of AL. Key lessons from this experience include the necessity for the participants to explore the possibilities for themselves, not only in the AL process (in their learning sets) but from the beginning – from the formation of the groups and deciding how they are going to interact, sharing experiences, backgrounds and organisational policies, practices and controls.

The tutor acts as the 'expert facilitator' on a post-experience or postgraduate programme of study for a cohort of students (or candidates depending upon the type of programme). It is usual to limit the group size to six to allow sufficient time and space for everyone to contribute. The facilitator manages a number of sets at a time. Each group starts with a presentation on a particular set of concepts, covering operations management, individual and team development, organisational behaviour and performance management. The managers then break out to discuss their own organisations in relation to the topic. They analyse current practice by identifying the relevant academic concepts and models that do or could apply to their individual organisations. They compare and contrast them across organisations – challenging each other over the applicability of the concepts to inspire each other's thinking and planning to map out their individual reports. These reports must both relate to the learning outcomes expected for the programme and be applicable to the development of their own work roles and organisational performance.

The authors have employed this approach in the UK and have adapted it for overseas programmes. Students from the UK as well as India, the Caribbean and China have found the approach stimulating and rewarding, if controversial at times! The feedback received from these groups has been that they have been inspired to 'rise above' their immediate working experiences and have been able to see things as they really are by sharing them with peers from other organisations as well as academic staff. However, as Marquardt (1999) points out, although there are many benefits from AL – suggesting it forms a good example of Type 2 learning – there are important cultural implications. Just as learning styles draw on an Anglo-American cultural context, so aspects of AL defer to the premium placed upon potential embarrassment from critical thinking and imply an expectation of a relatively equal relationship between facilitator and participant in contrast to 'teacher' and 'student'.

Action research and AL are interrelated. Carr and Kemmis (1986), cited in Brown and Jones (2001), see the former as self-reflective enquiry undertaken by participants (teachers, students or principals) in social situations (workplace or college) that can enhance the rationality and justice of their own work/educational practices and their understanding of these practices, as well as institutions and organisations in which these practices take place. To relate this definition to the main case study below, consider how each student may return to his or her workplace and reflect on his or her own attitudes and behaviour, both within the scenario and in previous working practices. This is where AL can lead to action research, which can then further inform AL, and so on around the cycle. In other words, it can be iterative and more beneficial than one-off training interventions.

Discussion questions

1   What are the four main types of development identified by Mumford?

2   Who are the key stakeholders involved with L&D at national and organisational level?

3   What types can you identify in your own organisation, or in an organisation that you are familiar with? How would you evaluate their effectiveness?

CONCLUSIONS AND FUTURE ISSUES

This chapter has investigated the key issues surrounding L&D in twenty-first-century organisations. The main theme is that there is a pressing need to transcend traditional 'training and development', with its emphasis upon formalised interventions disconnected from the workplace, towards a perspective that champions learning both as the acquisition of skills (ie experiential learning and the learning organisation) and as participation. The socio-cultural emphasis of learning as 'participation' is pertinent to contemporary IHRM because it has been suggested that IHRM research tends to de-emphasise softer cultural aspects as merely contingent factors, in favour of the 'hard' or 'core' functional issues, favouring generic idealised views of IHRM (Brewster and Suutari, 2005). There is a danger here of privileging formalised IHRM practices: no simple generic solutions exist through which to manage L&D, but what is clear is that there are key strategic issues that must be addressed.

It was noted that learning could be facilitated not only through formalised interventions (eg training courses) but through informal (eg international assignments). This chapter reveals that the most effective learning comes when both task and the lessons from it are combined – something upon which action learning in particular has focused. However, the cultural theme in this chapter reveals a need for caution in the adoption of L&D interventions in different cultural contexts. This means that HR practitioners, in their capacities as 'learning architects', have an even more complex role to play in IHRM.

CASE STUDY 22

ACTION LEARNING IN L&D: CULTURAL ISSUES

The following case study is a personal example of AL in practice. The interaction and outcomes from any learning set are personal and confidential to the individuals concerned and must remain so. The names have therefore been changed to protect their identities (and their organisations). Not all AL is this emotionally charged, but in general it is necessary to address feelings and assumptions in these kinds of learning contexts. It should also be borne in mind that this is a safe learning environment – more so than some managers find in-house L&D.

The cohort had been assigned a task to investigate L&D issues surrounding performance management, which would form an important part of their report towards their assignment grade and for their organisation. After a presentation by the facilitator (Carol), the sets went off to break-out rooms to explore these issues in their own organisations. One team of part-timers – a mix of ethnic groups and employed by various MNCs – began to indulge in some 'critical thinking'. They discussed the various models of performance management systems, and the subject of the impact of their implementation across cultures triggered some heated dialogue:

Ruth: 'But Candice, you can apply the principles of performance management to your team! I am sure they will respond to the idea of future goals and development more than they have on the retrospective "Have you achieved your targets?" '

Candice: 'You don't understand. We are talking about people whose first language is not English. I have people from all points of the globe – they cannot possibly understand what this is all about!'

Paul: 'Wait, both of you. I think we are talking about expectations. Don't you think that if these people were made to feel more valued about the work they do – rather than criticised for what they don't do – they would be happy to buy in to the principles?'

Candice: 'Paul, where are *you* coming from? You're white and English!'

Paul: 'But I have come from a very underprivileged background and never thought I would make it as a manager of people, responsible for their development. And I have a multiracial workgroup in the social services just as you have, nursing in residential care.'

Candice: 'But Paul, yours are all educated – unlike mine!'

Ashok: 'What's all the fuss about? I only employ my own kind in my factory, and their expectations are simply that they want a fair day's pay for a fair day's work. That's all that motivates them.'

Ruth: 'Ashok, are you saying that you wouldn't employ me in any of your team roles?'

Ashok: 'No, Ruth. You would expect far too much. You come from a privileged English background. You are well educated and have embarked on a high-flying career.'

Ruth: 'That is very racist – and also, I believe, classist. How you can possibly know how I feel and think if you can only see those things!'

At this point, Carol joined them and they focused on employee 'expectations' of L&D. Within a few minutes Candice disappeared and Ruth called Carol to one side to tell her that Candice was very upset and was feeling very undermined by Paul who exudes confidence, making her feel inadequate. Candice felt she was being stupid – after all, she was a mature woman who had had to become the breadwinner in her family following her husband's industrial accident.

Carol told Candice how valuable her contribution within the group had always been, but she felt she had failed to really convince Candice that she was able to contribute to the work of the group fully over these current issues. Carol then spent some time with the group and they began to challenge each other's assumptions about their staff's attitudes and expectations. Ashok began to wonder if his cultural identity was appropriate for other Pakistanis trying to make a new life in the UK.

Throughout the day, Candice took every opportunity to contribute to the wider plenary session when the individual groups brought their findings to the whole group. Her contribution was exceptional. The individual assignment results reflected the extent of each manager's learning and the new thinking they were able to apply to their work.

Carol's learning was as profound as was the learning within the groups that day. Action learning challenges the 'academic armour' tutors often develop for self-protection. Carol is a working-class woman, a late learner, and someone who has come to academia very late in her career. The welcome challenge of the risks associated with 'learning to learn' within a group of learners far outweighs any need to protect who she is, but of course there are some students who find this a serious problem. They want *someone* to be the *expert*!

Case study tasks

1   To what extent would this example of AL constitute Type 2 learning?

2   How does this case study demonstrate the importance of learning as 'acquiring skills' and learning as 'participation'?

3   What are the issues that might arise when action learning is applied to an international setting of your choice?

REFERENCES

Anderson T. D. (1998) *Transforming Leadership: Equipping yourself and coaching others to build the leadership organisation.* Baton Rouge, FL: CRC Press LLC.

Anonymous (2002) 'Are MBA grads learning the right stuff?', *New Zealand Management*, Vol. 49, No. 10: 6–7.

Argyris C. (1999) *On Organisational Learning.* Oxford: Blackwell Business.

Baruch Y. (2005) 'International careers, in M. Ozbilgin (ed.) *International Human Resource Management: Theory and practice.* New York: Palgrave Macmillan.

Bennell P. and Pearce T. (1998) *The Internalisation of Higher Education: Exporting education to developing and transitional economies.* Falmer: Institute of Development Studies: University of Sussex.

Black S., Morrison A. and Gregersen H. (1991) *Global Explorers: The next generation of leaders.* New York: Routledge.

Brewster C. and Suutari V. (2005) 'Global HRM: aspects of a research agenda', *Personnel Review*, Vol. 34, No. 1: 7–21.

Brewster C., Harris H. and Sparrow P. (eds) (2002) *Globalising HR.* London: IPD.

Brown J. S. and Duguid P. (1991) 'Organisational learning and communities-of-practice: towards a unified view of working, learning and innovation', *Organization Science*, Vol. 2, No. 1: 40–57.

Brown T. and Jones L. (2001) *Action Research and Post-Modernism: Congruence and critique*. London: Open University Press.

Buchanan D. and Huczynski A. (2004) *Organizational Behaviour: An introduction* (5th edition). London: Prentice Hall.

Calveley M. (2005) 'Competencies of *international human resource managers', in M. Ozbilgin (ed.) International Human Resource Management: Theory and practice*. New York: Palgrave Macmillan.

Chan S. (1991) 'The Chinese learner: a question of style', *Education and Training*, Vol. 41, No. 6/7: 294–304

Chartered Institute of Personnel and Development (2001) *CIPD Professional Standards*. London: CIPD.

Cundale K. (2005) 'East is east and West is west: Some perspectives on facilitating learning at, or across, the boundaries of culture', refereed paper presented at the 6th Organisational Learning and Knowledge Management (OLKM) Conference, Trento, Italy, 9–11 June 2005.

Currie G. and Knights D. (2003) 'Reflecting on a critical pedagogy in MBA education', *Management Learning*, Vol. 34, No. 1, March: 27–49.

Davis S. M. (1988) 2001 *Management: Managing the future now*. London: Simon & Schuster.

Denzin N. K. (1989) *Interpretive Biography*. Newbury Park, CA: Sage.

Drucker P. F. (1986) *The Frontiers of Management: Where tomorrow's decisions are being shaped today*. London: Heinemann Professional Publishing.

Drucker P. F. (1992) *Managing for the Future*. Oxford: Butterworth-Heinemann.

Edmondson A. (1999) 'Psychological safety and learning behavior in work teams', *Administrative Science Quarterly*, Vol. 44, No. 2: 350–83.

Elkjaer B. (2004) 'Organizational learning: the "third way" ', *Management Learning*, Vol. 35, No. 4: 419–34.

Engelhard J. and Nagele J. (2003) 'Organisational learning in subsidiaries of multinational companies in Russia', *Journal of World Business*, Vol. 38, No. 3: 262–77.

The European Commission (2004) 'Organisational learning: the role of SME clusters', http://www.pjb.co.uk/npl/bp19.htm [accessed 15 June 2004].

Evans G. and Keogh W. (2004) 'Issues in human resource development and the pressures faced by science park-based new technology-based firms', *International Journal of Human Resource Development and Management*, Vol. 4, No. 2: 128–43.

Friedson E. (1994) *Professionalism Reborn: Theory, prophecy and policy*. New York: Polity Press.

Gherardi S. (1999) 'Learning as problem-driven or learning in the face of mystery?', *Organization Studies*, Vol. 20, No.1:101–24.

Gibb A. (1997) 'Small firms training and competitiveness: building upon the small firm as a learning organisation', *International Small Business Journal*, Vol. 17, No. 1: 13–29.

Gibb S. (2002) *L&D: Processes, practices and perspectives at work*. Basingstoke: Palgrave Macmillan.

Gibb S. (2004) 'Arts-based training in management development: the use of improvisational theatre', *Journal of Management Development*, Vol. 23, No. 8: 741–50.

Habermas J. (1972) *Knowledge and Human Interests*. London: Heinemann.

Harrison R. (2004) *Learning and Development* (3rd edition). London: CIPD.

Heenan D. and Perlmutter H. (1979) *Multinational Organizational Development: A social architectural approach*. Reading, MA: Addison-Wesley.

Hofstede G. (1991) *Cultures and Organizations*. London: HarperCollins.

Honey P. and Mumford A. (1996) *Manual of Learning Styles* (3rd edition). Maidenhead: Honey Publications.

Ibbetson A. and Newell S. (1999) 'A comparison of a competitive and non-competitive outdoor management development programme', *Personnel Review*, Vol. 28, No. 1/2: 58–76.

Isaacs W. (1993) 'Taking flight: dialogue, collective thinking and organizational learning', *Organizational Dynamics*, Vol. 22, No. 2: 24–39.

Jackson T. (1995) 'European management learning: a cross-cultural interpretation of Kolb's learning cycle', *Journal of Management Development*, Vol. 14, No. 6: 42–50.

Jackson T. (1996) 'Understanding management learning across cultures: some east–west comparisons', paper presented at the Academy of International Business annual meeting, Banff, Alberta, Canada, September.

Jaw B. and Liu W. (2003) *Human Resource Management*, Vol. 42, No. 3, Fall: 223–41.

Kermani F. and Gittins R. (2004) 'Where will industry go for its high-calibre staff?', *Journal of Commercial Biotechnology*, Vol. 11, No. 1, October: 63–71.

Kolb D. (1984) *Experiential Learning*. Englewood Cliffs: Prentice Hall.

Langfield-Smith K. (1992) 'Exploring the need for a shared cognitive map', *Journal of Management Studies*, Vol. 29, No. 3: 349–68.

Lather P. (1991) *Getting Smart: Feminist research and pedagogy with/in the postmodern*. New York: Routledge.

Lave J. and Wenger E. (1991) *Situated Learning – Legitimate Peripheral Participation*. Cambridge: Cambridge University Press.

Lepak D. P. and Snell S. A. (1999) 'The human resource architect: toward a theory of human capital allocation and development', *Academy of Management Review*, Vol. 24, No. 1: 31–48.

Luoma M. (2000) 'Investigating the link between strategy and HRD', *Personnel Review*, Vol. 29, No. 6: 769–90.

Macpherson A. and Wilson A. (2003) 'Enhancing SMEs' capability: opportunities in supply chain relationships?', *Journal of Small Business and Enterprise Development*, Vol. 10, No. 2: 167.

Marquandt M. (1999) *Action Learning in Action*. Palo Alto: Davis Black.

McGill I. and Brockbank A. (2004) *The Action Learning Handbook*. London: Routledge Falmer.

Marshall J. (1995) *Women Managers Moving On*. London: Routledge.

Mendenhall M. E., Black J. S., Jensen R. J. and Gregersen H. B. (2003) 'Human resource management challenges in the age of globalization', *Organizational Dynamics*, Vol. 32, No. 3: 261–74.

Mezirow J. (1978) 'Perspective transformation', *Adult Education Quarterly*, Vol. 28: 100–10.

Mumford A. (1993) *How Managers Can Develop Managers*. Aldershot: Gower.

Mumford A. and Gold J. (2004) *Management Development: Strategies for action*. London: CIPD.

Murdock A. and Scutt C. N. (2003) *Personal Effectiveness* (3rd edition). Oxford: Butterworth-Heinemann.

Nonaka I. (1991) 'The knowledge-creating company', *Harvard Business Review*, November-December: 96–104.

Ozbilgin M. (2005) 'Aspects of international human resource management', in M. Ozbilgin (ed.) *International Human Resource Management: Theory and practice*. New York: Palgrave Macmillan.

Paul R. and Elder L. (2001) *Critical Thinking: Tools for taking charge of your learning and your life*. London: Prentice Hall.

Pedler M. (ed.) (2004) *Action Learning: Research and practice*, Vol. 1. London: Taylor & Francis.

Pedler M. (ed.) (2005) *Action Learning: Research and practice*, Vol. 2. London: Taylor & Francis.

Pedler M., Boydell T. and Burgoyne J. (1989) '*Towards the learning company*', *Management Education and Development*, Vol. 20, No. 1: 1–8.

Pucik V. (1998) 'Strategic alliances, organizational learning and competitive advantage', *Human Resource Management*, Vol. 27, No. 1.

Revans R. W. (1980) *Action Learning: New techniques for managers*. London: Blond & Briggs.

Reynolds M. (1997) 'Towards a critical pedagogy', in J. Burgoyne and M. Reynolds (eds) *Management Learning: Integrating perspectives in theory and practice*. London: Sage.

Rowe A. (2001) 'Exploring the Dance of Team Learning'. Unpublished PhD thesis, Essex University.

Senge P. (1992) *The Fifth Discipline: The art and practice of the learning organization*. London: Doubleday.

Shivers-Blackwell S. (2004) 'Reactions to outdoor teambuilding initiatives in MBA education', *Journal of Management Development*, Vol. 23, No. 7: 614–30.

Sparrow P., Schuler R. and Jackson S. (1994) 'Convergence or divergence: human resource practices and policies for competitive advantage worldwide', *International Journal of Human Resource Management*, Vol. 5: 267–99.

Thomson A., Mabey C., Storey J., Gray C. and Iles P. (2001) *Changing Patterns of Management Development*. Oxford: Blackwell.

Tranfield D., Rowe A., Smart P., Levene R., Deasley P. and Corley J. (2005) 'Coordinating for service delivery in public–private partnership and private finance initiative construction projects: early findings from an exploratory study', Proceedings of the Institute of Mechanical Engineers Part B: *J. Engineering Manufacture*, Vol. 219: 165–75.

Van Aken J. E. (2005) 'Management research as a design science: articulating the research products of Mode 2 knowledge production in management', *British Journal of Management*, Vol. 16: 19–36.

Vince R. (2003) 'The future practice of HRD', Human Resource Development International, Vol. 6, No. 4: 559–63.

Vinnicombe S. and Singh V. (2003) 'Women-only management training: an essential part of women's leadership development', Journal of Change Management, Vol. 3, No. 4, May: 294.

Von Glinow M. A., Drost E. A. and Teagarden M. B. (2002) 'Converging on IHRM best practices: lessons learned from a globally distributed consortium on theory and practice', *Human Resource Management*, Vol. 41, No. 1, Spring: 123–40.

Wenger E. (1998): *Communities of Practice: Learning, meaning and identity*. Cambridge: Cambridge University Press.

Zietsma C., Winn M., Branzei O. and Vertinsky B. (2002) 'The war of the woods: facilitators and impediments of organisational learning processes', *British Journal of Management*, Vol. 13: S61–S74.

Managing performance

CHAPTER 8

Carol Atkinson and Sue Shaw

CHAPTER OBJECTIVES

When you have read this chapter you should be able to:

- explain the role of performance management in developing human capital advantage for organisations

- analyse the nature of the processes associated with performance management (goal-setting, competence, development, 360-degree feedback, performance measurement and evaluation)

- discuss how performance management operates as a form of reward

- consider the issue of managing team – as opposed to individual – performance

- analyse international issues in performance management and consider the complexities of expatriate performance management

- critically examine the role of performance management.

PURPOSE AND SCOPE

In this chapter, we present a critical evaluation of performance management which begins with a consideration of the argued importance of performance management, moves through discussion of its inherent processes and associated key issues, and ends with a critique of such processes and their organisational contribution. This evaluation permits insight into why organisations adopt performance management systems (PMS) and the challenges they face in achieving their goal: the improvement of individual and organisational performance. We tackle a number of the book's over-arching themes, considering broadly the influence of globalisation and increased competition on an organisation's need to maximise performance, and discuss also more specifically the increasing need to devise PMS that apply to expatriate employees, the incidence of which has increased with globalisation. Technology and change are again broadly argued to have driven an enhanced need for organisational performance, and consideration is given within the final section on future issues to the emerging role of technology within PMS.

A key theme within this chapter is that of cultural variation which we address within most of our topic areas, drawing upon Hofstede's (2001) work on international cultures, and arguing that there is evidence of limited convergence within the PMS of many countries. In summary, we argue that performance management has the potential to make a significant contribution to individual and organisational performance, but for organisations to realise such potential, investment is required in the development and implementation of robust and consistent PMS.

1 CONCEPTUAL OVERVIEW

The idea of appraising performance has existed for many years and has revolved largely around an annual review of objectives between manager and subordinate. Such appraisal has been restricted often to management or supervisory groups, has been backwards-focused on historic performance, and has not typically sought to adopt a strategic approach. The concept of performance management, however, is a more recent development which adopts a future-oriented strategic focus and is applied to all employees in a workforce in order to maximise their current performance and future potential.

This increased focus on performance at all levels in an organisation arises from the pressures of globalisation and the associated requirement to create competitive advantage in order to survive in an international market place. Human capital, the value-creating skills, competencies, talents and abilities of an organisation's workforce (Elias and Scarbrough, 2004), is argued to be an essential component in creating such competitive advantage (Mayo, 2001). Performance management is argued to have a key role in developing such human capital (Tahvanainen, 2000). Organisational changes arising from competitive pressures, including flatter structures, leaner staffing levels and multiskilled cross-functional teams operating with considerable autonomy (Walsh *et al*, 2002), have had a great impact on performance management, not least because they have made the use of conventional top-down appraisal systems more difficult and led to, for example, the increased use of multi-source feedback (Fletcher, 2001) and many of the other issues that we discuss in this chapter.

The concept of performance management

This has developed over the past two decades as a strategic, integrated process which incorporates goal-setting, performance appraisal and development into a unified and coherent framework with the specific aim of aligning individual performance goals with the organisation's wider objectives (Dessler, 2005; Williams, 2002). Consequently, it is concerned with:

- how people work
- how they are managed and developed to improve their performance, and ultimately
- how to maximise their contribution to the organisation.

It is underpinned by the notion that sustained organisational success will be achieved through a strategic and integrated approach to improving the performance and developing the capabilities of individuals and wider teams (Armstrong and Baron, 2005). Although competitive pressures have been the driving force in the increased interest in performance management, organisations have also used these processes to support or drive culture change and to shift the emphasis to individual performance and self-development (Fletcher and Perry, 2001). There are a number of principles underlying the concept:

- Firstly, it is a strategic process in that it is aligned to the organisation's wider objectives and long-term direction.

- Secondly, it is integrative in nature, not only aligning organisational objectives with individual objectives but also linking together different aspects of human resource management such as human resource development, employee reward and organisational development, into a coherent approach to people management and development.

- Thirdly, it is concerned with performance enhancement in order to achieve both individual and organisational effectiveness. Performance enhancement is underpinned by two further principles: the ideas that employee effort should be goal-directed and that performance improvement must be supported by the development of employees' capability.

- A further feature relates to communication and understanding and the fact that performance management is based on an agreement between a manager and an individual, a shared understanding of and continuing dialogue about an individual's goals and the standards expected and the competencies needed, together with an appreciation of the organisation's wider mission, values and objectives.

- This is linked to a final point about the process, which is that performance management – unlike performance appraisal – is owned and driven by line management rather than by the HR function.

The theoretical basis for performance management

The underlying conceptual foundations for performance management lie in motivation theory and, in particular, goal-setting theory and expectancy theory. Goal-setting theory (Locke and Latham, 1984) suggests that not only does the assignment of specific goals result in enhanced performance but that, assuming goal acceptance, increasing the challenge or difficulty of goals leads to increased motivation and increases in performance (Mitchell *et al*, 2000). Expectancy theory hypothesises that individuals change their behaviour according to their anticipated satisfaction in achieving certain goals (Vroom, 1964). Both these theories have important implications for the design of performance management processes which are explored later in this chapter.

Clark (1998) suggests that both goal-setting and expectancy theory are founded on the premise that human beings think in a rational, calculative and individualistic way. Indeed, he argues that performance management is based on an extremely rationalistic, directive view of the organisation, which assumes not only that strategy can be clearly articulated but also that the outcomes of HR processes can be framed in a way that makes clear their links to the organisation's strategic objectives. He further argues that the approach assumes causal links between different parts of the process that can be readily identified and enable under-performance in one or more aspects of the process to be managed to ensure optimum functioning of the wider PMS. However, such assumptions not only ignore the debate about the nature of strategy and its formulation (Mintzberg, 1994), but also fail to recognise the context in which a PMS operates. The social processes and power systems within which organisations operate together with the broader organisational and country-cultural context are important mediating factors in the operation and success of any system (Clark, 1998).

The cultural context of performance management

Performance management is an essentially western development originating in the United States, and much of the research into its use and operation has been conducted in a domestic setting (Locke and Latham, 1984; Armstrong and Baron, 1998). Writers have suggested that it is cultural differences which make it difficult to standardise aspects of performance management practice (Pucik, 1985; Vance *et al*, 1992) and a number of studies have sought to examine the impact of country culture on aspects of the process. A common starting point has been Hofstede's (2001) dimensions (see Chapter 2 and, for example, Milliman *et al*, 1998; Fletcher and Perry, 2001; Mendonca and Kanungo, 1996):

- power distance
- uncertainty avoidance
- individualism/collectivism
- masculinity/femininity
- long-term/short-term orientation.

What is clear is that these contextual factors pervade all aspects of the performance management process, from the content or aim of the appraisal through the goal-setting stage to the evaluation stage, as well as influencing who provides the feedback and the process or style used to deliver it. The following section explores the different aspects of the performance management process and the ways in which the country context impacts upon them.

2 PERFORMANCE MANAGEMENT PROCESSES

Although there is no universal model of performance management, a review of literature and practice suggests there are a number of elements which might typically be found in a PMS. These elements are often depicted as a performance management cycle (IDS, 2003). In general, performance management models place objective-setting and formal appraisal systems at the centre of the cycle, and the literature suggests that these two areas might be particularly affected by the cultural context (Milliman *et al*, 1998; Fletcher and Perry, 2001; Lindholm *et al*, 1999). A typical cycle may be depicted thus in Figure 2.

Figure 2 Typical performance management cycle

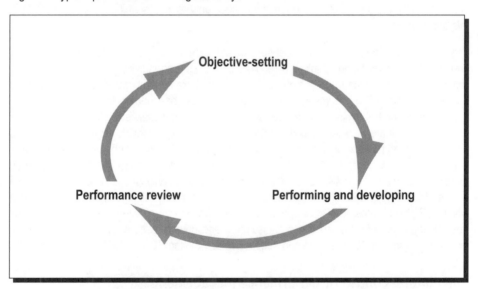

We consider issues relevant to this in what follows.

The role of objectives/goals

The performance planning process, where individual objectives are linked to organisational goals, is the typical starting point of the cycle and goal-setting usually occurs in line with annual standard review cycles (Suutari and Tahvanainen, 2002). Objectives are sometimes expressed as Key Result Areas or Accountabilities (KRA) and underpinned by performance standards and performance measures. Both practice and theory have focused on the nature of objectives, and how they are defined and expressed (see Mitchell *et al*, 2000, for a review of the theory and practice of goal-setting). Clark (1998) argues that although both goal-setting theory and expectancy theory emphasise the importance of setting a small number of relatively concrete goals, this may be difficult to achieve in practice because of either the lack of clear strategic organisational goals or their sheer volume, diversity or inherent instability (Fenwick, 2004). Defining objectives is not sufficient in itself. There has to be some agreement and understanding of how performance is to be measured, and this may be problematic. There has been considerable debate on the extent to which performance goals are 'hard', objective, quantifiable and capable of being directly measured, or 'soft', subjective and focused on such things as behaviours or traits – and many organisations use a mix of both hard and soft goals.

The impact of a particular national and cultural context may be reflected in the nature of the goals set, and writers have identified specific cultural differences in relation to competencies. It has been suggested that European managers rank 'drive for results' more highly than either their North American or Asia-Pacific counterparts (Rowson, 1998). The low individualism and low masculinity which characterise India's work culture, for example, prioritise personalised relationships and work well recognised over the accomplishment of job objectives (Mendonca and Kanungo, 1996). Moreover, in China evaluation criteria in the large state-owned enterprises where performance appraisal is widely practised not only relate to task but also to moral and ideological behaviour (Nyaw, 1995; Shen, 2004).

Setting objectives

Much of the literature and underpinning theory supports the idea that goal-setting should be a joint activity involving the individual and her or his line manager. However, the idea of employee participation in the process is essentially a western concept which does not readily transfer across cultures, particularly those with high power distance (Fenwick, 2004), and multinational corporations (MNCs) have been found to vary their practice in different national contexts. For instance, in her study of a Finnish MNC, Tahvanainen found that goal-setting was far more likely to be a joint process in Sweden and Germany, whereas in the USA goals were more likely to be assigned to individuals (Tahvanainen, 1998, in Fenwick 2004). Similar variations have been reported in the case of China, where aspects of Chinese culture such as respect for hierarchy and importance of 'face' have led MNCs not only to use assigned rather than jointly determined goals but also to modify both the nature and number of goals to ensure that they are easily attainable (Lindholm *et al*, 1999).

Development aimed at achieving objectives

The level of competence needed to achieve the objectives to a satisfactory level is another important consideration, and integration of a competency framework in a PMS supports identification of development needs and required resources. The manager plays an important role here not only in motivating, coaching and enabling performance, organising resources and facilitating any development opportunities, but also in monitoring and if necessary revising performance expectations and objectives (Torrington *et al*, 2005).

Performance review

Notwithstanding the need for ongoing informal review, formal assessment is a key component of any PMS and performance appraisal is one of the most common vehicles for reviewing performance against objectives (Redman, 2001). Country culture impacts on the appraisal process in a number of ways, and Table 3 illustrates the effect of individualism/collectivism and power distance on four different aspects of the appraisal process – who conducts the appraisal process, the manner in which it is conducted and the feedback given, the criteria or content, and the purpose of the appraisal.

Table 3 The effect of individualism/collectivism and power distance on the performance appraisal process

| Cultural dimensions | Performance appraisal process | | | |
	Who	How	Content	Purpose
Low power distance	Multi-source (eg peer, subordinate)	Participatory two-way communication Employee-initiated Appeals process	Unspecified	Unspecified
High power distance	Supervisor (someone with relatively more power)	Directive Supervisor-initiated No appeals process	Unspecified	Unspecified
Collectivist	Supervisor Third party	Subtle/indirect	Group level More positive tone Relationship-focused (criteria include loyalty, seniority, cooperativeness)	Developmental (increase loyalty)
Individualist	Unspecified	Direct/open	Individual level Job-focused	Administrative (make personnel decisions)

Note: Cells labelled 'Unspecified' indicate that there was little empirical or conceptual evidence of how the dimension would influence the performance appraisal process.

Reprinted by permission of Sage Publications Ltd from Fletcher, C. and Perry, E. L. (2001) Handbook of Industrial, Work and Organizational Psychology

Single-country studies have explored what this means in practice. For example, in his study of performance appraisal at Gandhi International Airport, Shaikh (1995) explains the tendency of managers to rate employees similarly in performance appraisal reports and the absence of counselling feedback in terms of the country's cultural tendency towards high power distance and high masculinity. The importance of the historical and political context is demonstrated in Lindholm et al's (1999) study of performance management in one western MNC in China. Their study reported perceived difficulties in receiving or giving direct feedback and providing criticism because of the indirect and reserved communication patterns which characterise the Chinese culture.

Functions of review

Performance review (or appraisal) is viewed as serving a number of functions. Milliman et al (2002) studied the aims of performance appraisal in 10 countries across the Pacific Rim, focusing on four specific purposes: documentation, development, administrative purposes (reward and promotion) and subordinate expression. In all countries they found that the purposes of appraisal were not being realised as intended or as was desired, and differences between countries were explained in terms of cultural difference. For instance, the four countries in the American continent together with Australia rated subordinate expression high compared with the other countries' moderate rating, and the high power distance orientation of Asian countries underplayed the role of subordinate input into the appraisal process. Shen (2004) also reports differences in the aims of performance appraisal in western and Chinese MNCs, suggesting that the major purpose in the latter is pay determination rather than individual and organisational development, thereby reflecting Chinese companies' current preoccupation with short-term business results rather than long-term strategic goals.

Clearly, there are a number of complexities both to performance management itself and to the consideration of performance management across national cultures. We turn now to consider in more detail the issues surrounding performance management and reward.

Discussion questions

1 To what extent do you think that setting specific objectives is both feasible and likely to enhance individual performance?

2 Outline the impact of individualism/collectivism and power distance on perform-ance review and consider the implications for the UK (or a country with which you are familiar).

3 To what extent do you think that it is possible to achieve the various functions of performance review?

3 PERFORMANCE MANAGEMENT AND REWARD

As we noted above, performance management may have a number of aims, the most common, however, being developmental and judgemental (Pullin and Haidar, 2003). In this section, we explore these aims and consider the implications for the relationship between performance management and reward. (See Chapter 9 for a more detailed discussion of the reward issues introduced below.) Here, we draw on Armstrong's (2002) conceptualisation of 'total reward', which comprises both financial and non-financial elements. With reference to performance management, financial (extrinsic) rewards relate usually to merit or contingent pay – that is, where an element of pay is at risk and dependent on performance, adopting performance management as the process by which decisions on the allocation of such reward are made. Non-financial (intrinsic) rewards include recognition, development, access to other assignments, career guidance and the quality of working life, many of which can be delivered by developmental forms of performance management. Debate continues as to the feasibility of a PMS that achieves both goals, Williams (2002) suggesting that in focusing on extrinsic reward there is a danger that the intrinsic is diminished. Indeed, Armstrong and Baron (2005) suggest, such is the tension between these two aims that PMS should be entirely developmen-tally focused, the allocation of merit pay or pay increases being made through other mechanisms.

Non-financial reward

In considering the non-financial rewards outlined above, it is not difficult to see how these will be delivered by a PMS focused on development. We outlined in the *Processes* section above how performance review, providing feedback and support for employees, is a fundamental part of the performance management process. Similarly, a PMS integrated with other HR processes will provide reviewees with an opportunity to access, for example, training to support their identified development needs, or advice on career opportunities open to the reviewee. Recognition for achievements, together with praise, will also flow naturally from a well-conducted performance review. Thus a PMS that has a developmental aim is likely to be successful in delivering non-financial, intrinsic rewards to the employees involved, at least in a western context. Other cultural contexts may, however, experience conflicts with a developmental approach to performance management. For example, in high power distance countries such as China, development through feedback may be less successful because managers are more likely to be reluctant to engage in two-way communication in the appraisal process or to provide counselling (Huo and von Glinow, 1995). Similarly, a collectivist approach in Russia means that direct feedback is perceived as being much less acceptable than in other cultures (Fletcher, 2001). A fundamental aim of performance management, the development of employees, may thus depend for its achievement upon cultural context.

Financial reward

A further complexity is the extent to which a PMS can be used to successfully drive financial reward. We should note at this point that we do not intend to discuss in detail here the mechanics of contingent pay (see Chapter 9), rather to consider the mechanisms through which performance management and financial reward can be linked. Performance management is goal-driven, using objectives and competencies, and reward is often attached to the achievement of such goals. Such links require robust systems of measurement of achievement, which is acknowledged as being highly problematic (Campbell *et al*, 1998). Measurement is usually expressed in terms of an overall rating, which gives rise to problems in respect of the validity and accuracy of such ratings (London *et al*, 2004). Further, it is argued that measuring people's performance is a form of control and is therefore likely to undermine, rather than contribute to, performance (Hendry *et al*, 2000).

Even setting aside difficulties in measurement, complexities of organisational operation render problematic the theoretical foundations upon which contingent pay is based. Lawler (1990) suggests that a clear 'line of sight' between achievement and reward is required. This derives from expectancy theory, whereby motivation only occurs when people expect that they will get worthwhile rewards for their effort and contribution. Hendry *et al* (2000), however, identify a number of problems with this requirement, not least the extent to which an individual has control over achieving his or her objectives in a rapidly changing organisation in which employees' efforts are usually interdependent. Despite questions on the effectiveness of the pay/performance link in motivating employees to achieve high levels of performance, many PMS in UK organisations nevertheless link to pay, albeit a declining number (Armstrong and Baron, 2005).

PMS and reward internationally

In considering comparative approaches to performance management and pay, we draw first on Milliman *et al*'s (2002) study of performance appraisal in a number of Pacific Rim countries. They suggest that performance/pay links are common in individualistic countries such as the USA, Canada and Australia, and that such links are increasing in the People's Republic of China, but from a low base. The pay/performance link is suggested, however, to be less common in cultures which place a high value on harmony, 'face', teamwork and factors such as off-the-job behaviours and attitudes towards superiors (McEvoy and Cascio, 1990). This means that a particular importance is placed on not disturbing group or interpersonal harmony through differentiation of employees in performance review and in merit pay, and Chinese cultures, such as Taiwan, and other collectivist cultures, such as Mexico, are less likely to tie appraisal to pay. In contrast, Snape *et al* (1998) suggest that Asian cultures are generally considered to be materialistic compared to western counterparts and demonstrate that monetary rewards are emerging as being of prime importance to workers in Hong Kong.

CASE STUDY 23

PERFORMANCE EVALUATION AND REWARD IN AUSTRALIAN LOCAL GOVERNMENT

The Victorian Local Government Act (1989) introduced fixed-term contracts in conjunction with performance evaluation for senior managers, although little detail is specified on the nature of the performance evaluation in the Act. The reported study seeks to explore the extent to which such performance evaluation is a meaningful process, considering the nature of performance evaluation, its strengths and limitations and its contribution, if any, to organisational performance.

The case study suggests that performance evaluation is an integral part of the management processes and systems, but questions the extent to which it has led to improved individual and/or organisational performance. The senior officers usually get their contracts renewed and most are reported to perform excellently in a collaborative and participative performance evaluation process. Continuous performance monitoring alerts those who fall behind on targets, allowing for the modification of targets which means that few managers fail to achieve their targets. However, there is a perceived lack of organisational commitment by some senior managers.

Whereas performance evaluation has in other cases been demonstrated to enhance commitment, in this case study the senior managers adjusted to the performance contracts by limiting their organisational commitment and developing contingency plans to maintain personal mobility, often seeking employment elsewhere towards the end of their employment contract. Incentive bonus payments linked to performance achievement were found to contribute little to organisational commitment, the 'at risk' bonus levels being a relatively small part of total remuneration, Further, the allocation process was considered to be divisive, such negativity arising from perceptions of unfairness in the rating and bonus distribution.

While the performance evaluation process was generally regarded as successful by the participants, the authors suggest that it demonstrates an emphasis on qualitative measures, adopting vague and at times unwritten criteria. There is also a political element to evaluation, Councillors having a (somewhat ill-defined) role in evaluation in addition to the Chief Executive's formal role of evaluating senior managers. It may be that these factors are representative of performance evaluation in the public sector, due to the inherent difficulty in establishing measurable objectives, coupled with the political desirability of not doing so, in order to avoid being judged on the 'success' or 'failure' of achieving those objectives.

The authors conclude that the performance evaluation process has led senior managers to be more results-oriented, yet their employment appears to be no less stable than under previous systems as they participate in the establishment of their goals and targets and are unlikely to agree to targets that are not achievable.

Source: Pullin and Haidar (2003)

Case study tasks

1   What are the key issues raised in the case study that may mean that performance evaluation does not contribute to improved performance?

2   Identify the tensions between performance-based contracts and employee commitment and suggest how these may be managed.

3   To what extent does linking performance to financial reward contribute to enhanced performance in this case study?

Discussion questions

1   Explain the tensions created in attempting to use a PMS to drive both development and reward.

2   Thinking of an organisation with which you are familiar, to what extent are its attempts to link PMS and financial reward successful, and why?

3   Outline the different approaches to the performance/pay link in the countries cited in this section, explaining the differences in terms of cultural variation.

Having considered in this section the tensions inherent in using performance management as a tool for both development and judgement, we turn now to consider another set of tensions – those created in managing individual and team performance.

4 PERFORMANCE MANAGEMENT AND TEAMS

While performance management has typically focused on individual performance, there is increasing recognition of the need to consider team performance. Teamworking has increased in prevalence in the past 20 years because it is argued to provide a source of competitive advantage, enabling cost reduction and improved quality, facilitating the completion of increasingly complex organisational tasks beyond the means of any one individual, and enabling the empowerment of employees as decision-making is decentralised (Torrington *et al*, 2005). Despite this, there is often a contradiction between a managerial discourse that emphasises the team and collective performance and the use of appraisal and reward tools that are above all individual (Emery, 2004). Further complexities arise when, in introducing teamworking, many western managers seek to emulate what they perceive to be a source of advantage in other cultural contexts – for example, in Japanese firms. Yet teamworking may not be compatible with all national cultural contexts (El-Kot and Leat, 2005), especially those which are predicated upon high levels of individualism.

Developments in managing team performance

Because there is limited empirical data on managing team performance, we draw here largely on Brumback (2003), who presents a detailed analysis of how, in the USA, attempts are being made to integrate both individual and team performance. He argues that performance not only of teams as a whole but of their individual members must be managed if a high standard of performance is to be achieved. He thus suggests the following:

■   Individuals should have standards communicated to them in terms of written objectives and competencies and thus maintain accountability for their own performance.

- Teams (via representatives) should, however, influence the firm's annual goals and the team goals thus agreed must inform individual goals.

- Further, the team becomes accountable for monitoring its own and individual members' performance, providing any mentoring and coaching that may be required.

- Performance review should incorporate the evaluation of both team and individual performance. Each team member should appraise his/her own performance and in so doing can appraise others'.

- The team reviews all individual appraisals and deals with any contentious issues and decides how to deal with, for example, any training needs identified.

- The team then appraises its own performance, with the assistance of at least one independent outsider to reinforce objectivity.

Brumback (2003) argues that this process meets the challenge of blending individualism with teamwork.

Suutari and Tahvanainen (2002) suggest that the use of team goals is increasing, up to 40% of their respondents indicating that they had goals set at the team level. Other studies demonstrate, however, that such processes are by no means widely applied. Emery's (2004) study of teams in the Swiss civil service demonstrates that the team aspect of performance (and reward) is rarely taken into account. He does suggest that the use of individual goals is widespread, but he claims that it makes a limited contribution to the performance and development of the team and that individual appraisal and reward generate competition and override the spirit of cooperation. Emery joins Brumback (2003) in calling for further developments in team performance management, arguing that essential elements in this are:

- a clear definition of team mission

- the negotiation of team goals and their understanding by all team members, and

- an assessment of team performance, combining self-assessment by the team members and assessment by a competent authority.

As we have noted, there is limited empirical data on managing team performance and the few studies that exist are derived from a western, individualistic context. In order to consider the issue from a collectivist perspective, we present below a case study on teamworking in Egypt. We draw the material from El-Kot and Leat's (2005) study of teamworking in this country, the inferences in respect of performance management being made by the authors of this chapter.

CASE STUDY 24

PERFORMANCE MANAGEMENT AND TEAMWORKING IN EGYPT

Changes to the Egyptian economy have led to human resources and their management becoming critical issues. In line with developments internationally, improving and measuring effectiveness has become a major concern for many Egyptian organisations as they seek to increase productivity, reduce costs and compete globally. Applying Hofstede's cultural analysis, Egypt – along with other Arabic-speaking countries – is classified as high power distance, moderately strong uncertainty avoidance, low individualism and moderate masculinity. The implications of this are that Egyptian workers are likely to accept an unequal distribution of power and expect to be directed by their supervisors whose authority they respect and with whom they may be afraid to disagree; they are unlikely to value or expect individual autonomy or to be consulted; decision-making is likely to be centralised; and the management style is likely to be autocratic or paternalistic. Job security is likely to be valued because employees see themselves as belonging to the organisation and work group. Employees are likely to use risk avoidance rather than risk-taking approaches at work, and to expect advancement to be based on seniority rather than individual performance.

El-Kot and Leat's (2005) study investigates teamwork, which is argued to be congruent with a collectivist culture based upon cooperative rather than competitive relationships. The above analysis, however, raises questions about the feasibility of autonomous self-managed teams, given the anticipated reliance on centralised decision-making and an autocratic management style. The study evidences an increased use of teams from the 1980s on, similar to that seen in the USA and the UK, the most commonly used team being the work team, but there are also examples of project teams, self-managed teams and cross-functional teams. El-Kot and Leat (2005) demonstrate that quite high levels of team autonomy exist, even if teams cannot be described as fully self-managing, and that there is decentralisation of task-oriented decision-making. As may be expected in a collectivist culture, the most common form of reward is team-based reward. Although some competitive elements exist, arrangements in the main required harmony and were congruent with low individualism. This study suggests that the key elements for successful teams are a suitable organisational culture, team member satisfaction, clear team goals and vision, and team responsibility in making decisions. Interestingly, while some of the study's results are consistent with Hofstede's cultural analysis, others are not. The authors suggest that cultural changes that have taken place over the past 20 years may make Hofstede's analysis increasingly problematic to apply. They provide evidence of a change in Egyptian values and expectations and suggest that there has been a shift to adoption of western values in certain instances.

While the cultural analysis provided above may be problematic for PMS with an individual focus – an autocratic management style affording little individual responsibility being likely to prevail, for example – it seems more promising in terms of team-oriented PMS. It may be supported by the collectivist elements of cooperation in working towards team goals, a value on harmony that emphasises team member satisfaction and a ready acceptance of team-based reward. Perhaps many of the challenges faced by those managing team-based PMS in individualistic cultures will not be relevant to those operating in more collectivist cultures.

Source: El-Kot and Leat (2005)

Case study tasks

1 Outline in detail the implications of the Egyptian culture for typical PMS.

2 To what extent is the analysis of teamworking in Egypt congruent with its suggested culture?

3 Identify the advantages and disadvantages of Egypt's culture and approach to teamworking for a team-oriented PMS.

In this section, we have demonstrated the complexities of managing at an individual and team level and the impact of national culture upon this. Thus far we have considered cultural influences within a given country, but we turn now to consider the implications for MNCs of managing across cultures, discussing issues relevant to the performance management of expatriate employees.

Discussion questions

1   Thinking of an organisation with which you are familiar, to what extent is its PMS team-based?

2   Outline a number of steps that could be taken to establish a team-based PMS.

3   What impact do you believe a country's culture will have on the likelihood of one of its organisations successfully operating a team-based PMS?

---

5 EXPATRIATE PERFORMANCE MANAGEMENT

In this section we consider the issue of expatriate performance management, given that effective performance management is particularly critical to MNCs which wish to make best use of expatriate employees, who play a central role in the global success of the company and whose use is typically expensive (Tahvanainen, 2000). The focus on expatriate performance management results from increasing levels of internationalisation and a greater number of companies operating globally and thus sending employees to work in a foreign country for an extended period of time. As noted above, performance management is essentially a western development and most performance data focuses on national, not international, settings (Suutari and Tahvanainen, 2002). This raises the question in the international context of how performance management works in MNCs and to what extent practices are standardised or localised.

The challenges of expatriate performance management

Shih et al (2005) suggest that contextual influences operate at the organisational, national and international levels and national culture is an important contextual variable that influences the implementation of performance management. Divergent practices are attributed to the culture of the nation in which head office is situated (Suutari and Tahvanainen, 2002). For example, Japanese companies in general possess a culture that emphasises collectivism and a desire to maintain harmony (Morishima, 1995), which leads to joint decision-making in appraisal rating, one-way feedback interview and compensation decided on tenure (Shih et al, 2005). Much of the literature on performance management of international staff, and particularly expatriate staff, is derived from western MNCs (Suutari and Tahvanainen, 2002; Fenwick, 2004; Dowling et al, 1999) although studies of international performance in MNCs from developing countries are beginning to emerge (Shen, 2004). These studies support the view that MNCs' performance management practices frequently represent a mix of home and local systems and concepts, which in turn are affected by various host-contextual factors such as country culture, economic, political and legal systems and organisation-specific factors such as strategy, structure and culture and country of origin (Entrekin and Chung, 2001; Shen, 2004; Mendonca and Kanungo, 1996).

There is also general agreement that performance management becomes more complicated with a move from a domestic to an international context. For instance, the location of an expatriate's boss in another country raises a range of communication issues about how the individual gets to know what is expected of him or her, what goals are appropriate to the particular context, and who will evaluate performance (Suutari and Tahvanainen, 2002). The situation relating to expatriates may be further complicated by the fact that both home- and host-country managers may be involved in the goal-setting process while the primary responsible manager is located not just locally but at a distance in a home- or even a third-country unit in the host country (Suutari and Tahvanainen, 2002). Once again, the matter of geographical distance and/or cultural difference increases the challenges in the provision of ongoing support and review of expatriates (Dowling *et al*, 1999).

Suutari and Tahvanainen (2002) demonstrate that managing performance at the team level is particularly appropriate given the complexity of cross-cultural assessment, close on half of the expatriates in their study operating with team goals. They also suggest that peer and self-assessment are likely to be useful, given the nature of expatriate assignments which often are reliant upon geographically dispersed reporting lines and involve as key elements team work and participation. We discuss peer assessment in more detail in a later section of this chapter.

Developments in expatriate performance management

Studies to date suggest that standardised performance management processes are typically adopted in expatriate performance management, relying on, for example, standardised forms (Shih *et al*, 2005). Also, that levels of formality are greater in the (usually) larger organisations dealing with expatriate performance management, more formal practices being required in matrix organisations with dual reporting relationships (Suutari and Tahvanainen, 2002). Tahvanainen (2000) argues, however, that regardless of the effectiveness or availability of performance management tools, expatriate success depends largely on the manager and expatriate in question: how well they both understand, internalise and accept performance management and how skilful they are in its implementation. To this end, appropriate training should be available for all expatriates, including their managers. Despite the tensions referred to in an earlier section of this chapter, it appears that the most common form of reward provided by MNCs to expatriate employees is contingent pay (Shih *et al*, 2005; see also Chapter 9 of this book).

We turn now to consider a case study on the performance management of expatriates, a study that focuses on the feasibility and desirability of attempts at standardisation of performance management processes.

CASE STUDY 25

EXPATRIATE PERFORMANCE MANAGEMENT AT NOKIA, FINLAND

Tahvanainen (2000) presents a case study of Nokia Telecommunications (NTC), a Finnish-based MNC. NTC operates a global, standardised PMS, meaning that all employees' performance should be managed on a similar basis. Her study in fact suggests that five expatriate groups emerged:

- top managers
- middle managers
- business establishers

- customer project employees
- research and development project personnel.

For each of these groups it was common performance management practice that all expatriates knew what was expected of them, that they knew how well they were performing, and that they received the opportunity to develop new competencies in order to meet the requirements of present and future job assignments. Differences in these processes also, however, emerged which centred mainly on the location of the manager who agrees to expatriate performance goals and then evaluates their performance; the type of goals set; the possibility of taking training courses while on assignment; and the type and clarity of linkage between performance and pay.

The case study demonstrates the key role of contingency factors when managing expatriate performance, differences in processes arising despite a standardised PMS. One implication of this is that in designing a PMS a firm must consider its specific circumstances, and that off-the-shelf solutions may not produce the desired improvements in expatriate and company performance. Further, a firm may have to supply several tools for the use of its various employee groups. While standardising the objectives of a PM process seems attractive, allowing diversity in the means and tools to achieve these objectives may be quite useful. In fact, the development of alternative PM tools, modified from a standardised global set, may result in more effective implementation of PM worldwide because it would be likely to formalise prevailing PMS, unify the different existing PM practices and provide appropriate tools for managing the differing expatriate experiences. Tahvanainen suggests at least two types of PM approaches: one for managing managerial and professional expatriate performance, and the other for customer and R&D expatriate performance.

Source: Tahvanainen (2000)

Case study tasks

1 Identify the key influences on the implementation of expatriate performance management processes and outline their implications.

2 Why is it important that MNCs design their own PMS?

3 To what extent are PMS customised to specific groups likely to help in managing expatriate performance?

We turn now to the penultimate section of this chapter to discuss what we consider to be one of the fundamental issues to performance management in contemporary organisations: multi-rater feedback.

Discussion questions

1 Explain why globalisation has rendered expatriate performance management more important.

2 What do you consider to be the key challenge in delivering successful expatriate performance management?

3   Describe the main cultural variations that could make managing expatriate performance across a range of countries difficult.

6 360-DEGREE FEEDBACK

360-degree feedback – also referred to as multi-rater or multi-source feedback – is the process whereby individuals receive feedback from a variety of stakeholders about the way they carry out their jobs. Performance feedback is typically collected from colleagues, direct reports, line managers, internal and external customers, as well as the individual. The rationale behind such multiple evaluations is that an individual obtains a breadth of information which would not normally be available, and that other people, beyond the immediate line manager, who observe or experience an individual's behaviour are in a strong position, and in some aspects uniquely qualified, to evaluate it (van der Heijden and Nijhof, 2004). It is argued that the result is greater validity in the assessment of individual performance (De Nisi and Kluger, 2000; Mabey, 2001).

Purpose

360-degree feedback was introduced initially for development purposes, and in this context the aim was to provide constructive feedback, greater awareness and, consequently, individual growth and performance enhancement, leading ultimately to organisational development and change. Although this is still one of its main functions, more recently it has been used to improve decision-making in performance appraisal, pay determination, succession planning, job placement and downsizing (Bracken et al, 2001). Originating in the United States, today the process is widely adopted, particularly in large organisations in developed countries (Luthans and Peterson, 2003) and also used with expatriates (Luthans and Farner, 2002; Woods, 2003). However, its use in geographically dispersed situations and cross-culturally presents certain challenges, not just in terms of rater knowledge about an individual's performance but also in terms of cultural difference and unfamiliarity with the concept or lack of understanding about what is expected of a person either as a rater or a ratee (Rowson, 1998). Moreover, despite its popularity, empirical evidence for the impact of this particular HR intervention on individual and organisational performance and development is limited (Mabey, 2001).

Process

The central feature of the process is a feedback instrument, typically a questionnaire, a common model being one in which the 360-degree instrument examines a number of skill areas or specific competencies or behavioural dimensions (Ghoparde, 2000). Many systems today are provided through sophisticated computer packages which enable all aspects of the process from questionnaire completion to feedback reports to be generated and delivered electronically. Notwithstanding the electronic possibilities for 360-degree feedback, it is suggested that individuals should be provided with social support in terms of interpreting feedback and development planning (Maurer and Tarulli, 1996).

Cultural differences affect not only how the process is viewed and whether it is accepted, but also the rating and feedback processes as well. Any system which delivers assessments across hierarchical boundaries may be problematic or even offensive in countries with high power distance and low levels of openness such as China, Japan, Korea, Mexico and India. For example, the respect for authority generally in high power distance cultures, together with more specific cultural values such as the importance of saving face in certain Far Eastern countries, might create concern for both the relevance and appropriateness of subordinate feedback (Entrekin and Chung, 2001), and result in overrating from subordinates (Rowson, 1998).

A critique of 360-degree feedback

360-degree feedback systems have been reported to have a number of benefits for both the individual, in terms of greater insight into how he or she is perceived by others, and for the organisation, in terms of increased organisational effectiveness and receptiveness to change. Many of the benefits are associated with improved rating reliability and validity using multiple sources over more traditional single-rater assessments, although the assumption that multiple evaluation perspectives result in greater objectivity and incremental validity when used for decision-making has been challenged. One particular problem is the mismatch between a line manager's rating and an individual's self-report – the individual generally having a higher self-image. Atwater et al (2005) found that in the United States, self-other ratings relative to other ratings were important in performance, and the authors attributed this to extreme individualism.

Notwithstanding the cultural issues associated with feedback discussed above, concerns have also been raised about the impact of feedback more generally. It has been argued that attention should be directed at the level of task performance and performance goals, rather than at the level of self, and that feedback should include specific recommendations for improvement and be accompanied by goal-setting interventions in order to be effective (De Nisi and Kluger, 2000).

Issues to address

The perceived benefits and the potential shortcomings have led writers to identify ways to maximise the effectiveness of 360-degree feedback. These fall into a number of categories:

- the system
- the people involved
- the implementation of the process.

There is a strong feeling that 360-degree feedback should be used for development purposes and not decision-making, and that it should be used regularly rather than be a one-off event (De Nisi and Kluger, 2000). Good design of all aspects, including the questionnaire, is critical, and Fletcher et al (1998) argue that a 360-degree feedback system should be developed and evaluated in the same rigorous way as psychometric tests, whether the purpose is development or appraisal.

There are a number of issues relating to the participants, including the general point that participants should be accountable and committed to the process (Bracken et al, 2001). Furthermore, it is argued that raters must be credible, be cooperative and be guaranteed anonymity (Bracken et al, 2001), commenting purely on the things they are qualified to comment on (De Nisi and Kluger, 2000). As far as the individual being rated is concerned, it is argued that the feedback should focus on the task, not the individual, that it should be developmental in nature and that help should be given in interpreting and reacting to the feedback through the incorporation of a goal-setting component (De Nisi and Kluger, 2000). 360-degree feedback is an inherently sensitive process, and research into practice in the United Kingdom suggests that inadequate attention is often given to this post-feedback stage

(Silverman *et al*, 2005). Good communication is paramount when implementing a system, together with guidance and training for all concerned and appropriate evaluation and review (van der Heijden and Nijhof, 2004). We illustrate some of the issues raised above in our final case study at the end of this chapter, which presents an overview of the introduction of a 360-degree feedback system in a New Zealand organisation.

Having considered in some detail the last of our specific performance management topics, we turn now to the final section of the chapter, its summary and an evaluation of performance management.

Discussion questions

1   To what extent do you think that 360-degree feedback is likely to achieve its aim of rendering feedback more valid?

2   Outline cultural variations that could render 360-degree feedback problematic in certain countries.

3   Outline the elements that are important to address in maximising the effectiveness of 360-degree and explain how these should be addressed.

CONCLUSIONS AND FUTURE ISSUES

In this chapter we have discussed performance management and its associated processes, adding a cross-cultural dimension which is under-explored (Fletcher and Perry, 2001). Here we present a critical review and a consideration of issues for the future.

Williams (2002) argues that there is limited evaluation of performance management, but many organisations are dissatisfied with their schemes as a means for developing and motivating people (Fletcher, 1997). Indeed, there is no conclusive evidence that performance management works (Winstanley and Stuart-Smith, 1996). The international dimension adds further complexity. For example, Milliman *et al*'s (2002) study in the Pacific Rim presents a mixed picture on whether PMS accomplish their intended objectives, and this is echoed in other studies (Pullin and Haidar, 2003; Winstanley and Stuart-Smith 1996).

Such managerialist critiques, focusing on problems of operationalisation, have been accompanied by radical critiques. These propose that performance management constitutes a new form of 'Taylorism' which seeks to control the labour process via performance evaluation and evidence-gathering (Newton and Finlay, 1996). In addressing managerialist critiques, it is argued that the purposes of PMS must be realistic and that organisations need to focus more on implementation (Milliman *et al*, 2002). Radical critiques have been addressed by authors such as Winstanley and Stuart-Smith (1996), who argue that PMS must have as a basis respect for the individual, procedural fairness and transparency of decision-making.

A further issue is the extent to which PMS devised largely for a western – specifically US – culture can be extended to other cultures (Fletcher and Perry, 2001). As noted, cultural variations impact significantly on performance management, there being limited evidence of cultural convergence. In their comparative study of Hong Kong and the UK, Snape *et al* (1998) suggest that PMS are adapted to suit the cultural characteristics of a society and that western practices need not necessarily operate under the same assumptions when translated to a different culture. While this does not mean that PMS will be any less effective in different cultures, it does make its evaluation more problematic given that objectives and processes may differ between locations.

There is much work still to be done to demonstrate the effectiveness of PMS and to ensure their effective implementation. One of the primary foci will be research in cross-cultural issues. Fletcher and Perry (2001) suggest that this is an area of limited understanding and one which, given the increasing internationalisation of business, is key to ensuring the success of PMS. Organisations must consider whether a 'one model fits all' approach is appropriate, and we may see a move away from a western model to one that reflects broader cultural concerns.

Technology is likely to play an increasing role (Sulsky and Keown, 1998), particularly in the electronic monitoring of performance, in providing feedback on performance to individuals (Kruger and Adler, 1993; Fletcher, 2001), and in supporting implementation. Call centres are a classic example of technology that provides monitoring data on employee performance (Stanton, 2000). Information is available faster, in greater quantity and in respect of jobs that have not typically been subject to formal performance management, raising a whole new set of concerns about the implementation and adaptation of PMS.

We argue throughout this chapter that in theory, performance management can make a vital contribution to enhancing individual and organisational performance in a highly competitive business environment. We recognise, however, the complexities of operationalising performance management, especially in a cross-cultural context, in order to achieve this potential. Clearly, there remains much to be done to ensure that performance management delivers on its promises.

CASE STUDY 26

INTRODUCING 360-DEGREE FEEDBACK TO ELECTRICITY GENERATION IN NEW ZEALAND

This case study focuses on the introduction of 360-degree feedback to the Electricity Corporation of New Zealand Ltd (ECNZ). Until the late 1990s ECNZ was responsible for the country's electricity generation. [In 1999 ECNZ's assets were transferred to three new generating companies: Genesis Power, Meridian Energy and Mighty River Ltd. The 360-degree programme is still in operation in the three new generating companies, and has continued to develop and evolve.]

Background
At the time that 360-degree feedback was introduced in 1996, the Corporation had a turnover of $3 billion and employed around 3,000 people. In addition to a corporate head office, there were five geographic regions. The HR function had 45 employees, of which six were based at head office undertaking a strategic corporate HR function; the balance of HR staff, undertaking an operational role, were located in the regions. The HR function was headed up by an HR director who was a member of the ECNZ management team. The HR director had responsibility for leading organisational change and for capability and culture development, and the corporate HR staff focused on policies and systems, particularly performance management, development, and remuneration.

A number of regionally developed PMS were in existence at the time of the implementation of 360-degree feedback, and annual conventional appraisal schemes were part of these. However, none of them incorporated 360-degree feedback.

The initiative was introduced as part of a broader strategy to build overall capability and embed wider culture change. The aim was to ensure that the organisation had the managers it needed to operate successfully in a complex and changing environment. The organisation's strategy to assess and deliver the structure and type of organisation it needed to be for the future was driven through a major organisational capability project led by a team which included McKinsey Consultants and the most upwardly mobile young managers in ECNZ. Key stages in this project were to assess alternative potential futures for ECNZ, to identify the critical organisational capabilities required for each potential scenario, to identify the common capabilities across all options, to assess managers' capability to move the organisation forward, and to implement an effective performance management process to link people closely with forward business and organisational development plans.

360-degree feedback was the means by which managers' capability was identified and developed within this broader strategy. The drive came from the HR director and the Chief Executive who both understood the critical importance to organisational success of managerial capability. Their aim was to use 360-degree feedback to build effective behaviours into the organisation and impact on the culture. The underlying assumption was that as managers exhibited appropriate behaviours, the rest of the workforce would follow.

The scheme
The scheme had both an assessment and a developmental focus. The purpose was to assess managers' effectiveness both in terms of achievement of goals and their behaviour in the eyes of others and to provide the managers with feedback which would inform their self-development. Its underlying aims were to help managers develop, or to remove those who were not appropriate for the future of the organisation. Although ECNZ made use of competencies for key roles, this 360-degree system was based on the core values (critical organisational competencies) of the organisation and it measured people's behaviour against those values. The core values were a definition of the critical organisational behaviours that the company believed were strategically essential for its future and its culture.

HR managed the whole project. Corporate HR designed both the system and the tools, which were electronic, and intranet-based, and regional HR staff implemented and managed the process. A number of features informed the design. Above all the aim was to provide something that was easy to understand and operate from each of the stakeholders' perspectives. The organisation was particularly keen to ensure that the people giving feedback were not overloaded in terms of the information they had to provide through the questionnaire. It also wanted to ensure not only that the managers had support in the early stages in understanding their 360-degree feedback, but that the process led to some positive outcomes which fed into those managers' personal development plans.

The first stage was to develop a pilot system which was tested with a small group of people, and their feedback was used to tweak the design. The 360-degree programme itself was introduced over a three-month period. Managers were briefed on its introduction as part of the overall major strategic capability project, and the view was that they would implement and use it effectively if they easily understood why it was needed. Consequently, there was a lot of up-front communication via newsletters (for the main capability project) and team briefings about what it was for and why it was needed. At the same time, it could be implemented with no specific training, which made it very effective from the user's point of view.

The way the 360-degree system operated was by sending short questionnaires to respondents via the organisation's intranet. These respondents were chosen jointly by the person receiving the feedback and his or her manager to ensure as much objectivity as possible. The results were collected in an Access database and analysed, and simple reports produced automatically, summarising the information. Actions were then incorporated into an individual's personal development plan. Although training in the system's operation was minimal, when people received the results for the first time, a person skilled in the interpretation of the results was closely involved to provide support and guidance. The cycle of operation was annual, and on a rolling basis, to ensure that people responding were not constantly being asked to fill in questionnaires. Results were reviewed locally and nationally.

Initially, the scheme was introduced to the first three levels of management in the organisation, and subsequently it was rolled out through to supervisor level. Although participation was not voluntary, both the scheme's objectives and the fact that feedback was a measure of other people's perceptions and not necessarily reality were made clear to participants. The aim was to get them to acknowledge that if people had a view, then it was relevant to take it on board and aim to understand it. The scheme was introduced without too many problems. One issue that did surface was the question of skewing results to personally benefit an individual manager – and this presented challenges for ECNZ's senior team. For instance, there was a situation where one manager threatened his staff with low 360 scores for themselves if his were low. The commitment of the Chief Executive was critical in this kind of situation and he worked closely with the HR director to ensure that this type of manager was handled individually on a performance basis.

The impact and success of the initiative more generally was measured in the results of the annual culture survey, which was run for the three years up to the time that ECNZ was split up. The results of that survey demonstrated a significant change in the way the culture performed.

Acknowledgement: the authors would like to thank Kevin Gaunt, Chief Executive, New Zealand Institute of Management, for his help with this case study

Case study tasks

1　What factors do you think contributed to the success of this initiative?

2　Evaluate the roles of the different stakeholders in the process.

3　In what way might country or organisational cultural factors impact on the introduction and operation of 360-degree feedback?

REFERENCES

Armstrong M. (2002) Employee Reward (3rd edition). London: CIPD.

Armstrong M. and Baron A. (1998) *Performance Management: The new realities*. London: CIPD.

Armstrong M. and Baron A. (2005) *Managing Performance: Performance management in action*. London: CIPD.

Atwater L., Waldman D., Ostroff C., Robie C. and Johnson K. M. (2005) 'Self-other agreement: comparing its relationship with performance in the US and Europe', *International Journal of Selection and Assessment*, Vol. 13, No. 1: 25–39.

Bracken D. W., Timmeck C. W., Fleenor J. W. and Summers L. (2001) '360 feedback from another angle', *Human Resource Management*, Vol. 40, No. 1: 3–20.

Brumback G. B. (2003) 'Blending the "we/me" in performance management', *Team Performance Management: An International Journal*, Vol. 9, No. 7/8: 167–73.

Campbell D. J., Campbell K. M. and Chia H.-B. (1998) 'Merit pay, performance appraisal and individual motivation: an analysis and alternative', *Human Resource Management*, Vol. 37, No. 2: 131–46.

www.cipd.co.uk/subjects/perfmangmt/

Clark G. (1998) 'Performance management strategies' in C. Mabey, G. Salaman and J. Storey, *Human Resource Management: A strategic introduction* (2nd edition). Oxford: Blackwell.

De Nisi A. S. and Kluger A. N. (2000) 'Feedback effectiveness: can 360-degree appraisals be improved?', *Academy of Management Executive*, Vol. 14, No. 1: 129–39.

Dessler G. (2005) *Human Resource Management* (10th edition). Upper Saddle River, NJ: Pearson Education Prentice Hall.

Dowling P. J., Welch D. E. and Schuler R. S. (1999) *International Human Resource Management: Managing people in a multinational context* (3rd edition). Cincinnati, OH: South-Western College Publishing.

Elias J. and Scarbrough H. (2004) 'Evaluating human capital: an exploratory study of management practice', *Human Resource Management Journal*, Vol. 14, No. 4: 21–40.

El-Kot G. and Leat M. (2005) 'Investigating teamwork in the Egyptian context', *Personnel Review*, Vol. 34, No. 2: 246–61.

Emery Y. (2004) 'Rewarding civil service performance through team bonuses: findings, analysis and recommendations', *International Review of Administrative Sciences*, Vol. 70, No. 1: 157–68.

Entrekin L. and Chung Y. W. (2001) 'Attitudes towards different sources of executive appraisal: a comparison of Hong Kong Chinese and American managers in Hong Kong', *International Journal of Human Resource Management*, Vol. 12, No. 6: 965–87.

Fenwick M. (2004) 'International compensation and performance management', in A.-W. Harzing and J. V. Ruysseveldt, *International Human Resource Management* (2nd edition). London: Sage.

Fletcher C. (1997) *Appraisal: Routes to improved performance* (2nd edition). London: CIPD.

Fletcher C. (2001) 'Performance appraisal and management: the developing research agenda', *Journal of Occupational and Organizational Psychology*, Vol. 74: 473–87.

Fletcher C. and Perry E. I. (2001) 'Performance appraisal and feedback: a consideration of national culture and a review of contemporary research and future trends', in N. Anderson, D. S. Ones, H. K. Singali and C. Viswesvaran (eds) *Handbook of Industrial, Work and Organisational Psychology*, Vol. 1: *Personnel Psychology*. London: Sage.

Fletcher C., Baldry C. and Cunningham-Snell N. (1998) 'The psychometric properties of 360-degree feedback: an empirical study and a cautionary tale', *International Journal of Selection and Assessment*, Vol. 6 No. 1: 19–34.

Ghoparde J. (2000) 'Managing five paradoxes of 360-degree feedback', *Academy of Management Executive*, Vol. 14, No. 1: 140–50.

Hendry C., Woodward S. and Bradley P. (2000) 'Performance and rewards: cleaning out the stables', *Human Resource Management Journal*, Vol. 10, No. 3: 46–62

Hofstede G. (2001) *Culture's Consequences* (2nd edition). London: Sage.

Huo Y. P. and von Glinow M. A. (1995) 'On transplanting human resource practices to China: a culture-driven approach', *International Journal of Manpower*, Vol. 16: 3–15.

IDS (2003) *Performance Management*. IDS Studies No. 748, April, London: IDS.

www.incomesdata.co.uk/studies/perfman.htm

Kluger A. N. and Adler S. (1993) 'Person- versus computer-mediated feedback', *Computers in Human Behavior*, Vol. 9: 1–16.

Lawler E. E. (1990) *Strategic Pay: Aligning organisational strategies and pay systems*. San Francisco: Jossey-Bass.

Lindholm N. (2000) 'National culture and performance in MNC subsidiaries', *International Studies of Management and Organization*, Vol. 29, No. 4: 45–66.

Lindholm N., Tahvanainen M. and Borkman I. (1999) 'Performance appraisal of host-country employees: Western MNEs in China', in C. Brewster and H. Harris (eds) *International HRM: Contemporary Issues in Europe*. London: Routledge.

Locke E. A. and Latham G. P. (1984) *Goal-Setting: A motivational technique that works*. Englewood Cliffs, NJ: Prentice Hall.

London M., Mone E. M. and Scott J. C. (2004) 'Performance management and assessment: methods for improved rater accuracy and employee goal-setting', *Human Resource Management*, Vol. 43, No. 4: 319–36.

Luthans F. and Peterson S. J. (2003) '360-degree feedback with systematic coaching: empirical analysis suggests a winning combination', *Human Resource Management*, Vol. 42, No. 3: 243–56.

Luthans K. W. and Farner S. (2002) 'Expatriate development: the use of 360-degree feedback', *Journal of Management Development*, Vol. 21, No. 10: 780–93.

Mabey C. (2001) 'Closing the circle: participant views of a 360-degree feedback programme', *Human Resource Management Journal*, Vol. 11, No. 1: 41–53.

Maurer T. and Tarulli B. (1996) 'Acceptance of peer/upward appraisal systems: role of work context factors and beliefs about managers' development capability', *Human Resource Management*, Vol. 35, No. 2: 217–41.

Mayo A. (2001) *The Human Value of the Enterprise: Valuing people as assets – monitoring, measuring, managing*. London: Nicolas Brealey.

McEvoy G. M. and Cascio W. R. (1990) 'The US and Taiwan: two different cultures look at performance appraisal', in G. R. Ferris and K. M. Rowland (eds) *Research in Personnel and Human Resource Management*, Supplement 2. Greenwich, CT: JAI Press.

Mendonca M. and Kanungo R. N. (1996) 'Impact of culture on performance management in developing countries', *International Journal of Manpower*, Vol. 17, No. 4/5: 65–75.

Milliman J., Nason S., Gallagher E., Huo P., von Glinow M. A. and Lowe K. B. (1998) 'The impact of national culture on human resource management practices: the case of performance appraisal', *Advances in International Comparative Management*, Vol. 12: 157–83.

Milliman J., Nason S., Zhu C. and De Ciere H. (2002) 'An exploratory assessment of the purposes of performance appraisals in North and Central America and the Pacific Rim', *Human Resource Management*, Vol. 41, No. 1: 87–102.

Mintzberg H. (1994) 'The rise and fall of strategic planning', *Harvard Business Review*, Jan-Feb: 107–14.

Mitchell T. R., Thompson K. R. and George-Falvy J. (2000) 'Goal-setting: theory and practice', in C. L. Cooper and E. A. Locke (eds) *Industrial, Work and Organisational Psychology*. Oxford: Sage.

Morishima M. (1995) 'The Japanese human resource management system: a learning bureaucracy', in L. F. Moore and P. D. Jennings (eds) *Human Resource Management on the Pacific Rim: Institutions, practices and attitudes*. Berlin: Walter de Gruyter.

Newton T. and Finlay P. (1996) 'Playing god? The performance of appraisal', *Human Resource Management Journal*, Vol. 6, No. 3: 42–58.

Nyaw M. K. (1995) 'Human resource management in the People's Republic of China', in L. F. Moore and P. D. Jennings (eds) *Human Resource Management on the Pacific Rim: Institutions, practices and attitudes*, Berlin: Walter de Gruyter.

Pucik V. (1985) 'Strategic human resource management in a multinational firm', in H. V. Wortzel and L. H. Wortzel (eds) *Strategic Management of Multinational Corporations: The essentials*. New York: John Wiley & Sons.

Pullin L. and Haidar A. (2003) 'Performance contract management in regional local government', *Asia Pacific Journal of Human Resources*, Vol. 41, No. 3: 279–97.

Redman T. (2001) 'Performance appraisal', in T. Redman and A. Wilkinson, *Contemporary Human Resource Management: Text and cases*. Harlow: Pearson Education.

Rowson A.-M. (1998) 'Using 360-degree feedback instruments up, down and around the world: implications for global implementation and use of multi-rater feedback', *International Journal of Selection and Assessment*, Vol. 6, No. 1: 45–8.

Shen J. (2004)' International performance appraisals: policies, practices and determinants in the case of Chinese multinational companies', *International Journal of Manpower*, Vol. 25, No. 6: 547–63.

Shih H.-A., Chiang Y.-H. and Kim I.-S. (2005) 'Expatriate performance management from MNEs of different national origins', *International Journal of Manpower*, Vol. 26, No. 2: 157–76.

Silverman M., Kerrin M. and Carter A. (2005) *360-Degree Feedback Beyond the Spin*. IES Report No. 418. Brighton: Institute of Employment Studies.

Snape E., Thompson D., Ka-Ching Yan F. and Redman T. (1998) 'Performance appraisal and culture: practice and attitudes in Hong Kong and Great Britain', *International Journal of Human Resource Management*, Vol. 9, No. 5: 841–61.

Stanton J. M. (2000) 'Reactions to employee performance monitoring: framework, review and research directions', *Human Performance*, Vol. 13: 85–113.

Sulsky L. M. and Keown J. L. (1998) 'Performance appraisal in the changing world of work: implications for the meaning and measurement of work performance', *Canadian Psychology*, Vol. 39: 52–9.

Suutari V. and Tahvanainen M. (2002) 'The antecedents of performance management among Finnish expatriates', *International Journal of Human Resource Management*, Vol. 13, No. 1: 55–75.

Tahvanainen M. (2000) 'Expatriate performance management: the case of Nokia Telecommunications', *Human Resource Management*. Vol. 37, No. 4: 267–75.

Torrington D., Hall L. and Taylor S. (2005) *Human Resource Management* (6th edition). Harlow: FT/Prentice Hall.

van der Heijden, B. I. J. M. and Nijhof A. H. J. (2004) 'The value of subjectivity; problems and prospects for 360-degree appraisal systems', *International Journal of Human Resource Management*, Vol. 15, No. 3: 493–511.

Vance C. M., McClaine S. R., Boje D. M. and Stage D. H. (1992) ' An examination of the transferability of traditional performance appraisal across cultural boundaries', *Management International Review*, Vol. 32, No. 4: 313–26.

Vroom V. H. (1964) *Work and Motivation*. New York: John Wiley & Sons.

Walsh P., Bryson J. and Lonti Z. (2002) 'Jack be nimble, Jill be quick: HR capability and organisational agility in the New Zealand public and private sectors', *Asia-Pacific Journal of Human Resources*, Vol. 40, No. 2: 177–92.

Williams R. (1998) *Performance Management*. London: International Thomson Business Press.

Williams R. (2002) *Managing Employee Performance: Design and implementation in organisations*. London: Thomson Learning.

Williams V. (2001) 'Making performance management relevant', *Compensation and Benefits Review*, Vol. 33, No. 4: 47–51.

Winstanley D. and Stuart-Smith K. (1996) 'Policing performance: the ethics of performance management', *Personnel Review*, Vol. 25, No. 6: 66–84.

Woods P. (2003) 'Performance management of Australian and Singaporean expatriates', *International Journal of Manpower*, Vol. 24, No. 5: 517–34.

Reward

CHAPTER 9

Gill Homan and Stephen Taylor

CHAPTER OBJECTIVES

When you have read this chapter you should be able to:

- explain the strategic significance of reward, and the different forms that reward can take

- understand the impact of national, regional and global issues on reward strategies

- identify the options available for rewarding people for international and expatriate working, and the issues driving change in this area

- outline the process of building a reward strategy for a global workforce.

PURPOSE AND SCOPE

This chapter looks at three aspects of reward in an international context:

- how the practice of reward management varies in different countries

- how organisations reward those employees required to work outside their home country

- how organisations that employ local people in more than one country can manage their reward strategy.

In exploring these issues we address a number of the book's themes as they relate to reward. Cultural variation underpins differences in the way in which reward is understood, managed and experienced in different countries. Globalisation, technological change and the rise of the emerging economies impact on the changing context in which organisations seek to manage reward beyond their home-country boundaries.

Managing reward in an international context is not a new issue – much of the wealth of the developed economies has been built on the exploitation of raw materials from the developing world and the use of expatriate expertise to resource and manage production. In the past the global expansion of an organisation has been a natural progression from a domestically mature business (Dunn and Rumberger, 1996), but in the last 25 years there has been a substantial increase in the number and type of organisations requiring their employees to work in other countries, often at earlier stages in the corporate life-cycle. Similarly, continual pressure to be competitive on costs (of which employment costs are a significant part) has seen many organisations relocate production and service provision. This means that many more organisations now grapple with the issues associated with employment and reward in other countries. In this chapter we identify these issues and explore the ways in which organisations approach them. We start by defining reward, before looking at the impact of culture and context on how reward is approached in different countries. We then examine how this understanding can inform the management of reward by organisations operating globally.

1 REWARD IN AN INTERNATIONAL CONTEXT

The nature of reward and its strategic significance

We normally think of reward as the money we receive in our pay packet and maybe one or two of the more substantial benefits. However, the recognition of people as the inimitable source of competitive edge, in addition to the effects of skills shortages, have seen a resurgence of interest in both the composition and the presentation of the reward package and the commodification of aspects of work and employment not previously regarded as having an exchange value. This can best be observed in the rise of the concept of 'total reward'. There is no definitive model of total reward. For example the CIPD (*Research Review*, 2005) identifies four consultancy models:

- Hay Group (www.haygroup.com) inspiration/values; quality of work; enabling environment; tangible rewards; work–life balance; future growth and opportunity

- Towers Perrin (www.towers.com) pay; benefits; learning and development

- Schuster, Zingheim & Associates (www.paypeopleright.com) individual growth; total pay; compelling future; positive workplace

- World at Work (www.worldatwork.org) compensation; benefits; the work experience.

Each of these models contains different aspects and combinations of reward, but together they illustrate the range of rewards available – beyond base pay to allowances, variable or contingent pay, financial and non-financial benefits. The key point is that organisations have choices in how they define total reward to fit their own context. The art and science of reward management lies in making these choices. It is also important to recognise that these choices are strategic ones. Reward is an area of HRM practice that is regarded by all theorists as of strategic significance, and is included in all the major models of HRM (see Chapter 3). It is also one of the most difficult for a number of reasons. These are outlined below:

- It forms a substantial – sometimes *the most* substantial – component of organisation costs and often drives location decisions. Issues include the calculation of true costs and on-costs, flexibility, control, risk, predictability, and 'hidden costs' such as turnover and absence.

- The concept of employee voice – pay is acknowledged to have the 'loudest' voice.

- It is a powerful force for behavioural change and achieving organisational change.

- There are a number of key stakeholders with variable power and influence – employees, trade unions, professional bodies, government bodies, etc.

- It is a key factor in the success of other HR strategies – for example, the ability to attract and retain required skills and knowledge.

- It is a key component in the drive for effective organisational and individual performance by flagging up and encouraging appropriate behaviours.

- It is bounded by government in both structures and processes – for example, entrance and exit from the labour market, collective bargaining arrangements, the minimum wage, taxation law, etc.

■ It has to be right first time.

Making these strategic choices in an international context adds an extra series of challenges. Dowling *et al* (1999) identify six factors that complicate HRM in a global context. They are: a larger number of activities, the need to adopt a wider view of people issues facing the organisation, an increased involvement in the lives of employees, greater exposure to risk generally both direct and indirect in nature, and an increased number of external influences as a result of the variety of national contexts involved. These factors certainly apply to reward, and this adds to the strategic significance of managing reward in an international context.

National influences in international reward

In this age of the 'global village' in which fashions in clothing, music and entertainment span the world in weeks and ever larger numbers of the world's population travel both for work and pleasure, it is easy to forget that fundamental differences between national groups mean that some issues are looked at quite differently. Schuler and Rogovsky (1998) identify four areas which impact on human resource policies and practices. They are: legislation, the employment relationship context or climate, national patterns of compensation, and national culture. Later, we explore some of these differences and their implications for the practice of reward management. However, there are also some fundamental similarities, and we must deal with them first. As Harris *et al* (2003) point out, the basis for pay throughout the world is attendance, and the basis for progression is experience or length of service (Harris *et al*, 2003). There are also cross-cultural similarities in terms of motivation. Thierry (1998) suggests that the process of pay satisfaction and the way in which it affects behaviour is generic. He identifies four ways in which people derive meaning from reward:

■ motivation – the extent to which pay offers a means of achieving important objectives

■ relative position – the extent to which pay recognises achievement of goals and performance relative to personal comparators

■ individual control – the extent to which the individual can exert control over the reward package through the different systems and components

■ utility – the extent to which reward can be exchanged for goods and services.

The level of meaning derived is influenced by the structure and mix of components of pay and by the climate of the organisation, all of which vary substantially between organisations. We now move on to explore the differences

Culture

Sparrow (2000) defines three ways in which national culture can influence reward: distributive justice, the strength and orientation of values, and social alignment. Distributive justice (see also Chapter 13) concerns the rules and factors that determine the way in which resources are allocated and whether those decisions are perceived to be equitable – the source of the 'felt fair' and 'parity' perceptions. These rules reflect the values and social alignment of a society. Thus they influence decisions about financial and non-financial rewards and the degree of acceptance of societal boundaries around pay differentials such as the minimum wage and the gap between shop floor and senior executives.

Hofstede's (2001) work on culture (see Chapter 2 for a detailed discussion) offers a framework to understand national cultural differences, and we use this framework below to explore the impact of these on reward. Chiang (2005) explored national cultural perceptions of reward practices in four countries. His research largely supported Hofstede's work but found that contextual issues – for example, economic strength, and the provision of a national system of healthcare – profoundly affected perceptions of what was desirable in a reward package.

Organisations use their reward and benefits policies as a means of reinforcing organisation culture throughout the world – often, corporate culture is considered more important than national culture – but Hempel (1998) argues that 'blind transplantation' can create substantial difficulties locally. If strategies are adjusted to reflect national cultural values, they are more likely to deliver predictable behaviours and improved performance (Schuler and Rogovsky, 1998). Thus an understanding of national culture is essential to the practice of international reward management. In the remainder of this section we explore this in relation to four of the main building-blocks of reward strategy that we identified above: base pay, variable or contingent pay, benefits, and non-financial benefits.

Base pay

Many countries have taken steps to protect those earning at the lowest levels by introducing a minimum wage, sometimes differentiated by age or trainee status, and by attempting the redistribution of wealth via the taxation and social service systems. Most countries that support the Organisation for Economic Co-operation and Development (OECD), including a third of the advanced industrialised nations, offer a minimum wage (Edwards and Rees, 2006). One might therefore expect the gap between the lowest and highest earners to be decreasing as a general world trend. This does not seem to be the case. Both OECD data (Edwards and Rees, 2006) and research by Galbraith and Kum (2003) show that irrespective of national policies, changes in the global economy are generating a climate of higher inequalities almost everywhere.

Pay inequality differs substantially between different countries. For example, the difference between the top and bottom 10% of earners during the 1990s was:

- USA – 4½ times
- France – 3½ times
- UK – 3½ times
- Japan – 3½ times
- Norway – 2 times.

Factors that contribute to these variations include density of union membership, centralisation of collective bargaining (Rueda and Pontusson, 2000) and the political positioning of governments in relation to taxation policies and employment protection. Seniority-based pay systems and skills-based pay systems are more likely to be found in cultures with high uncertainty avoidance. For example, in Germany wage levels link to hierarchical levels very explicitly, whereas in the United States there are higher intra-level variations in wage differentials (Grand, 2005). Spain has seen a rising trend in remuneration based on capacities, competencies and abilities but still retains rigid salary hierarchies with little transparency and a short-term orientation (Valle *et al*, 2001).

The principle on which base pay is calculated also differs by country. For example, Spain, South Africa and many other countries offer a 'thirteenth month', some offer fourteen months' pay. An extra month's pay is received usually at the time of summer holidays. Although no longer mandatory in Spain, it is still custom and practice. In other countries, such as Saudi Arabia, it is mandatory to pay for rest days as well – that is, for seven days of the week (Briscoe and Schuler, 2004).

Harris *et al* (2003) found an almost universal preference for individually focused pay, and systems based on skill, competence or performance preferred to those based on age, experience or seniority. This view is gaining ground as organisations recognise the significance of capability and the flexible exercise of that capability (Harris *et al*, 2003).

Variable or contingent pay

Variable or contingent pay, particularly individual performance-related pay, is viewed as having originated within the USA. However, it is now more widespread, and a focus on the individual is stated as a preference by employees across the world (Lowe *et al*, 2002; Harris *et al*, 2003). Variable or contingent pay is difficult to compare meaningfully across countries because of the variety of different forms and lack of cross-national research evidence. What research there is suggests that it is a significant component of pay, although limited to about 10%, within the western industrialised nations, but offers little variation in amounts generated between different employees in the same scheme.

Europe
In the private sector, evidence suggests coverage in the UK of about 60% of the workforce; in Germany, a social market economy, over 50%; in Italy and the Netherlands 40% (Edwards and Rees, 2006). In France, Cardin *et al* (2001a) found a wide use of collective bonuses and exceptional work premiums, a recent rise in the use of gainsharing, and a predicted rise in employee shareholding over the next decade – but also an increase in questions of security and equity. In all cases the use of variable pay in the public sector is about half of that in the private sector and concentrated in more senior jobs.

Canada and Australia
Long and Shields (2005) looked at 13 different forms of variable pay and found that in both of these two countries the most important positive predictor of variable pay was larger size, with the degree of unionisation a negative predictor. The most popular form was individual performance-related pay whereas group-based variable pay had the lowest take-up in both countries. Their research supported Pfeffer's hypothesis (in Long and Shields, 2005) that there is a trend towards convergence in international pay, at least in the developed economies, but that contextual and firm-specific factors are also important.

Asia
Variable pay tends to be contingent on group performance rather than individual. Appraisal-based pay in China or Japan might be hampered by the practice of not normally giving feedback in order to save 'face', and maybe this is one of the reasons why group schemes are favoured (Shen, 2005).

There has always been and still is a substantial debate about the merits and applicability of pay for performance, especially individual performance-related pay. Arguments centre on perceived equity, its encouragement of a short-term focus, inappropriateness for teamworking and other interdependent forms of working, its inapplicability to difficult-to-measure jobs, and its overall unsuitability for those whose values are at odds with the ethos of pay for performance. It tends to have a better fit and widest spread in cultures that are highly individualistic and masculine, such as the United States, the UK, Australia and Canada, Japan and Germany, and less fit and spread in those countries that register uncertainty avoidance, such as the Latin nations.

Financial participation is a particular form of pay for performance which attempts to involve employees in the performance of the organisation by offering either profit-related pay or the opportunity to buy stock at favourable prices, or both. Stock option plans tend to be found in cultures which combine high individualism with low uncertainty avoidance and low power distance (Schuler and Rogovsky, 1998). This form of variable pay is subject to considerable political influence, ranging from encouragement via taxation systems to statutory prohibition.

Benefits

Employee benefits 'lie at the heart of the employment relationship' (Hempel, 1998) and should reflect a society's general value system and be congruent with national culture. However, they tend to be driven by political and legal issues. Factors that significantly affect the benefits package are differences in national benefit provision and in job and income protection – for example, healthcare provision ranges from none at all to complete provision – economic factors, demographics, historical factors and culture.

Culture has been found to affect benefit preferences to a significant extent, and is considered relatively stable and therefore not easy to manage (Hempel, 1998). Using examples of Hofstede's (2001) dimensions, high levels of power distance favour benefit packages related to status; low power distance scores tend towards harmonised benefits. High masculinity is associated with a lower use of flexible benefits and those associated with quality of life but a high concern for benefits that reflect status and personal success. High individualism is associated with increasing use of flexible benefits. Universal healthcare provision, paradoxically, seems unrelated to culture but closely connected with national wealth.

Pensions offer striking variation in national provision, even within the same region. For example, pensions in Singapore are completely government-provided via a mandatory savings plan towards which employer and employee contributions total 40% of pay, whereas the system in Hong Kong, at least until the demise of British governance, was completely voluntary. In Italy the government replaces 80% of earnings after 40 years of work, and only senior executives tend to have supplementary pensions. More often there is a mix of government, employer and individual provision as in the UK and the USA.

Social pensions – those provided or mandated by government – have two important characteristics: generosity and income distribution. Both can be measured by income replacement rates (Hempel, 1998). This is the proportion of working income replaced by a pension after retirement. Income redistribution takes two forms. Intergenerational redistribution occurs when pensions are paid out of current government income, as in the UK. There, the income is redistributed from the working generations to the retired generation. Income can also be redistributed within a generation when low earners receive a greater proportion of income replacement than higher earners. In cultural terms low power distance societies tend to use social pensions as a means of redistributing wealth. Norway has a power distance rating of 31 and an income replacement ratio of 72%. This relationship applies generally across the power distance spectrum.

Income protection in the form of sickness and unemployment benefit is more valued in countries with high scores for uncertainty avoidance and femininity, as for example Spain, whereas the Republic of Ireland has low uncertainty avoidance and high masculinity, and has low levels of income protection.

Non-financial benefits

Contractually required weekly hours of work show little variation across the world. They vary between 48 in Hong Kong and 35 in France (Briscoe and Schuler, 2004), but a remarkable number of countries lie within the 37–40 range. Contractual hours worked may bear little relation to actual hours worked, however. For example, within Europe the UK is acknowledged to have a 'long hours culture' in which both employers and employees have resisted the introduction of the EU Working-Time Directive.

Key in this area is the masculinity/femininity dimension. High masculine cultures value work, competition and success whereas feminine cultures value quality of life. This can be seen in measures of security such as job protection, which is valued in cultures with a high uncertainty avoidance and high masculinity such as Greece. Conversely there is little job protection in countries with low uncertainty avoidance and high masculinity scores as in the case of the Republic of Ireland. This pattern can also be seen in hours of work: high masculinity usually equates with long working hours, as in the UK, whereas high femininity equates with shorter working hours, as with France. To some extent the influence of national culture is being eroded in Europe as the EU legislates on matters of working environment and benefits. EU laws combined with those of national governments make these areas very difficult for multinationals (Taft and Powell, 2005).

Discussion questions

1 What theories of motivation might explain the current interest in the work environment of non-financial aspects of total reward?

2 What might be the impact on reward packages of ignoring national cultural values?

3 Should governments pursue employment law strategies that are aimed at attracting inward investment or that are aimed at employee protection?

2 EXPATRIATE PAY

Having examined issues of definition, strategy and context, we now turn our attention to the management of reward across international boundaries. We start with the issue of expatriate reward and then move on to look at global reward strategies in Section 3.

The management of expatriate pay is a difficult balancing act between cost, attractiveness, flexibility and equity (Fenwick, 2004). This is becoming increasingly complex as organisations use a variety of approaches to international working in an effort to minimise costs (Briscoe and Schuler, 2004). The Cranfield Centre for Research into the Management of Expatriation (CReME) identifies four types of international assignment.

Types of international and expatriate assignments

Frequent flyers
These are employees whose role requires them to travel extensively on business. Mobility and flexibility may be encouraged by mobility payments and additional benefits, while from the perspective of the employee the management of work–life balance may become an issue (Harris et al, 2003).

Short-term assignments

These are of three to twelve months' duration, usually with one or two key objectives: the transfer of knowledge, skill and/or control to the host country, or management development. The use of short-term assignments since the early 1990s (Latta, 1999), particularly in organisations with an established presence in a country (Allard, 1996), appears to be continuing to increase (ORC, 2005a; Mercer, 2003). Short-term assignments are perceived as less disruptive to home and social life and circumvent the problems of dual career families, and can be more cost-effective. They do, however, raise issues of long hours, family separation, frequent assignment extension and control (Harris *et al*, 2003). Reward in short-term assignments tends to take the form of fully-paid accommodation and frequent travel home combined with very generous 'per diem' allowances. Some organisations offer an additional bonus on successful assignment completion.

Commuter assignments

These involve employees who work away from home on a Monday-to-Friday basis and who return home for the weekend, or some other variation on this theme. The system is mostly used in short-term assignments to minimise the disruption of the family and social life of the employee. Accommodation is usually in hotels and a 'per diem' allowance made to defray daily costs (IDS, 2002); a mobility allowance may also be paid and more frequent trips home to visit the family funded. Harris *et al* (2003) indicate the problems with this group as burnout, travel fatigue, poor work–life balance and cultural issues.

Expatriate assignments

These are assignments that generally last more than a year. They are more complex than the other assignment types listed above because they often require the relocation of the family for the period (IDS, 2002) of the assignment and involve assistance and support extending to the spouse in the case of dual-career couples. Even within this category there are a number of variations on the personnel involved. They include experienced managers with specific expertise, younger managers on developmental assignments, international managers who move from one overseas assignment to another, and permanent expatriates who to all intents and purposes have relocated to the host country (Briscoe and Schuler 2004). This adds a further level of complexity because each of these variations needs a different reward package.

The objectives of expatriate pay

In setting expatriate pay organisations have a number of goals including the ability to attract, recruit, retain and motivate the best people to fill these important roles (Briscoe and Schuler, 2004; and see Chapters 6 and 8 of this book) and protect any sustainable competitive advantage (Fenwick, 2004). Objectives vary according to the stage of internationalisation that the organisation has reached. During the start-up or launch phase the organisation must establish its presence and communicate vision and purpose (Allard, 1996), which requires entrepreneurial skills. At this time controlling costs and consistency in pay policy and strategy may not be a key issue. During subsequent phases of growth, objectives are concerned with the transfer of knowledge into the local environment and the management of a mature presence. Placements may be more focused on the development of a cadre of international managers, while there is increasing need for the substantial costs of expatriate placements to be controlled. During all phases expatriate pay must meet, or at least go some way towards meeting, the expectations of the expatriates concerned.

Many organisations (Sims and Schroeder, 2005) seek to achieve an outcome in which the expatriate is neither worse nor better off by undertaking the expatriate placement. The expatriate may, however, expect an incentive to undertake an overseas assignment, especially to a very different culture or an environment in which he or she may experience some 'hardship' such as extreme weather or political instability.

Factors that affect the pay of expatriate employees

There are a number of factors that affect the pay of expatriate employees. They include:

- the cost of living in the host country – considered the most important factor and potentially the most costly for the organisation, especially if the posting is to a high-cost-of-living country such as Japan

- hardship – compensation received for living in a country which is, for example, remote, dangerous, politically unstable (see the box below)

- currency fluctuations – one of the major issues in protecting the value and consistency of expatriate pay over time

- healthcare – a primary concern of expatriates ... and a high cause of dissatisfaction according to Frazee (1998)

- housing – estimated to account for about 25% of total expatriate costs (ORC, 2005); housing includes assistance in finding accommodation in the host country, a contribution towards housing costs, relocation costs (ORC, 2005) and the expenses of utilities such as power and telephone. Many organisations also provide property management services for those employees that retain their original home

- taxation – one of the most complex and difficult areas of expatriate pay because it is li

- t   vision of an appropriate
  c   ment?

SO
EXP
Sourc   try of origin of the
expat

- ack of cultural and
  nd other essentials

- itions, risk of natural

- isk of disease, poor

- ption, human rights
  on

- oor housing quality,

Components of expatriate pay

Base pay

As with domestic pay this is the main component of expatriate pay, but it has a wider significance because other allowances and benefits may be directly related to the level of base pay (Dowling and Welch, 2004). It is also more complex in that decisions have to be made about whether it will be related to home pay, local pay, or an international pay system; what percentage will be paid into home (to cover continuing commitments) and host-country bank accounts; and what currency it will be paid in.

Allowances

These can be many and varied. The most significant allowances, in terms of cost, are the cost-of-living allowance (COLA), which compensates for higher costs of living in different countries, and the housing allowance. There are many other allowances, including those for the education of children, for the provision of cars and, in some countries, drivers, for home visits, for goods and services, and for relocation expenses. One of the more contentious is the 'hardship' allowance. This is meant to compensate for difficult conditions and separation from family and social networks. Now that expatriate placements are increasingly being viewed as development opportunities, however, hardship allowances are in decline in the developed world. They are nonetheless still an issue in the case of assignments in emerging economies and areas where conditions may be less favourable in many ways than the home country.

Variable or contingent pay

There is evidence that an increasing proportion of expatriate pay falls into this category, particularly for senior managers. It can take any of three forms – the renaming and restructuring of the hardship allowance as mobility allowance part-paid on acceptance of the assignment, with the remainder on completion and contingent upon success; pay for perform- ance (see Chapter 8 for a detailed discussion); and financial participation. Performance is usually assessed by the host-country manager but the level of pay for performance often remains within the home-country scheme. This applies at both Cadbury-Schweppes and Smith & Nephew (IDS, 2002). Maintaining expatriates in financial participation schemes that involve stock ownership can be particularly difficult because of the legal frameworks of both the home and host countries and the tax implications.

Benefits

One of the most difficult decisions is whether to maintain home benefits or to transfer into host-country schemes. This is particularly important where the decisions may have implica- tions for the future quality of life or when membership is mandatory, for example, as in pensions and social security schemes where there are wide variations between countries. Many of these areas also have significant tax implications for the organisation.

Healthcare is an essential element of the expatriate package because poor medical care can equate to a failed assignment either through the need to return home for treatment or through recruitment and retention issues. There are three key factors that inform decision-making, according to Frazee (1997): the availability of healthcare of a sufficient standard, coverage in the host country and the home healthcare plan for dependants remaining at home, and endeavours towards health education and disease prevention because expatriates are particu- larly vulnerable to health problems and accidents in unfamiliar environments. Healthcare has also become an issue in all forms of international assignment following evidence of a significant rise in travel-related stress and other mental health issues (Frazee, 1997). Control of healthcare costs is of increasing corporate concern.

Other benefits include holidays. In areas of hardship holidays may include 'respite' leave to relatively local but more congenial places. Both normally include flight costs. Statutory or national holidays tend to be taken as in the host country. Policy can vary from a standard allowance for all expatriates – at ICI, for example, this is 25 days – to an entitlement in line with the host country but subject to a minimum. Others offer home or host, whichever is the more advantageous (IDS, 2002).

Company cars tend to be awarded in line with the host-country benefits rules, the requirements of the assignment, and personal security needs, which may extend to the spouse and the provision of security staff (Hume, 1995).

Non-financial benefits
Increasingly, an expatriate assignment is seen as a development opportunity and an essential step for corporate 'high-fliers', particularly during early career. The 'career value' is seen as having an exchange value in reward terms, which reduces the need for financial incentives. This is discussed further in the section on cost minimisation. Despite this, many expatriates express dissatisfaction with this aspect of their package (Briscoe and Schuler, 2004) – particularly with career planning during the assignment and on repatriation, and with the availability of support for cultural adjustment. The appraisal of the expatriate forms a key component of this section of total reward because of its links to career progression, recognition and performance-related pay.

Suutari and Tornikoski (2001) found that the main sources of dissatisfaction amongst expatriates were the overall level of expatriate pay, the scarcity of data on local costs of living, currency-rate risks, social security and pension issues, spouse-related issues, and repatriation costs. Sources of satisfaction were the lower levels of taxation, allowances (particularly car allowances), clear compensation principles, and sufficient information to be able to negotiate the expatriate's own package.

Calculating expatriate pay

There are a number of frameworks or models that can be used.

The balance-sheet approach
This is the most popular – at least 85% of organisations in the USA use this approach (Watson and Gangeram, 2005; IDS, 2002). It retains the expatriate on the home-country payment structure while protecting the standard of living in the host country; it is underpinned by tax equalisation.

The balance-sheet approach provides:

- a base for home-country continued benefits such as pension and social welfare payments

- ease of repatriation by maintaining home parity

- a fairly straightforward basis for transfers from country to country

- relative transparency for the recipient.

However, it can cause great disparity in salaries paid to host-, parent- and third-country nationals who are performing the same role in the same location, but who have different base salary levels (Dowling and Welch, 2004). It can also carry a high administrative burden in terms of managing the tax equalisation and social security contributions, and may need regular updating and recalculation where there are large currency fluctuations (IDS, 2002).

The host-country approach

Sometimes called the market rate approach (Dowling and Welch, 2004), this method links base pay to the market rate prevailing in the host country for similar jobs. In low-pay countries additional allowances may be added. The advantages of this method are:

- Expatriates are paid on the same basis as local employees, and this avoids any resentment towards 'overpaid' outsiders. Research (Peters, 1994) indicates that salaries can range from three times (Poland and Hungary) to 20 to 50 times (China) those of local employees in similar jobs (Bonache and Fernandez, 2005). Inevitably, this gap will narrow over time and there is evidence to show that some local managerial salaries are rapidly catching up. This issue is particularly important when home-, host- and third-country nationals have to work in multinational teams (Herod, 1997).

- The method is relatively transparent when there are expatriates from different countries of origin in the same location.

It does have some disadvantages in that local taxation may significantly affect purchasing power and lead to some locations being regarded as financially advantageous, whereas less advantageous locations become difficult to fill. It works well for younger employees and for senior jobs where market salaries are similar across the world (IDS, 2002).

Other approaches

Negotiation/ad hoc – When organisations first engage with international activities the number of expatriates will be relatively small and reward packages generally be determined on an individual or ad hoc basis and be generous because cost control is not a major consideration (Briscoe and Schuler, 2004).

The higher of home or host pay – A balance-sheet calculation is undertaken and then compared with the host-country net salary. This enables salaries to be compared more easily, particularly when there are large variations in the home and host regimes.

Lump sum – This follows the balance-sheet approach but allowances are 'bundled' and paid as a lump sum – usually paid half in advance and the remainder on completion. This approach allows the expatriate more discretion over how he/she uses the money, and has some tax efficiency (Fox and Phillips, 2003).

Cafeteria selection – This approach provides choice from a range of benefits up to an agreed limit. It is advantageous to both organisation and expatriate in that it can be tax-efficient for both.

Regional systems – These standardise the treatment of pay and allowances within a geographical region such as Europe or Asia. For example, Portal Software Europe has standardised car allowances and other benefits in eight of their Eurozone bases (Fenwick, 2004).

Global – A common global total reward package is applied across a global job-grading system. This approach is discussed in more detail below.

Selecting the appropriate approach

In general it is administratively more efficient to treat the majority of assignees with the same approach. However, variation may be required to recognise, for example, the level of responsibility of the expatriate, the purpose of the assignment and the destination (IDS, 2002). Frazee (1998b) believes that equity is a key decision for the organisation. If equity with home-country peers is the most important factor, the balance-sheet approach is the most appropriate choice; for equity with local peers, the host-country approach; and for equity within an international cadre an internationally based approach may be needed. Bonache and Fernandez (1997) use Gupta and Govindarajan's (1991) framework to classify expatriate roles and align them with the use of incentives and performance management strategies. They argue for a 'best fit' approach between expatriate compensation and the strategy in the subsidiary organisation, maintaining that differentiated and appropriate behaviours are best achieved by a differentiated approach to compensation.

Taxation

Once resident in a country for a specific period of time, an expatriate becomes liable for host-country taxation in addition to or instead of home-country taxation. Organisations can adopt any of a number of different approaches to this issue.

Tax equalisation ensures that the expatriate employee pays no more or less tax than he/she would at home, so there is no financial advantage to being in one country or the other (Reynolds, 1997). This is achieved by deducting the home taxes from pay in the normal way while the organisation pays all taxes in the host country (Dowling and Welch, 2004; Fenwick, 2004). The organisation retains any tax advantage or bears the additional cost. This usually underpins the balance-sheet approach (IDS, 2002).

Tax protection ensures that no more tax is paid than in the home country but allows the employee to benefit from any tax savings that accrue from being located in a lower tax economy. This method may limit mobility, especially if the move is from a low- to a high-tax host country, and does not allow the organisation to offset the gains in one country with the losses in another (IDS, 2002).

An alternative option is for the organisation not to interfere, but let the expatriate deal with this issue.

Tax equalisation is by far the most popular method: 91% of organisations surveyed utilised it (Latta, 1999).

Finally, allowances will be treated differently in home and host countries for tax purposes. Some may be taxed in both, and companies will usually ensure that the expatriate's net income is 'protected' by meeting additional taxation costs.

Issues in expatriate pay

Dual-career families
Expatriates increasingly have spouses with careers that may be disrupted by an expatriate assignment. This has two aspects – firstly, loss of a second income; secondly, a possible negative effect on the spouse's career which may jeopardise both future advancement and earnings potential. These may result in the overseas assignment looking far less attractive and lead to overall difficulties in recruitment. A survey (ORC, 1999) found that consideration for loss of spousal income had risen from 15% to 25.5% of participating companies in the period

1989–1999, and spousal assistance in job-search activities had increased from 7% to 25% within the same period. A recent study by Cranfield (Harris *et al*, 2003) showed that only 9% of expatriates are women – a small but increasing percentage that will only add to the dual-career problem

Cost minimisation
Estimates of expatriate costs range from three times to a possible four-and-a-half times (Myers, 1995; Briscoe and Schuler, 2004) the cost of a host-country national in the same job. Changing practices aimed at reducing expatriate costs include removal of the 'foreign service' inducement, usually about 15% of base pay (Latta, 1998) for developmental assignments, providing different inducements for different types of assignment (as at AT&T: Myers, 1995) and paying inducements as lump sums (split at the beginning and end of the assignment) to simplify payroll administration and maintain incentives to complete (also AT&T: Myers, 1995).

Evaluating the return on expatriate investment

There is a consensus that the cost of expatriate assignments is high (Johnson, 2005; Bonache and Fernandez, 2005), but little research evaluating the return on investment (ROI), and a lack of definition as to what constitutes the 'success' or 'failure' of an expatriate assignment. This makes the calculation of a return on investment difficult. Latta (2003) suggests a stakeholder approach to defining success and failure in expatriate assignments. He identifies five groups each with their own criteria for success:

- senior management – contribution to business objectives; cost-effectiveness
- 'sending' management – flexibility and mobility of expatriates; cost-effectiveness at unit level
- 'receiving' management – as for 'sending' management
- human resources – satisfaction of internal customers' needs; ability to meet expatriates' needs; administrative simplicity; transparency of systems; ability to meet tax and legal compliance requirements in all countries
- expatriates – relocation with minimum disruption; satisfactory economic rewards on assignment; contribution of the assignment to future career.

Failure is equally difficult to define, but the most common causes of failure are:

- early return
- failure to meet assignment objectives
- integration problems at the assignment location – for example, management style, language, family problems, and cultural issues
- unmet career development objectives.

It may also be important to measure wider system problems because they may indicate flaws in the compensation package or approach chosen. These include the numbers of employees who refuse assignments and the retention rate of returning expatriates.

To establish the ROI the true costs of the assignment must be established (Johnson, 2005) including the costs of preparation training and recruitment. Added to these are the overhead administrative costs for both home-based and location-based support – for example, HR services. Clear and measurable objectives must be set for the assignment. This may be difficult when these might be as diffuse as enabling knowledge transfer in joint venture situations or establishing the company culture and values in a relocated unit. In the case of an assignment undertaken for development purposes, the key competencies to be developed can be identified and measured, but return only realised when put to work for the organisation. In this case, the measurement of retention on return becomes key to ROI. Bonache and Fernandez (2005) suggest using the theory of transaction costs and Bartlett and Goshal's (2000) objectives of international business – local responsiveness, global integration and developing innovation and organisational learning – to pursue a more strategic assessment of the return on expatriate investment. Assignment benefits include those from the actual assignment and knowledge transfer and the utilisation of experience on repatriation which is dependent on the retention of the employee.

CASE STUDY 27

CADBURY-SCHWEPPES' ASSIGNMENT POLICY

Context: one of the world's largest confectionary and soft drinks groups with a global workforce of approximately 38,000 and 140 employees on international assignments in 28 countries, mainly in Europe, the USA and Asia.

Base pay

- A balance-sheet approach is adopted to a home-base pay established at the outset of the assignment.
- An efficient purchaser-index cost-of-living allowance is applied.
- A location adjustment of up to 35% of gross basic salary is applied for difficult living conditions.
- A foreign service premium of 10% of gross basic salary.
- A tax equalisation is applied.
- An additional responsibility allowance may be paid if the expatriate assumes a role more senior than his/her base salary reflects. This is not consolidated into base pay.

Variable or contingent pay

- Annual incentive payment (AIP) based on host business unit performance, but applied to the home AIP target and calculated in the home currency.
- Expatriates continue in the home-country share plans.

Benefits

- Expatriate remains in home-country pension scheme.
- Where possible expatriate remains in the home-country social security scheme.
- A company car is provided subject to the host-country policy. An allowance may be paid if the expatriate does not qualify under the host policy.
- The company pays all costs and insurance relating to the shipping of a reasonable quantity of household goods.

- A relocation allowance of 10% of basic salary is paid at the beginning and end of the assignment for accompanied expatriates, 5% for unaccompanied.

- Medical and dental cover are provided.

- Travel is provided at economy for flights up to six hours, business class for longer flights, at the beginning and end of the assignment.

- Temporary accommodation costs are paid, if necessary, for up to six weeks at the beginning and end of the assignment.

- Accommodation is provided appropriate to seniority and family size. No assistance is given with the home property.

- Normal utility costs are paid – with the exception of personal telephone calls.

- Expatriates receive home- or host-country annual leave, whichever is the better.

- One return airfare per twelve months is provided for expatriate and family, under the same terms as the initial assignment flight.

- An allowance of up to £5,000 is available for spousal professional development.

- School fees and uniform costs are reimbursed according to agreed limits for children.

- In difficult living conditions the company may provide up to five days' additional leave and one extra flight.

- In markedly different cold-climate conditions a one-off contribution to appropriate clothing for the assignee and family may be made.

Non-financial benefits

- Cultural awareness training for expatriate and family.
- Language training.
- Pre-assignment trip with orientation programme.

Source: abbreviated from IDS Study No. 728, Special Issue on International Assignments

Case study tasks

1 Identify two areas in which the organisation could explore cost minimisation strategies.

2 Suggest ways in which the organisation could seek to enhance its non-financial benefits.

3 How would you evaluate whether the organisation was achieving 'value for money' from its expatriate investment?

Discussion questions

1 What would you see as the problems for the HR function associated with having employees on all four types of international assignment?

2   Why does the balance-sheet approach remain the most popular method for calculating expatriate reward packages?

3   How might flexible benefits contribute to an expatriate reward strategy?

3 GLOBAL REWARD STRATEGY

When an organisation becomes a 'global' player, the management of expatriate reward presents a more complex and substantial challenge (White, 2005). An organisation may have home employees based in several countries, employees from several countries in one location, and home- and third-country nationals in multiple locations. In addition, the organisation may be using all of the types of assignment outlined earlier in this chapter. Traditional forms of calculating expatriate compensation may no longer be 'fit for purpose' and a more strategic approach required. This approach must (Dowling and Welch, 2004):

■   recognise national differences in taxation, social security and standards of living

■   take into account the variations in culture and values which differentiate national attitudes to components of the total reward package

■   achieve administrative economy and support global strategy.

Other factors that influence the development of a global reward strategy include:

■   As organisations develop a cadre of managers with global careers, the maintenance of parity with 'home' becomes more difficult and costly (Watson and Gangeram, 2005; White, 2005).

■   The impact of highly paid expatriates on the morale of local managers in similar jobs, particularly when expatriate assignments are not time-bounded.

■   The growth of ad hoc compensation systems that have developed over time to deal with local issues. These eventually contain contradictory measures providing little integration with corporate strategy and also lack any internal integration and synergy (Stredwick, 2000).

A survey of 90 US and European multinationals (Mercer, 2004) found that 85% had a global strategy in place, 45% of them having had that strategy in place for less than four years. External factors, such as the development of the 'Euro zone', may also push organisations towards reconsidering their strategy on a more global basis. Many organisations have created a more centralised 'Euro band' within their global systems, and moved to harmonise benefits packages as disparities between countries in the zone have become more obvious and less easy to justify (Shonfield, 1999). Edwards and Rees (2006) see a concentration of global strategy at management levels such that the total value of managers' reward packages, however calculated, become 'increasingly detached from those of non-managerial employees'.

The objectives of a global reward strategy include:

■   the development of flexible systems that facilitate the effective movement of expatriates around the world (Watson and Gangeram, 2005; Dowling and Welch, 2004)

■   equity in pay for similar jobs across the globe

- cost-efficiency (Dowling and Welch, 2004)

- ease of management and administration (Burns, 2003)

- that it should reflect organisational structure, culture, values and strategy (Krupp, 2002; Dowling and Welch; 2004; Stredwick, 2000)

- that it should attract and retain a global cadre of employees (Edwards and Rees, 2006)

- that it should facilitate different forms of international working

- that it should be able to react and develop as the organisations develops.

A successful global reward strategy must ensure a balance between organisational consistency and local compatibility. This requires the organisation to research and understand a number of the issues and prevailing conditions that will impact on local implementation and effective operation, thus acquiring a substantial amount of local information (see the box below).

RESEARCHING NATIONAL INFORMATION

Economic conditions – levels of economic growth: inflation, and unemployment; the level of taxation; national insurance costs; government agendas relating to employment

The legal environment – terms and conditions; minimum wage legislation; equal pay legislation; working time information; holidays; sickness benefit; pensions; maternity/ paternity pay and leave; premium rates of pay; social security levels; health coverage. Labour legislation

Local labour market information – benchmark comparisons against potential competitors' pay and benefit levels; skills levels and shortages; educational system levels and output; standards of working practices; local mobility

Pay practices – standard components of benefit packages; payroll practices; cultural acceptance of the various forms of contingent and variable pay; stock/share plans.

Balancing the tensions between achieving the benefits of a global strategy and the requirements to comply with national mandatory requirements is one of the key difficulties encountered by organisations (Edwards and Rees, 2006). Global consistency offers the advantages of transparency, ease of communication, ease of design, and internal equity, and it facilitates mobility. The disadvantages of being unresponsive to local labour market conditions include inefficient use of company resources by offering standard benefits that are not culturally valued locally or utilising systems that will be ineffective because of lack of cultural 'fit' (White, 2005).

Local market design offers external equity and local labour market responsiveness, a more effective use of resources and application of systems, but lacks the advantages of transparency, is more challenging to both communication and mobility, and is more complex to design. Lowe *et al* (2002) report that a recent 'best practices in international HRM' study suggests that 'understanding what employees from a given culture want from a compensation system rather than replicating current cultural norms might be a more effective way of designing global systems'.

Differential approaches to this issue exist, as becomes more evident during acquisitions. Some organisations go to great lengths to reflect national culture and even variations within a country, particularly in countries which cover a vast geographical area with many different cultures.

Others absorb an acquisition into their existing compensation processes as a matter of priority, seeing integration as a way to maximise competitive edge.

Some organisations may seek accommodation from national governments, in terms of their adoption of strategies not consistent with national policy, by using the substantial leverage that the intention to locate or invest within a country offers (Fox and Phillips, 2003). Conversely, the use of global strategies may be limited by factors such as collective bargaining and the statutory representation of employees – although some companies (notably McDonald's) go to great efforts to try to avoid employee representation in any form (Edwards and Rees, 2006). Other strategies – such as pay for performance – may be limited by varying levels of managerial capability in the subsidiary units.

Reconciling these competing factors requires strategic accommodation. Milkovitch and Bloom (1998) suggest a threefold approach, using strategic flexibility to balance transactional (financial) with relational (non-financial) returns to develop commitment to common values while reflecting multiple employment relationships that reflect local needs. The first element is base salary which reflects organisational values, although these may be interpreted to reflect local market values. The second element is the 'crafted' menu of compensation strategies that enable each operating unit to gain advantage in its operational market. The final element, the 'choice' strategies, offers flexibility to individuals as in flexible benefits. Milkovitch and Bloom suggest the need to realign total reward strategy to gain maximum advantage, a promotion of 'joined up' thinking in reward.

Developing a global reward strategy

Base pay
Base pay should reflect the organisation's values and key objectives of its reward strategy. These decisions must be framed to guide but not constrain local circumstances. One such decision is the positioning of base pay in relation to the labour market. For example, Glaxo-Wellcome (Stredwick, 2000) made a strategic decision to place its salaries in the upper quartile of the labour market in order to be able to attract and retain the best-qualified research staff. This decision can be implemented in relation to each national labour market cost-effectively, thus adhering to a global strategy without a 'one size fits all' approach. Structures must be flexible enough to contain the various units in the organisation, and broad bands can help to facilitate this (Fox and Phillips, 2003). Volkswagen and ICL use job evaluation based on competencies, whereas Texton uses skills-based pay to achieve maximum flexibility (Stredwick, 2000). Even those organisations which pursue a policy of international consistency in all aspects of their business – such as McDonald's – find that in order to compete in the local labour markets they have to pay local rates, thus in Scandinavia pay is about 50% higher than in the UK.

In the case of senior managers, fewer constraints exist to inhibit a global approach. Briscoe and Schuler (2004) advocate a strategy of classifying all employees above a certain level as 'international' and applying a global approach to all aspects of their reward package. For those employees classified as 'local' the application of a global strategy may simply consist of decisions in principle, such as where the organisation will position itself in the labour market, the mechanisms used to structure pay, and its stance on issues of equality.

Variable or contingent pay
At senior levels organisations' pay for performance schemes are more widely used to achieve managerial commitment to a consistent set of values, objectives and performance indicators.

There is some evidence that in the 'international cadre' of managers variable or contingent pay is becoming a more significant proportion of total reward. Figures quoted range from 10 to 50% both individual performance-related pay and financial participation schemes being utilised. At lower levels, pay-for-performance strategies are more likely to reflect national values.

There has been a trend in recent years for financial participation schemes to be rolled out internationally, particularly stock option plans. The objectives are to achieve increased employee commitment, to enhance entrepreneurial attitudes and to gain increased cooperation in 'partnership' via a financial high-involvement strategy (Poutsma *et al*, 2003). The potential for this is limited by legal constraints. In some countries the private ownership of shares is illegal. Others are constrained by national cultures that do not easily recognise the concept, as in Greece. DuPont found that in 25 of the 53 countries in which it operated laws banned or limited the ownership of foreign shares. Conversely, in the USA and many European countries stock ownership is encouraged and incentivised by tax law to a greater or lesser extent. Government objectives appear to be the wider distribution of wealth and the enhancement of organisational competitiveness (Poutsma *et al*, 2003). There is evidence of greater interest in stock options from emerging, developing and developed economies, and it has been identified as an area of future growth in international reward (Briscoe and Schuler, 2004).

Benefits

The benefits package represents a significant cost to employers and a substantial value to employees but is one of the most complex and variable areas of reward. This is because it interacts with the organisation's systems, with regulating authorities, with employees, and with trade unions (Oliver and Cravens, 2001) in each country. It therefore presents a challenging issue in expanding global operations (Hempel, 1998).

The organisation has to decide whether the benefits package should be developed locally or be delivered using a standard or global approach across the organisation as a whole (Frazee, 1997). GE, for example, uses local plans designed to meet labour market practice in each company. In one survey (Asinta, 2003, n = 77, in 44 countries) 21% of the companies surveyed offered a global benefits package whereas 73% of companies used locally designed packages. However, 69% of these reported seriously considering a move to a global benefits package within the next few years.

The advantages of taking a local perspective include the ability to reflect local norms and expectations as to what the benefits package should contain, particularly where it is subject to union negotiation (Jeske, 1997). The package can also be constructed to compete more effectively in the local labour market, as well as to incorporate the differing mandatory requirements in each country (Oliver and Cravens, 2001). Standard or global packages can be more cost-efficient through the pooling of risk in areas such as life insurance and healthcare, and can promote the culture and values of the organisation internationally (Taft and Powell, 2005).

Healthcare is one of the benefits most susceptible to change, for two major reasons. Firstly, more governments are opting out of healthcare provision, especially in Europe, as medical costs rise faster than inflation (LaSorte, 1996; Frazee, 1997). And secondly, in many areas provision is inadequate in terms both of the quality and of the time taken to access care.

Healthcare costs are a growing concern (Jeske, 1997) and organisations are using a number of strategies to achieve cost containment. These include managed care, including the use of preferred suppliers (Frazee, 1997; Jeske, 1997), self-insurance by organisations, networked insurance plans using global providers, health education, international administration to lower costs, and benchmarking competitors.

Pensions are perhaps the most difficult area of benefits to contain within a global benefits strategy. They are extremely costly, subject to very different mandatory conditions and the legal position in any country can be complex. Conversely, together with life assurance, pensions are one of the areas in which it is possible to gain substantial cost savings in both administration and premiums by consolidating national plans with an international provider, without necessarily reducing benefits for members (Taft and Powell, 2005).

Annual holidays are often mandated and have immense national variation. They range from an entitlement after one year's service from six days in Mexico to 31 days in Denmark. Global strategy usually consists of a minimum annual allowance or the mandatory national allowance, whichever is the greater. Maternity, paternity and family leave, with or without pay but with guaranteed retention of employment, is mandatory in about two thirds of all nations, including most developed countries. Costs may be borne by the government, the employer or both, but the amount of leave varies from six weeks in Australia to 28 weeks in Denmark. An interesting anomaly here is the USA in which this benefit is still not fully provided in all states.

Flexible benefit plans, which originated in the USA, are now becoming more popular worldwide and may provide a mechanism to forward global strategy in benefits as well as catering for the diversity in individual needs and national differences.

Non-financial benefits

Recognition of the significance and exchange value of non-financial benefits in the reward package is of relatively recent origin and little real research exists to guide organisations, but it is an area of increasing creativity. A scarcity of talent worldwide has led employers to pay attention to this area in order to 'brand' the organisation as an 'employer of choice', acknowledging that financial rewards alone will not attract the best employees (Zingheim and Schuster, 2002). The importance of the psychological contract is accepted, and strategies in the areas of involvement, communication, career development, flexibility, work–life balance and training and development all form a part of this section of total reward. It is also the area with the least constraint, and organisations can more easily implement truly global systems in areas such as talent development and performance appraisal. This approach is often explicit within corporate objectives, as in Serono (Coleman and Chambers, 2005), a medical research and drug manufacturing organisation which has an objective of 'creating a work environment that attracts the best talent'.

Managing reward on a global basis

As global reward becomes more complex the administrative and management control systems must be robust enough to meet the requirements of organisational strategies and of the numbers of international assignees (Burns, 2003; Crandall, 1992), and flexible enough to cope with the variation in types of international assignment. Because pay requires robust administrative and control systems, it is more conducive to being extended to units or subsidiaries in other countries (Edwards and Rees, 2006).

The objectives of administrative and management control systems vary but almost certainly include (Danielson and Stagnitta, 2005):

- to reduce the administrative burden
- to link effectively with corporate accounting and payroll systems
- to improve processing times of transactions
- to meet the requirements for income tax and social insurance

- to provide clear cost information for control purposes
- to provide timely and accurate information for corporate reporting
- to keep track of diverse international assignments.

At regular intervals an organisation may 'outgrow' its management system. Major international changes, such as the introduction of the euro in 2002 (Cummins, 2002; Shonfield, 1999), may reveal the inadequacies of systems and the need for administrative savings. Challenges to communication may necessitate updating or replacement of the system. Issues involved in the design and selection of a new system involve planning to ensure a smooth transition, system definition, links to other systems, the timing of the changeover, communication and information for employees (Crandall, 1992), costs, and the adaptation of policies to include changes necessitated by the new systems.

Discussion questions

1   Summarise the arguments for and against a global reward strategy.

2   List and describe three ways in which a global approach to benefits can gain cost savings without reducing value to employees.

3   Why is it easier to adopt a global strategy for senior managers' reward than it is for other employees' reward?

CONCLUSIONS AND FUTURE ISSUES

In this chapter we have examined the different and changing international contexts in which organisations are required to develop their reward strategies, and explored some of the key decisions that they have to make and some of the alternatives available to them. Although it may be true that globalisation, and the convergence it will inevitably bring, will reduce some of the complexities of managing reward internationally, other issues are likely to emerge to increase this complexity. These may include the increasing importance of knowledge transfer, innovation and organisational learning across national boundaries, the increasing number of women expatriates and dual-career couples, and the changing role of expatriates as localisation becomes a more cost-effective option. All of these will present challenges to those tasked with developing reward strategies.

Although there is a large body of literature and research in the field of international reward, much of it is concentrated in the area of expatriate reward, and there remain substantial gaps. Aside from the developing areas outlined below, further research could usefully examine, *inter alia*, the integration of compensation in international acquisitions, mergers and joint ventures, the evaluation of expatriate reward strategies, and approaches to reward in voluntary organisations and SMEs operating internationally. Finally, although the reward practices of many countries are detailed in IDS International Documents, there is little research in some of the developing countries, particularly those in Africa and some parts of Latin and Central America.

As research in these (and other) areas develops it is to be hoped that those managers responsible for international reward strategies will have an increasingly solid and broad evidence base on which to draw.

CASE STUDY 28

INTRODUCING A GLOBAL REWARD STRATEGY AT ANYWHERE CORPORATION

Anywhere is a high-tech multinational that has grown rapidly over the last ten years by acquisition. It operates in 58 countries and employs 40,000 staff worldwide.

Until two years ago its structure was fragmented and strategy decentralised to the local units. In the past two years a new structure has been integrated which has established business units in each location dealing with all company products for that country or region. Some subsidiary company names have been retained for marketing purposes but the majority have gone. A global job structure has been introduced, based on job families and broad bands to give maximum flexibility to recruit and retain the highly skilled knowledge-rich workforce. A global total reward strategy has been introduced by a full-time multinational project group who have put great emphasis on communication and consultation.

Base pay is market-focused, which has required each job group to have its own defined labour market category. There are four in all:

- local – the lowest-paid workers who are all drawn from a defined radius from the operating unit

- regional – the second tier of labour market, defined by travelling times to the unit by car and public transport

- national – these are employees, mainly professional and managerial, who would relocate to move jobs

- international – this comprises senior management roles for which there is an international demand – senior staff who are willing to move countries for jobs both within and outside the company.

The major issue with this exercise has been the difficulty in obtaining data worldwide.

Variable or contingent pay

- short-term pay – At unit management level this is a pay-for-performance scheme linked to individual capability and contribution to unit objectives defined by operational and financial measures.
  For employees below management level an individual performance-related pay scheme was introduced.
  The performance indicators for both schemes are drawn from the organisation's balanced scorecard which is devolved to business units and then devolved within each unit utilised by the performance management scheme.

- long-term pay – No long-term incentives are available below management level. Those that were in place under the previous structure have been closed and a new share option scheme introduced for management. They constitute a higher proportion of senior management pay, thus tying more closely to business performance in the marketplace.

Benefits
A worldwide flexible benefits scheme has been introduced which allows individuals to select their own benefits package online to suit their needs. Points are awarded to reflect base salary and service as a retention tool. One striking feature is the abolition of company cars for all including the CEO. The company has negotiated an advantageous lease-buy scheme which is open to all employees within their points. The only exception to this is where transport is required for personal security reasons. Local mandatory provision above the minimum outlined in the strategy is reflected in the points awarded to each employee.

Work environment
This section of the reward package has a focus on individual growth, career development at all levels and recognition for outstanding contribution. For example, there are stock option awards for important contributions by Research and Development staff.

The organisation has introduced a standard family-friendly policy which is different from the existing policies and on the whole more generous.

Throughout the whole period of the introduction of the new reward strategy an emphasis was placed on communication and consultation. A member of the integration team was drawn from each country and a member of the senior management team from headquarters visited each site at least once.

The introduction went well – but there were still some lessons to be learned.

Case study tasks

1   The area that gave the most problems was short-term pay for performance. Why do you think that was?

2   Can you pick out those areas of the reward package employees will find most difficult to understand?

3   What could the organisation have done to avoid these problems?

REFERENCES

Allard L. A. C. (1996) 'Managing globe-trotting expats', *Management Review*, May, Vol. 85, No. 5: 38–43.

Anonymous (2003) 'Global stock options: a complex tax issue', *HR Focus,* Vol. 80, No. 5: 4–5.

Asinta (2003) *Global Benefit Strategies Survey*, available at: *www.clearpoint.com/pe/asinta.pdf* [accessed November].

Bartlett C. and Goshal S. (2000) *Transnational Management: Text, cases and readings in cross-border management* (3rd edition). Boston: McGraw-Hill.

Baruch Y. (2004) *Managing Careers: Theory and practice*. Harlow: FT/Prentice Hall.

Blau G. and Bordia P. (1998) 'Pay referent comparison and pay level satisfaction in private versus public sector organisations in India', *International Journal of Human Resource Management*, Vol. 9, No. 1: 155–67.

Bonache J. and Fernandez Z. (1997) 'Expatriate compensation and its link to the subsidiary strategic role: a theoretical analysis', *International Journal of Human Resource Management*, Vol. 8, No. 4: 457–75.

Bonache J. and Fernandez Z. (2005) 'International compensation: costs and benefits of international assignments', in H. Scullion and M. Lineham, *International Human Resource Management: A critical text*. Basingstoke: Palgrave Macmillan.

Bonache J., Brewster C. and Suutari V. (2001) 'Expatriation: a developing research agenda', *Thunderbird International Review*, Vol. 43, No. 1: 3–20.

Briscoe D. R. and Schuler R. S. (2004) *International Human Resource Management* (2nd edition). Oxford: Routledge.

Burns S. M. (2003) 'Flexible international assignee compensation plans', *Compensation and Benefits Review*, May-June, Vol. 35, No. 3: 35–44.

Chiang F. (2005) 'A critical examination of Hofstede's thesis and its application to international reward management', *International Journal of Human Resource Management*, Vol. 16, No. 9: 1545–63.

Coleman T. and Chambers T. (2005) 'Serono case study: global performance, evaluations and compensation', *Compensation and Benefits Review*, Vol. 37, No. 4: 61–5.

Crandall L. P. (1992) 'Getting Through the global pay maze', *Personnel Journal*, Vol. 71, No. 8: 76–8.

Cummins S. (2002) 'The implications of the euro for expatriate policies and practices', *Compensation and Benefits Review*, July-August, Vol. 34, No. 4: 6–13.

Danielson T. A. and Stagnitta S. V. (2005) 'Beyond pay: administrative hotspots of international HR management', *Mobility*, February: 71–5.

Dowling P. J. and Welch D. E. (2004) *International Human Resource Management: Managing people in a multinational context* (4th edition). Cincinnati, OH: South-Western College Publishing.

Dowling P. J., Welch D. E. and Schuler R. S. (1999) *International Human Resource Management: Managing people in a multinational context*. Cincinnati, OH: South-Western College Publishing

Dunn B. and Rumberger J. C. (1996) 'Equity-based compensation plans for multinationals: compensation in a worldwide environment', *Tax Executive*, Sept.-Oct., Vol. 48, No. 5: 373–80.

Edwards T. and Rees C. (2006) *International Human Resource Management: Globalisation, national systems and multinational companies*. Dorchester: FT/Prentice Hall.

Engle A. D. and Mendenhall M. E. (2004) 'Transnational roles, transnational rewards: global integration in compensation', *Employee Relations*, Vol. 26, No. 6: 613–25.

Fenwick M. (2004) 'International compensation and performance management', in A. W. Harzing and J. Van Rysseveldt, *International Human Resource Management* (2nd edition). Trowbridge: Sage.

Fox M.A. and Phillips L. (2003) 'Competitive strategy in transnational organisations', *Management Decision*, Vol. 41, No. 5: 465–76.

Frazee V. (1997) 'It's inevitable: managed care is going global', *Global Workforce*, Vol. 76, No. 1: 24–9.

Frazee V. (1998a) 'Keeping your expatriates happy', *Global Workforce*, Vol. 6: 18–23.

Frazee V. (1998b) 'Is the balance sheet right for your expats?', *Workforce*, Vol. 3, No. 5: 19–22.

Galbraith J. K. and Kum H. (2003) 'Inequality and economic growth: a global view based on measures of pay', *CESifo Economic Studies*, 49: 527–56.

Grand C. (2005) 'The wage policy of firms: comparative evidence from the United States and Germany from personnel data', *International Journal of Human Resource Management*, Vol. 16, No. 1: 104–19.

Gupta A. K. and Govindarajan V. (1991) 'Knowledge flows and the structure of control within multinational corporations', *Academy of Management Review*, Vol. 16, No. 4: 768–92.

Harris H., Brewster C. and Sparrow P. (2003) *International Human Resource Management*. London: CIPD.

Hempel P. S. (1998) 'Designing multinational benefits programmes: the role of national culture', *Journal of World Business*, Vol. 33, No. 3: 277–88.

Herod R. (1997) 'Integrating expatriate and local national compensation', *Benefits and Compensation International*, Vol. 26, No. 10: 14–18.

Hofstede G. (1991) *Cultures and Organisations: Software of the mind*. London: McGraw-Hill.

Hume D. A. (1995) *Reward Management*. Oxford: Blackwell.

IDS (2002) *International Assignments*. Special Issue No. 728, May. London: Income Data Services Ltd.

Jeske H. J. (1997) 'A global healthcare prescription', *Business Insurance*, Vol. 3, No. 38: 35–7.

Johnson L. (2005) 'Measuring international return on investment', *Compensation and Benefits Review*, March/April, Vol. 37, No. 2: 50–4.

Krupp N. B. (2002) 'Global compensation planning – establishing and maintaining a competitive edge', *Compensation and Benefits Management*, Vol. 18, No. 2: 54–6.

LaSorte J. A. (1996) 'The next front in healthcare', *Financial Executive*, July-August: 39–41.

Latta G. W. (1998) 'Expatriate incentives: beyond tradition', *HR Focus*, Vol. 75, No. 3: 53–4.

Latta G. W. (1999) 'Expatriate policy and practice: a ten-year comparison of trends', *Compensation and Benefits Review*, Vol. 31, No. 4: 35–9.

Latta G. W. (2003) 'Expatriate compensation policies and programs: how do you measure performance?', *ORC Worldwide*, www.worldatwork.org.

Long R. J. and Shields J. L. (2005) 'Performance pay in Canadian and Australian firms: a comparative study', *International Journal of Human Resource Management*, Vol. 26, No. 10: 1783–1811.

Lowe K., Milliman J., De Cieri H. and Dowling P. (2002) 'International compensation practices: a ten-country comparative analysis', *Human Resource Management*, Vol. 41, No. 1: 45–66.

Mercer Consulting (2003) *International Assignment Survey*. Mercer Human Resource Consulting, www.mercerhr.com.

Mercer Consulting (2004) *Global Strategy Survey*. Mercer Human Resource Consulting, www.mercerhr.com.

Milkovitch G. T. and Bloom M. (1998) 'Rethinking international compensation', *Compensation and Benefits Review*, Vol. 30, No. 1: 15–23.

Misano G. and Del Boca A. (2004) 'Profit-related pay in Italy', *International Journal of Manpower*, Vol. 25, No. 5: 463–78.

Myers R. (1995) 'When in Rome, pay as the Romans pay', *CFO*, Vol. 11, No. 10: 93–5.

Oliver G. S. and Cravens K. S. (2001) 'An international comparison of employee welfare plans', *Thunderbird International Business Review*, Vol. 43, No. 4: 501–24.

Orcworldwide (2005a) *Global Survey of Short Term International Assignment Policies*, www.orcworldwide.com/surveys/shortterm.html, 14 June 2005.

Orcworldwide (2005b) *Global Survey of Expatriate Housing Policies*, www.orcworldwide.com/surveys/housing.html, 14 June 2005.

Peters S. (1994) 'Expatriates pay exceeds nationals' in Central and Eastern Europe', *Personnel Journal*, Vol. 73, No. 5: 19–20.

Poutsma E., De Nijs W. and Poole M. (2003) 'The global phenomenon of employee financial participation', *International Journal of Human Resource Management*, Vol. 14, No. 6: 855–62.

Reynolds C. (1997) 'Expatriate compensation in historical perspective', *Journal of World Business*, Summer, Vol. 32, No. 2: 118–33.

Rueda D. and Pontusson J. (2000) 'Wage inequality and varieties of capitalism', *World Politics*, Vol. 52, No. 3: 350–83.

Schuler R. S. and Rogovsky N. (1998) 'Understanding compensation practice variations across firms: the impact of national culture', *Journal of International Business Studies*, Vol. 29, No. 1: 139–77.

Shen J. (2005) 'Effective international performance appraisals: easily said, hard to do', *Compensation and Benefits Review*, Vol. 37, No. 4: 70–9.

Shonfield D. (1999) 'The euro's impact on pay and HR policies', *Compensation and Benefits Review*, July-August, Vol. 31, No. 4: 75–9.

Sims R. H. and Schroeder M. (2005) 'Expatriate compensation: an exploratory review of salient contextual factors and common practices', *Career Development International*, Vol. 10, No. 2: 98–108.

Sparrow P. R. (2000) 'International reward management', in G. White and J. Drucker (eds) *Reward Management: A critical text*. London: Routledge.

Stredwick J. (2000) 'Aligning rewards to organisational goals – a multinational experience', *European Business Review*, Vol. 12, No. 1: 9–18.

Suutari V. and Tornikoski C. (2001) 'The challenge of expatriate compensation: the sources of satisfaction and dissatisfaction among expatriates', *International Journal of Human Resource Management*, Vol. 12, No. 3: 389–404.

Taft F. P. and Powell C. (2005) 'The European pension and benefits environment: a complex ecology', *Compensation and Benefits Review*, Vol. 13, No. 1: 37–50.

Thierry H. (1998) 'Compensating work', in P. J. D. Drenth, H. Thierry and C. J. De Wolf (eds) *Handbook of Work and Organisational Psychology*, Volume 4: *Organisational Psychology*. Brighton: Psychology Press.

Valle R., Martin F. and Romero P. M. (2001) 'Trends and emerging values in human resource management: the Spanish scene', *International Journal of Management*, Vol. 22, No. 3: 244–51.

Watson B. W. and Gangeram S. (2005) 'Global pay systems and compensation in support of a multinational strategy', *Compensation and Benefits Review*, Vol. 37, No. 1: 33–6.

White R. (2005) 'A strategic approach to building a consistent global rewards program', *Compensation and Benefits Review*, Vol. 37, No. 4: 23–40.

Zingheim P. K. and Schuster J. R. (2002 'Pay changes going forward', *Compensation and Benefits Review*, Vol. 34, No. 4: 48–53.

Regulation and employment relations

Employee voice

CHAPTER 10

Hamish Mathieson and Andrew Pendleton

CHAPTER OBJECTIVES

When you have read this chapter you should be able to:

- list the meanings of 'employee voice'

- outline the various rationales for employee voice

- identify the dimensions and forms of employee voice

- analyse trends in employee voice in an international context, and the factors that influence them

- appreciate the important role played by institutions in mediating the effects of wider environmental forces

- evaluate contemporary initiatives designed to extend employee voice in a transnational context.

PURPOSE AND SCOPE

This chapter examines employee voice in an international context, focusing primarily on the themes of globalisation and convergence and divergence, but also touching on cultural variation, emerging economies and EU enlargement. The meaning of 'voice' is defined. There is then a discussion of humanistic, power-sharing and efficiency justifications for voice. The main dimensions of voice and features of particular voice mechanisms are discussed. A framework for analysing developments in voice within an international context is suggested. International trends in employee voice are reviewed and explanations given. Attention is paid to voice within multinational companies. The chapter concludes by considering the future of employee voice against a background of globalisation. Various attempts to extend employee voice transnationally are discussed.

1 INTRODUCTION TO EMPLOYEE VOICE

Employee voice can be defined as the ability for employees to have an input into decisions that are made in organisations. It is something of an umbrella term that is 'increasingly used to cover a whole variety of processes and structures which enable, and at times empower, employees, directly and indirectly, to contribute to decision-making in the firm, and occasionally in the wider society' (Boxall and Purcell, 2003: 162).

Voice can take a variety of forms, and serve a number of functions (Dundon *et al*, 2004). First, it can be the expression of individual dissatisfaction, with the aim of resolving a specific grievance. Second, it can be an expression of collective organisation among employees aimed at correcting imbalances in employee–employer power-holding. Third, voice may contribute to management decision-making by facilitating improvements in work organisation, quality and productivity. Fourth, voice may take the form of mutuality and partnership with the aim of achieving long-term viability for the organisation. In the first and second cases voice is expressed around an essentially 'contested agenda', whereas in the third and fourth instances it is expressed within the context of a 'shared agenda' (Wilkinson *et al*, 2004).

Rationales for voice articulation

In his discussion of organisational participation Strauss (1998: 8–14) presents a threefold justification for employee voice.

1   Voice is advocated on *humanistic* grounds. By developing voice mechanisms, organisations can satisfy employees' non-pecuniary needs for creativity, achievement and social approval, thereby contributing to self-actualisation. For employees, 'having a voice in how they do their work may be as important as how much they are paid for it' (p.8).

2   Voice can rest on a *power-sharing* rationale embedded in democratic values. This view of voice rejects autocratic authority relationships and related 'command-and-control' management practices as incompatible with the democratic ethos. Advocates of this approach have seen voice as an important element of 'industrial democracy'. For some, industrial democracy is about a new economic order in which workers secure control over the means of production and become the decision-takers in industry. For others, it has a more limited meaning. Industrial democracy is seen as workers' participation in management, a means of influence over management decisions.

3   Employee voice may be justified because of its *impact on organisational efficiency*. In economies where employee knowledge is becoming more critical to competitive success, the capacity for employees to share this knowledge with management (and other employees) can have a substantial effect on organisational performance. The process of information-sharing may also enhance employees' commitment to the organisation, leading to better work performance and lower employee turnover. Hirschman (1970) argued that voice can be a positive efficiency-enhancing alternative to employee 'exit' where employees are dissatisfied with some aspect of their jobs. In a similar vein, Freeman and Medoff (1984) show how unions can aid efficiency and productivity by providing voice mechanisms, which 'safeguard investments in training, provide an impetus towards more efficient management and even through raising the minimum costs of labour provide incentives towards efficiency-increasing technical progress and investment' (Rubery and Grimshaw, 2003: 50).

Discussion questions

1   What are the relative strengths of the 'humanistic', power-sharing' and 'organisational efficiency' rationales for extending employee voice in decision-making?

2   Employee voice may be viewed as one of the principal contributors to the quality of an employee relations system. What might other elements be?

3   What are the potential business benefits which accompany the articulation of employee voice?

2 DIMENSIONS OF EMPLOYEE VOICE

Although employee voice can be reduced to simple terms of 'having a say' or 'exercising influence' in decision-making, there is considerable variation both within and between countries in the ways that voice may be expressed.

In analysing this diversity a helpful starting point is the degree or depth of employee influence or voice over final decision-making. The strength of employee voice may range from *none*, through relatively *low* degrees represented in the receipt of information and two-way communications, to *medium* intensity via more influential representative-based forms of consultation and collective bargaining. A *high* degree of voice occurs in the (rare) circumstances where employees exercise full control over decisions. The absence of employee voice reflects the exercise of managerial prerogative while low-intensity voice is characterised by a lack of active involvement in the decision-making process. By contrast consultation and collective bargaining permit employee representatives to exert, respectively, advisory and co-decision-making influence. Employee control over higher-level decisions is typically confined to workers' cooperatives (Blyton and Turnbull, 2004; Marchington *et al*, 2001).

It is usual to distinguish also between forms of employee voice, and a common contrast is between direct and indirect forms of employee voice systems:

- *Direct voice* means 'that the individual employee takes over or is drawn into certain managerial decisions which have traditionally been taken by management alone' (Knudsen, 1995: 5). The other main feature is the largely localised orientation of voice around 'lower-level' decisions at workplace and department levels concerning the organisation and performance of the immediate work task. Direct voice mechanisms operate within the predominantly unitarist rationale of employee involvement initiated by management.

- *Indirect voice* refers to the participation of employees collectively in decision-making through reliance on union or non-union representatives to deal indirectly with management on their behalf. Indirect voice mechanisms operate within a predominantly pluralist rationale and are initiated and sustained mainly by trade unions and legislation.

A further dimension is the focus of employee voice. Boxall and Purcell (2003: 168–9) identify three types of decision:

- *Power-centred* decisions focus on the authority of management and the context within which operational decisions are made. Here the focus is management strategy and policy decisions.

- *Task-centred* decisions focus on the operational work situation and particular jobs.

- *Ownership-centred* decisions focus on employees' economic participation in the enterprise.

This suggests a framework for analysis which combines forms of voice mechanisms in terms of different sorts of decisions.

Direct voice

Power-centred direct

Direct voice can be articulated in power-centred forms. First, *disclosure of information* to employees, whether through face-to-face briefings or via written or electronic media, ranks as the weakest of the direct voice forms. However, it qualifies for inclusion because although the provision of information in itself does not bestow any influence over decision-making, it may provide the foundations for gaining influence in the future. As Knudsen remarks, 'If employees do not know the plans of management, they are also unable to influence them' (1995: 9). Attitude survey findings may feed into senior managerial deliberations on employment strategy decisions.

Task-centred direct

Second, there are a range of task-centred *upward problem-solving* techniques such as suggestion schemes, project teams and quality improvement groups which are concerned to encourage employees to voice their opinions and views, either individually or in small groups, in generating ideas to help solve operational production problems rather than to contribute to employment policy formulation.

On the other hand task-centred *delegative participation*, reflecting the adoption of a 'responsible autonomy' strategy, may be seen as a potentially more powerful vehicle for employee voice than its 'consultative' counterpart because responsibility for the organisation of work is placed directly in employees' hands and is not an advisory (and possibly discontinuous) process wherein management retains the final decision. The principal ways for achieving delegative participation are through *semi-autonomous work groups* and *self-managed teamworking* the combined features of which – responsibility for a complete task, working without direct supervision, discretion over work methods and time, encouragement for team members to organise and multi-skill, influence over recruitment to the team – lead Marchington and Wilkinson (2000) to describe these forms of direct participation as management's most radical initiatives, 'most notably in terms of the centrality to the work processes and the level and scope of subject matter which are within the control of employees' (2000: 349).

Ownership-centred direct

Direct employee voice can also be articulated in terms of individualised forms of ownership. Employees may acquire shares in the company in which they work, possibly through company schemes. Once shares are fully held by employees, they have certain rights, such as the right to vote their share (assuming it is a voting share) and to attend the company Annual General Meeting. The practical significance of this is limited in most cases because the proportion of equity owned by employees tends to be small.

Indirect voice

Indirect voice can also be articulated through power-centred, task-centred and ownership-centred mechanisms.

Power-centred indirect

This voice mechanism has traditionally been exercised through trade unions and collective bargaining machinery. Trade unions exist in most countries, but there are big differences in their role and influence, and in general the European countries are more unionised than others (Harris *et al*, 2003). In many European countries unions are recognised as social partners, working alongside government and employers' bodies in the regulation of employment, and as we have seen, the concept of social partnership has been adopted by the EU. In the USA there is a strong anti-union feeling amongst many employers, although the union role is important in some industries and in some parts of the country. In Japan the large companies usually deal with a single employer-based union. In autocratic regimes unions may be creatures of the state, or a centre for political opposition. In some countries there is a unified national union movement, whereas in others the union movement is divided on ethnic or religious lines. While these national differences can be described, it is more difficult to measure and compare the *effective* influence of unions, since this is dependent on perceptions within different cultures (Harris *et al*, 2003: 117).

Collective power-centred employee voice may also be expressed through representative channels other than trade unions and collective bargaining. Employee representatives (who may or may not be union members) may have the opportunity to exercise voice on behalf of their constituents via *consultation*, which takes place in employer-created bodies such as joint consultative committees and company councils, or via legislatively created works councils. Similarly employee reps, whether affiliated to a union or not, are afforded *co-decision-making* powers through legislatively created employee/worker-director arrangements and works councils in a number of continental European countries.

Task-centred indirect

Indirect employee voice *centred on the immediate work task* may be exerted through employee representatives who succeed in building a strong bargaining relationship with departmental managers. The strength of voice over decisions on issues such as job allocation and staffing levels depends, however, on the power resources that work groups possess, which in turn are related to a range of factors such as the position of the group in the production process.

Ownership-centred indirect

Indirect voice may also be articulated through *ownership-centred channels*. First, there are employee share ownership plans (ESOPs) in which shares are held by trustees of an employee benefit trust, and these trustees may be directly elected by the employees. Apart from the financial investment, this form of ownership can provide for indirect representative voice and co-decision-making, although this does not always happen (see Pendleton, 2001). Second, the most extensive form of ownership-centred voice is found in the worker cooperative firm where in theory employees have an equal say in making major decisions and enjoy overall control of the organisation.

Discussion questions

1 How is the extent of employee influence related to managerial control strategies?

2 Is the aim of facilitating the expression of employee voice a matter of concentrating on direct or indirect forms, or a mixture of both?

3 Analyse your own work organisation (or one with which you are familiar) in terms of the framework discussed above. What accounts for the pattern of employee voice that you have revealed?

---

3 EMPLOYEE VOICE IN AN INTERNATIONAL CONTEXT – FRAMEWORK FOR ANALYSIS

Employee voice differs considerably between countries. For instance, in Germany – a 'coordinated market economy' – employees enjoy strong voice based on extensive legal rights, whereas in the UK – a 'liberal market economy' – employees have had much fewer powers. In Germany, indirect employee voice occurs through a 'dual channel' system involving collective bargaining on the one hand and codetermination through works councils and employee representation on supervisory boards on the other. The UK, by contrast, has had a single-channel system as far as indirect voice is concerned. In the USA firms have either a union-based system of indirect participation, in which unions have won certification elections, or a non-union system of participation, typically involving mainly direct forms of participation.

Corporate and expatriate managers from multinational companies originating in countries with strong unions may have no difficulty in operating in other countries where unions are strong. However, managers from multinationals who do not recognise unions may find dealing with unions elsewhere difficult, and will have to rely on the expertise of local managers. There are some multinationals, mostly from the USA, with a corporate philosophy that is opposed to unions and any collective representation, and headquarters managers from such enterprises may have difficulty in reconciling their corporate approach to ER with legal or social requirements in other countries. McDonald's (Royle, 2002) is a good example of a US company that when established in European countries with legal requirements related to union recognition and employee consultation, has tried to ignore the law or to implement it so that employee representation is ineffective. A common view of US managers is that employees will not feel the need for representation by an independent union or works council if they are being well managed.

A framework for analysing patterns of employee voice

In this section we identify the factors that influence the variety in patterns, structures and processes of employee voice across countries. One methodological approach that is useful in providing a framework to account for and explain such diversity derives from the 'institutionalist' school of thought (see Rubery and Grimshaw, 2003: 37–9). This focuses on the ways in which the set of institutional arrangements and societal structures in which organisations are embedded can explain differences between societies. Institutions play a mediating role between pervasive pressures for change, such as globalisation, and actual experience within a particular employee relations system. An institutional framework challenges a view of globalisation which posits a process of convergence in national patterns of employee relations (Bamber, et al, 2004).

From within an institutionalist perspective Poole et al (2001) have developed a framework which identifies four sets of analytical variables to explain local diversity against a backdrop of wider 'macro' influences. The variables are:

- macro-level structural economic and technical conditions, cultural and ideological variables, and the politico-legal framework
- the strategic choices of the parties
- the power of the parties
- organisational structures and processes at the level of the enterprise.

In this model all the factors or variables affect the development and expression of employee voice in either favourable or unfavourable ways. Taken together they constitute the infrastructure which through institutional interaction will either promote or constrain the articulation of employee voice in a given instance. However, the macro-level factors do not exercise a determinant influence on actual employment outcomes because of the crucial mediating role played by the strategic choices of management, trade union and the state, the distribution of power among the actors and organisational innovations at enterprise level.

Economic conditions

The contemporary period is one of widespread and profound change in the international economy often referred to as 'globalisation'. Definitions of globalisation abound but it is commonly taken to refer to a combination of a number of interconnected developments and processes such as the opening and integration of product and labour markets, technological innovation, and political reform around a 'neo-liberal' agenda. Several prominent components of globalisation are:

- heightening of competition flowing from the liberalisation of trade and financial markets and the emergence of new market economies in the wake of the collapse of the centrally planned 'state socialist' economies of Central and Eastern Europe

- rapid change in information technology which has increased the pace and extent of information exchange and altered production, distribution and management structures

- enhancement of the role of multinational companies and with it associated substantial growth and importance of foreign direct investment and global production chains

- the increasingly coordinating role of international financial institutions such as the World Bank, the International Monetary Fund (IMF) and the World Trade Organisation (WTO)

- increased inequalities between countries (ie in industrialised and developing regions) at different stages of integration into the global economy.

Given that employment regulation was traditionally developed within the context of national economies and markets, the advent of globalisation entails some significant challenges for employee representation and voice. A recent assessment by the International Labour Organisation (ILO, 2000: 9–12) identifies a range of issues:

- the possibility that regulatory and institutional forms of employment protection are perceived as impediments to competitiveness and deterrents to inward investors

- the effects of mobile capital 'upping sticks' and exiting from regions where collective bargaining is extant to those where it is absent

- the effects of labour market segmentation around flexibility and contracted-out work that are 'causing the employment relationship increasingly to resemble a commercial relationship, making it difficult to identify the real employer for the purposes of collective bargaining' (ILO, 2000: 10)

- the significant expansion in the numbers in the 'informal economy', many of whom are not employees, who experience extreme representational insecurity.

With particular regard to developing countries Jose (1999: 7) identifies a number of trends which mirror changes occurring in the labour markets of the developed world:

- the disintegration of large workplaces and the growth of smaller geographically dispersed workplaces

- an expansion of the labour market beyond urban areas

- a skills-based differentiation of the labour force

- a rise in significant wage disparities.

In sum, many of the implications of globalisation appear to shift the power balance in the employer's favour and throw the increased vulnerability of labour in the new world order into sharp relief.

Cultural values and ideologies

The cultural features of a particular country predispose it to promote or constrain the development of employee voice and to influence its articulation in particular ways. A society's culture is composed of the values and beliefs held by citizens which translate into their attitudes and behaviour (see Chapter 2). A good example is provided in a study comparing workers' participation in Germany and Taiwan. Han and Chiu (2000: 160) see German culture as valuing communication and consensus among social actors, and showing a preference for participation, interdependence and reciprocity. This contrasts with Taiwanese culture, where there is 'a high degree of distance in terms of power relations, subordination and docility of the managed'. According to Han and Chiu the effects of these traditional cultural values are seen in the ways in which management and workers interact and in the inferior status of labour relative to capital and the state. Cultural differences therefore facilitate employee voice in Germany and impede it in Taiwan.

The politico-legal context

The prevailing politico-legal context has a profound conditioning impact on the policies and practices which regulate the employment relationship and the provision of worker voice. One way of examining the nature of the context in a comparative way is to look at the attitude of the state to organised labour. Cella and Treu (2001: 461–5) categorise approaches in terms of four regimes:

- *'Repression'* – in many of the developed economies of Europe the experience of trade unions in their early years was one of legal prohibition. Repression remains a marked feature of the official stance taken to trade unions in a considerable range of developing countries in Africa, South America and Asia.

- *'Tolerance'* – in which state tolerance of trade union activity is based on a tenet of state abstention in the employment relations arena and an acceptance of the desire of employers and trade unions for voluntary rather than legal regulation of relations.

- *'Intervention'* – in which the state actively intervenes through legislation to support employee voice. An example of such an interventionist stance is the role of the European Union acting under its Community Charter of Social Rights for Workers adopted in 1989. Directives passed under the Social Charter range over individual employment rights issues such as anti-discrimination, health and safety at work and transfer of undertakings protections, and also confer collective rights on trade unions and other representative bodies relating to the receipt of information and consultation on major changes at work (see Chapter 11).

- *'Neo-corporatism'* – in which 'peak level' representatives of unions, business and government are involved in making deals on major economic and social issues affecting the country as a whole. Such arrangements provide trade unions with an institutional-ised voice in the determination of societal priorities. Such features of 'social partner-ship' are to be found in countries such as the Republic of Ireland, Austria, Denmark, the Netherlands and Norway.

Strategic choice

Boxall and Purcell note that 'choices on voice arrangements, while to a lesser or greater degree are constrained by legislation and wider beliefs on legitimacy, are taken by management in the sense of wishing to avoid, live with, or embrace forms of partnership with representatives and with employees directly' (2003: 179). Thus, for example, multinational firms might adopt one of three broad strategies in relation to unions and employee representation.

Paternalistic
The objective of this strategy is to treat employees well so that they do not feel the need to join a union or seek its recognition. This is sometimes the result of an ideological antagonism towards unions. MNCs pursuing this strategy will deal with unions or set up consultation bodies if the legal or institutional framework of a country gives them no choice, but they will generally be looking to marginalise the independent representation structure. Companies with this strategy may be subdivided between those that try to maintain good two-way communication with employees individually or in teams, and those organisations that provide no effective form of employee voice.

Partnership
This strategy may be followed by MNCs that have a corporate philosophy that employment relations will be improved by recognising employees as stakeholders in the business. These firms may be proactive in establishing effective forms of employee voice, including union recognition where this is appropriate in relation to local ER norms.

Pragmatic
This strategy is to accept and adapt to the forms of employee representation that are found in different countries. In the absence of any particular corporate ideology, local managers tend to determine the forms of employee representation if any.

Power of the parties

Poole *et al* (2001) see the distribution of power between management, trade unions and the state as of 'critical consequence' in establishing the conditions for voice articulation. Union strength tends to lead to collective bargaining becoming the main channel of employee voice. However, as Olney (1996) and Jose (1999) show in their international studies of trade unionism, a combination of external factors and forces are in play which may affect the ability of unions to realise their goal as the dominant channel of employee voice in a given situation. These range from the 'friendliness' of the prevailing legislative climate to employers' and employees' attitudes towards unions, and from changes in the structure of employment to the rise of unitarist human resource management approaches. An illustration of the key role of the strength of unions is provided by Cook (1998), who studied the shift to neo-liberal economic policies and associated labour law changes in Latin American countries in the 1980s and 1990s. Whereas all countries were subject to similar pressures for flexibility, she found that weak labour movements in some countries were less able to resist flexible reforms than was the case in countries with stronger unions. Although in no case did unions block changes in labour law regimes, those labour movements which were stronger were able to shape outcomes through mobilisation, coalition-building and insistence on having a voice in the reform process.

Organisational innovations

Other important influences on voice articulation flow from organisational changes in firms such as downsizing and de-layering, which can create conditions for individual task-level empowerment initiatives rather than more centralised power-centred approaches to voice expression. As traditional command-and-control hierarchies are dismantled employees are assigned a broader span of responsibilities crossing task boundaries and within teamwork formations. Such trends place emphasis on the development of participation and voice articulation at the micro task level (Markey *et al*, 2001).

Discussion questions

1 With reference to your country of origin, what influence do national cultural factors have on the development and articulation of employee voice in organisational decision-making?

2 What other factors might one usefully refer to in explaining variations in employee voice between countries?

3 What factors may influence the stance taken by multinational companies towards employee voice expressed through trade unions?

CASE STUDY 29

EMPLOYEE VOICE AND RESTRUCTURING AT LUFTHANSA AND BRITISH AIRWAYS

This case examines the factors influencing the effectiveness of partnership working by comparing the experience of two airlines: British Airways (BA) (based in the UK) and Lufthansa (based in Germany). Over the past 20 years these carriers, in common with all other European airlines, have been subject to a number of significant external shocks, such as the liberalisation of the airline sector, severe fluctuations in passenger demand, and variations in fuel costs. As a result European airlines have been engaged in a prolonged period of restructuring with many implications for employment relations.

Restructuring at Lufthansa
The process of restructuring has been undertaken within the framework of long-standing social partnership institutions. In accordance with national law, half of the members of the Lufthansa supervisory board, which appoints the executive board and oversees general company strategy, are employee representatives from the different occupational groups in the workforce. A multi-layered system of works councils at different levels of the company completes the framework of employee representation. In addition, a complex system of company-level collective agreements sets substantive terms and conditions for ground staff, flight staff and apprentices.

A number of large-scale restructuring exercises have been carried out in recent years. The company's main restructuring initiative in the 1990s during and after privatisation was centred on the creation of six subsidiary companies which management wished to designate as separate businesses with different terms and conditions of employment. One implication would have been the dismantling of the long-standing company-wide collective agreements specifying uniform basic conditions of service. However, an important outcome of 'de-liberation' was a decision by the company to recast itself as an 'integrated' aviation group. This preserved the company-wide framework agreements across the subsidiaries. Rationalisation did occur, but through agreement with unions: jobs were cut, but only through early retirement, non-replacement of leavers, and job-sharing rather than via compulsory redundancies. Substantial pay concessions were made, with pay increases below the rate of inflation agreed, while work pressure intensified for some groups such as check-in staff where lower staffing levels were introduced.

Following the '9/11' attacks the company was forced to cut transatlantic route capacity but again avoided large-scale compulsory redundancies. Instead, a process of consultation and negotiation yielded changes in working-time arrangements including the use of voluntary unpaid leave. In response to the growth of low-cost airlines, collective agreements have been concluded which preserve existing employment levels in return for concessions including pay freezes and working-time flexibility. Finally, sources of savings in costs which do not impact on terms and conditions of employment and job loss have been pursued, such as common handling arrangements and shared maintenance arising from Lufthansa's strategic alliance with other airlines.

Restructuring at British Airways

Restructuring has been most pronounced in the domestic (European) operations. Within the context of a market-led strategy developed after privatisation in 1987, the airline was reorganised into a divisionalised structure with separate terms and conditions of employment for each subsidiary, and market rates of pay for each company benchmarked against low-cost competitor airlines. In addition BA sought to increase productivity and labour utilisation by the introduction of new shift patterns and duty rosters. BA has detached various services from the core business through leasing and franchising arrangements. The philosophy of the 'virtual airline' where only the minimum number of back office and front-line customer-facing staff are employed directly has led BA to initiate a process of outsourcing. Remaining in-house services must be cost-competitive against external service providers. The strategy of cutting labour costs has resulted in substantial redundancies, numbering 20,000 between 2001 and 2003.

The airline's approach to trade unions and collective bargaining has tended to oscillate between harder and softer stances. Immediately after privatisation, BA emphasised direct communications with individual employees while leaving intact the national bargaining structures inherited from state ownership. During the 1990s BA moved to restructure its collective bargaining arrangements, replacing negotiated agreements for the workforce as a whole by separate bargaining for different occupational groups. In 1996 the company threatened to replace pilots if they took strike action. In a dispute with cabin crew the following year, BA threatened to de-recognise their union.

In the aftermath of these disputes and in an apparent reversal of its adversarial approach, the company responded positively in 1997 to an initiative taken by the pilots' union to conclude a 'partnership agreement' based on principles such as information exchange, communications, and problem-solving. Then BA took the initiative itself and proposed a similar partnership-based approach to the other main airline unions. However, partnership working has proved to be more a case of rhetoric than reality. The unions representing staff other than pilots did not sign the agreement. The agreement covering pilots has also decayed because of lack of grass-roots commitment.

Following the crisis created by the 2001 terrorist attacks, BA appears to have reverted to its earlier strategy of unilateral cost-cutting. Job losses were announced after a company communication exercise rather than by consultation and negotiation with union representatives. Similarly, the company's 2001 strategic review was undertaken without any involvement of its trade unions (or indeed HR executives).

Sources: Turnbull *et al*, (2004); European Industrial Relations Observatory (2005b)

Case study tasks

1   How did the different market contexts in Germany and the UK affect the two airlines' approach to restructuring?

2   Why did partnership founder in BA and not in Lufthansa?

3   How would you assess the relative strength of employee voice in restructuring in the two airlines?

4 INTERNATIONAL TRENDS IN EMPLOYEE VOICE

We now turn to assess patterns of employee voice internationally in terms of 'power-centred', 'task-centred' and 'ownership-centred' voice mechanisms.

Power-centred voice

Employee voice can be fed into an organisation's policy-making process in two ways: directly and individualistically through channels such as attitude surveys and company communications arrangements, and indirectly via employee representatives who are elected to serve on co-decision-making and either joint union-management or employee-only consultative bodies.

Direct power-centred voice
Direct forms of employee voice transmission have traditionally been widespread in firms in the USA and Japan. More recently, research evidence from Europe confirms its spread in this region. The EU-funded Employee Direct Participation in Organisational Change (EPOC) project which surveyed direct participation practice in 10 countries in the 1990s found that 82% of workplaces reported using at least one direct participation practice (Gill and Kreiger, 1999). The scope of power-centred direct voice mechanisms – termed 'consultative participation' in the EPOC survey – was measured in terms of the number of issues on which managers asked employees for advice. The greater the number of issues consulted over, the further along a scale of 'low' , 'medium' and 'high' they scored in terms of the strength of participation. In only 5% of the workplaces surveyed did consultative participation score at a high level. A more recent survey examined employee perceptions in four EU countries of how frequently they were consulted directly by managers over important work decisions, and also how much influence they had over important work decisions (Kessler *et al*, 2004). The authors conclude that 'employees in all four countries saw themselves as having a limited direct influence over important work decisions' (2004: 528).

Indirect power-centred voice

Kuruvilla (2003) identifies a range of indicators to assess the extent and strength of indirect power-centred voice. The 'common and universal measures' are trade union density – ie the number of union members expressed as a percentage of wage and salary earners – and collective bargaining coverage, which is an indicator of the number of workers who are actually covered by collective bargaining arrangements. However, it should be borne in mind that these measures do not necessarily translate straightforwardly as indices of union strength. Where unions are not independent (as in China), for instance, high membership figures do not indicate strength (Clarke *et al*, 2004).

Trade union density

Data collected by the ILO (1997) on changes in international union density levels point to a situation of widespread de-unionisation in the decade from 1985 across the world. For example, in Africa the percentage decline in union density ranges from 23.9% in Egypt to 59.6% in Kenya. In Asia and Oceania declines range from 18.0% in South Korea to 56.6% in New Zealand. In Latin America the relevant figures show declines from 37.3% in Colombia to 47.9% in Argentina. Data from other sources show declining densities in Europe and North America. In Western European countries declines in density from 1980 to 1995 ranged from 1.0% in Sweden to 65.3% in France (Verma and Kochan, 2004). In the countries of Central and Eastern Europe which joined the European Union in 2004, where densities in the Communist era were over 90%, recent estimates put union density at approximately 20–25% (EIRO, 2003; Mailand and Due, 2004). Between 1980 and 1995 union density declined by 39.8% in the USA (Verma and Kochan, 2004).

Union density levels also vary widely *within* each region of the world. For example, in Europe the density range is from over 70% in Belgium, Denmark, Finland and Sweden to under 20% in France and Spain. Contrary to the general trend, increases in union density have been recorded in individual countries in each region of the world except North America. Examples are in South Africa, Hong Kong, the Nordic States (except Sweden), Ireland and Chile. However, despite the upward trends in some countries, the overall picture is of 'stagnation and decline' (Verma and Kochan, 2004).

Collective bargaining coverage

Collective bargaining coverage varies considerably between regions and countries, as Table 4 shows. In broad terms higher rates of coverage tend to be associated with centralised bargaining, although other factors such as management support for bargaining is also important. Collective bargaining coverage in most EU states where sectoral agreements are in place exceeds 80%, while coverage is significantly lower in countries where bargaining is decentralised or patchy – for example, in the UK and the 2004 EU accession states (EIRO, 2005a).

In developing and industrialising economies coverage tends to be relatively low. ILO figures show coverage in Asia ranging from 2% in India to 19% in Singapore and 33% in the Philippines. In Latin America the variation is between 3% in Costa Rica and 65% in Argentina. In Africa the average rate is estimated at 30%, although in South Africa coverage is estimated at 50% (ILO, 2004).

Table 4 Average union density and collective bargaining coverage

Region	Average % union density	Average collective bargaining coverage % for which data is available (number of countries)	Percentage of world population in each region (2000)
Americas	14.50	30.90 (12)	13.7
Asia and Oceania	15.58	18.53 (10)	61.3
Europe	42.64	72.89 (13)	12.0
Africa	14.00	30.00 (8)	12.9

Source: ILO, *World Labour Report* 1997–98

Such trends may be said to reflect a global erosion of 'representational security' which 'comes from the existence of organisations able to defend the interest of those in vulnerable positions, giving those subject to controls a collective voice to bargain with controllers' (Standing, 1999: 194). The main explanations for and origins of this decline are:

■ *Structural economic and labour market changes*

Pressures for flexibility and competitiveness have promoted changes in the composition of the labour force (see Chapter 4). This has resulted in an increasing proportion of non-standard jobs of which the occupants, by virtue of their more marginal participation in the workforce, are less likely to join or remain in unions. A further development which has impeded unionisation has been the decline of the large conglomerate company with its institutionalised employment relations arrangements.

In a study of union decline in Asian countries in the 1990s, Kuruvilla *et al* suggest that a common feature was that 'almost without exception the economic environment poses threats to unions' (2002: 449). Declining union influence is related to the strengthening of the 'logic of competition' associated with foreign direct investment and trade, 'causing a reconfiguration of IR institutions, practices and policies, which in many cases changed the balance of power between management and unions' (2002: 440). The spread of numerical flexibility in the labour markets of India and the Philippines, for instance, has casualised the workforce and weakened unions.

■ *Management strategies*

Managers in some countries have taken steps to suppress unions. According to one study in the USA, employers use a range of tactics including mandatory 'captive-audience' meetings in company time during which a strong anti-union message was delivered and threats that the workplace would close or be relocated should workers vote for union representation (AFL-CIO, 2005).

An alternative strategy is *union substitution* where company-dependent 'in-house' enterprise unions are encouraged as an alternative to independent unionism. Such organisations have spread to industrialising countries such as Korea and Malaysia (Standing, 1999).

■ *Attitude of government to unions*

The decline or absence of legislative protection for union organisation or violations of worker's rights to organise are other key reasons for underdeveloped employee voice. State action can range from the restriction of union liberties by narrowing legal immunities, as in the UK, via the integration of trade unions into the management decision-making apparatus as in China, to the brutal repression of trade unionism and individual trade unionists in other parts of the world. Government control of trade unions is also a feature of a number of African countries including Sudan, Egypt and Libya. In Nigeria the government is seeking to outlaw the independent Nigeria Labour Congress, while in Zimbabwe trade unionists have experienced harassment, intimidation, arrests, dismissals and persecution. The Middle East is identified as the region where workers' rights are least respected. Trade unions are prohibited in Oman and Saudi Arabia while in Kuwait, Yemen, Syria and Jordan only a single government-approved union organisation is allowed (International Confederation of Free Trade Unions, 2005).

Other forms of indirect power-centred voice

Apart from trade-union-based collective bargaining, indirect employee voice can be expressed in two other ways: through works councils based on legislation, and through 'voluntary' initiatives taken by management, such as 'company councils' or 'joint consultative committees'.

Works council systems based on national legislation
As noted in Chapter 2, these are a predominant feature in the industrial relations systems of the majority of EU member states. Elected by employees, such bodies have a range of information and consultation rights (extending to co-determination rights on some issues in some countries) on a variety of matters relating to a company's financial, economic and employment situation, and also in relation to personnel and employment issues. In addition, legislation in the majority of EU states provides for forms of worker representation on company boards of directors.

The general consensus is that legislatively based national works councils have strengthened employee voice. For example, a survey of works councils in subsidiaries of national Dutch firms found that they exercised a 'reasonable to large influence' on personnel, organisational and (to a lesser extent) general policy (Looise and Drucker, 2002).

However, works councils face a number of challenges in terms of their coverage and influence. First, works councils have tended to be a feature of larger enterprises and have, as a consequence, strengthened the voice of only some sections of the workforce. Second, growing internationalisation of production poses threats to national systems of employee representation. In the Dutch study referred to above, the strongest reduction in influence of works councils occurred in companies which were subsidiaries of Dutch, and especially foreign, multinationals (Looise and Drucker, 2002: 39–48).

Voluntary approaches to indirect employee representation
These are features of the 'Anglo-Saxon' approach to employment regulation characteristic of the UK and the USA. In the context of a severe decline in UK trade union density and representation since 1980, attention has focused on initiatives taken by some employers to set up non-union employee representation structures (NERs) (Gall, 2003; Gollan, 2003).

One question posed by such developments is whether non-union forms of voice articulation are as effective as union-based forms. On one side it is argued that non-union channels are essentially restricted in scope and of limited value in representing employee voice. This is because employer-initiated arrangements inevitably reflect employer interests and objectives. Gollan's study of Eurotunnel notes that managers saw the the company council as a means to persuade employees of the benefit of change. The alternative view is that NERs can advance employees' interests by providing a forum for the development of a 'mutual gains' climate.

Dundon *et al* (2005), reporting on managers' perceptions of employee voice in seven non-union organisations, argue that that 'employee voice acted as the gateway to a more open and constructive IR climate'. Moreover, 'voice structures set up to facilitate business improvements may also have consequences beyond those that management had in mind at the outset. What is significant is that such processes take on a life of their own and evolve over time' (2005: 317–18).

Task-centred voice

Task-centred direct voice mechanisms comprise two sorts of schemes. First, there are upward problem-solving groups such as quality circles and suggestion schemes where the employer consults employees individually and in small groups on their ideas concerning possible solutions to production problems. Second, there are 'delegative' mechanisms, such as teamworking and semi-autonomous work groups, which are designed to increase the degree of autonomy which workers have over decision-making in the performance of their allotted work tasks. In both types of arrangements the aim is to turn workers from passive rule-followers into active and empowered agents in the work process. Historically, task-centred initiatives of these kinds were associated with the 'Japanese' model of industrial practice and with the Scandinavian Quality of Work/Life Movement (Oliver and Wilkinson, 1992; Strauss, 1998). Evidence from a range of surveys suggests a growth in this approach to hearing employee voice.

In the cross-Europe EPOC survey two measures of delegative participation were used: 'individual delegation' based on the number of rights of individual employees to make decisions about how the work task was performed without reference to the immediate manager, and 'group delegation' which focused on a group's autonomy to allocate work, to exercise quality control, in job rotation, in coordination of work with other groups, and in choice of group leader (Gill and Kreiger, 1999). Overall, the survey findings show limited use of delegative participation, but in particular restricted use of the more radical form of group delegation.

Ownership-centred voice

Several different 'generic' types of financial participation can be observed in Europe and the USA:

Stock option plans
These provide a mechanism for shares to be acquired by employees at some point in the future based on current market prices (though often at a discount).

Stock purchase plans
These are where employees purchase shares, often on favourable terms.

There are also arrangements whereby employees are awarded shares in the company free of charge ('free shares').

Employee share ownership plans (ESOPs)
These are plans that provide for substantial amounts of company equity to be passed to employees. Typically, this equity is held collectively on behalf of employees, and may provide for indirect voice. In many cases, however, the collective arrangements are in place to satisfy regulatory requirements on holding periods (shares are required to be held in trust for a period before distribution to employees) rather than to support industrial democracy.

The UK and the USA have been seen as pacesetters in the use of equity-based plans. The ESOP concept was pioneered in the USA, and there are around 10,000 companies with ESOPs (see Pendleton, 2001). Both the UK and the USA have had well-developed regulatory frameworks for employee share plans for some years, and the availability of tax concessions to employees and companies has undoubtedly stimulated the use of these plans.

In the UK, share option plans and free shares arrangements, with supporting tax concessions, have been established for over 20 years. The most common stock option plan – Save As You Earn or 'Sharesave' – enables firms to grant options to employees at up to 20% discount on current market prices so as to acquire shares in three or five (extendable to seven) years' time. In the meantime, employees save up to exercise the options using a savings contract. The Share Incentive Plan introduced in 2000 enables employees to purchase shares with highly advantageous tax arrangements and to receive free shares awarded by the employer.

Influences on employee financial participation

In the last few years, there has been growing interest and use of share plans in Europe. The European Commission has advocated the use of financial participation for a number of years, and several European governments have revised or introduced legislation in the last ten years to facilitate the use of equity-based plans. For instance, German company law generally prohibited the use of stock options until the passage of the Kon Trac legislation in 1998. Recent research indicates that equity plans are most common in the UK, followed by the Netherlands, France and the Republic of Ireland. The Scandinavian countries then follow. Share ownership plans are least common in southern Mediterranean states such as Italy, Spain and Portugal (Pendleton *et al*, 2001).

Another influence on the use of share plans has been the spread of Anglo-American business practices and philosophies. American multinationals operating in Europe, and American institutional investors with equity holdings in European firms, have encouraged the use of equity-based rewards and participation.

Limitations of employee share plans

There are several potential limitations of employee share plans as a form of involvement in ownership.

- A key issue is the extent of employee eligibility. Are plans open to all employees or are they aimed primarily at executives? Even where they have broad-based eligibility, do all or most employees participate? Share-ownership plans need employees to consciously opt in (to meet securities legislation) while contributory plans (such as the Save As You Earn plan) are voluntary. In many companies, fewer than half of employees participate even though plans are open to all.

- A limitation of most plans in the listed company sector is that only a small proportion of equity is available to employees. In the UK case, this is partly because of corporate governance rules operated by investor trade associations, such as the Association of British Insurers. As a result, employees (either individually or collectively) have little clout in corporate governance, even though their shares entitle them to vote. Few employees attend company Annual General Meetings. Even where they do, the reality of UK corporate governance is that the influence of shareholder power takes place elsewhere (Pendleton, 2005). An exception to this, however, is France, where employee equity holdings in excess of 3% entitle employees to elect a main board director.

- Finally, a key consideration is employee expectations of employee share plans. The evidence indicates that most employees enter most share plans as a way of saving rather than as a means of exercising control over the company. Perhaps unsurprisingly, a substantial proportion of employees (around 40%) choose to exercise options and sell immediately rather than to become employee share owners.

Discussion questions

1   Are non-union forms of collective employee representation an effective substitute for union-based forms?

2   How far do 'task-based' schemes for employee participation enhance employee influence over work?

3   To what extent does financial participation give employees a stake in the company?

CASE STUDY 30

THE CROSS-BORDER TRANSFER OF EMPLOYEE RELATIONS PRACTICES – SUBSIDIARIES OF US MNCS IN THE UK

Despite the apparent similarities between the UK and the US business systems (the relatively weak regulatory framework, and attitudes towards unions), there are some significant differences between the employment practices of indigenous UK firms and those of UK-based subsidiaries of US MNCs. For instance, a recent representative survey of such companies found that the UK-based subsidiaries of US MNCs were significantly less likely than indigenous UK firms to rely solely on unions as the means by which employees can voice their concerns and make suggestions. Moreover, the UK-based subsidiaries of US MNCs were more likely than indigenous UK companies to have direct-voice mechanisms in place. Such mechanisms range from information-sharing and consultation through to employee-participation schemes. However, US MNCs in the UK are no more likely than indigenous companies to combine representative and direct forms of voice in a partnership. Overall, the evidence suggests that in spite of similar legal frameworks, companies operating in different countries may develop very distinct approaches to employee relations that persist in their overseas subsidiaries.

Source: partly derived from H.-J. Tüselmann et al, (2006)

'The emerging approach to employee relations in German overseas affiliates: a role model for international operation?',
Journal of World Business, Vol. 41, No. 1: 66–80

Case study tasks

1   How easy is it for US MNCs to transfer their preferred employment policies to the UK?

> 2   What might explain the different employment practices in indigenous UK compa-
>   nies and the UK-based subsidiaries of US MNCs?
>
> 3   Are direct or indirect forms of voice likely to be more beneficial to firm
>   performance?

5 GLOBALISATION AND THE FUTURE OF EMPLOYEE VOICE

The IMF describes globalisation as 'the growing economic interdependence of countries worldwide through the increasing volume and variety of cross-border transactions in goods and services and of international capital flows, and also through the more rapid and widespread diffusion of technology' (1997: 45). Globalisation has serious implications for employees. Leisink (1999: 14–20) has identified the principal trends:

- a growing unemployment rate, including an increasing proportion of structural unemployment in the industrialised economies

- a growth in new non-standard and less secure jobs such as contract labour, agency work and self-employment

- increased locational freedom of multinational companies as states, anxious to secure or retain foreign direct investment, seek to reduce the burden of regulation, including labour regulation

- redesign of labour relations arrangements on a neo-liberal basis with an emphasis on deregulation, decentralisation and reduction in labour costs through greater flexibility

- reduction in the power and influence of organised labour as measured in terms of union density.

Growing economic internationalisation is shifting the global balance of power in favour of capital and highlights the importance of developing transnational legal and other frameworks to protect employee voice. A number of initiatives have taken place which aim in different ways to promote and articulate employee voice on an international basis. Budd (2004) suggests that we can differentiate between mechanisms to protect employees' rights and mechanisms of transnational voice articulation.

Mechanisms to protect employees' rights to free association

There are mechanisms which lay a foundation for employee voice through protecting the rights of employees to free association. The ILO, an agency of the United Nations to which virtually every country in the world is a member, lays down minimum – though not legally enforceable – labour standards. In 1998 all ILO member states committed themselves to a set of basic standards enshrined in the ILO Declaration on Fundamental Principles and Rights at Work. The principles are: freedom of association and the effective recognition of the right to collective bargaining; the elimination of forced labour and child labour; and the ending of discrimination in employment (ILO, 2000). The espoused advantages of a 'minimum standards' approach through government regulation are that employment rights are not dependent on the uncertainties of self-policed corporate compliance with voluntary codes of conduct or on variations in trade union organisation and influence around the world. However, compliance with the ILO standards is reliant on 'publicity, diplomacy and technical assistance, not legal or economic punishment' (Budd, 2004: 169). Further discussion of the ILO is contained in Chapter 11.

Mechanisms of transnational employee voice articulation

International trade union cooperation

Trade union internationalism has a long history (at least in rhetorical terms). However, in the current situation in which multinational companies occupy a dominant role in the global economy, strong international links between unions are more important than ever. Lillie and Martinez Lucio (2004: 160–2) suggest that initiatives are taking place across six dimensions. First, there has been a growth in networking, information exchange and coordination between union representatives within multinational companies. Second, supra-national union bodies such as the European Trade Union Confederation (ETUC) have emerged and been influential in the formulation of the EU's industrial relations policy. Third, organisations like the ICFTU have shed their 'cold war mentality and Anglo-American domination' and have opened out their field of vision. Fourth, new formal organisational links have been forged between individual unions operating in the same sector in different countries (eg unions in the UK and German finance sector). Fifth, there has been a proliferation of mutual learning between unions in areas such as recruitment strategies and workers' education. Sixth, there has been a shift away from traditional hierarchical and bureaucratic union internationalism, which saw its primary goal as the establishment of collective bargaining in multinational companies, to embrace engagement and coalitions with wider social movements such as feminism, consumerism, environmentalism and human rights.

Although union networks do exist, the extent of international union cooperation is limited. In general, unions are parochial, and seek to protect the interests of their own members in their own country. There are also obvious practical difficulties in developing effective international cooperation amongst employee representatives from different countries, including language and cost. Sisson (2006), for example, describes the difficulties the European Metalworkers' Federation went through in producing a working-time charter to be pursued by affiliated unions in Europe. Despite this, Europe is the region in which greater international cooperation between unions is most likely to develop, spurred by the creation of the Euro zone, and the recognition by the EU of the union movement as a social partner.

European Works Councils

European Works Councils (EWCs) are transnational company-level committees of employee representatives drawn from differing EU member states. The EU EWC Directive of 1994 requires every company employing more than 1,000 workers in the EU, with over 150 in at least two member countries, to establish an EWC. EWCs have minimum specified rights to information and consultation, but not co-decision-making, on a range of issues relating to the structure, economic and financial situation, future business developments, employment and investment trends, substantial changes in organisation, the introduction of new working methods, transfers of production, mergers, closures and collective redundancies. Issues such as the size of the council, the sort of information to be conveyed to council reps, the procedures by which reps are selected, and procedures for consultation are devolved to 'local' decisions taken in the member states. Approximately 1,300 companies have set up EWCs. Although EWC representatives need not be trade unionists, the councils are nevertheless strongly supported by European trade unions who see them as the basis for developing regional union solidarity and the 'Europeanisation' of industrial relations (Taylor, 1999: 8).

The effectiveness of EWCs can be judged by the extent to which they are perceived as performing an 'active' or merely 'symbolic' role. A symbolic role involves a low level of information provision and no formal consultation, little or no contact between reps, or with management, between meetings resulting in little influence over management decision-making (Budd, 2004; EIRO, 2004). An example of the latter type of EWC is reported by Royle (1999), whose study of the McDonald's Restaurants' EWC shows how the company rendered the council ineffective by using loopholes in the legislation to marginalise trade union presence.

Alternatively, EWCs can be placed on a continuum of activity (Lecher et al, 2001). 'Service' EWCs confine their activities to networking and passing on European-level information gleaned via council meetings to the national union. More active EWCs are those which are 'project-oriented', which can lead them to be transformed into 'participative' bodies where there is regular contact and liaison between reps and management outside the annual meeting.

A recent study suggests that a key factor determining the extent to which an EWC is 'active' rather than 'symbolic' is management structure and management policy. If there is a close fit between management structure and the EWC, it s more likely that the council will influence management decision-making. Second, there is a positive association between the ability of an EWC to exercise influence and a proactive management stance toward the council. Where management perceives that the EWC can assist in the legitimation of management actions and attainment of its objectives, the EWC is likely to enjoy greater influence (Marginson et al, 2004).

Unions have themselves always benchmarked as a way of putting pressure on low-paying employers to raise wages. There is some evidence that this is beginning to happen at the European level. As we have seen, a large company operating in more than one European country has to establish a EWC if requested to by employees. Although these are not bargaining bodies, they do facilitate contact and information exchange between employee representatives that may help them in negotiations over pay and conditions (Hancké, 2000).

World works councils
The automotive sector is the location for the establishment of bilateral relations with employers through 'world works councils' (WWCs). Building on its EWC and on sustained pressure from its employee representatives Volkswagen set up its 'world group council' in 1998. This is a joint employee representative body covering the entire VW global workforce which is 80% unionised and spread across 35 production sites. In 2002 Daimler-Chrysler followed suit by the establishment of its World Employee Committee, which consists of employee representatives from plants in Europe, North America, Latin America and South Africa. It provides for the exchange of information amongst employee representatives, and between representatives and company management. In both cases the parties have underlined the role of the councils in establishing core global employment rights as well as contributing to the cooperation needed to achieve sustained profitability in a competitive world context (EIRO, 1998, 2002).

Transnational collective bargaining
Although a long-held goal of international trade union organisations, the extension of collective bargaining from the national to the international level remains unfulfilled. However, one exception is the global agreement reached in 2003 between the shipping employers and the International Transport Workers' Federation (ITF) covering wages and working conditions on flag-of-convenience ships.

International framework agreements
IFAs or 'global agreements' have been described as 'accords' that are signed by the management of a multinational company and by 'global union federations' (GUFs) bringing

together trade unions in different countries in the same sector. The agreements commit the company, joint ventures, suppliers and subcontractors to respect basic principles such as freedom of association and collective bargaining as established, for example, by ILO Conventions (EIRR, 2005). While the agreements resemble codes of conduct on corporate social responsibility (CSR), they are distinctive in two main respects. First, whereas codes of conduct are unilateral management pledges principally aimed to address wider public concerns, framework agreements demonstrate a company's commitment to discuss issues of fundamental concern to both unions and management. Second, whereas codes of conduct are typically self-monitored by the company, framework agreements normally include a procedure for the signatories to jointly monitor their operation and outcomes. Framework agreements allow the establishment of the right to organise and negotiate which otherwise might not have been available to workers. This has led the ICFTU to claim that global agreements can be seen as 'the start of international collective bargaining' (ICFTU, 2003).

A recent survey shows that framework agreements have been signed by 48 companies, predominantly headquartered in the EU, with the highest proportion in Germany. Agreements are most common in the manufacturing, processing and primary sectors (EIRR, 2005). There is a particular concentration of agreements in the automotive sector, including accords between the WWCs and the managements of VW and Daimler-Chrysler. In both these cases the agreements embody a flavour of labour-management 'partnership' thinking. The VW talks of the company and unions working together openly in the spirit of 'constructive and cooperative conflict management' (Bibby, 2002).

Discussion questions

1   Why have trade unions tended to be internationally fragmented?

2   To what extent are transnational works councils effective channels of employee voice within multinational enterprises?

3   What are the relative strengths of the alternative methods by which the 'global workplace' may be governed?

CONCLUSIONS AND FUTURE ISSUES

This chapter defined employee voice and identified varying underpinning rationales for it. Important influences on the extent and character of employee voice in decision-making are globalisation, culture, and European integration. The principal dimensions of employee voice were identified in terms of degree of influence over the final decision, forms of voice articulation, and the focus on different types of decisions. The usefulness of an 'institutional' framework comprised of macro- and organisational-level variables whose interaction influence the expression of voice was outlined. International trends in employee voice were examined in terms of power-, task- and ownership-centred foci. Evidence points to the erosion of power-centred representative forms of voice, with some growth in task-centred and ownership-centred types. The context of advancing globalisation emphasises the importance of transnational channels of employee representation and voice articulation. While the prospects for a radical extension of collective bargaining beyond national boundaries and in the developing world are slim, an interesting development is represented by the advent of IFAs. Neither collective agreements or voluntary corporate codes of conduct, IFAs are nevertheless the outcome of union–management negotiations and typically establish the principle of freedom of association and the right to organise in otherwise unpropitious circumstances. The pace at which IFAs develop will be a function of the degree of acceptance accorded them by multinational companies on the one hand and the capacity of international trade union federations on the other to promote cohesive relations between their affiliates. A favourable conjuncture would appear to underpin a promising step toward the extension of representative employee voice for those workers who need it most acutely.

CASE STUDY 31

THE INTERNATIONAL FRAMEWORK AGREEMENT AT CHIQUITA BRANDS

In June 2001 an international framework agreement (IFA) was concluded between the multinational banana company Chiquita and the Latin American Coordination of Banana Workers' Unions (COLSIBA).

The international banana industry is dominated by five companies covering more than 82% of world exports. They are Chiquita Brands (USA) with 25–26%, Dole Standard Fruit (USA) with 25–26%, Del Monte Fresh Produce (USA/Chile/United Arab Emirates) 16%, Noboa (Ecuador) 10%, and Fyffes (Ireland) 6%. The leading companies are involved in production, packing, transport and ripening, which gives them a high degree of control over the production end of the commodity chain. At the retail end of the chain, the leading companies are in fierce competition due to saturated markets and oversupply, and are under pressure on price from the highly concentrated retail sector. Faced with such pressures and the additional policy of the European Union to favour bananas from former European colonies in Africa, the Caribbean and Pacific States, a common response of the companies has been to restructure their operations by increased outsourcing and rationalisation of the production process. Another important strategy for Chiquita has been to strengthen its market position through campaigns directed at consumers and retailers which emphasise the company's social and environmental credentials.

COLSIBA has members in seven different countries (Ecuador, Colombia, Costa Rica, Panama, Nicaragua, Honduras and Guatemala) that together account for 78% of world banana exports. COLSIBA represents 42 unions covering around 45,000 workers. It was formed to exchange information and develop a coordinated strategy to confront the multinationals in the region. The problems facing Latin America banana workers and their unions are:

- the threat of relocation of production to non-union low-pay supplier plantations and the attendant erosion of bargaining power

- a move to looser contract forms and anti-union policies such as discrimination, dismissals and black-listing as well as continued support for 'solidarismo' organisations introduced by employers in the 1980s to replace the independent unions

- working conditions which include long working hours, health hazards from agricultural chemicals, and dismissals without compensation.

The IFA was signed following several years of work in which COLSIBA joined with, among others, 30 European non-governmental organisations under the banner of the European Banana Action Network in a media and consumer campaign which targeted Chiquita in its key markets demanding the right to organise, the right to collective agreements, and protection of the environment. Although Chiquita was initially reluctant to conclude an agreement with COLSIBA, a framework agreement was concluded in 2001. The agreement was the first of its kind in agriculture and the first such agreement negotiated and signed by a coordinating body of unions from developing countries.

The main features of the agreement are:

- the right of each worker to choose to belong to and be represented by an independent and democratic trade union, and to bargain collectively

- a commitment by Chiquita to respect ILO Conventions on forced labour, freedom of association, the right to organise and collective bargaining, discrimination, child labour, and protection and facilities guaranteed to workers' representatives

- a requirement that Chiquita's suppliers, contract growers and joint venture partners are bound to comply with the above standards

- the establishment of a review committee composed of representatives desig-nated by the IUF, COLSIBA and the company which meets at least twice a year to review the application of the agreement

- a commitment by the company to share information

- the establishment of guidelines on the procedures to be invoked in the event of changes in the volume of employment, type of contracts, or transfers of production

- undertakings that the parties avoid actions which could undermine the process spelled out in the agreement, such as public international campaigns or anti-union retaliatory tactics.

Implementation of the agreement

In the agreement, the parties commit to publicising the agreement in all the company's banana operations in Latin America. However, dissemination of and knowledge about the agreement was patchy with, in general, information to workers about the contents of the agreement coming exclusively from the union side. Yet the extent to which unions publicised the agreement varied between countries. Sparse dissemination in Costa Rica, Nicaragua and Guatemala contrasted with the situation in Honduras where the agreement, combined with extensive dissemination of knowledge through radio pro-grammes, meetings and leaflets and local organising activities, led to the establishment of a new union with 47 members at the Buenos Amigos plantation (a supplier to Chiquita). Local organising activity pre-dated the signing of the agreement by a year but had been frustrated by a refusal to allow union representatives on to the plantation to address the workers. News that the IFA negotiations were well advanced was exploited by the Honduran unions to gain access to the plantation for organising purposes.

In terms of agreement compliance, basic workers' rights such as the right to organise have been generally respected on Chiquita-owned plantations, although violations were reported in Costa Rica and Nicaragua. But the biggest problems both with violations and lack of improvements in working conditions have been on supplier plantations. Part of the problem is that although the agreement stipulates Chiquita's obligations to secure its suppliers' respect for the agreement, actual enforcement depends on the influence the company can exert over suppliers. The agreement commits Chiquita to require its suppliers, contract growers and joint venture partners only to provide 'reasonable evidence' that they respect national legislation and core labour standards.

The agreement provides for a review committee to monitor implementation and to deal with complaints. The committee gives unions access to the corporate management of the company and thereby potentially makes it possible to override local management hostility. However, problems have hindered the work of the committee. First, a lack of communication in replying to complaints lodged with it for action poses threats to the level of trust which local unions may have in its effectiveness as a monitoring agency. Second, a lack of the strategic use of the committee was evident in the failure of COLSIBA to hold pre-meetings to discuss priorities in dealing with complaints and to consider preferences in how to resolve problems of violation of the agreement. Third, unions have little experience as partners in an international agreement with a company.

The agreement has been instrumental in securing union recognition at a supplier plantation in Honduras. Elsewhere in the region, unions have reported that the agreement has been instrumental in recruiting 2,000 new members and in signing three new collective agreements (Colombia). It has acted as catalyst for new dialogue between unions and suppliers (in Equador). Finally, when Chiquita's banana plantations in Colombia were sold, unions were consulted prior to the sale and a memorandum of understanding negotiated between the unions and Chiquita. This committed the company to insist that the buyer preserved existing collective bargaining agreements and the IFA itself.

Source: Riisgaard (2005)

Case study tasks

1 In the context of globalisation, how significant are International Framework Agreements?

2 What are the strengths and weaknesses of the IFA at Chiquita?

3 How robust is a strategy based on IFAs for unions in developing countries in seeking to deal with the challenges presented by multinational enterprises?

REFERENCES

American Federation of Labour-Congress of Industrial Organisations (2005) 'The silent war: the assault on workers' freedom to choose a union and bargain collectively in the United States', *Issue Brief*, October.

Bamber G., Ryan S. and Wailes N. (2004) 'Globalisation, employment relations and human resource indicators in ten developed market economies: international data sets', *International Journal of Human Resource Management*, Vol. 15, No. 8: 1481–1516.

Bibby A. (2002) 'Clause and effect', *People Management*, Vol. 8, No. 20, 10 October: 46–7.

Blyton P. and Turnbull P. (2004) *The Dynamics of Employee Relations* (3rd edition). London: Routledge.

Boxall P. and Purcell J. (2003) *Strategy and Human Resource Management.* London: Routledge.

Budd J. W. (2004) *Employment with a Human Face: Balancing efficiency, equity and voice.* Ithaca: Cornell University Press.

Cella G. P. and Treu T. (2001) 'National trade union movements', in R. Blanpain and C. Engels (eds) *Comparative Labour Law and Industrial Relations in Industrialised Market Economies.* The Hague: Kluwer Law International.

Clarke S., Lee C. and Li Q. (2004) 'Collective consultation and industrial relations in China', *British Journal of Industrial Relations*, Vol. 42, No. 2: 235–54.

Cook M. L. (1998) 'Toward flexible industrial relations? Neo-liberalism, democracy, and labor reform in Latin America', *Industrial Relations*, Vol. 37. No. 3: 311–36.

Dundon T., Wilkinson A., Marchington M. and Ackers P. (2004) 'The meanings and purpose of employee voice', *International Journal of Human Resource Management*, Vol. 15, No. 6: 1149–70.

Dundon T., Wilkinson A., Marchington M. and Ackers P. (2005) 'The management of voice in non-union organisations: managers' perceptions', *Employee Relations*, Vol. 27, No. 3: 307–19.

European Industrial Relations Observatory (1998) 'Volkswagen sets up a world group council', www.eiro.eurofound.ie/1998/06/inbrief/de980627in.html

European Industrial Relations Observatory (2002) 'Daimler-Chrysler establishes World Employee Committee', www.eiro.eurofound.ie/2002/09/inbrief/de0209204n.html

European Industrial Relations Observatory (2003) 'Industrial relations in EU member states and candidate countries'.

European Industrial Relations Observatory (2004) 'Developments in European Works Councils', www.eiro.eurofound.ie/2004/11/study/tn/0411101r.html

European Industrial Relations Observatory (2005a) 'Changes in national collective bargaining systems since 1990', www.eiro.eurofound.ie/05/03/study/tn/0503102s.html

European Industrial Relations Observatory (2005b) 'Industrial relations in the airline sector', www.eiro.euroufound.ie/2005/08/study/tn0508101s.html

European Industrial Relations Review (2005) 'Global agreements: state of play', October: 14–16.

Geary J. (1994) 'Employees' participation: enabled or constrained?', in K. Sisson (ed.) *Personnel Management.* Oxford: Oxford University Press.

Gill C. and Kreiger H. (1999) 'Direct and representative participation in Europe: recent survey evidence', *International Journal of Human Resource Management*, Vol. 10, No. 4: 572–91.

Gollan P. (2003) 'Faces of non-union representation in the United Kingdom: management strategy, processes and practices', *International Employment Relations Review*, Vol. 9, No. 2: 1–28.

Hall P. A. and Soskice D. (eds) (2001) *Varieties of Capitalism: The institutional foundations of competitive advantage.* Oxford: Oxford University Press.

Han T.-S. and Chiu S. (2000) 'Industrial democracy and institutional environments: a comparison of Germany and Taiwan', *Economic and Industrial Democracy*, Vol. 21: 147–82.

Hancké B. (2000) 'European Works Councils and restructuring in the European motor industry', *European Journal of Industrial Relations*, Vol. 6, No. 1: 35–60.

Harris H., Brewster C. and Sparrow P. (2003) *International Human Resource Management*. London: CIPD

Hirschman A. (1970) *Exit, Voice and Loyalty*. Cambridge, MA: Harvard University Press.

International Confederation of Free Trade Unions (2000) *A Trade Union Guide to Globalisation*. Brussels: ICFTU.

International Confederation of Free Trade Unions (2003) *A Trade Union Guide to Globalisation* (2nd edition). Brussels: ICFTU.

International Confederation of Free Trade Unions (2005) *Annual Survey of Violations of Trade Union Rights*. www.icftu.org.displaydocument [accessed 21/10/05].

International Labour Organisation (1997) *World Labour Report 1997–98: Industrial democracy and social stability*. Geneva: ILO.

International Labour Organisation (2000) *Your Voice at Work*. Geneva: ILO.

International Labour Organisation (2004) *Organising for Social Justice*. Geneva: ILO.

International Monetary Fund (1997) *World Economic Outlook*. Washington, DC: IMF.

Jose A. V. (1999) 'The future of the labour movement: some observations on developing countries'. International Institute of Labour Studies Discussion Paper DP/112/1999. Geneva: ILO.

Kessler I., Undy R. and Heron P. (2004) 'Employee perspectives on communication and consultation: findings from a cross-national survey', *International Journal of Human Resource Management*, Vol. 15, No. 3: 512–32.

Knudsen H. (1995) *Employee Participation in Europe*. London: Sage.

Kuruvilla S. (2003) 'Social dialogue for decent work', International Institute of Labour Studies Discussion Paper DP/149/2003. Geneva: ILO.

Kuruvilla S., Das S., Kwon H. and Kwon S. (2002) 'Trade union growth and decline in Asia', *British Journal of Industrial Relations*, Vol. 40, No. 3: 431–61.

Lecher W., Platzer H.-W., Rub S. and Weiner K.-P. (2001) *European Works Councils: Developments, types and networking*. Aldershot: Gower.

Leisink P. (ed.) (1999) *Globalisation and Labour Relations*. Cheltenham: Edward Elgar.

Lillie N. and Martinez Lucio M. (2004) 'International trade union revitalisation: the role of national union approaches', in C. M. Frege and J. Kelly (eds) *Varieties of Unionism*. Oxford: Oxford University Press.

Looise J. K. and Drucker M. (2002) 'Employee participation in multinational enterprises: the effects of globalisation on Dutch works councils', *Employee Relations*, Vol. 24, No. 1: 29–52.

Mailand M. and Due J. (2004) 'Social dialogue in central and eastern Europe: present state and future development', *European Journal of Industrial Relations*, Vol. 10, No. 2: 179–97.

Marchington M. and Wilkinson A. (2000) 'Direct participation', in S. Bach and K. Sisson (eds) *Personnel Management* (3rd edition). Oxford: Blackwell.

Marginson P., Hall M., Hoffman A. and Muller T. (2004) 'The impact of European Works Councils on management decision-making in UK- and US- based multinationals: a case study comparison', *British Journal of Industrial Relations*, Vol. 42, No. 2: 209–33.

Markey R., Gollan P., Hodgkinson A., Chouraquai A. and Veersma U. (eds) (2001) *Models of Employee Participation in a Changing Global Environment: Diversity and interaction*. Aldershot: Ashgate.

Oliver N. and Wilkinson B. (1992) *The Japanisation of British Industry*. Oxford: Blackwell.

Olney S. (1996) *Unions in a Changing World*. Geneva: ILO.

Pendleton A. (2001) *Employee Ownership, Participation and Governance*. London: Routledge.

Pendleton A. (2005) 'How far does the UK have a market-based system of corporate governance?' *Competition and Change*, Vol. 9: 107–26.

Pendleton A., Poutsma E., van Ommeren J. and Brewster C. (2001) *Employee Share Ownership and Profit-Sharing in the European Union*. Luxembourg: European Foundation for the Improvement of Living and Working Conditions.

Poole M., Lansbury R. and Wailes N. (2001) 'A comparative analysis of developments in industrial democracy', *Industrial Relations*, Vol. 40, No. 3: 490–525.

Riisgaard L. (2005) 'International framework agreements: a new model for securing workers' rights?', *Industrial Relations*, Vol. 44, No. 4: 707–37.

Royle T. (1999) 'Where's the beef: McDonald's and its European Works Council', *European Journal of Industrial Relations*, Vol. 5: 327–47.

Royle T. (2002) 'Multinational corporations, employers' associations and trade union exclusion strategies in the German fast-food industry', *Employee Relations*, Vol. 24, No. 4: 437–60.

Rubery J. and Grimshaw D. (2003) *The Organisation of Employment: An international perspective*. Basingstoke: Palgrave Macmillan.

Sako M. (1998) 'The nature and impact of "employee voice" in the European car components industry', *Human Resource Management Journal*, Vol. 8, No. 2: 6–13.

Sisson K. (2006) 'International employee representation: a case of industrial relations systems following the market?', in T. Edwards and C. Rees (eds) *International Human Resource Management*. Harlow: Prentice Hall.

Standing G. (1999) *Global Labour Flexibility: Seeking distributive justice.* Basingstoke: Macmillan.

Strauss G. (1998) 'An overview', in F. Heller, E. Pusic, G. Strauss and B. Wilpert (eds) *Organisational Participation: Myth and reality*. Oxford: Oxford University Press.

Taylor R. (1999) 'Trade unions and transnational industrial relations', Labour and Society Programme Discussion Paper DP99/1999. Geneva: ILO.

Turnbull P., Blyton P. and Harvey G. (2004) 'Cleared for take-off? Management–labour partnership in the European civil aviation industry', *European Journal of Industrial Relations*, Vol. 10, No. 3: 287–307.

Tüselmann H.-J., McDonald F. and Thorpe R. (2006) 'The emerging approach to employee relations in German overseas affiliates: a role model for international operation?', *Journal of World Business*, Vol. 41, No. 1: 66–80.

Verma A. and Kochan T. (2004) 'Unions in the 21st century: prospects for renewal', in A. Verma and T. Kochan (eds) *Unions in the 21st Century: An international perspective*. Basingstoke: Palgrave Macmillan.

Wilkinson A., Dundon T., Marchington M. and Ackers P. (2004) 'Changing patterns of employee voice: studies from the UK and Republic of Ireland', *Journal of Industrial Relations*, Vol. 46, No. 3: 298–322.

Employment law

CHAPTER 11

Stephen Taylor and Rosemary Lucas

CHAPTER OBJECTIVES

When you have read this chapter you should be able to:

■ explain the basis of different legal traditions and regimes across the globe

■ understand how dismissal law diverges across nations

■ appreciate differences in working-time regimes across countries

■ describe the principles which underpin the convergence of employment law in Europe and internationally

■ suggest how far future global legal developments may lead to more or less convergence or divergence

---

PURPOSE AND SCOPE

Employment law differs very considerably from country to country across the world. The approaches used vary, sometimes in quite fundamental ways, because the legal systems in which they originate have evolved differently over the centuries. However, the extent of this diversity has reduced somewhat in recent decades. Each jurisdiction has influenced the evolution of the others, leading to a degree of convergence, while the introduction of international standards has also necessarily brought about a degree of harmonisation. Care must thus be taken not to over-emphasise the differences. Increasingly, it is accurate to state that the aims and objectives of employment regulation are the same or similar across much of the world, even if the methods used to achieve them vary. It is also true to state that in the vast majority of countries the extent to which the employment relationship is regulated is increasing steadily year on year. There are one or two examples of governments who are embarked on genuine (as opposed to rhetorical) journeys of de-regulation (eg Australia from 2005), but these are relatively few and far between.

In this chapter, while we address the themes of globalistion, labour market change, cultural variation, European Union (EU) enlargement and emerging economies, our primary focus is divergence and convergence. In respect of divergence we start by explaining how and why employment law differs from country to country by examining different legal traditions and different law regimes. The next two sections use the examples of dismissal law and the regulation of working time to illustrate the major contrasts between systems. The final two sections consider convergence in which we outline the respective roles being played by two international organisations – the EU and the International Labour Organisation (ILO) – in promoting convergence in regimes of employment regulation. Related material on the regulation of the collective employment relationship and on discrimination law can be found in

Chapters 9 and 14. In the final section we assess how far legal developments may lead to greater convergence or may remain divergent, concluding that greater convergence may not be desirable if it drives down standards, and that global improvements may be better effected from the spread of good employment practice by transnational corporations.

1 COUNTRY-BY-COUNTRY DIVERGENCE

Different legal traditions

Scholars are divided about how to categorise the various systems of law that operate around the world. A common approach has been to identify legal families or clusters of systems that operate similarly. This is a useful concept because it allows the identification of 'parent' systems that have heavily influenced the evolution of law in developing countries following decolonisation in the later twentieth century. One of the most widely quoted categorisations derives from the work of the German scholars Zweigert and Kotz (1998), who argue that the major legal families are:

- Romanistic (France, southern Europe and former colonies of these countries)

- Germanic (Germany, Austria, Switzerland – also Taiwan, South Korea and Japan)

- Anglo-American (English-speaking countries and former British colonies)

- Nordic (Scandinavian countries)

- Chinese

- Islamic.

In addition they point to the existence of 'hybrid' systems in some countries which have been influenced in their histories by two or more of the above parent systems. The Indian and Israeli systems are examples of hybrids, as is the law evolving in the former socialist countries of Eastern Europe and Asia. Indeed, the Chinese system, as moves are made away from a socialist approach, is increasingly developing features that owe as much to western as to longer-established Confucian traditions.

While care must be taken not to over-simplify the categorisation of complex legal systems, it is helpful to think in terms of the existence of three clusters of traditions in the area of private law:

- common law systems

- codified systems

- theocratic systems.

Common law systems
Common law approaches are those that have traditionally been used in England and Wales (less so in Scotland) and in former colonies of the UK such as the United States, Canada (not including Quebec), Ireland, Australia, New Zealand, South Africa, Singapore, Hong Kong and Malaysia. The major distinguishing feature of common law legal systems is the idea that law is made by judges building on custom and tradition. As cases are brought before them, the judiciary applies the doctrine of precedent and bases its decisions on principles established by other judges in previous cases. Appeals against decisions on questions of law are then made

to higher courts onwards up a hierarchy of courts until ultimately the case comes before a supreme court (eg the House of Lords in the UK) which makes a definitive ruling on the question of law which is disputed. The law evolves steadily and consistently in common law systems because the decisions of higher courts are binding on the courts that are lower down the hierarchy. So once a point of law has been decided, it is applied by all judges faced with the task of making a decision about a similar matter.

In England the common law has been evolving in this way for centuries and continues to do so. In common law systems parliaments pass statutes which adapt or even override established common law principles, but statutes tend to be quite short and only contain the minimum amount of detail that is necessary. They are interpreted according to the common law and will often draw extensively on established common law principles. Once an interpretation of a statute has been made by a higher court, as with the common law itself, this becomes a binding precedent on the lower courts in the system. Until this has happened, if an action has not been declared unlawful, it is lawful.

The way that justice is enforced is also different in common law systems from the approach used under codified and theocratic legal regimes. The major distinguishing feature is the adversarial system whereby the parties to a dispute come to court and present their cases in great detail, also examining and cross-examining all the witnesses. The judges listen to the evidence which is presented to them during the trial or hearing and then give a reasoned decision. The judge will typically know very little about the case which he or she is to hear ahead of the hearing. In presenting their cases, the advocates representing each party are also expected to set out for the judge the basis of their legal case. They present their interpretation of any statutes or past case law which they consider to be relevant to the case. The judge then goes on to weigh the relative strength of the competing cases which have been presented.

Codified systems

Codified systems (also sometimes referred to as civil systems) are the major alternative forms of legal jurisdiction used in industrialised countries. Based on Roman law and, in more recent times, on the Napoleonic codes developed in France following the Revolution in the 1790s, the approach is wholly different. Instead of the law evolving over time as cases are brought before courts and precedents established, detailed codes setting out exactly what the law is and how it should be interpreted are drawn up and issued by governments. This is the established approach in France, Spain, Portugal, Italy, Germany and the rest of continental Europe, and in the countries colonised by these powers over the past centuries (ie in South America and much of Africa). There are significant differences between the codes used across the different countries, but they are all in one way or another codified systems. Faced with a case, a judge will look first and foremost to the relevant code when making a decision and justifying it. Decisions made in past cases will influence the outcome of cases, but they are not legally binding in the way that they are in common law jurisdictions. Moreover, appeals to higher courts can be made on questions of fact as well as law.

In codified systems there is no adversarial approach as is the case in common law systems. Instead, the judge takes a more active, inquisitorial role in proceedings. Judges do not sit back and listen as the two sides question one another's witnesses. Rather, they undertake the questioning themselves and gather together any relevant documents. A single, long, continuous trial or hearing is less common than a series of hearings held over time as the judge completes each stage of his or her investigation.

Theocratic systems

Theocratic systems are also codified, but they differ from those described in the previous paragraphs in that their principles are immutable. In other words, they are derived from sacred texts and cannot thus be changed over time – although interpretations can evolve. In recent years some established theocratic systems have been diluted to a great extent as other principles have become more widely used. Hence in India there remain only remnants of traditional Hindu law which has force in certain circumstances (Zweigert and Kotz, 1998: 313–22), while in Israel principles of Talmudic law are present alongside codes and common law approaches. Islamic Sharia law is the major extant example of an operating theocratic legal system. It covers 500 million people (around a sixth of the world's population), but is applied in different ways in different countries. For example under the more conservative regimes such as Saudi Arabia, women are prevented from taking up permanent employment, while dress codes and religious holidays are observed strictly. Elsewhere (eg Pakistan and Egypt) the underlying principles of Sharia law are applied in a far more liberal way.

Different employment law regimes

From legally binding to voluntary

In most European countries employment law is set out in extensive codes which detail how different classes of employees are to be treated, specify substantial involvement for trade unions or works councils, and to a great extent determine terms and conditions of employment. Moreover, collective agreements are enforceable in court. In the UK and the Republic of Ireland employment statutes increasingly regulate aspects of the employment relationship, but they remain far more limited in their effect than continental European labour codes. Employers and employees are far freer to establish their own terms and conditions, while collective agreements in 99% of cases are 'binding in honour only' and cannot be enforced legally. Moves towards codification have also occurred elsewhere in jurisdictions where common law traditions prevail. We therefore see substantial anti-discrimination law in the USA and Canada and a complex statutory framework of employment protection legislation in Australia and New Zealand. Yet these remain regimes in which the state plays a far lesser role in determining what happens between employers and employees in their workplaces than is the case in France, Spain, Germany or Italy. This is partly because European labour codes are far more detailed than the employment statutes passed by parliaments in the common law countries, but also partly because of a fundamental difference in the way that much employment law is enforced.

Enforcement mechanisms

In the countries that have a common law tradition it is customarily an injured party (ie an aggrieved employee, ex-employee or failed job applicant) who brings a case to court seeking an injunction or compensation from the employing organisation. This is the case in codified jurisdictions too, but a greater role tends also to be played by inspectorates and government offices of one kind or another. Not only is the law itself more restrictive from an employer's point of view, but it is also more rigorously (and effectively) enforced. There is not just a risk that an employer acting unlawfully may be sued by a worker who suffers as a result, there is also a major risk of civil (or indeed criminal) actions being brought by a state-funded inspectorate.

In some countries labour inspectors, accountable to government ministers, wield substantial power and have wide-ranging responsibilities. In France, Spain, Portugal and their former colonies inspectors are generalists, overseeing a range of employer activities in a locality. They typically have responsibility for health and safety issues, working time, conditions of employment, some wage issues, compulsory vocational training, illegal employment issues and some social security matters. They also routinely get involved in the mediation of employee grievances and industrial disputes (von Richthofen, 2002: 38–43). It is not uncommon for inspectorates in these regimes to levy fines when employers refuse to comply with their rulings.

Coverage in other jurisdictions, as well as the extent of the inspectors' powers, is a great deal less substantial. In many countries inspectorates only deal with health and safety matters (eg the USA and Scandinavian countries) and are accountable to commissions that are independent of government. Fines are levied by the courts to which inspectors can bring cases, and not by the inspectors themselves. This used to be the case in the UK, but in recent years limited powers of inspection have been spread beyond the Health and Safety Executive (who still cannot levy fines themselves) to others, notably the Information Commissioner who has responsibility for policing data protection law, and to the statutory bodies charged with promoting equality at work and in the provision of goods and services.

Economic, social, and political challenges to the legal traditions and legal regime of Bulgaria form the basis of Case study 34 at the end of this chapter.

Discussion questions

1   How far do the three different types of legal systems establish frameworks to guide fair managerial action *and* protect employees from exploitative employment?

2   To what extent does the adversarial method of law enforcement produce a more equitable and just outcome than the inquisitorial and inspection methods?

3   Should employment law apply equally to all organisations and all employees, or is there a case for some variation and exemptions?

2 DISMISSAL LAW

The extent to which workers are protected from dismissal varies very considerably across the world. This is not an area of practice about which international standards have had much to say, largely because it would be very difficult indeed to get any measure of agreement on whether or not the law should restrict an employer's right to dismiss, let alone in what ways and circumstances. The EU, for example, has so far resisted the temptation to harmonise this fundamental area of employment law in all its member states. The same is true of the ILO.

Highly prescribed

At one extreme of the spectrum is the Dutch system. In the Netherlands, except in limited situations (end of fixed-term contracts, gross misconduct, termination by mutual consent, etc), employers are not permitted to dismiss their employees without first gaining written consent from a government official, the Director of the local District Labour Office (Rojot, 2001: 440; Hepple, 1998: 291–2). The same is true when employees wish to resign. The resignation only takes effect once it has been approved by this official. Any dismissal that occurs without the sanction of the Director is void in law, so the employer must continue paying wages until the dismissal is approved. Dismissals are only approved (which they are, in 95% of cases) if the

District Labour Office is satisfied that they are for one of the lawful reasons recognised in law, and that the matter has been handled in a procedurally correct way. But the process takes time – typically six to eight weeks (IDS/IPM, 1995: 277–8). Once permission to dismiss has been granted, the dismissal has to take place within two months, or else a fresh application to dismiss must be made. Where permission to dismiss is refused, the employer must go to court in order to be able to terminate the contract.

Highly permissive

At the other extreme is the USA which, for the most part, retains its long-held principle of 'employment at will', meaning that employers have the right to terminate employment whenever they wish and for whatever reason, which forms the basis of Case study 32. The principle was established by a Tennessee judge, who declared that someone could be lawfully fired 'for good reason, bad reason, or no reason at all'. There are, however, important exceptions. First and foremost, unionised workplaces (around 15% of the total) are not effectively covered. This is because collective agreements invariably contain provisions to ensure that workers are only dismissed with 'just cause'. Because collective agreements are legally enforceable in the USA, union members in such workplaces cannot normally be fired unless there is a good reason to justify their dismissals. In addition, there is extensive protection for women and minority groups provided through discrimination law, and for those who are dismissed for exercising their statutory rights in areas such as health and safety law or the payment of minimum wages (Rojot, 2002: 441). Furthermore, in the USA you cannot be lawfully dismissed for reporting for jury service or for refusing to take a lie detector test. A further group who are effectively protected are those individuals whose labour market position is powerful (members of the head-hunted classes) because they are in a position to ensure that restrictions on the employer's right to terminate without good cause are written into their individual contracts of employment.

Interestingly, because of the 'employment at will' doctrine and the lack of any general statutory protection for US workers who are fired, the common law has been developed extensively in such a way as to provide some measure of protection. For example, in some states employment contracts have been held to contain the implied term 'good faith and fair dealing'. Dismissals which breach these principles can thus be challenged in court and damages won where the plaintiff is successful. More significantly, the tort of defamation is increasingly used across the USA as a means of gaining redress following a dismissal, particularly where claims are made about poor conduct or performance which may be untrue to justify a dismissal.

The number of defamation-based lawsuits has grown in number since it was ruled in the case of *Milkovich v Lorain Journal Co* (1990) that employers could no longer deploy a defence of 'opinion'. From that time employers have not therefore been able to sidestep defamation laws by arguing that it was reasonable opinion to suggest that a particular employee was lazy, dishonest or incapable of performing his job (Carrell *et al*, 1995: 712). If the result of a dismissal is to damage an individual's reputation and this occurs because of a defamation, the person concerned can sue. It can be argued that these common law rights, in some respects at least, provide employees in the USA with a greater level of protection than their counterparts in Europe where the employment at will doctrine does not prevail. This is simply because the level of damages that can be obtained by American litigants is so high as to represent a stronger deterrent than is provided by the statutory unlawful discharge schemes operated in Europe.

CASE STUDY 32

EMPLOYMENT TERMINATION IN THE USA – THE ISSUE OF 'EMPLOYMENT AT WILL'

The USA is alone among industrialised nations in providing no legal protection against wrongful termination of employment. As many as 85% of all US employees are covered by the doctrine of 'employment at will' that allows employers to dismiss them at any time, for any or no reason, and the courts will not generally intervene to protect an ex-employee from allegedly unfair treatment. Solely employees with just-cause contracts can be dismissed only for a good reason, such as poor job performance.

Although since the 1980s there has been some limited erosion of this doctrine, the following examples illustrate an employee's hazardous situation:

- An employee who claimed he had been fired for reporting for jury service lost his appeal on the grounds that even though this might be true, he was an at-will employee whose employment could be terminated at any time.

- An employee who was fired because he shared his opinion that 'blacks have rights too' with a colleague was rightfully fired if his boss didn't like his sympathetic views on African-Americans.

The main erosions to the at-will doctrine have a public policy implication:

- *civil rights laws* – older employees can be fired, but not because they are older

- *contracts* – where there is a formal employment individual or collective contract with a just-cause requirement. Collective bargaining contracts apply only to trade union members and limit terminations to those with good reasons

- *whistleblowing* – eg where employees provide testimony in agency investigations

- *public sector protections* – where any federal, state or local laws require just-cause before a government employee can be terminated

- *good faith and fair dealing* – California and some other states have an implied contract to this effect between employers and employees that allows the courts freedom to exercise some discretion of judgement. Firing an employee to avoid paying a Christmas bonus is an example of violation

- *implied contract* – these are based on other evidence. For example, Blue Cross-Blue Shield's HR manual contained a just-cause clause that its representatives were unaware of when defending its at-will policy in court.

Employment-at will is highly institutionalised. There is no strong lobby to press the case for change. Employers are happy with the status quo, there is no employee cohesion in a highly individualised society, and trade unions are not bothered about the rights of non-union private sector employees. The courts are unwilling to intervene, and it is unlikely that any statutes will be introduced to make employment-at-will unlawful.

Employment-at-will is justified by commentators who support its continuation on the grounds that regulation of dismissal distorts the free operation of labour markets, making them less efficient and flexible. The more cumbersome and expensive it becomes to fire someone, the less incentive there is for an employer to hire people in the first place. The result is higher unemployment than there otherwise would be. Moreover, the additional costs imposed on employment mean that wages are lower than would be the case without the regulation.

Sources: Epstein (1984), Siegal (1998), Carrell *et al* (2000) and Standler (2000)

Case study tasks

1   To what extent are US employees' fundamental rights at work being infringed?

2   As the HR manager of a British-owned firm operating in the USA, how would you ensure that the organisation's HR policies and practices conform to fair and just employment standards?

3   As legal adviser to the policy-makers in a liberal state, with reference to dismissal legislation in other countries, how can you best make a case for a change in state law to ameliorate the effects of employment-at-will?

Half-way houses

Most dismissal laws fall somewhere in between the two extremes outlined above. Nearly all industrialised countries offer a degree of protection for employees who are dismissed unjustly or without compensation that is owed to them under their contracts, but it is rare for managers to have to seek permission before they can dismiss. The UK system is typical. Here, employers are restricted in law, once someone has completed a year's continuous service, from dismissing 'unfairly'. This means that the reason for the dismissal must be one of those listed as lawful in the relevant statute (capability, redundancy, misconduct, etc) and that it must be handled in a reasonable fashion. 'Reasonableness' in this respect means employing a proper procedure, giving adequate warnings and acting consistently in the way that different individual employees are treated. The incentive to act lawfully is provided by the ever-present threat that an employee who believes himself or herself to have been unfairly dismissed might take the case to an employment tribunal.

Discussion questions

1   As HR manager of a US organisation opening new branches in the Netherlands, China and the UK, what factors would you take into account in drawing up a dismissal policy that applies in all four countries?

2   Where an employee is wrongfully or unfairly dismissed, how should he/she be compensated for past and future loss?

3   How can you ensure that line managers act consistently in the way individuals are disciplined and dismissed?

3 WORKING TIME

The question of whether or not the state should intervene to regulate how long employees are required to work each day, week or year, and the extent to which this should happen, is one of the most controversial in employment law. Views differ very widely among commentators about what such laws achieve in practice, on their wider economic impact, and about how (if at all) they benefit employees. The issue is by far the most controversial in the employment arena as far as the EU is concerned, but it is also very divisive within those countries which have placed the greatest restrictions on working time.

Limited regulation

These substantial differences of opinion derive from the long-established diverse approaches to the regulation of working time used in different countries. The extent of these is clear from a search of the labour law database provided on the ILO website (www.ilo.org). In many countries there are no laws at all limiting working time or providing for paid annual leave. Elsewhere, the extent of regulation is very limited. In Singapore, for example, the only restrictions relate to the employment of pregnant women between 11.00 at night and 6.00 in the morning, while in India the three protected groups are employees in shops, restaurants and theatres, workers in beedi and cigar establishments, and children. The latter are restricted to a maximum of six hours' work a day and cannot work at all between 7pm and 8am, but all restrictions are removed once they reach the age of 14. In several other countries the only limitations are for workers in particular industries – mining and road transport being the most commonly protected sectors.

Detailed regulation

Elsewhere in the world regulation restricts working hours to a far greater degree. In Japan, for example, the law requires that everyone gets at least one day a week off work and prescribes an hour's break during any shift of eight hours or more. Officially, weekly working hours in Japan are limited to 45 (40 normal hours and up to five hours' overtime), but in practice many Japanese employees work many more hours than this. It is made worth their while by regulations which stipulate that overtime is paid at 125% of the normal hourly rate, rising to 135% for work undertaken between 10.00pm and 5.00am or on a designated rest day. The Japanese labour inspectors monitor payments of overtime and can bring charges against companies which underpay. Workers in Japan are also entitled to between 10 and 20 days' paid annual leave each year, depending on their length of service, but this only applies to people whose attendance records are good in their first months of employment with a new employer. Poland has a similar regime, workers being limited to 40 hours a week unless there are special circumstances that permit overtime. Even then, though, workers are limited to 150 hours' overtime a year paid at a 50% premium hourly rate.

The most protective regimes are found in those Western European countries such as France and Italy where working time has been regulated for centuries. All EU countries are required to limit working time to 48 hours a week and to give everyone a legal right to four weeks' paid annual leave each year, but the way that these rules are enforced varies greatly from country to country. In France there is a limit of 35 hours' work per week, which is quite rigidly enforced in practice but has been a source of increasing controversy since its introduction in 2000 (see Case study 33 below, and also Case study 8 in Chapter 4). Elsewhere, within the limits set out in EU regulations, the law requires that agreement about normal hours of work, overtime and rest periods is negotiated or even co-determined with trade unions or works councils. This is the case in Denmark, Germany, Austria and Sweden. In the UK, working-time regulations provide for the 48-hour working week to be averaged over 17 weeks, thus allowing employers a great deal of flexibility in practice. Moreover, as matters stand, employers can require their employees to sign 'opt-outs' as a condition of being offered a job which puts them outside the

48-hour working week altogether. The fact that such employees are entitled in law to opt back in without suffering any detriment, provided they give three months' notice, is not widely known or publicised by employers.

CASE STUDY 33

THE 35-HOUR WEEK IN FRANCE AND ITS APPLICATION TO MANAGERS (*CADRES*)

France is the first European Union country to have adopted a 35-hour week. Arguably, one of the most fundamental changes was the inclusion of managers and professional staff (*cadres*) within the scope of this law, because they had previously been exempt. The term *cadres* does not translate directly into English and refers to a very diverse category of upper-echelon white-collar workers, including engineers, foremen, managers, executives and, sometimes, secretaries. Previous case law had established their exemption from the statutory working week because their duties and levels of responsibility prevented them from adhering to any specific schedule.

The 2000 law established three groups of *cadres*:

- Senior managers (*cadres dirigeants*) – exempt from all provisions except paid holiday and mandatory maternity leave. In practice, the numbers of employees covered are likely to be small because their definition must conform to three criteria: they have considerable freedom to organise their work schedule, they take independent decisions frequently, and they have remuneration at the highest level relative to others in the company or establishment.

- Managers and professional staff working within a team in accordance with the employer's collective agreement (*cadres intègres dans une unite de travail*) – covered by all the working-time provisions including the statutory 35-hour week, overtime, night work, time off, holidays and supervision of working time. If their working week regularly exceeds 25 hours, a lump sum must be agreed to cover a certain number of hours.

- Other managers and professional staff – these are staff as defined in collective agreements, whose hours must be reduced in accordance with those specified in the agreement. There are two types of arrangement. One is based on the number of hours worked (*forfait annuel en heures*), if the employee works to a timetable calculated in hours. The other is calculated in days (*forfait annuel en jours*) where managers enjoy considerable work autonomy such that working time cannot be calculated in hours (up to 217 days maximum). There must be a system for monitoring cadres' workload.

These *cadres* are entitled to 11 consecutive hours of rest per day and 24 hours' consecutive rest per week.

Initially, some *cadres* feared that they would lose out from an annual 217-day flat rate working-time package because it imposed no limit on working hours, and could actually increase the length of working time – eg 13-hour days and 78-hour weeks. It was agreed to institute a scheme exempting working time calculated in days from the law, so that it could be challenged by the trade unions. Following a complaint to the Council of Europe's European Social Committee of Social Rights, France was found to be in violation of the European Social Charter, particularly on failing to limit weekly hours. However, any subsequent decision by the Council of Europe's Committee of Ministers would not be binding on the government.

By 2002 a majority of managerial staff perceived an improvement in their working conditions, and further reform of the legislation in 2005 included some benefits for *cadres*.

Source: Euroline: France (www.eurofound.ie, 1998, 1999, 2000, 2002a, b, 2005d); Mayne and Malyon (2001)

Case study tasks

1 What are the benefits and drawbacks of exempting managers from any or all of the working-time provisions? Should the most senior managers always be exempt from a maximum hours limit?

2 If you were to differentiate between categories of managers in terms of how working-time regulations should apply in a different country, how would you categorise managers and which working-time provisions would apply to each group?

3 Are the EU's enforcement powers adequate where a country fails to implement a Directive in accordance with the European Social Charter?

To regulate or deregulate?

The rights and wrongs of regulating working time are controversial all around the world. In recent years the extent to which hours should be restricted by law has been by far the most contested social policy issue in the European Union, where the impact of the regulations on employers, employees and on economies more generally has been both negative and positive. There is always pressure from trade unions to reduce hours, by decree or statute if not by agreement, and there is always resistance from employers. The issue has, however, moved up the agenda recently in many countries because of technological developments and the increase in global economic competition. The rise of consumer-led service-oriented industries with relatively low barriers to entry means that flexibility and efficiency in terms of service delivery are key to an organisation's survival. Customers expect to be able to get what they want, when they want, at the lowest possible price. This means longer hours of operation for organisations in most industries and a high degree of unpredictability when it comes to demand (see Chapter 5 for a broader discussion of the impact of this). The result is summed up by Karsten and Leopold (2003: 405):

'Working-time patterns are moving away from the traditional pattern of regularity, standardisation and coordination to a new triptych of individualism, heterogeneity and irregularity.'

In modern economies there is thus a great deal of extra pressure for people regularly to work longer hours, often without a great deal of notice and at times which (for most people) have traditionally not been occupied by work (evenings, night time, Sundays, etc).

There is thus a strong argument based on economic efficiency for minimal regulation. If a government wants its economy to thrive, it should not take steps to reduce the flexibility and efficiency of its organisations to compete effectively – particularly when other governments have chosen not to restrict working hours in their economies. On the other hand, it is also argued by many economists that reducing working hours can serve to increase productivity over the longer term because the quality of a person's work tends to diminish the longer he or she is required to perform it. Without adequate rest we all tire and find ourselves unable to perform our roles to the highest standards. We make more mistakes, slow down, and become less accommodating to others if required to overwork. Linked to this is the debate that thrives in France over the effect of working-time laws on unemployment levels. The major argument advanced for the introduction of the French 35-hour week was that it would reduce unemployment. If employers could not pay overtime to existing staff, they would hire new people instead. The case is persuasive in principle, but its opponents believe that they have been proved right in practice as unemployment levels have remained high in France despite the fact that its people work for 8% less time than the average EU worker. Reduced flexibility and increased training costs, it is argued, have lowered competitiveness, resulting in a negative impact on job levels overall.

The other major arguments in favour of restricting working time are social rather than economic in nature. In the EU, regulation in this field comes under the heading of health and safety. Working excessive hours, it is argued, creates undue stress, which over time increases the incidence of heart disease, high blood pressure and depression. There are further health and social consequences resulting from increased stress-induced consumption of alcohol, tobacco and other substances. Yet there is also evidence to suggest that for some people underwork is just as stressful as overwork. Provided they enjoy what they are doing and can exercise a degree of control over their work, depriving them of the opportunity to work long hours is likely to lead to adverse health consequences. Similar arguments can also be made in relation to work–life balance issues. A strong case can be put in favour of limiting working hours to help ensure that employees are free to spend time with their partners and families (see the discussion on this issue in Chapter 4). This is important to maintain social cohesion and results in fewer instances of breakdowns in relationships. Yet for many people, particularly those who are low-paid, the economic consequences of being deprived of the opportunity to earn overtime bring similar threats.

Discussion questions

1   What are the advantages and disadvantages of a maximum working week?

2   To what extent is the regulation of working time a health and safety issue rather than a work–life integration issue?

3   What are the effects of regulating working time on efficiency and productivity?

4 REGIONAL CONVERGENCE: EU LAW

We have already made reference in this chapter to the significance of EU law on member states. It is the major example in the contemporary world of a serious and sustained attempt to establish common regulation in the employment field across a number of different countries and hence to reduce diversity and bring about a degree of convergence. European employment law has evolved steadily over three decades, the pace of new regulation increasing somewhat since 2000. The aim is to create a Europe in which each member state observes the same basic minimum standards as far as employment law is concerned, and hence to create a situation in which institutional differences become less and less significant over time. Some countries will always want to regulate aspects of the employment relationship more than others, so EU law sets minimum standards and does not prevent member states from offering greater levels of social protection if they wish to.

In the Treaty of Rome, which originally established the EU, all the signatories signed up to some clauses which established core principles regarding the rights of workers. Treaty articles make direct reference to the following:

■ equal pay for equal work as between men and women

■ decent levels of health and safety practice in organisations to protect workers

■ the need to ensure that there is free movement of people (ie workers) within the borders of the EU

■ the improvement of working conditions generally.

These articles formed the underlying principles of the first European law in the employment field in the 1970s and 1980s, but it is only since the later 1980s that we have seen the development of a really meaningful social dimension. The first big impetus for faster movement came in the run-up to 1992 and the creation of a single market in goods and services across the EU. The view was expressed by Jacques Delors, then the EU's president, that social policy had to be harmonised between the member states alongside trade policy:

> **'There can be no social progress without economic progress, and no economic progress without social cohesion.'**

For the single market to operate effectively, he argued, there had to be an accompanying programme of social measures introduced in addition to those designed to promote trade and competition between member states. Moreover, without extensive social regulation there would be a tendency for 'social dumping' to occur. Member states would compete with one another to attract overseas investment by de-regulating and hence reducing overheads on business. The result would be steadily less social protection for employees over time. A third argument deployed related to a perceived need on the part of the EU's institutions to garner positive support for its projects among a sceptical and disinterested public. It was believed that harmonising employment regulation and setting high minimum standards would help to create 'a people's Europe' which would have widespread, positive and enthusiastic support.

Parts of this agenda were not especially controversial. For example, it was possible for the EU to get unanimous agreement for many health and safety measures (eg the Control of Substances Hazardous to Health Regulations in 1987) and for the measures designed to ease the movement of workers across borders (eg the recognition of equivalent qualifications). However, the idea that employment in general should be regulated by the EU, and not by member states themselves, was (and still is) hugely controversial. It was resisted by many business organisations and was opposed vigorously by the UK government of the time.

In 1989 the EU drew up a Social Charter which was signed by all member states except the UK. It had no legal effect at all, but was a statement of intent. It set out the core aims of the proposed 'social dimension' and to this day remains the framework around which new social policy measures are developed. It has 13 headings:

1   The improvement of living and working conditions (including those of seasonal and part-time workers)

2   The right to freedom of movement

3   The right to exercise any trade or occupation on the same terms as those applied to nationals of the host state

4   The right to fair remuneration for all employment

5   The right to social protection

6   The right to freedom of association and collective bargaining

7   The right to vocational training

8   The right of men and women to equal treatment

9   The right to information, consultation and worker participation

10 The right to health, protection and safety at the workplace

11 The protection of children and adolescents

12 Provisions for elderly people

13 Provisions for disabled people.

The next key step in the development of EU social policy came in 1993 with the signing by all the EU's member states of the Maastricht Treaty, which committed them all to make progress towards 'ever closer union'. The Social Charter was included here as a separate protocol called the Social Chapter, from which the UK had an 'opt-out'. This meant that the chapter and legislation brought forward under it would apply everywhere in the EU except the UK, but that EU institutions could be used to generate and subsequently enforce it. Following the election of the Blair government in 1997, the UK opted in to the Social Chapter, and so since then all EU employment regulation has applied across the whole of the union.

To date several dozen Directives have been issued and agreed, giving effect to the principles set out in the Social Charter, the most significant being:

■   measures preventing unjustified discrimination on grounds of sex, race, national origin, sexual orientation, religion or belief, disability and age

■   health and safety measures

■   protection for employees when their organisations are transferred from one owner or controlling body to another (the transfer of undertakings regulataions)

■   regulation of working time (see above)

■   requirements for employers to share information and to consult with employee representatives over major employment decisions such as redundancy

■   the establishment of European Works Councils in larger transnational companies

■   equal rights for 'posted' workers employed overseas within the EU

■   protection from discrimination for part-time workers and fixed-term workers

- rights for workers to take periods of parental leave and time off to make arrangements for the care of dependants

- substantial data protection law restricting what information employers can hold on employees and to whom it can be communicated.

Views differ on how to evaluate the development of EU employment regulation to date. On the one hand it is possible to look at the above list and conclude that substantial progress has been made towards the creation of a single body of employment law applying across 25 very different economies. But it is equally possible to look at the detailed picture and conclude that remarkably little progress towards that aim has actually occurred over a 30-year period. The playing-field is not level and a degree of social dumping continues to occur as a result. More importantly, unemployment rates remain stubbornly high across most of the EU and are especially high where employment regulation is most advanced. Pressures to de-regulate, or at least to halt further regulation, are thus growing. The big central questions thus remain unanswered: Is it wise to restrict employers' freedom to manage people as they see fit in a highly competitive world economy? Is it possible in an age of globalisation to enjoy high standards of social protection and high levels of economic dynamism?

Discussion questions

1 To what extent do you share Jacques Delors' view that social cohesion and social progress are prerequisites to economic progress in Europe?

2 Which are the three most important and the three least important of the Social Charter's principles?

3 Should member states be allowed more scope to regulate their own affairs – and if so, how could this be achieved?

5 INTERNATIONAL CONVERGENCE: THE INTERNATIONAL LABOUR ORGANISATION (ILO)

The ILO was established in 1919 in response to the growing momentum among countries in Western Europe to ameliorate poverty and harsh working conditions in a rapidly industrialised world. International social regulation based on fundamental basic principles was seen as both humanitarian and economically desirable. Starting from the premise that labour is not simply a commodity, these principles enshrine freedom of association for workers, the payment of decent wages, an eight-hour working day and 48-hour working week, weekly rest, the elimination of child labour and the regulation of young persons' work, equal pay for work of equal value, equivalent economic treatment for foreign workers, and the organisation of inspection services.

These principles, in the form of international standards, aim 'to establish minimum standards as a goal for some, while serving as a trampoline for others to allow them to improve their own legislation by comparing it with standards that are considered to be minimal at the international level' (Bartolomei de la Cruz et al, 1996: 26). Mindful of concerns that minimum standards may increase labour costs, ILO standards on wages, for example, do not impose wages at a predetermined level, but instead provide for minimum working conditions. Minimum standards are designed to mitigate any indirect effects on labour costs in two main ways. Firstly, they can raise productivity by protecting against inefficient, dangerous work environments and exploitative working conditions. Secondly, protective measures can promote the rationalisation of work organisation to compensate for any increase in costs.

The ILO now embraces a wider set of objectives designed to shape the future by:

- contributing to the possibility of lasting peace through a programme of social justice

- helping to mitigate the potentially adverse effects of international market competition by establishing minimum standards

- assisting in the social and economic development of countries through the implementation of programmes including vocational training, labour legislation and social security.

Constitution and scope

The ILO is an intergovernmental body whose membership more or less coincides with that of the United Nations (UN), and comprises 178 nations. It is a legal entity to the extent that is has privileges and immunities within member states that enable it to carry out its work, but is not a supra-national entity because it cannot impose any obligations on member states, except to the extent that they have agreed them – ie ratified a Convention. Member states may withdraw by giving two years' notice. South Africa is the most notable example, returning after a 30-year absence in 1994 after holding its first multi-racial elections. The USA also withdrew briefly between 1977 and 1980. There are no provisions for forced suspension or expulsion.

The ILO is made up of three principal bodies:

- The International Labour Conference (ILC) is tripartite and comprises four representatives – two from government, one employer, and one worker – who are assisted by technical advisers. This supreme body meets two to three times a year to discuss and adopt international standards – ie Conventions and Recommendations. Regional conferences meet periodically in the major continents to discuss regional issues, and may adopt less formal resolutions that serve their particular needs.

- The Governing Body is the executive, and is also tripartite comprising 56 members, half of whom are equal numbers of employer and worker members. Ten of the 28 governmental members represent countries of major industrial and agricultural importance – Brazil, China, India, Japan, the Russian Federation, the USA, and four Western European nations. The remaining governmental members are elected every three years. It selects the Director-General of the ILO, and meets three times per annum to set the ILC's agenda.

- The International Labour Office in Geneva is the permanent secretariat. Officials from over 100 countries collect and disseminate information, carry out studies and mount investigations, and publish studies and reviews.

The tripartite structure by which employers and trade unions together have the same number of representatives as governments is regarded as a major strength because it produces more realistic decisions. Nevertheless, there have been tensions in former socialist and Communist regimes whose employer and worker delegates could not legitimately claim true independence from government.

Policy instruments

Three main policy instruments have different effects (www.ilo.org).

Conventions are international treaties that can be considered a type of international law, although they have to be ratified, like a treaty, to become binding on the member state. This contrasts with the powers of the Commission of the European Communities, whose regulations have compulsory legal application in member states. Eight Fundamental Conventions underpin the basic rights of human beings at work. They cover subjects dealing with freedom of association and collective bargaining, the elimination of discrimination in respect of employment and occupation, the elimination of forced and compulsory labour and the abolition of child labour. Four Priority Conventions are concerned with matters of essential importance to labour institutions and policy. In total there are over 180 Conventions.

In 1995 a campaign was launched to achieve universal ratification of the Fundamental Conventions. By mid-2005 86% of the possible number of ratifications had taken place, and Tajikistan, St Kitts and Nevis, Bolivia, São Tomé and Principe, Mauritius, Chad, Israel, Mongolia and Colombia were among countries that finally ratified all Fundamental Conventions (www.webfusion.ilo.org). Countries that have yet to complete this process include Australia (abolition of child labour), Bahrain (freedom of association and collective bargaining), Lao People's Democratic Republic (elimination of discrimination) and Vietnam (elimination of forced and compulsory labour) (www.ilo.org/ilolex).

Recommendations also create obligations, but are non-binding instruments that set out guidelines for national policy and practice. There are over 185 Recommendations.

Other forms include codes of conduct, resolutions and declarations that are intended to have normative effects but are neither obligations nor international standards.

Enforcement and compliance

Enforcement is based on the ratification of a labour standard and an obligation to provide regular, periodic reports on measures taken to implement the standard. The Committee of Experts is responsible for examining these reports and for securing any additional information required by the Governing Body. The Committee comprises 20 eminent legal experts from different cultures, legal systems and regions across the world. Any observations arising from an evaluation of these reports are published in the Committee's annual report.

While modes of implementation vary according to countries' institutional arrangements, ascertaining compliance does not take account of prevailing economic and social conditions. Gaps in the observance of Conventions are not exclusive to developing countries, and may arise in different circumstances. One example is where governments propose reforms, such as in Australia, where the Government's proposals to abolish protection from unfair dismissal for 3.6 million workers employed in companies with fewer than 100 workers and individualise contracts have been opposed by the Australian Council of Trade Unions (ACTU) (www.actu.asn.au/public/news). Existing policies may be found wanting: the UK introduced in 2006 a new action plan to tackle sexual harassment in the Armed Forces (www.eoc.org.uk/cseng/news). The box below provides other examples of the ILO's influence in bringing countries' law and practices into line with ILO Conventions and Recommendations.

THE INFLUENCE OF ILO STANDARDS

Poland
From 1980 the primary goal of the 'Solidarity' trade union movement was to see the application of ILO Convention No. 87 (freedom of association and the right to organise),

which Poland had ratified. In advising the trade union and the government, the ILO contributed to the overthrow of Communism in the country.

South Africa
The ILO played a major part in fighting *apartheid*. In addition to providing sustained criticism of the regime and offering practical help to workers' organisations, the ILO conducted the only international investigation under apartheid. Its recommendations for non-discriminatory industrial relations and labour laws provided the foundation for the country's new policies in the post-apartheid era after 1994, and help has been extended to employers' organisations.

Brazil
Following ILO criticisms of the country's failure to prevent employers from demanding sterilisation and non-pregnancy certificates before the hire of women, in contravention of Convention No. 111, new legislation was adopted forbidding these practices in 1995.

Child labour
The ILO continues to draw attention to countries including Peru, India, Bangladesh and Thailand where children are enslaved to work in brothels and factories, and exploited in other industries such as carpet-making. Practical help is given through the ILO's International Programme for the Elimination of Child Labour.

Regional policy
ILO standards formed the basis for the European Social Charter of the EU and the social dimension of the common market among Argentina, Brazil, Paraguay and Uruguay.

Recommendations of the Committee on Freedom of Association
This is recognised as one of the most effective international human rights bodies. It has helped to remove measures for dismissing workers for trade union activity in Chad, to allow for the free election of trade union leaders and the recognition of a miner's union in Fiji, the release of trade unionists from prison in China, and the repeal of rules overriding collective agreements in Sweden.

Source: derived from Bartolomei de la Cruz *et al* (1996: 30–3)

Discussion questions

1 Evaluate the role of the ILO in a global economy.

2 Are the subjects covered by the Eight Fundamental Conventions sufficient to underpin the basic rights of human beings at work in the twenty-first century?

3 How could the work of the ILO be more widely publicised and made more effective?

CONCLUSIONS AND FUTURE ISSUES

In this chapter we have introduced comparative employment law, explaining how and why we observe patterns of both convergence and divergence. But what of the future? Are we likely to see more convergence driven by international (or supra-national) institutions, or is the globalisation of trade likely to lead to de-regulation as national governments compete with one another to attract investment from international companies and to maximise the flexibility of home-based employing organisations? Ultimately, everything depends on the judgement of the governments that come to power in the future and on the strength of interest groups such as trade unions. But there is a third possibility that is worth flagging. This has recently been articulated very effectively by Bob Hepple (2005) in his work on the place of labour law in a global economy. He argues that transnational regulation may not actually be the best way of protecting the interests of workers over the long term. He argues that this inevitably involves developing a sanctions regime whereby states that do not comply with internationally defined standards are punished economically in some way for their non-compliance. Except in the case of rogue states, Hepple argues that such an approach is likely to be counter-productive from the point of view of the workers who labour laws are intended to protect. Instead, he argues pragmatically for more positive encouragement from interest groups, international organisations and consumers. He also argues for an acceptance that labour law must vary considerably from country to country. Genuine harmonisation is not practically achievable, but the spread of good employment practice is.

Hepple believes that transnational corporations have a positive role to play as they tend to observe higher standards in employing people than local organisations in the developing world. Encouraging improvements via local contracting arrangements will help to create a 'race to the top' as employers increasingly realise that observing high standards increases their productivity over the long term. Major transnational corporations have a key role to play because of their market power (smaller organisations who supply them rely wholly on them) and because their international brands need to maintain a positive image with consumers (see Chapter 12). It is not in the interests of these companies to get their supplies from bad employers.

It may well be the case, therefore, that further harmonisation of labour laws across national boundaries and enforced by supra-national bodies is not likely to occur in the near future. But this does not necessarily mean that labour standards need fall or remain poor in countries where protective employment legislation is undeveloped. We could see, through the market-leading activities of multinational companies, local campaigns and encouragement from international bodies, steady improvement in the standards that organisations maintain in practice. The idea that the logic of globalisation points to ever-increasing reduction in employment standards and that the imposition of international labour standards are the necessary solution, may itself be flawed.

CASE STUDY 34

THE BULGARIAN LABOUR CODE – WAGES, SOCIAL PARTNERSHIP AND ILO AND EU COMPLIANCE

Since the end of Communist rule in 1989, the Bulgarian Labour Code 1986 has been amended regularly, the most important amendments occurring at least biennially. This is to bring it into line with the principles of a democratic market economy and, more recently, to make it compliant with EU social legislation embodied in the Council of Europe's European Social Charter to enable Bulgaria to secure successful accession to the EU in 2007.

The main areas regulated by the Code relate to the constitutional arrangements for tripartite cooperation and social partnership between the government, employers' organisations and trade unions, arrangements for collective bargaining, employment contracts, obligations of the parties to the employment relationship, working hours and rest, paid and unpaid leave, work discipline, employers' and employees' financial liability and other types of compensation, professional qualifications, labour remuneration, safe and healthy conditions at work, social benefits within the enterprise, special protection for some categories of employees, termination of the employment relationship, service record and length of service, labour disputes, and enforcement mechanisms and penalties.

Changes to the Labour Code follow from discussions within the National Council for Tripartite Partnership (NCTP) established in 1993 as the main body for national-level social partnership. This government-convened body has been subject to considerable tensions between the partners – the largest trade union confederations and employer's organisations and government representatives, the latter dependent on the government of the time.

Wages

The non-payment or late payment of wages has been a major source of industrial conflict since the early 1990s, leading the Confederation of Independent Trade Unions in Bulgaria (CITUB) to convene a tripartite meeting in 2003. The ILO Committee of Experts on the Application of Conventions and Recommendations, with reference to ILO Convention No. 95 and Recommendation No. 85 on the protection of wages, suggested that the phenomenon of unpaid wages was spreading and that it had created an 'ingrained culture of non-payment'.

Jeliazko Hristov, CITUB's president, criticised successive governments for ignoring this serious problem. He alleged that employers frequently do not pay wages to increase their cash flow – many companies do not even observe the minimum wage stipulated by the Labour Code – and employees prefer to keep their jobs with no pay, rather than to have no job at all. Employers countered these allegations by attributing the problem to insolvency of the firm's clients, lack of available cash, high levels of debts to the state and high social insurance and ineffective management. Nevertheless, the outcome of the meeting was a recognition of the need to reduce the number of the 'working poor' by introducing legislation to provide wage guarantees and protect workers' rights in this area.

Later in 2003 the government created a new fund to guarantee employees' pay claims in the event of their employees' insolvency. This reflected ILO Convention No. 173 on the protection of workers' claims (employer's insolvency) and the EU Directive (80/987/EEC) on the protection of employees in the event of their employer's insolvency. Payment of part of a worker's unsettled claim comes from a special fund financed by employers' contributions.

In 2003 average hourly remuneration for Bulgarian employees was extremely low, at around 1.35 euro per hour compared to an EU average of 23 euros per hour among the then 15 countries. Unpaid wages amounted to more than 75 million euros in 2003. The minimum wage is determined by the government in compliance with Article 244 of the Labour Code, and represents the lowest guaranteed remuneration for working hours of normal duration. The Ministry for Labour and Social Policy prepares proposals for amendments to the levels of the minimum wage, which are discussed by the social partners of the NCTP. Since 1989 the minimum wage has lost much of its purchasing power, and in 2004 it was set at 61.5 euros per month – some 40% below the average wage.

Many private SMEs declare pay levels near the official minimum wage but actually pay higher remuneration. Their motivation appears to be to reduce their tax and social insurance contributions and to cut their labour costs. As a result, national pay statistics are unreliable and the state budget and social security funds do not receive their due contributions.

In 2004 the Ministry for Labour and Social Policy embarked upon an ambitious wage-raising programme affecting the minimum wage and pensions. The proposals were to increase the minimum wage by 25% to 77 euros per month and the guaranteed minimum income below which people are entitled to social assistance by 50% to 31 euros per month. Both changes would take effect from 1 January 2005. A subsequent report by the World Bank found that one in seven people in Bulgaria are poor – ie with an income below 52 euros per month.

The Labour Code was also amended in 2004 following discussions in the NCTP, although the employers had initially been negative about some of the changes. The main area of contention related to overtime work where an employer orders an employee to work during the two-day rest period. In addition to the relevant wage premium, employers have to give the employee an additional period of at least 24 hours' uninterrupted rest in the following week.

The Bulgarian trade unions regarded the 25% raise in the minimum wage as inadequate, demanding that its level be linked with an 'official' poverty threshold. They also opposed (as did the employers) the government's plans to abolish the system that allows employees to transfer their mandatory length of service allowance between jobs, in the absence of any new measures linking pay to skills, experience, quality and performance. The unions further believed that other 'liberalisation' measures aimed at creating a more flexible labour market were unreasonable, including the abolition of severance pay on retirement, without apparently having realised that some aspects of flexibility could be beneficial.

The two main trade unions, CITUB and the Confederation of Labour Podkrepa (CLP), believe that the government is reacting to the pressures of international financial institutions and big business, and could endanger the positive findings of the European Commission and the ILO with regard to Bulgaria's compliance with EU and international standards. For example, the unions claimed that the abolition of some compensatory allowances will reduce the pay of those affected by 160 euros per month.

In January 2005 the government imposed the new minimum wage of 77 euros per month, despite some employer and trade union opposition over the lack of consultation and particular employer concern at its unduly high level for businesses in some sectors of the economy. Nevertheless, all the social partners agreed that there was an urgent need to develop a method for fixing the minimum wage that is consistent with 'objective criteria' embodied in ILO Conventions and Recommendations. In March the trade unions CITUB and CLP withdrew their participation from the NCTC, blaming the government on the grounds that proceedings had become too formalised and inefficient, a process that had been exacerbated by the admission of three 'unrepresentative' bodies – one trade union and two employers' organisations – to the NCTC in late 2004. In February John Monks, the General Secretary of the European Trade Union Confederation (ETUC), highlighted Bulgaria's failure to observe appropriate tripartite and social dialogue to the

European Commission as one factor that could jeopardise Bulgaria's chances of EU accession in 2007, although the abolition of some compensatory allowances remains highly contentious.

Source: Eironline: Bulgaria (www.eiro.eurofound.eu.int, 2003a,b; 2004a, b, c, d, e, f, g; 2005a, b, c, e); Ivanov (2005)

Case study tasks

1 What are the implications of this situation for:
   a. the state?
   b. business performance?
   c. HR policy and practice?
   d. workers' protection?

2 How far have the ILO and the European Commission been able to bring about change in Bulgaria, and how they can they contribute to further improvements in the future?

3 How can the minimum wage in Bulgaria be fixed and adjusted more equitably?

REFERENCES

Bartolomei de la Cruz H. G., von Potobsky G. and Swepston L. (1996) *The International Labor Organization: The International Standards System and basic human rights.* Boulder, CO: Westview.

Carrell M. R., Elbert N. F. and Hatfield R. D. (1995) *Human Resource Management. Strategies for Managing a Diverse and Global Workforce* (5th edition). Englewood Cliffs, NJ: Prentice Hall.

Carrell M. R., Elbert N. F. and Hatfield R. D. (2000) *Human Resource Management. Strategies for Managing a Diverse and Global Workforce* (6th edition: Chapter 16, Discipline and Counselling). Orlando, FL: The Dryden Press.

Epstein R. A. (1984) 'In defense of the contract at will', *University of Chicago Law Review*, Vol. 51: 947–82.

European Industrial Relations Observatory On-line (Eironline):

(1998) 35-hour week adopted, June

(1999) Discontent spreads among managerial staff on 35-hour week, December

(2000) Law on 35-hour week is in force, January

(2002a) 35-hour week law challenged by Council of Europe Committee, March

(2002b) Government issues assessment of 35-hour week legislation, October

(2003a) Social partners and government discuss unpaid wages, August

(2003b) New law establishes insolvency fund, December

(2004a) 2003 Annual Review for Bulgaria, May

(2004b) Pay developments over 2003–4 examined, June

(2004d) Government proposes to increase incomes, July

(2004e) Labour Code amended, August

(2004f) Trade unions oppose government wage restraint, November

(2004g) Compensation for hazardous work under debate, November

(2005a) New social partnership organisations recognised as representative, January

(2005b) Minimum wage increased without tripartite consensus, February

(2005c) Tripartite partnership under threat, April

(2005d) Reform of 35-hour week under way, April

(2005e) Round table on working poor in Bulgaria, May

Hepple B. (1998) 'Flexibility and security of employment' in R. Blainpain and C. Engels (eds) *Comparative Labour Law and Industrial Relations in Industrialised Market Economies* (6th edition). The Hague: Kluwer Law International.

Hepple B. (2005) *Labour Laws and Global Trade*. Oxford: Hart Publishing.

IDS/IPM (1995) *Contracts and Terms and Conditions of Employment*. London: Incomes Data Services and Institute of Personnel and Development.

Ivanov A. (2005) Information provided by the Director of the Law Department, Ministry of Labour and Social Policy, Bulgaria.

Karsten L. and Leopold J. (2003) 'Time and management: the need for hora management', *Personnel Review*, Vol. 32, No. 4: 405–21.

Labour Code (2001) *State Gazette No. 25*, Sofia, Bulgaria.

Labour Code (2004) *State Gazette No. 52*, Sofia, Bulgaria.

Mayne S. and Malyon S. (eds) (2001) *Employment Law in Europe*. London: Butterworths Students.

Rojot J. (2001) 'Security of employment and employability' in R. Blainpain and C. Engels (eds) *Comparative Labour Law and Industrial Relations in Industrialised Market Economies* (7th edition). The Hague: Kluwer Law International.

Siegal M. (1998) 'Yes, they can fire you', *Fortune*, Vol. 138, No. 26, October: 301.

Standler R. B. (2000) History of at-will employment law in the USA. (www.rbs2com/atwill.htm)

von Richthofen W. (2002) *Labour Inspection: A guide to the profession*. Geneva: ILO.

Zweigert K. and Kotz H. (1998) *An Introduction to Comparative Law* (3rd edition, translated by T. Weir). Oxford: Oxford University Press.

Useful websites

www

www.actu.asn.au

www.eoc.org.uk

www.eu-employment-observatory.net

www.eurofound.ie

www.ilo.org

www.ilo.org/ilolex

Gorporate governance, justice and equity

Corporate social responsibility and human resource management

CHAPTER 12

Richard Warren and Hamish Mathieson

CHAPTER OBJECTIVES

When you have read this chapter you should be able to:

■ define and be able to describe corporate social responsibility (CSR)

■ understand why this has become an important part of the global business agenda

■ articulate and criticise some of the arguments for and against CSR

■ identify and understand the contribution of the HRM function to the CSR agenda

■ understand and appreciate the requirements of a CSR management system

■ appreciate and evaluate the HRM function's contribution to CSR reports

■ benefit from what you have learned from case studies and other examples of best practice in CSR in the international context.

PURPOSE AND SCOPE

This chapter is about corporate social responsibility (CSR) and the contribution the HRM function can make to this new agenda in business. For many companies, the attention that has had to be devoted to social responsibility issues is proving to be costly and time-consuming. Most companies now allocate some of their budget to social responsibility issues. What was once perhaps a public relations stunt is now a serious part of many firms' business strategy.

This chapter will examine the implications of these developments for HRM, focusing primarily on the themes of globalisation, cultural change and EU integration and enlargement, and is organised in four broad sections. The first section explains how CSR can be understood as a voluntary activity, the integration of social and economic concerns and a part of a company's multiple responsibilities to a range of stakeholders. In Section 2 the authors argue that HRM departments have not driven this development, but many are now actively involved and have made innovative and creative contributions to company CSR-led policies and activities through initiatives in the areas of pay, working time and employer branding. Section 3 discusses how CSR can be organised and integrated into the HRM function, emphasising that the trend has been for firms to become more open, transparent and concerned about non-shareholder interests or stakeholders in society. Section 4 then turns to the role that the HR function can play in CSR reporting activities and how this is manifested in different contexts. Accounting and reporting on corporate social responsibility is a new field and many imaginative experiments are taking place in this area of disclosure, and these are likely to help shape new conventions and procedures in the future.

1 WHAT IS CSR?

A new agenda

CSR is the idea that companies should consider the interests of society and the environment when making decisions. The importance of CSR in the operational strategies of business firms is apparent to most consumers today. The controversy surrounding obesity and fast food chains such as McDonald's in recent times is a real sign that consumer pressure has come of age and is a potent force that companies are obliged to take into account (see box below).

HEALTHY AND HAPPY EATING AT MCDONALD'S

A clever and amusing critique of the McDonald's fast food diet made in the film *Super Size Me* by Morgan Spurlock, and other health-based criticisms, have brought about revisions in the menus and marketing of McDonald's in double-quick time. Weeks after the screening of this film, McDonald's introduced its new salad meals and a new children's menu with 108 'healthy' happy meal combinations. McDonald's and many other global brands are only too well aware that they need to retain public approval if they are to remain profitable businesses.

And yet, a large number of people, it would seem, still have an uneasy relationship with many of these companies. In the UK, MORI opinion polls have tracked the public approval rating for big business over the last 30 years and find it to be at an all-time low, only a quarter of the public considering it a 'good thing' for large companies to make profits (Lewis, 2003). Many people in these surveys are concerned that companies do not behave 'ethically'. Companies are aware of this fact, and have in recent times been searching for ways to improve their standing and legitimacy with the public without losing sight of their private self-interest.

Many companies in response to these pressures have developed policies on corporate social responsibility. A quick reading of the report and accounts for many large companies reveals that stakeholders, accountability and sustainability have become the slogans of the new millennium. Many companies are now publishing operating and financial reviews alongside their mandatory accounts, and some have actively welcomed independent auditors and pressure groups such as Friends of the Earth as verifiers of their sustainability statements and achievements. The failure of a company to take swift action in the face of social pressure can be enormous – it is much harder for managements to get these decisions wrong than right. In 1995, Shell abandoned its sinking of the oil storage platform, the Brent Spar, in the face of pressure from Greenpeace and its supporters, much to its own and the British government's embarrassment.

Defining corporate social responsibility

'Corporate social responsibility' is a fairly recent term but it is becoming a well-known expression for what, in the recent past, has been a collection of different and yet related terms: corporate philanthropy, corporate citizenship, business ethics, stakeholding, community in-volvement, corporate responsibility, socially responsible investment, sustainability, triple-bottom line, corporate accountability, corporate social performance. Some of these terms have a family resemblance to each other, but many of these expressions have other connotations as well. All these words have different meanings and emphases, and some companies are more wedded to some of these expressions than to others (Table 5).

Table 5 Examples of company terms for CSR

Company	Term
Co-operative Group	'corporate responsibility'
Ford Motor Company	'connecting with society'
United Utilities	'social and environmental impact'
Shell	'sustainable development'
P&O	'environment and community'

These phrases and terms have to some extent been in competition for dominance in describing and giving name to the range of concerns of firms in this new field of responsibility. In many ways, it does not matter which term becomes dominant as long as there is some agreement about what firms mean by it, so that they do not talk past one another. For the moment, CSR seems to have gained dominance as the collective term for this new set of initiatives and responsibilities. Many of the expressions listed above are contributory or complementary activities to the central message of CSR. Some of them are discussed in later sections of this chapter, but for now it may be useful to try to define what themes and activities CSR describes, and then to examine some of the different interpretations of this phrase.

Authoritative definitions of CSR are hard to come by in this developing area of responsibility because there is, as yet, so little orthodoxy in both theories of CSR and in its practice (Carroll, 1999). There seems to be no general theory of CSR, although many academics have sought to establish the fact that such a responsibility exists, and some academics are leading advocates and campaigners for its adoption in business (Zadek, 2001). In fact, CSR is perhaps better understood as a new concern or activity that has been pioneered by business, and then discovered by the academy, and finally recommended to the state for validation and endorsement. This process has now moved on a stage further, beyond the academy and the nation-state, to the supra-national level in Europe and the United Nations. The European Union (EU) is now embracing CSR, and in the Green Paper *Promoting a European Framework for CSR* has defined CSR as (EU Comm, 2001: 6):

> **'a concept whereby companies integrate social and environmental concerns in their business operations and in their interaction with their stakeholders on a voluntary basis.'**

There are three points to note in this definition:

- This activity on the part of companies is held to be a voluntary initiative.
- These social and environmental concerns should be integrated.
- All businesses should interact with their stakeholders.

Let us consider these points in turn.

CSR as a voluntary activity

The EU at the moment is encouraging firms to embrace CSR as a voluntary activity, which is a move above and beyond what is required by company law. Firms are urged to do this as a matter of enlightened self-interest, but as yet, most states (and in particular the supra-national EU) do not want to force this responsibility on to firms or require that it becomes legally enforceable. This reflects a political compromise within the EU, as firms in some states are finding that certain aspects of CSR are now almost mandatory and are increasingly becoming integrated into some states' frameworks of company law. For example, CSR reporting is virtually compulsory for UK firms that want to maintain stockmarket listings and the approval of large investment funds. So, although the EU definition defines CSR as an added value or voluntary activity, this may be a transition phase prior to its incorporation into the regulatory framework of business. On the other hand, CSR may just be a passing fad, as it has been in the past, that the EU is happy enough to endorse and encourage at present but that will in due time be allowed to drop away so that its incorporation in company law will not then arise. The voluntary character of CSR will also allow it to be dropped by business in a few years if the public pressure for CSR begins to subside. The designation of CSR as voluntary in the EU definition indicates, then, that it is still a tentative and a contested political issue that has succeeded in gaining the attention of the EU but has not yet managed to become an institutional fixture in business.

Social and environmental agendas

The EU definition indicates that two responsibility agendas ought to be integrated: the social and the environmental.

- The environmental agenda for business has been around since the 1960s, and in Europe some states are much further along the road of making business more environmentally conscious than others. The movement towards sustainable business has a long way to go but consciousness of the perils of ignoring these matters is now with us. Many of these requirements are making their way into state and EU regulations, but once again business is being urged to take this responsibility further than mere compliance.

- The social responsibility agenda that is being integrated with the environmental or green agenda has arisen more recently, but represents the growing need for business to act ethically, transparently and responsibly in its dealings with customers, and in the communities where it operates.

The integration of these two agenda reflects the globalisation of business and the fact that the social and the environmental are ultimately connected and must be embraced as a single concern for sustainability in business.

Stakeholders

The notion of stakeholders is also referred to in the definition, and this reflects some of the debate in business that developed in the 1990s about the different ways to embrace capitalism – sometimes characterised as a choice between the Rhennish (stakeholder) and the Anglo-Saxon (stockholder) view of the firm. The term 'stakeholder' is contrasted with 'shareholder' – or in the USA, 'stockholder' – as the signifier of the differing perspectives at issue. Shareholders are often held up as the beneficial owners of the company because they are the major risk-bearers and are therefore entitled to the profits of the business after all other contract payments have been made. The creation of shareholder value is said by many commentators to be the raison d'être of the business and is therefore the primary duty of the shareholder's agents, the managers of the company. The substitution of the term 'stakeholder' in place of the shareholder is an explicit questioning of this first duty assumption, effectively redefining the duties of management as pluralist or multiple. Stakeholder advocates are seeking to define business as an endeavour shared with many participants, all of whom have a stake in its success, and in the firm's good governance.

As yet, 'stakeholding' is a term used mainly by public relations departments and in some management literature in large organisations, but there is now a push to see this conception of responsibilities incorporated into company law. In the so-called Rhennish model of firms in countries such as Germany and the Netherlands, stakeholder representatives drawn from the workers have boardroom seats in the company. The demand to enfranchise more stakeholders in the company would substantially alter the institutional nature of business and the model of governance that sets its purpose and function. The introduction of stakeholder language into the EU definition is indicative of the radical potential the CSR concept has and indicates that this will be a contentious and momentous change in the institutional structure of capitalism should this view come to prevail.

Before we consider what CSR activity involves and what guides its development, it is important to explore some of the contentious arguments underpinning this conception of business responsibility.

Why has CSR become such a prominent issue in the new millennium?

The adoption of CSR language and activity in business is now substantial and widespread. These changes are an indication that there has been a response by business to social, political and ecological pressures that are largely instinctive, ad hoc, and to date have had little guidance or direction from a justifying theory. In initiating policies and activities demonstrating concern for CSR business has made all the running and business school academics are often struggling to catch up, such schools being mainly content with describing and categorising these initiatives rather than directing them. However, in recent years several interesting explanations have emerged that can help us to understand business's response to these new social and political pressures.

The rise of the 'bimoral' society

John Hendry, in his book *Between Enterprise and Ethics*, offers perhaps one of the most eloquent explanations (Hendry, 2004). As he sees it, we now live in a 'bimoral' society in which social conduct is influenced by two contrasting sets of principles. On the one hand there are the principles associated with traditional morality and the maintenance of hierarchical order in society. Although these rules of conduct allow individuals a modicum of self-interest, their emphasis is on our duties and obligations to others: to treat people honestly and with respect, to treat them fairly and without prejudice, to help others and to be there for them when in need, and ultimately, to put the needs of others before one's own. On the other hand there are the principles associated with the entrepreneurial self-interest of individuals in a competitive society. These also impose obligations, but of a much more limited kind. Their emphasis is competitive rather than cooperative: to advance our own interests rather than to meet the needs of others.

Three aspects of Hendry are noteworthy:

- Hendry demonstrates in a richly textured analysis of changes in Britain that both sets of principles have always been present in society but that in recent years traditional moral authorities have lost much of their force and the morality of self-interest has acquired a much greater social legitimacy, over a much wider field of behaviour, than ever before. The modern moral dilemma is that in many situations it is no longer at all apparent to many people which set of principles should take precedence.

- Hendry carefully explores how the cultural and historical origins of the 'bimoral' society have also led to new, more flexible forms of organising, which have released people's entrepreneurial energies and significantly enhanced the creative capacities of business. He notes that working within these organisations, however, is fraught with moral tensions because traditional obligations and individual self-interest conflict and workers are pulled in all sorts of different directions at once. Consequently, organisation and governance in business are much more problematic and are posing new moral challenges for business leaders, and this is therefore putting a new focus on business ethics. The raison d'être of management becomes institution-building and stakeholder-balancing: determining purposes and priorities, reconciling divergent interests, and nurturing trust in interpersonal relationships.

- Hendry identifies the issue of business legitimacy as one of the challenges posed for all societies as they seek to regulate and govern an increasingly powerful and global business sector. In this respect the issue of CSR and its influence on public opinion is of crucial importance in the national and increasingly in the global context.

A crisis of business legitimacy

The importance of the public acceptance of business as a legitimate set of interests that contribute to the good of society has also been stressed by Warren in his analysis of this change in the business climate (Warren, 2000). 'Legitimisation' is a term used to analyse the relationship of power that exists between an institution and society. In society, a legitimisation crisis arises when the power of an institution is challenged or where it comes into conflict with other groups who ask questions about the authority and scope of the institution. Because such institutional authority rests upon a kind of power, there is a need to gain assent or deference on the basis of a claim recognised as of right by those both inside and outside the institution. Authority can be swiftly eroded when this assent disappears, and at times this can happen very quickly – for example, the authority of the Communist governments in the Eastern European countries in 1989.

The movement towards a legitimacy crisis for business institutions in recent years can be seen to derive from a diverse combination of factors. Some are new and circumstantial, others are the legacy of a prolonged period of political change designed to make societies more enterprising and market-based. The legitimacy of companies as creators and distributors of wealth is beginning to be questioned as greater inequalities are emerging. The employee's sense of security which comes from working in a company has been shaken in recent years through cost-cutting redundancy programmes and the subcontracting and outsourcing of the supply chains across the globe. The welfare states in many societies are now struggling to cushion the blow of uncertainty, and increasingly divided and unequal societies are growing. In the face of these pressures and drivers, CSR has been moving to the top of the corporate agenda in recent years.

Arguments against the CSR response

These trends towards the embracing of CSR particularly on the part of big business have not been without their critics in recent years (Vogel, 2005; Sternberg, 1994). Such tendencies were subjected to criticism as long ago as in the 1970s by the Nobel Prize-winning economists Friedman and Hayek.

CSR as 'global salvationism'

In recent years the CSR movement has been criticised and viewed with dismay by the noted economist David Henderson in his pamphlet *Misguided Virtue* (Henderson, 2001). Henderson claims that CSR is a form of 'global salvationism', which advocates acceptance of alarmist views on the state of the environment and the damage done to it by business-related activity, and that business has done little to improve the lot of the poor – in fact, on the contrary, it has exacerbated inequality and social divisions. He claims that these assumptions are wrong, and that the adoption of CSR policies carries with it a high probability of increasing business costs and impaired business efficiency. This is because CSR requires managers to take account of a wider range of goals and concerns in new processes of engagement with stakeholders. Also, new methods of accounting, monitoring and auditing are required, adding to the firm's costs. Then the adoption of more exacting than are legally required social and environmental standards becomes a compliance requirement of partners, firms, suppliers and other contractors, adding to the total cost base of industries. CSR initiatives assume that the direction of progress lies in making social and environmental norms and standards more stringent and more pervasive. Henderson thinks this takes too little account of costs and benefits at the margin, and of the differences in circumstances in which firms find themselves. The enforcement of global standards and contract compliance has the effect of limiting competition and worsening the performance of the economy as a whole. Consequently, CSR policies will make people poorer in the long run.

Henderson suggests that the primary role of business is *to act as a vehicle for economic progress*, which is best achieved by a smoothly functioning market economy in which firms' profits are related to how well consumers' demands are met. Profits are the indicator of success in this system and measure the firms' contribution to the welfare of society. Business has ethical obligations to serve the limited and specific purpose that firms were created for, and to do so within the legal framework of society. Real CSR concerns should be focused upon greater liberalisation of the global economy, and international institutions should put their efforts into widening market opportunities and increasing the competitive framework.

CSR as public relations

A second line of argument against CSR is that these policies are *more about public relations and marketing than about serious intentions to do good*. A report by the Institute for Public Policy and Research (IPPR) in 2003, using data from a survey of 500 leading firms, claimed that many of the firms' claims about CSR were tokenistic (Joseph, 2003). The report highlighted that although 75% of directors said their firm promoted equal opportunities, only 50% collected information on how many women worked for them, and only 40% did so for ethnic minority employees. And although 60% of directors said that environmental impact was important, fewer than 30% collected information on their greenhouse gas emissions. The IPPR noted generally that there was a real gap between the rhetoric and reality of CSR reports, and that there were limits to what voluntary action on CSR could achieve.

CSR policies are also *a kind of insurance policy*. Companies with well-known brands, healthy profits, and old sites in the developed world and significant activities in the developing world have significant value at risk. A commitment to CSR can reduce these risks and act as an insurance against reputation damage if something goes wrong.

Whether these arguments will deflate the CSR movement remains to be seen, but even a small sample of today's business literature tends to indicate that CSR is an element in a much-used vocabulary of motive and is now widely adopted in many organisations. Whether CSR will provide the necessary boost to business legitimacy and will therefore become a permanent fixture in the institutionalisation of the corporate form depends upon the sincerity with which these initiatives are pursued by business leaders.

Discussion questions

1　Could you write a better definition of what CSR is all about?

2　What have been the major drivers of CSR in recent years?

3　Why should we be sceptical about the CSR agenda?

2 THE CONTRIBUTION OF HRM TO THE CSR AGENDA

CSR requires business to acknowledge that its responsibilities extend beyond maximising profitability to meeting the demands of other stakeholders. One of these key stakeholder groups is the firm's employees and potential employees. Consequently, the HRM function has an important contribution to make on the CSR agenda with these sets of stakeholders. This contribution has been acknowledged by the Chartered Institute of Personnel and Development (CIPD) in the UK, which has issued a guide to its members, stating (CIPD, 2002) that:

'CSR does not change so much as broaden the HR agenda, and focuses on effective implementation.'

Employees today are more discerning in the jobs they choose, and increasingly prefer to work for companies whose values they share. Also, to attract the best staff firms have to appeal to prospective employees by reputation and standing up for the right values. Moreover, if employees are treated well and share the ethos of the company, they are more likely to treat customers and suppliers well and help to build the reputation of the company. For example, evidence from recent research conducted in the financial services industry (Brammer, 2006) suggests that employees' perceptions of the firm's corporate social responsibility activities had a major impact on organisational commitment. Firms can demonstrate their commitment to CSR by involving employees directly in company philanthropic activities and in community engagement through employee volunteering schemes. A large number of companies in the UK operate schemes by which employees can donate part of their salaries to charitable causes through the payroll system. Companies may match or exceed the sums given by employees. Another form of corporate community involvement is where firms 'donate' their employees' time and skills by setting up volunteering programmes. These may enable employees to contribute to the local community either in structured projects during company time or in ad hoc activities outside working hours (IDS, 2001).

CSR and a wide HRM agenda

The human resource CSR agenda concerning employees and potential employees is very wide-ranging. CSR initiatives can be included in the following aspects of HRM many of which are explored in detail in other chapters of this book:

- recruitment and the cultivation of the labour market
- the payment of fair remuneration and benefits
- the provision of good training and development opportunities
- good communications
- health and well-being initiatives
- consideration of employees' work–life balance
- exemplary health and safety procedures
- listening to the employees' voice through representation.

Best practice in HRM goes a long way in helping a firm to fulfil its CSR agenda with its employee stakeholders. Of course, much depends on the level of commitment on the part of human resource managers to embedding CSR in their day-to-day professional work. In this respect there is some encouraging evidence. For example, a 2004 survey of HR managers in 51 UK organisations showed that in 45 cases there was 'agreement' or 'strong agreement' that the HR function had a positive role to play in improving the ethical stance of the organisation through the promotion of appropriate behaviour and relationships in the workplace. Some 35 of the organisations had policies relating to the fair and ethical treatment of employees, and 27 of those policies were represented by formal written statements. The most common areas covered by the policies were diversity, health and safety, anti-harassment, flexible working and decisions around dismissals, while the least common was the right to collective representation (IRS *Employment Review*, 2004). Some examples of how CSR considerations may influence aspects of HR practice are presented by focusing on what Sisson and Storey term 'two issues at the heart of the employment relationship: pay and working time' (2000: 117).

Pay and reward

CSR issues are of contemporary relevance to this area in four main ways.

1 Directors' pay

There has been considerable controversy relating to the growth in directors' remuneration relative to the pay of other staff. This has been most pronounced in the 'liberal market economies' of the USA and the UK where the pay ratio of Chief Executive Officers to staff increased, respectively, from 325:1 to 600:1 and from 18:1 to 20:1 between 1997 and 2002. The debate turns on the question of 'where fair pay ends and where over-compensation begins' (Kakabadse *et al* 2004) and of the need for executives to practice 'corporate temperance' (Warren, 1994).

2 The 'new pay' model

Heery (1996) has drawn attention to ethically questionable features of the 'new pay model', which has come to prominence in the USA and the UK in the past 20 years. The key characteristic of 'new pay' is its emphasis on reward's being contingent on business strategy and closely linked to measures of performance (see Chapter 9 for a full discussion of this trend). Pay is at once seen as strategic, flexible and variable. One effect of such an innovation is to deliberately increase employee risk, which is unacceptable on various counts. First, on utilitarian grounds new pay poses a threat to employee well-being because it is incompatible with needs for stability and security of income. Second, it offends against the principles of both distributive and procedural justice because t increases the exposure of employees to inequitable treatment and it is a vehicle for transferring financial risk from employer to employee. A further effect of new pay practice is that it restricts the scope for the exercise and intervention of representative voice and thus poses a threat to employee rights. There is apparently little room for representation of employee interests via trade unions and collective bargaining in new pay theory.

Heery suggests a list of ways in which HR practice informed by ethical considerations might respond to new pay: by using variable pay as a supplement and not a replacement for a 'fair' base salary; by commitment to maintaining the value of employee benefits and particularly those which provide for economic security; by basing contingent pay systems on rigorous measures of performance which are subject to employee control; by the regulation of management decision-making about pay, supported through training, strict guidelines and review; by transparency and full communication of pay system rules; by the regular monitoring and periodic audit of pay systems to ensure consistency of application and an absence of discrimination; by effective due process mechanisms for employees to appeal against management judgements; and by the full involvement of employee representatives in the design, application and review of payment systems (1996: 63).

3 The gender pay gap

As noted in Chapter 14, a persisting gender pay gap is a feature of the US and UK economies (and those of many others). Despite 30 years of equal pay legislation in the UK, working women still earn only around 80% of the earnings of full-time men, although the gap has been gradually narrowing. In the case of part-time workers the gap is even wider. At the current rate of change it has been estimated that it will take a further 30 years to completely eliminate the gap.

Reasons for the gender gap's continuance range from the effects of biased pay systems, occupational segregation, and the unequal impact of women's family responsibilities, to weaknesses in equal pay legal enforcement procedures and the limited effect of collective bargaining. Whatever the exact mix of causal factors, the existence of the gender pay gap directs attention to the lack of equity and fair treatment of employees and to a deficit in procedural and distributive justice. Where such a gap prevails it cannot be said that rewards are being fairly distributed and balanced across different groups in the workforce. Moreover, it is a sign of discriminatory treatment of employees. See Chapter 14 for a fuller examination of this issue than is possible here.

An HR approach for tackling the gender pay informed by CSR principles is reflected in the practice of companies who voluntarily commit themselves to conducting fact-finding equal pay audits to assess whether pay structures are discriminatory and as a catalyst for corrective action to close any gap revealed in the exercise. A further possible initiative is for companies to comply with the recommendation of the government-appointed Kingsmill Review of women's pay and employment in 2002, that equal pay be an issue included in annual company reporting procedures on human capital management (Incomes Data Services, 2002).

4 Low pay

Low pay remains a significant feature of the service-based economies of both the USA and the UK. In separate studies of low pay in the two countries a common finding is the extent to which poverty is actually 'earned': in the UK the largest single group of poor citizens are in work (Ehrenreich, 2002; Toynbee, 2003).

One remarkable 'bottom-up' response to low pay rooted in ethical considerations that work should be fairly rewarded and that no one who works should live in poverty, has emerged in the USA. In 1994–5 a local coalition of labour, religious, community activists and business leaders in the city of Baltimore successfully lobbied the city council to adopt a 'living wage' ordinance requiring that companies which had substantial contracts with the city authority must pay a 'living wage'. The ordinance defined a living wage as the amount of money required to lift a family of three over the federal poverty line. Thus was born the Living Wage movement, which has been successful in persuading over 80 other city councils (including ten of America's 20 largest cities) and 18 state governments to enact similar ordinances within their territories. Most apply only to local authority contractors, but in one case – Santa Fe, in New Mexico – the ordinance applies to employers of 25 employees or more (www.responsiblewealth.org).

Inspired by the US example The East London Communities Organisation (TELCO) – a coalition of religious groups, schools and trade unions – has campaigned for the establishment of a living wage in London, with growing success. The Mayor of London has set up a living wage unit at the Greater London Authority and set a living wage level for GLA contractors. Further, both Barclays and HSBC have agreed to pay the living wage to their cleaning staffs in the capital, and in both cases have justified their employment decisions on CSR grounds. For example, a Barclays spokesman said of the living wage that 'It is a CSR issue in that we want to be fair across the board, but it's also an HR issue because we want to attract the right people as well' (Donovan, 2004). By adopting the living wage HR can contribute to the CSR agenda of treating employees fairly, which in turn helps fulfil HR goals of attracting a better standard of applicant and delivering a more satisfied employee with associated benefits in terms of retention, motivation and productivity.

Working time

While pay is a measure of self-esteem for employees as well as being a form of compensation, working-time patterns shape the very experience of work itself (Sisson and Storey, 2000). Of all the issues currently relating to working time probably the one to have gained the highest public profile is 'work–life balance' or 'work–life integration (WLI)' (see also Chapters 4 and 11). In her book *Willing Slaves* (2004) on the effects of contemporary working-time patterns in the UK, Madeleine Bunting points to what she calls an 'overwork culture'. The time spent at work has grown steadily longer and longer (as in the US experience) to the point where UK employees work the longest hours in the European Union.

A number of factors are perceived to contribute to the trend:

- Managers are encouraging employees to work long hours by setting deadlines, by explicit monitoring and inspection of work performance, and by setting a personal example of 'presenteeism'.

- Measuring employees' performance in terms of working hours is easier than some of the alternatives, particularly in the case of knowledge-based occupations.

- There are competitive pressures among work colleagues to keep pace with or exceed the hours worked by each other.

- Cultural values, such as individualism in the USA, can strongly colour employee attitudes in relation to the acceptability of working long hours (Walsh, 2005).

According to Bunting a major effect of such influences is that the traditional boundaries between working time and individuals' private and social lives have become blurred and in some cases 'erased'. She argues that individuals are having to 'live simultaneously in two different time frames: the timelessness required by their employer and the "timeliness" required by intimate human relationships – most markedly, the routine of children's daily lives – and how that connects to a wider network of family and friends and social activities' (2004: 16–17).

An example of how an organisation can respond positively through HR policies to the problems created by work–life imbalance is the case of MSN UK, the UK arm of a global web/IT company owned by Microsoft. Despite the company's enjoying considerable business success measured in terms of revenue growth, a staff attitude survey recorded low levels of morale and there was also a high staff turnover rate. These were traced back to the long-hours culture in the firm. In response the company mounted a culture-change programme which integrated work–life balance into business, work team and individual objectives backed up by a range of options open to all staff and a formal policy with constant 'evidence-based' monitoring. A raft of elements make up a work–life balance package, including flexi-working, home-working, an employee assistance programme and a well-being centre. Of particular significance is the role model adopted by the organisation's senior leaders who all embrace work–life balance and work flexibly. Research by the company following the culture-change programme provides evidence of the benefits to MSN in terms of positive working attitudes, reduced stress, higher efficiency and staff retention, and improved corporate image and reputation (Foster, 2005).

Employer branding

A further important way in which the HRM function can further a CSR agenda focuses on the concept of employer branding and the importance of employees' finding their work meaningful.

Positive employer 'brand' can be a very effective way of differentiating one company from another and help to create a distinctive reputation for customers, employees and shareholders. Good HRM policy can help to do this, but a deeper impact can be made if congruence between the values of the stakeholder and those projected by the company is forged. For example, more companies are placing emphasis on their CSR performance in their recruitment literature to enhance their attractiveness to recruits and those who will invest in them.

The Work Foundation conducted a study to examine the impact of CSR on employer brand based upon 1,050 interviews with economically active adults in 2001 (Bevan *et al*, 2004). The main findings were that 20% of employees found employers with a positive socially responsible image more attractive. Younger employees between 18 and 24 years old, and employees aged over 45 years were more likely to take into account CSR performance in determining their attitudes towards their current or prospective employer. There was a statistically significant relationship between employee loyalty and the organisation's CSR rating among employees. Also, employers that matched the company's values with those of its employees increased retention. Retention was also affected by the extent to which promises at the point of recruitment were kept, again reflecting the contribution good HRM practice can make to company performance.

Imaginative CSR policies can also become drivers for improving employee satisfaction, commitment and loyalty. The opportunity to make CSR an important part of the attractiveness of the company to employees as well as customers is supported by research from the Roffey Park Institute (Holbeche and Springett, 2004). Their study was based on responses from more than 750 managers, and it found that 63% of board directors, 72% of middle managers and 69% of directors and senior managers were looking for a greater sense of meaning in their working lives. For many of these managers the search for meaning was born out of disenchantment with the way their working lives were going. Many complained about a ruthlessly competitive ethos at work, the lack of mutual trust and loyalty, the intensity of working life, poor leadership, constant restructurings, and a decline in autonomy as targets supplanted individual conscientiousness. The study also found that younger managers were the most sensitive to the search for 'meaning in work': some 82% of those aged 20–30 years expressed a desire for a sense of meaning, compared with 33% of those aged 51–60 years.

People working in large organisations were least likely to find meaning in their work. Participants in the survey linked meaning with a variety of actions: work–life integration, a sense of higher purpose, leaders who act in accordance with values statements, workplace involvement, and the ability to serve customers. For many of the participants, work, at its best, could provide a sense of peace and fulfilment. The firm's commitment to CSR, along with the implementation of HRM best practice, could do much therefore to create more meaningful work for many employees.

Discussion questions

1   Does the 'living wage' represent a better approach to tackling low pay than the minimum wage?

2   What solutions may be proposed to deal with the 'overwork culture'?

3   Is it ethically justifiable for HR departments to participate in employer branding initiatives in fulfilment of their CSR remit?

3 ORGANISING CSR AND INTEGRATING IT INTO THE HRM FUNCTION

Very few companies have set up full CSR management systems. Creating and building a successful system is a complex long-term project for any company. This is because it involves a shift in the way a company conducts business and is very much like trying to implement a Total Quality Management approach. The commitment to CSR starts with assigning responsibility for CSR within the company, followed by a process of engagement with stakeholders to discover what their concerns are, and how they can be worked with to create partnerships. Many companies have made CSR a boardroom responsibility either by appointing a new director with CSR expertise or by creating a committee to oversee this area of responsibility (see Table 6).

Table 6 Handling CSR at boardroom level

Company	Method
Ford Motor Company	an environment and public policy committee led by the company's chairman
Pfizer	the full board takes decisions on CSR and periodically reviews the company policies and practices
British Telecom	the board has created a social policy unit

In whichever way responsibility for CSR is organised, it is important that a company builds mechanisms for communication between its business functions and units. In this respect, cross-functional teams can play an important part in integrating CSR and can encourage feedback from supporters and sceptics.

The involvement of the HRM function in CSR is particularly beneficial because employee involvement in helping to determine the CSR agenda and what causes are to be pursued helps counter the danger that these causes might be chosen solely by the management of the firm.

Accusations of managerial self-indulgence and personal aggrandisement or political bias can then be avoided, and it could be argued that this gives the CSR agenda more legitimacy in that it has been made more democratic.

Challenges for the HR function from CSR

Developing CSR capability in a company presents many challenges for the HRM function. The following characteristics must be developed in the organisation's members: awareness of stakeholders and their needs, the capacity to create partnerships, being open to new ideas and creative ways of thinking, taking a strategic view, and taking action on the variety of CSR initiatives. The HRM function can help managers and employees understand the role of different stakeholders and how to implement CSR policies in many different ways. For example, the supermarket retailer Tesco actively offers employment opportunities to people who have been out of work for several years, lone parents, older people made redundant, and young unemployed people. This initiative both enlightens store managers and staff regarding the good characteristics of these often marginalised workers, as well as creating goodwill in the local community.

Some companies are using their appraisal and compensation systems to encourage CSR awareness in employees. For some managers bonuses and share allocations depend partly on how well they perform on various measures of corporate citizenship that are seen as essential to protecting or enhancing the reputation of the business. Statoil, the largest Norwegian oil company, links indicators related to health, safety, environment and employee satisfaction to managers' remuneration packages.

The organisation's total engagement with CSR has to be both transparent and accountable. It is therefore particularly important that shareholders and other stakeholders are informed about these policies so that the effectiveness can be monitored and enhanced through a feedback process. The HRM function has an important contribution to make in CSR reporting too.

Discussion questions

1   What differences are there in managing for total quality and CSR?
2   What competencies must those managing CSR develop?
3   What design features would you incorporate in a procedure for involving employees in CSR decisions?

4 CSR REPORTING

CSR reporting has come a long way in the last decade, and over 2,500 companies have now joined the early pioneers such as BodyShop and the Co-op Bank. Recent converts to CSR reporting now include McDonald's and British American Tobacco. In 2003, 132 of the leading FTSE 250 companies reported on their performance in at least one area of CSR.

In most countries reporting is still a voluntary activity. But, slowly, legislation is beginning to make it mandatory. For example, in the UK, the Pension Fund Amendment Act has raised the profile and importance of socially responsible investment and has encouraged companies to report on their CSR criteria. Large companies in the UK are now voluntarily producing an Operating and Financial Review, which includes reporting on CSR issues. In France, new economic regulations require companies to disclose information on social and environmental issues such as stakeholder dialogue and human rights. The EU is in the process of considering the question of making reporting requirements mandatory for all European companies.

At the moment those companies wanting to communicate with their stakeholders face a bewildering array of reporting standards and frameworks. There is the United Nations Global Compact, standards such as AccountAbility 1000 and Social Accountability Standard 8000, and multinational guidelines such as those of the Organisation for European Cooperation and Development. The Global Reporting Initiative is emerging as one of the leading frameworks because of its broad foundations and international reach. The GRI is a UN-backed organisation that has brought together governments, business, campaign groups, trade unions, accountants and academics to develop reporting guidelines applicable to any organisation anywhere. Another advantage of GRI is that it is compatible with other systems and standards. GRI covers three components of CSR sustainability reporting: environmental, social and economic performance. Companies are asked to report on a wide range of indicators from greenhouse gas emissions and waste management to human rights, child labour, bribery payments and customer data privacy. In all, there are 57 core indicators of performance and 53 voluntary ones. The GRI is also producing sector-specific supplements in sectors such as financial services, tour operators, mining, and car manufacturing. The next issue for greater clarification and standardisation is that of the verification and auditing of these reports.

Reporting HRM aspects

Observers of business in recent years will have witnessed an increase in company social reporting and disclosure from the HRM function. Reporting on employee matters is examined below first, followed by the more general topic of social responsibility reporting, and finally reporting on the company's human rights record is covered in the third subsection.

Employee reporting practice

Some firms are trying to move away from treating employees in accounting terms as costs; some firms are attempting to report on their employees as potential assets. One theoretical approach, noted in Chapter 2, is that of human resource accounting. The attempt is made to measure the contribution of employees to the firm so that this information can then be published. Investments made in training and development can then be related to improvements in operating performance, and the payback on these activities – previously only classified as a cost to the business – can be noted. The concept and implications for practice have been developed most fully by Likert, and have been applied to some companies in the USA (Likert, 1967). However, the use of these techniques in wider accounting practice has generally failed to materialise, although the movement towards knowledge-based companies may, in time, rekindle this interest. There is nonetheless new interest in this debate in the accounting journals. For example, ideas have been put forward for assessing the 'worth' of employees to the company, and trying to estimate what it would cost the company if an employee was to leave. This technique would require the use of 'soft' accounting information, which puts a value upon the employees' tacit knowledge and skills and their contribution to organisational knowledge and learning. It has been argued that this form of accounting is beneficial to the employees by showing them as valuable assets of the firm in the hope that it might lead to a more considerate leadership style and a more sophisticated system of HRM (Roslender and Dyson, 1992).

Comparing practice

In the UK, the disclosure of information to employees and their trade unions gained a great deal of support from employment legislation. This put on a statutory basis the requirement to disclose information to trade unions that would help them in drawing up their claims in the collective bargaining process. However, the encouragement to disclose information which was in the interests of promoting good industrial relations has still some way to go in the UK. A study by Gray, Owen and Adams has shown that the number of UK companies disclosing information to employees on issues such as health and safety, pensions, and employee share ownership schemes has increased in frequency every year since the late 1980s (Gray *et al*, 1996). The Department of Trade and Industry (DTI)-commissioned report on *Accounting for People* has recommended that companies make much more extensive and detailed reports about human capital investments and employment policies in UK firms. It could also be that the movement to be closer to EU standards is slowly bringing British companies into line with the practices of their European counterparts which are much more extensive. Many companies in Europe are obliged to go much further in terms of information disclosure to employees, and this greatly assists the role of trade unions in collective bargaining and more general representation within the company.

In the case of Germany, there is a long tradition of reporting on employee matters, many firms producing social reports which contain descriptions of goals, actions taken and achievements in the fields of employment and social concern, a value-added statement indicating the distribution among the various stakeholders, and a social account providing a quantitative presentation of all measurable employment and societally oriented corporate expenditures and revenues. Despite these extensive disclosure requirements, many pressure groups in Germany, including the trade unions, are pushing for the development of social reporting to be taken further. A general review of reporting trends in the EU has concluded, however, that there is still much to be done to take these issues forward on a mandatory basis rather than allow some companies to make all the running with innovative voluntary initiatives. Consequently, what many commentators claim is needed are EU-wide social policies and laws that cover CSR reporting practices. The EU has been engaged in trying to resolve the dispute about the proposals for a European company statute for some years. The aim is to allow companies with operations in more than one member state to establish themselves as 'European companies' governed by one law that is applicable throughout the EU. At present, companies have to tailor their activities to comply with different company laws in the member states – a requirement that adds to administration costs.

EU proposals
An interesting development which could increase the need for more detailed employee reporting by companies in the EU is a proposal from the Commission to create performance league tables for large companies based upon best employment practices. These could also be used by socially responsible investors to reward and to penalise 'bad' employers who fail to comply with notions of good HRM practice (*Financial Times*, 27 October 2005). Penalised companies would also be denied access to grants, public procurement and public aid for research and development by the EU Commission.

The challenge for companies in HRM reporting is to foster the recognition that CSR represents good business practice for the HRM function, and so should not be confined to programmes in the public relations and marketing departments. Company excellence can only be achieved through adopting an integrated approach to CSR, embracing the needs of all stakeholders. The HRM function has an important part to play in this effort and can help to demonstrate that CSR is no longer an added extra but is now an essential component in delivering improved performance, in a sustainable business.

CASE STUDY 35

PIONEERS IN REPORTING HRM ASPECTS OF CSR – THE CO-OPERATIVE BANK'S PARTNERSHIP REPORTS

The (Co-operative) Co-op Bank was created in 1872 as part of the Rochdale Pioneers Co-operative movement. In recent years it has reinvigorated its appeal by becoming one of the first banks to offer free banking, and in 1992, after analysing some market research on ethical attitudes, it launched an ethical banking policy aimed at securing its long-standing customers and at gaining new business. The Bank committed itself to a range of self-imposed restrictions on its investments. For example, it will not invest in repressive regimes abroad, not finance the manufacture and sale of weapons, not provide financial services for tobacco product manufacturers, not invest in exploitative factory farming methods, fur trading, blood sports, drug-trafficking or money laundering. It also aims to seek out and support fair trade and those firms that have a proactive stance on the environment, and pledges not to speculate against the pound in the currency markets. The policy has been aggressively marketed and has been spectacularly successful in generating a lot of new customers and improving the profitability of the Bank in every year since the policy was declared. In 1997 the Bank won a prestigious Corporate Conscience Award from the Council on Economic Priorities in the USA. The first of its annual Partnership Reports was published in 1998 so that its ethical claims could be held up to scrutiny. These reports are conducted by a specialist department in the Bank in an audit process that considers the various Bank partners: staff, customers, suppliers and the wider community. The reports attempt to measure the extent to which the Bank delivers value to its partners and to assess whether it lives up to its social responsibilities as well as meeting the claims made in its ethical mission statement. The audit process involves conducting interviews and sending out questionnaires, and then analysing the results. In terms of the ethical policy, the reports examine whether the bank follows through on commitments not to finance the arms trade, oppressive regimes, exploitative factory farming, the fur trade, blood sports or businesses that use animals for testing cosmetics. The procedures for implementing the Bank's ethical policy are also checked and any decisions to refuse to take on new customers scrutinised to see whether this was for reasons specified such as involvement with environmental damage or animal welfare. The Bank has continued to produce these annual partnership reports and has improved and updated the range and quality of its CSR performance indicators and the independence of the verification process.

Case study tasks

1 What criticisms would you make of the Co-op's approach to CSR?

2 Has it identified all the right partners to report to?

3 What further developments in CSR would to recommend to the Co-op?

Reporting on human rights issues

Most of the pressure to get companies to take their responsibilities seriously on CSR also involves a requirement that companies pay attention to human rights issues, particularly if they are multinationals. Human rights violations have often been regarded as a product of domestic politics and therefore beyond the sphere of influence of international companies. But with the globalisation of the economy and the sourcing of consumer products in the developing world and the increasing role and influence of multinationals as the engines of economic development, companies can no longer stand aside with impunity in a critical world in which information about what they do is widely available.

Retailers whose supply chains contract to buy products from tens of thousands of sources in the developing world often confront difficult ethical problems in relation to human rights, such as child labour, debt slavery, hostility to trade unions, sweatshops, starvation wages, and racial and ethnic discrimination. Companies which make direct investments in foreign countries face the threat of their security arrangements having an adverse impact and of being accused of complicity if they are seen to benefit from silence in the face of oppression. Some companies such as BodyShop, Levi-Strauss, Toys "R" Us, Avon Cosmetics and the Co-operative Bank have built human rights commitments into their decision-making policies, and this number is likely to be increasing as campaigning groups increase the pressure. Added pressure is also coming from consumers through the supermarkets and other stores in the field of clothing, footwear, toys, sports goods and cosmetics.

Measuring corporate ethical commitment
The Council on Economic Priorities, a New-York-based research consultancy, has drawn up the SA 8000 Social Accountability Standard for the measurement of the ethical commitment of companies in this area. It is designed to mirror the International Standards Organisation (ISO) 9000 and ISO 14000 standards for manufacturing quality systems and environmental quality systems. SA 8000 sets out specific provisions on issues such as trade union rights, the use of child labour, working hours, health and safety at work, and fair pay and conditions, as well as the necessary management systems to deliver them.

Each company applying for certification is given an independent verification by an outside auditor such as the Société Générale de Surveillance – International Certification Services (SGS–ICS), the world largest certification company. The standard is modelled on universal quality standards and based upon the conventions laid down by the International Labour Organisation (ILO), the (UN) Universal Declaration of Human Rights, and the UN Convention on the rights of the child. SA 8000 has two other elements to help with social auditing: the auditors are required to talk to and learn from interested parties – trade unions, workers and charities, etc – and a complaints and appeals process allows for interested parties to bring up issues of non-compliance at certified companies. Accreditation is valid for a span of three years, with surveillance and observation audits every six months, covering each and every country where the certification body audits ten or more companies. It might be only be a matter of time before the call for companies to publish comprehensive information on their compliance with the likes of SA 8000 is made.

Soon, other standards for corporate community involvement are likely to be developed and they are also likely to be made a formal accounting requirement for companies. This is likely to take the issue of social responsibility into the mainstream of HRM practice. For companies that trade upon their ethical reputations, the auditing and reporting of the veracity of their claims is a very important part of preserving their reputation, which will always be under scrutiny because it represents a high-risk business strategy in very competitive markets for reputations and brands. Research by the Future Foundation found that companies operating in a responsible way are nearly always more successful in commercial terms because such behaviour has an impact on customer trust and perceptions (Future Foundation, 1997).

Discussion questions

1 Should CSR reporting be voluntary?
2 Should countries with poor human rights records be excluded from the supply chain?
3 What new issues should be included in the CSR agenda?

CASE STUDY 36

HUMAN RIGHTS COLLABORATION – THE WORLD COCOA FOUNDATION

The chocolate industry created the World Cocoa Foundation in 2000 with the aim of supporting training and education for cocoa farmers and to promote projects to grow cocoa in a sustainable and ethical way. The foundation's members include manufacturers such as Mars, Nestlé, Kraft Foods, and Hershey Foods, exporters such as Cargill and Archer Daniels Midland Cocoa Company (ADM Cocoa), and retailers such as Starbucks. The Foundation is trying to do something about child labour, which is endemic in the industry and has to be eliminated according to an ILO protocol. Much of this effort is focused on West Africa where more than two thirds of the world's cocoa is grown and nearly 2 million small farmers are employed. It has been estimated that over half a million children were involved in this industry, often on hazardous labour such as clearing brush with machetes or applying pesticides. The trafficking of children to work in this industry has caused a great deal of bad publicity and was the catalyst for the formation of the World Cocoa Foundation. The Foundation has set up a network of local schools to help educate some of the children working on these farms, and to try to improve the understanding of the farmers with regard to helpful insects and pests to prevent excessive pesticide-spraying. However, these initiatives are hampered by low commodity prices, which put pressure on farmers to use cheap child labour, and the unstable political situation in many west-coast African states such as Ivory Coast (www.worldcocoafoundation.org).

Case study tasks

1 Has the World Cocoa Foundation gone far enough in CSR?
2 What other human rights should it try to protect?
3 What is the role of consumers in this campaign?

CONCLUSIONS AND FUTURE ISSUES

This chapter defined CSR and identified the drivers that have put this on to the global business agenda. The main drivers are globalisation, legitimacy, inequality, cultural change and the influence of European integration. The arguments for and against CSR were examined. The role of HRM in achieving CSR outcomes was explored, and the integration of CSR into HRM policies and practices in a variety of areas was discussed. Several international case studies of good CSR practice were identified, and the future direction of CSR developments was speculated upon.

A new trend in CSR with implications for HRM is for companies to work together alongside governments and development agencies on problems that are too big for any one company to handle, such as the HIV/AIDS pandemic, and corruption. The UN is helping to forge some of these collaborations with its initiative called Growing Sustainable Business for Poverty Reduction in Africa. This initiative aims to encourage businesses to target poor consumers and improve the links between big and small companies in the continent. The Shell Foundation is also exploring collaborative solutions to social and environmental problems in Africa (www.shellfoundation.org). It has set up two investment funds that provide loans to small businesses in Uganda and South Africa. The fund is trying to tackle two common problems in Africa: the lack of access to energy among poor rural households, and the fact that small business growth is often hampered by poor governance, corruption and the unwillingness of banks to make risky loans. Using the Royal Dutch Shell Group's reputation the Foundation is encouraging local banks to put up capital alongside its own finance. Other micro-finance initiatives are also focusing on poor people as a potential market for goods and services.

Most recently, the Shell Foundation has suggested that international development aid should be focused more closely on enterprise and small business development using business principles to evaluate the success of these investments. And, it argues, who better to devise and help make these interventions than private businesses, which have untapped reservoirs of skills, assets and experience, that if deployed, via partnerships and the development of best practice, could significantly enhance the efforts of the aid community? This could extend the scope and impact of CSR quite considerably and, importantly, is an initiative that business is itself promoting – a further sign that corporate social responsibility could really be coming of age in the new millennium.

CASE STUDY 37

HRM AND CSR BEST PRACTICE IN BRITISH TELECOM

British Telecom (BT) has many strands to its CSR activity, but a notable one was the commissioning of independent experts to assess the morality of its offshoring policy.

BT commissioned Sustainability, the independent CSR consultancy group, to scrutinise its decision to outsource its call centres and software development to India (Kuszewski, Prakash-Mani and Beloe, 2004). This trend for offshoring has been growing in the UK, and critics have complained that companies that do this are being disloyal to their workers in the UK, and are trying to take advantage of exploitative labour practices in the third world to reduce costs. A similar process of 'flagging-out' has been common practice in the UK shipping industry for many years, has effectively destroyed the employment prospects of many UK seafarers, and has often caused a race to the bottom in terms of safety standards on 'flag-of-convenience' tonnage. With the availability of modern computer and communications equipment and highly educated but cheap labour in India, many other businesses are moving parts of their operations offshore. Sustainability was asked to report on three issues: to examine the trend of offshoring and evaluate the implications for CSR; to study the specific impacts of BT's offshoring decisions in the UK and India; and to give strategic advice to BT in the light of these investigations.

In terms of the first point, Sustainability's report notes that some companies can save as much as 70% of their labour costs by moving their call centres offshore to countries such as India. The UK's Communication Workers' Union (CWU) has estimated that as many as 200,000 jobs are at risk of being moved offshore. And while the obvious loss to the UK is in terms of jobs and tax revenues, local communities supporting the call centres also lose out. On the other hand, the export of jobs and wealth-creating opportunities is much welcomed in India. It is difficult to morally criticise companies for making this move if in utilitarian terms the net benefit to the global common good could be greater. However, Sustainability noted that a company with a commitment to CSR policies must work to reduce the pain and stress of the disruption this relocation decision will cause in both countries – the loss of jobs in the UK, and the fair treatment of workers in India. In India, the treatment of the call centre workers is a particular concern. Will they be free to join unions? Will they be treated decently and paid a fair wage? And will they have to adopt new names and tell lies about their culture and identities? Moreover, Sustainability asks, will the drain of well-educated workers into the call centres impoverish public services and the longer-term development of the Indian economy?

In terms of the BT operations in India, Sustainability reports that its two call centres in Delhi and Bangalore employed around 2,200 people. In the UK around 2,000 jobs had been lost, but BT operated a policy of no compulsory redundancies and helped relocate or find jobs for the displaced employees. However, many of the UK call centres were in areas of high unemployment and the loss of tax revenues and local opportunities for young people and other suppliers was keenly felt. Many of these benefits have been transferred to the operations in India where tax revenues and contracts for local suppliers have boosted the local economy. Investments in technology and infrastructure were made, with standards for working conditions and employee management informed by BT's policy on *Sourcing with Human Dignity*. BT has set up extensive training and development for the Indian employees and has made philanthropic contributions to schools and charities in the communities surrounding the call centres. Sustainability also acknowledged that the cost savings for BT may have helped it improve its services to customers and the provision of new services.

Sustainability's considered view was that BT's offshoring decision was ethical because, on balance, it improved the lot of overseas workers and helped with the development of an underdeveloped economy. Nevertheless, Sustainability recommended that employers such as BT should consult with employees, trade unions, communities and other affected stakeholders *before* making the decision to move operations offshore; that as much lead-time notice as possible should be given to all stakeholders; and that the basis of the decision should be made clear and transparent to everyone concerned. Compulsory redundancies should be avoided in the home country, and investments made in training and in advice to help displaced employees find new jobs. The employers should also work closely with the affected suppliers and communities to help them find new sources of employment and income. In terms of the recipient country, the firm should work with local suppliers to develop skills and adhere to global best practice guidelines on operations and employment. The offshore employer should make sure that wages, benefits and working conditions and workers' rights are respected. This includes upholding the workers' rights to freedom of association. They should engage with stakeholders locally and become good citizens in their host community. In particular, they should attempt to understand and respect the local customs and culture, and assist with the development of the economy generally. Importantly, Sustainability recommends that the offshore call centres should not try to deceive customers into thinking that the operations are still based in the home country, or ask employees to adopt false identities and scripts.

In terms of BT's offshoring decision, Sustainability's specific judgement was that 'much good practice is evident in the way the company has sought to protect workers and maintain high standards. But the decision to engage in offshoring itself did not apparently include any CSR element to it' (p.35). In other words, this enquiry was something of a post-hoc response to the discontent raised by BT's offshoring critics. Nevertheless, it is a bold move on BT's part to open itself up to criticism in this way, and may be a positive sign that the organisation intends to adopt a CSR-based business strategy in the future.

Case study tasks

1 Has BT done enough to live up to its CSR commitments?

2 How could standards for offshoring be made universal?

3 What further follow-up activity should BT undertake?

REFERENCES

Bevan S., Iles N., Emery P. and Hoskins T. (2004) *Achieving High Performance: CSR at the heart of business.* London: Work Foundation.

Brammer S. (2006) 'Feel-good factories', *The Guardian* ('Work' section), 21 January: 3.

Bunting M. (2004) *Willing Slaves: How the overwork culture is ruining our lives.* London: HarperCollins.

Carroll A. B. (1999) 'Corporate social responsibility', *Business and Society*, Vol. 38, No. 3: 268–95.

Chartered Institute of Personnel and Development (2002) *CSR and HR's Role.* London: CIPD.

Chartered Institute of Personnel and Development (2005) *Making CSR Happen: The contribution of people management*, Research Report. London: CIPD.

Dahl R. (1985) *A Preface to Economic Democracy.* Berkeley: University of California Press.

Donovan P. (2004) 'The rise of the living wage', *People Management*, Vol. 10, No. 14, 15 July: 14–15.

Ehrenreich B. (2002) *Nickel and Dimed: Undercover in Low-Wage USA.* New York: Granta.

European Union Commision (2001) *Promoting a European Framework for CSR.* Brussels 18.7.2001 Com (2001) 366 Final.

Financial Times (2005) 'The measure of a great employer', 27 October.

Foster, C. (2005) 'MSN UK – tackling the long-hours culture', *Equal Opportunities Review*, No. 140, April: 15–19.

Friedman, M. (1962) *Capitalism and Freedom.* Chicago: Chicago University Press.

Future Foundation (1997) *The Responsible Organisation.* London: Future Foundation.

Gray R., Owen D. and Adams C. (1996) *Accounting and Accountability.* London: Prentice Hall.

Hayek F. (1969) 'The corporation in a democratic society', in H. Ansoff, *Business Strategy*. Harmondsworth: Penguin.

Heery E. (1996) 'Risk, representation and the new pay', *Personnel Review*, Vol. 25, No. 6: 54–65.

Henderson D. (2001) *Misguided Virtue.* London: IEA.

Hendry J. (2004) *Between Enterprise and Ethics.* Oxford: Oxford University Press.

Holbeche L. and Springett N. (2004) *In Search of Meaning in the Workplace.* London: Roffey Park Institute.

IDS (2001) *Secondments and Volunteering.* Incomes Data Services Studies No. 704, February: 1–7.

IDS (2002) *The Equal Pay Challenge.* Incomes Data Services Report No. 856, May.

Joseph E. (2003) *A New Business Agenda for Government.* London: IPPR.

Kakabadse N., Kakabadse A. and Kouzmin A. (2004) 'Directors' remuneration: the need for a geo-political perspective', *Personnel Review*, Vol. 33, No. 5: 561–82.

Kempner T., Macmillan K. and Hawkins K. (1974) *Business and Society.* Harmondsworth: Penguin.

Kuszewski J., Prakash-Mani K. and Beloe S. (2004) *Good Migrations: BT, Corporate Social Responsibility and the geography of jobs.* London: Sustainability/BT.

Likert R. (1967) *The Human Organisation.* New York: McGraw-Hill.

Lindblom C. (1977) *Politics and Markets.* New York: Basic Books.

Roslender R. and Dyson J. (1992) 'Accounting for the worth of employees: a new look at an old problem', *British Accounting Review*, Vol. 24, No. 4: 311–29.

Sisson K. and Storey J. (2000) *The Realities of Human Resource Management.* Buckingham: Open University Press.

Sternberg E. (1994) *Just Business.* London: Little Brown.

Toynbee P. (2003) *Hard Work: Life in Low-Pay Britain.* London: Bloomsbury.

Vogel D. (2005) *The Market for Virtue.* Washington: Brookings Institution.

Walsh J. (2005) 'Work–life balance: challenging the overwork culture', in S. Bach (ed.) *Managing Human Resources: Personnel management in transition* (4th edition). Oxford: Blackwell.

Warren R. (1994) 'Corporate temperance: a business virtue', *Business Ethics: A European Review*, Vol. 3, No. 4, October: 223–32.

Warren R. (2000) *Corporate Governance and Accountability.* Wirral: Liverpool Academic Press.

Wolff C. (2004) *Ethics in Employment: Social responsibility begins at home.* IRS Employment Review No. 805, 6 August: 9–15.

Zadek S. (2001) *The Civil Corporation.* London: Earthscan.

Ethics and organisational justice

CHAPTER 13

Richard Warren and Rosemary Lucas

CHAPTER OBJECTIVES

When you have read this chapter you should be able to:

- explain the meaning of ethics and how they relate to business life

- apply the main theories of ethics to decision-making processes

- evaluate how ethical principles inform managerial behaviour in cross-cultural comparisons

- appreciate the role of ethics in HRM practice

- understand the principles of organisational justice and how cultural differences impact upon justice behaviour.

PURPOSE AND SCOPE

This chapter takes a closer look at ethics and its relationships to business and HRM. Although we focus on secular ethical theories that have their basis in western moral philosophy, we nevertheless place emphasis on the themes of cultural variation, globalisation, and convergence and divergence in order to reflect some of the challenges that are arising from the internationalisation of business, particularly in emerging economies. We also touch upon the themes of technological change and the knowledge economy and labour market change.

The first section introduces the notion of ethics and identifies the new business ethics agenda. The second section outlines the major theories of ethics that are used to analyse business ethics dilemmas and presents examples of how these apply in practice in shaping managerial decisions in cross-cultural situations. The third section provides a justification for paying greater attention to ethics in HRM practice. The fourth section explores how employers, through the HR function and line managers, can apply an ethical approach through a framework of organisational justice in terms of its three component parts: distributive justice, procedural justice and interactional justice. We also reflect how employee perceptions of justice are affected by cultural differences in selected countries. We conclude by arguing that it is engagement in the process of analysis and rational argument that is the key benefit to be gained by HRM professionals who explore ethical issues in this context, and that the building of ethical conduct on these principles will enable HRM to rise to the challenge of globalisation.

1 ETHICS AND BUSINESS

What is ethics?

A general appreciation of philosophy can be invaluable to the HRM professional – but of particular relevance is that branch of philosophy called ethics. This opens up a whole new world and provides a language in which the question of ends and means can be discussed and put into perspective. Ethics, or as it is often called, moral philosophy, has very ancient roots and in the western tradition of philosophy owes more to the Greek philosophers Socrates, Plato and Aristotle than any other branch of the subject. The word *ethics* in classical Greek means the sense of propriety in the people. Ethics is the study of what is right and good in human conduct and the justification of such claims. Not surprisingly, there is considerable disagreement about what is right and good, and even more disagreement about how ethical theories can be justified on a rational basis.

The two terms 'ethics' and 'morals' ought to be distinguished, although they are often used interchangeably in common usage:

■ *Morals* is used to refer to particular norms or beliefs that are supposed to govern conduct in a social group or society and have developed as a social institution.

■ *Ethics* is a theoretical endeavour to uncover the fundamental principles and basic concepts of human conduct.

In the light of this, whether people behave according to ethical principles has not been of much concern to the moral philosopher, so in this sense they are not to be confused with the pronouncements and pretensions of moralists.

Ethics in western philosophy is itself a stratified subject:

■ *Meta-ethical analysis* is concerned with the concepts and status of the language used in ethical theories, and whether there can be such a thing as ethical knowledge.

■ *Normative ethics* is concerned with the formulation and defence of theories about what ought to be done in moral life.

■ *Applied ethics* is the use of these theories to examine and try to resolve moral problems such as abortion, war, racial discrimination, cruelty to animals, etc. Business ethics, as we shall see, can be thought of as a subset of applied ethics.

In practice, ethical analysis involves aspects from all these strata using as the prime tool reasoned argument. The main insights to be had come mainly from the discoveries we make on the journey rather than in the reaching of any destination. Perhaps this is why Aristotle called ethics 'practical reason' and assigned it more importance than 'speculative reason' (science) because it dealt with the fundamental question of how one should live, and that a person who understood the nature of ethics would know that right conduct was a necessary condition both for self-fulfilment and in order to lead the good life (Aristotle, 1961).

Connecting ethics and business

We now examine the use of practical reason in the business context, and consider what the connection is between ethics and business, and how ethical problems in business can be analysed.

Can a corporation be held to be ethically responsible?

Some commentators argue that only people are ethically responsible and that a corporation is not a person and so is not a responsible moral agent. Others argue that corporations are organisations that are recognised under the law as legal persons and so can be treated as moral agents for the purposes of making them accountable for the deeds and misdeeds committed in their name.

Is there a corporate social responsibility?

One of the early denouncers of this notion, Milton Friedman, the economist, argued that the social responsibility of business began and ended with the duty to increase profits, that it was the shareholders who should then decide what their personal ethical stance was, and that this right should not be subverted by management, nor should managers try to second-guess the ethical preferences of the shareholders (Friedman, 1970). As discussed in Chapter 12, this view is challenged by those who stress that the separation of ownership from control in the corporation is an undeniable fact, and that the accountability of the modern firm is increasingly tenuous in terms of shareholders and nation-states. The corporation is a structure of enormous power in society and so should recognise its responsibilities to its various stakeholders which are dependent upon and subject to the actions of the corporation. To maintain a social mandate, therefore, the managers of the corporation must be mindful of these responsibilities and act accordingly.

Is business ethics different?

Business ethics is the study of the conduct of people in the business context – and this raises the question of whether this behaviour should be judged by the same standards of ethical behaviour we apply to the rest of life. Some commentators claim that personal ethics are unrelated to business ethics. But we should be careful that business ethics does not allow people to use the cloak of corporate legal personality to avoid moral responsibility when doing business. Indeed, if business ethics becomes, as Peter Drucker puts it, a form of discredited excuse-making, then it will not last long, and 'it will have become a tool of the business executive to justify what for other people would be unethical behaviour rather than a tool to restrain the business executive and to impose tight ethical limits on business' (Drucker, 1981: 43). Ethical conduct should be consistent in all contexts and there is no fundamental separation between personal and business ethics.

Ethical problems are part of business life. They are as old as business itself (arguments about a fair price, a just wage and usury are found in the Bible and the Koran), but today they are more complex, because business has expanded and become truly global. The Bhopal disaster, the Exxon Valdez oil spill, the BCCI banking fraud, the collapse of Barings Bank, the Enron, WorldCom and Parmalat scandals are all the stuff of current public concern over the morals of businesspeople. But ethical issues are also part of everyday business life and ordinary transactions could not be performed if certain moral norms did not prevail. For example, the making of contracts, while legally enforceable, depends for its efficacy upon the ethical behaviour of truth-telling, keeping promises and acting in good faith. In fact, it is impossible to think of an employment contract purely as a legal contract, for it would be meaningless and quite useless as a contract unless it is built upon a whole raft of moral and social norms which both parties leave unacknowledged in the contract. These issues form the basis of Case study 38 in an Asian cultural context, and Case study 41 at the end of this chapter, which explores the Enron scandal.

CASE STUDY 38

WHISTLEBLOWING IN SOUTH KOREA – CONFUCIAN ETHICS AND COLLECTIVISM

Scandals in a number of major corporations have caused their employees to take actions against wrongdoing by disclosing practices they believe to be illegal, immoral or illegitimate to an external authority they perceive can take appropriate action. This practice, commonly known as whistleblowing, may be done openly, particularly where the individual has attempted unsuccessfully to seek resolution for the problem internally. Alternatively, individuals fearing victimisation may choose to remain anonymous, although a number of more individually based western societies including the USA, Canada, the UK and Australia have legislated to afford protection against victimisation or dismissal to workers who blow the whistle on criminal behaviour or other wrongdoing.

Asian societies are typically characterised by Confucian ethics and collectivism. The teachings of Confucius form a core part of the ethical content for guiding good behaviour in East Asian countries. However, Confucian ethics can be used both to justify and reject whistleblowing. On the one hand, a noble man is one with virtue and courage who speaks up for righteousness. On the other hand, filiality and deference are the foundation of nobleness ... Rare is the person who ... harbours designs to challenge the authorities. Collectivism embraces group-based values such as harmony, cooperation, loyalty and conformity where employees subvert their own goals to those of the organisation and avoid expressing opinions that may be disruptive. Confrontation and conflict are undesirable and unacceptable.

Source: derived from Park *et al* (2005)

Case study tasks

1   In what circumstances are employees justified in blowing the whistle? Differentiate between situations where resolution of the problem can be pursued internally as a first option and those that where disclosure to an external authority is necessary.

2   How can the principle of whistleblowing be incorporated into societies where it conflicts with prevailing philosophical and cultural norms?

3   How can major corporations assert moral authority in a global economy?

Any business issue that relates to human values is of interest to business ethics. Its scope of concern can be divided up into four levels of analysis which, together with the sorts of questions that can be explored at each level, are:

1   The ethics of the social system: do capitalism and the market mechanism contribute to a good society and reflect our most important social values?

2   The ethics of the business organisation: does business have other sorts of obligations because of its vast power or relationship to other elements of society?

3   The ethical issues that arise in the course of business activity: what is honesty and fair dealing?

4   Can ethical conduct in business be improved?

The analysis of such issues requires the use of ethical theories to investigate in a systematic way specific business practices including HRM practices. The language, concepts and arguments of those facing ethical dilemmas in business are examined and the moral choices identified. Of course, not all moral dilemmas are resolvable, nor can ethical analysis make us agree about what to do – but at least we can be clear about what we are doing when we act, what the contending viewpoints are, and how they are being justified.

Discussion questions

1　Are ethics and morals about the same thing?

2　Is business ethics separate from the ethical norms of society?

3　Can all ethical issues ultimately be decided by courts of law?

2 WHAT ARE ETHICAL THEORIES?

One of the problems in looking for guidance in the judgement of conduct is that there are various ideas about what is good and right and a variety of ways of life which underpin different notions of the good and the right. This problem sometimes goes by the name of relativism, and can lead to scepticism and the view that there is no such thing as morality, and that it is only another name for the struggle for power and domination (Reidenbach and Robin, 1988). These arguments cannot be explored or resolved here but some indication of the variety of normative ethical theories can be given and their differences in outlook indicated. On many issues there is a good deal of agreement between the various approaches, and even when they differ, it is often instructive to examine why and on what grounds.

The basis of theories

For many business people, their membership of one or other of the great world religions – including Judaism, Christianity and Islam – provides them with ethical principles that can be applied in business. But the difficulty about theistic ethics is that the ethical principles and rules derived from religious beliefs have very little to say to people who do not share those beliefs. We therefore only explore secular theories which try to offer reasons and arguments about what is good, and which are the right and wrong ways for human beings to treat each other. That there are still problems in securing the foundation of such secular attempts to place ethics on a rational footing has to be acknowledged, but as with science, we have to work with the best theory that is presently known to us, and with the proviso that a better theory with a more secure foundation may be found in the future.

The ethical theories that you might read about in most business ethics textbooks are drawn from the major traditions in western moral philosophy. These are the *consequentialist* and *duty theories*. They constitute the orthodox approach to business ethics analysis, which tends to concentrate on ethical dilemmas and decisions in business and the generation of rules that should guide people in deciding these matters. However, there is also another tradition in the history of ethics which has been lost from view until fairly recently but is in the process of being recovered in business ethics. This is the tradition which directs our attention to the moral agent, or the person who is faced with moral choices, and asks not just what action should be taken but what it means to be an ethical person. This approach goes by the name of *virtue theory*, and is perhaps particularly useful to the HRM practitioner whose professional orientation is concerned with questions of character and the just community. We now briefly outline each of these basic ethical theories in turn.

Consequentialist theories

Sometimes called teleological theories of ethics, these hold the view that the moral worth of an action is determined by the consequences of the action. The rightness of an action is determined by the results that are produced by that action. What makes the action right or wrong is the good or evil that is produced by the act, not the act in itself. Thus all acts must be evaluated in terms of the good and bad consequences they produce and have no intrinsic value in themselves as acts. The box below outlines a practical example in relation to business regulation.

A BRIEF CONSEQUENTIALIST ANALYSIS OF THE EFFECTIVENESS OF REGULATION IN BUSINESS

Regulation is effective to a degree in improving the conduct of businesses perhaps more because of the fear or cost of prosecution or loss of reputation than because businesses are taking a principled moral stance to honour the spirit and letter of the regulations. However, there are several problems with regulation. One of the most significant is the cost to business and society, which is often paid for by general taxation, or by increases in product and service overheads that are then passed on to consumers. There is also the loss of productivity in business as a result of compliance and monitoring activity. This can lead to loss of competitive performance and the loss of capital stock formation. Regulation can also stifle innovation in some industries and can be said to divert management from the task of running the business. Many firms may devote their attention to evading and exploiting loopholes in regulations and so distort the framework of competition in the market. Regulation can also become a self-fulfilling tendency: regulations that are inadequately complied with can lead to the demand for the appointment of more regulators, who in turn produce more regulations which again have to be complied with. The major beneficiaries of regulations become the regulators and lawyers who service the system. At some point in the debate about the degree and coverage of regulation of industry (the political left calls for more: the political right for less) the absolute need for a degree of self-imposed regulation or control is encountered. In fact, there is almost no hope of better business conduct unless a degree of self-control is exercised over moral behaviour in business.

There are several consequentialist theories to choose from. Ethical egoism is the view that whether an act is right or morally wrong depends upon how good or bad the results of the action are *for oneself*. How other people are affected is irrelevant to the decision unless the other people affected alter the consequences for oneself. Ethical altruism is the position that actions are right or wrong dependent upon the effect they have on everyone else *except* oneself. Ethical egoism is criticised because few people would totally ignore the effects of their actions on other people; it is also difficult to believe that a totally selfless approach can be rigorously applied.

A consequentialist theory that has elements of both these approaches is utilitarianism, developed by Jeremy Bentham and advocated with ingenuity by J. S. Mill (Bentham, 1971; Mill, 1972). This is the view that an action is right or wrong depending upon the good or bad consequences produced for everyone affected by the action. This gives the theory a universal component. Utilitarianism requires a careful consideration of the options available, because an action is judged to be right if it leads to the greatest possible balance of good consequences or the least possible balance of bad consequences for everyone affected by the action when compared with the other actions that could be taken, including that of doing nothing. The utilitarian approach is depicted in the following box.

UTILITARIANISM: STEPS TO MAXIMISING HUMAN HAPPINESS BY MINIMISING UNHAPPINESS

1 Identify the action options available in any specific decision.

2 Estimate the costs and benefits that a given action would produce for each and every person affected by the action.

3 Choose the best option that produces the greatest sum of utility or the least amount of disutility.

4 Utilitarianism's most famous maxim for decision-making is that of producing the greatest good for the greatest number.

Utilitarianism is orientated towards a view of the 'good', which in the case of hedonistic utilitarians is pleasure, or in the case of pluralist utilitarians is made up of a range of elements like friendship, knowledge, beauty, health, courage, etc. There is also a distinction to be found between 'act' and 'rule' utilitarians. Act utilitarians hold that in all situations the act to be performed should be that which maximises utility for all the persons affected by the action. This means that different situations may require different acts and that all situations have to be analysed afresh. Rule utilitarians, however, hold that utility can be best served by rules of action rather than by giving consideration to each individual action. Rules to guide action are formulated which, when followed, tend to maximise utility in similar situations. For example, the rule of not breaking promises, if kept, will tend to maximise social utility in the long run. Whereas an act utilitarian is prepared to break promises if the balance of utility favours this decision, rule utilitarians claim that people do not have time to weigh the consequences of every action, so the formulation of rules is more realistic. The disadvantage is that rules can become inflexible and outdated in new situations and so lead to perverse consequences.

The major criticisms made of utilitarianism are that by concentrating on consequences, some human rights may be overridden in the interests of general welfare, and that the distribution of utility may be socially unjust. There is also the problem of finding a common measure of utility so that units can be added and subtracted from each other. Moreover, to what extent is the full range of consequences of an action knowable and predictable? In spite of these criticisms, the use of utilitarian theory in social and economic life is pervasive because it maps easily on to supply-and-demand price-fixing mechanisms in economics and cost-benefit calculations in social policy.

Duty theories

Often called deontological theories, these hold that actions can be right in themselves regardless of the consequences. The value of an action lies in the motive behind its doing, which should be based upon duty rather than on self-interest. Duty can be derived from divine command, reason or intuition, or from a social contract between members of a society. Examples of acting according to duty would be keeping promises and paying one's debts even when it may not be in one's own interests to do so.

One of the most influential theories of duty derives from Immanuel Kant, the great German philosopher who tried to provide the foundations for a system of ethics on the basis of reason rather than intuition, consequences or conscience (Kant, 1964). Morality for Kant was to be founded upon individuals' ability to reason which they possess in common with humanity. This gives an objective basis to moral claims outside our personal preferences and interests based upon what reason demands of us. Kant calls the demand of reason the 'categorical imperative' because it admits of no exceptions and is absolutely binding, requiring that a certain act be performed regardless of circumstances or consequences. If one wants to be a rational human being, one is duty-bound to follow the categorical imperative.

Kant explained the categorical imperative as follows: 'Act only in that way that the maxim of my action should become a universal law.' This is a rule regarding the form a moral principle should take rather than the content of the principle. So for example 'Do not tell lies' is a maxim that could be adopted as a moral imperative, and it demands that you never tell a lie in any circumstance or to any person, and it stipulates that you would wish other people to behave in the same way regardless of motives or consequences. As it happens, most people would find it very difficult to live according to this particular maxim, which would make social interaction very uncomfortable. A similar dilemma occurs in relation to bribery (see the box below). Nevertheless, we can see that for an action or principle to be regarded as moral it must be capable of being made consistently universal: it must show respect for other people as rational beings and ends in themselves and be respectful of the autonomy of rational people. Kant claims that our moral laws can be self-imposed (so there is free will) and so people should be respected and valued as autonomous law creators who are participants in a realm beyond the world of appearances.

WOULD BRIBERY BE ACCEPTABLE TO A KANTIAN?

Bribery in business occurs when property or personal advantage is offered, without the authority of the law, to another person with the intent that that person should act favourably towards the offerer. A Kantian approach is likely to regard this behaviour as deeply immoral for some of the following reasons. The maxim of treating like cases alike in business means that we should treat others with fairness and not allow some persons to get ahead or gain favours that others would not gain. So bribery is wrong both at home and abroad. More than likely bribery offends the sensibilities of the foreign country as well, but even if that were not the case, the bribery is still wrong for it breaches the maxim that people should be treated alike and with fairness. It also damages the social institution of promise-making and keeping trust in business transactions, which can also be held to be maxims of a Kantian.

Actions and principles that match up to these criteria are valid moral laws and so should be obeyed by the person of goodwill who lives by the demands of the categorical imperative.

The major criticism made of duty theories is that if the system of reasoning upon which they are founded is rejected, the authority of the categorical imperative is undermined. There is also the problem of how choices should be made between conflicting principles which conform to the requirements of the categorical imperative. For example, giving consideration to others' feelings as a maxim conflicts with that of telling the truth at all times. How should this conflict of maxims be resolved? Another problem is the difficulty of separating out actions from the consequences they may give rise to. For example, should you tell the truth to bad people when the consequences of your action could be devastating for a good person?

The strength of this approach is that it highlights the call of duty for the ordinary person and prescribes some actions absolutely. Its weaknesses are that it ignores consequences and allows of no exceptions in any circumstances. However, it should be noted that an attempt to establish moral duties without regard to consequences is the basis of human rights or natural law theories. These hold that certain human rights are fundamental or natural and cannot be overridden and create corresponding duties in others to uphold those rights. The basis of these rights is sometimes established on religious arguments about what God intends for humankind, or on the basis of a shared human nature which revolves around the needs to survive, procreate and respect others, and more recently on the appeal to the existence of a social contract or conventional agreement which establishes certain human rights as essential for a flourishing society.

But again the major problem involved in the theory of human rights is how one can prove that rights actually exist such that all human beings, without exception, have valid grounds for making certain claims on how they ought to be treated. Also, the motives or consequences of an action are not held to be sufficient reasons to allow infringement of certain rights but the problem then becomes what happens when rights conflict and a judgement between rights claims has to be made. Take, for example, the case where the rights of AIDS sufferers not to be discriminated against in employment clashes with the rights of other employees to protect themselves from the risk of HIV infection. Motives and consequences are considered together in virtue theory, the third of our theories of secular ethics.

Virtue theories

This is a view of ethics that has ancient roots in the work of Plato and Aristotle and is based on the character and actions of the virtuous individual. Ethics is not perceived as a set of rules to determine what is the right action to perform but as the motives and actions of people who are concerned to further the common good. The central question which informs the person's actions are about how one should live and what constitutes the life worth living in a human community. The development of virtue takes place in a community which has a clear conception of what makes for human flourishing and what virtues are to be commended and what vices scorned. Virtuous people strive to develop dispositions and character traits which predispose them to act in the right way in any circumstance, as guided by their practical wisdom. This means that circumstances and consequences will be weighed up by persons of discernment who know what they want to achieve and take pride in doing it or would be shamed if they failed to do the right thing – hence the choice dilemma posed in the box below.

SHOULD LOYALTY COME BEFORE HONESTY IN BUSINESS?

This is a complex issue to analyse briefly. It may be best to take an example of a conflict between these two virtues, such as the case of whistleblowing where the act of disloyalty to the company is in conflict with the person's need to tell the truth. The judgement of whether the breach of trust is justified is a difficult one to make. From the position of the virtuous person who hopes to exercise practical wisdom it will depend upon whether the virtue of loyalty is to override the virtue of justice and honesty in the circumstances of the case. For example, in cases where harm could be done to the public and the company has failed to respond adequately to the complaints of the employee made through internal procedures, then as a matter of justice it would be morally right to tell the truth and ignore the damage done to the company by such disloyalty. If the whistleblower experiences retaliation from the company in these circumstances, the company itself must be judged as being a community without virtue.

There is a good deal of variation between virtue theorists as to what constitutes the ideal set of virtues, but most would agree that they are the product of a shared conception of the good life to be aspired to by a society. So, for example, Aristotle thought that the key virtues were courage, temperance, justice and wisdom, and that these were character traits fixed in people by habitual training such that virtuous persons aim at moderation between the two extremes of excess and deficiency and that the proper balance is determined by people of practical wisdom who develop judgement and discernment in making their choices (Aristotle, 1961). Virtuous people grow up knowing what to do because they know what is worth having and doing, and it has become second nature to them that they should exercise their practical wisdom in every situation that confronts them. In the middle ages, Aquinas tried to supplement this view of the virtues by placing the good of humankind as the knowing and doing of God's will and the virtues of faith, hope and love as the central traits in a community which debates what kind of life it is good to lead. Ethical conduct is therefore anchored in the dispositions of character rather than in a decision procedure or according to formal rules.

The main criticism of virtue-based ethics is that it is unclear what action might be judged to be right or wrong in a particular circumstance: two virtuous persons may decide on different courses of action. Because virtue ethics enables notions of justice and fairness to be addressed, does being fair to a majority make a collective outcome more virtuous and ethical? Moreover, the fact that a virtuous person chooses a certain action does not in itself make that action moral. In other words, it might be thought to be sufficient to judge actions by the character of their doer rather than the consequences of their actions. Accordingly, this approach still needs to be supported by careful thought and analysis over what is ethical, and why, in the various situations and circumstances of life, some actions are the right ones to perform while others are morally questionable.

The ethical theories above constitute only some of the range of approaches that can be brought to bear upon ethical problems in HRM. But it should be remembered that the various theories tend to focus on different aspects of the ethical question and the selection of a theory is a matter of preference depending upon what aspect of ethics is considered to be more important: consequences, obligations or character.

Cross-cultural issues

Differences in ethical values may lead to opposite conclusions of what is right or wrong, evoke different moral implications, and cause decision-makers to interpret a common situation differently, even where there is some overlap in national values (Hendry, 1999). At best, managers working across national borders may face barriers to progress, and at worst, overt hostility to decisions that are deemed to be culturally unethical.

Yet cross-cultural comparisons of convergence and divergence in the ethical content of business decisions have only begun to be explored recently. Our first example considers Beekun et al's (2003) assessment of the influence of justice and utilitarianism criteria (Reidenbach and Robin, 1988) in managerial decision-making in Russia and the USA. These countries manifest extreme differences in economic and business development and cultural characteristics along four of Hofstede's (2001) dimensions of culture (see Chapter 2). The main contrasts lie in power distance (the degree of inequality that a society considers normal in areas such as prestige, wealth and power) and uncertainty avoidance (the extent to which a society feels threatened by ambiguity and tries to avoid uncertainty), in which the US scores are low and the Russian scores are high, and in individualism (the degree to which people prefer being individuals to being members of a group) where the US score is high and the Russian score is low. The difference in masculinity (hard and soft work-related cultural values such as assertiveness compared to nurturing) is much less marked.

Focusing on the two dimensions of power distance and individualism that exhibited the largest differences, Americans were found to have stricter guidelines when assessing ethics and to assess certain actions as less ethical when applying justice or utilitarianism criteria. For example, wrongful disclosure of information by an auditor in a bankruptcy case would be unethical in the knowledge that the auditing profession is subject to a professional code of conduct regardless of whether justice or utilitarian criteria were employed. When applying justice criteria Russians considered it unethical for a person to be granted important private information about an individual by a third party without the individual's approval or knowledge. This is explained by a history of government intrusion into individuals' lives, with a legacy of 'big brother' having sensitised Russians to the dangers of acting in such a way.

The second example relates to Beekun *et al*'s (2005) follow-up study, in which Reidenbach and Robin's (1988) multi-criteria ethics instrument is used to conduct the first empirical test of Robertson and Crittenden's (2003) macro-level moral philosophy model of cross-cultural ethics. Issues of ethos, relativism, virtue ethics and utilitarianism can thus be explored in Case study 39.

CASE STUDY 39

WHAT ETHICAL CRITERIA GOVERN BUSINESSPEOPLE'S BEHAVIOUR IN RUSSIA AND THE USA?

Different moral philosophies are used as the basis for ethical decisions
Americans place more emphasis on virtue ethics, whereas Russian managers favour utilitarianism. The Americans found the ethical dilemmas depicted by a series of given scenarios to be considerably more unacceptable – for example, where an accountant accepted a job to audit the accounts of a major corporation for which his sister was treasurer. Americans have a different perception of virtue ethics, view justice broadly and tend to include equity and fair treatment as well as equality, whereas Russians focus solely on equality. Nevertheless, Russians have different ethical standards for impersonal and personal relationships, so that deceiving someone in a business transaction is not unethical but deceiving a friend would be unethical.

Multiple philosophies were used simultaneously
Russians combined relativism with a utilitarian perspective, whereas Americans emphasised virtue ethics in combination with a relativistic approach.

Cultural convergence appears to be developing
Economic rapprochement between the USA and Russia and in their styles of capitalism may eventually lead to similarity in use of moral philosophies in guiding norms and behaviour.

Source: derived from Beekun *et al* (2005)

Case study tasks

1   How can American managers persuade their Russian counterparts that a universal standard will benefit a larger group collectively and that due process should not be ignored?

2   How can Russian executives help Americans to understand that what is good and fair for the majority may also be good and fair for the few, provided due process is observed and the rules of justice are not subverted?

3   Is greater convergence of moral philosophies desirable?

In the third example, Vynoslavska *et al* (2005) unequivocally demonstrate more lenient ethical attitudes among Ukrainian managers compared to their US counterparts which are explained by a remarkable deterioration in social-moral attitudes during the period of economic transition in the Ukraine, based on a general questionnaire about people's attitudes to a series of statements shown in Table 7. The deteriorations in respect of the first and last statements are deemed 'truly remarkable' when the economic system in 1982 was planned with few incentives for individual effort and little opportunity for entrepreneurship. Similarly the 'old regime', in spite of well-known corruption, provided fewer opportunities for corruption and law-breaking. In short, the development of a highly unstable business climate within a moral vacuum and weak institutional framework has made for difficulties in establishing any sort of moral or ethical underpinning for businesses. Inefficiencies have been introduced into the system, the cost of doing business has increased, and foreign investors shun the country. Western aid is called for to instil ethics training into business school curricula and professional development programmes.

Table 7 Changes in social-moral attitudes in the Ukraine

[figures are percentage majorities in agreement with the statements]

Ukrainian managers ...	1982	2002
Can exercise initiative in job and community life	62	37
Are open-hearted and always ready to help	83	36
Are not indifferent to the violation of laws and regulations	61	20
Disapprove of bribes	71	49
Think only of themselves and their own well-being	20	65
Are interested in buying things	41	60
Can achieve success and well-being by honest labour	87	32

Notes:

Based on Ukrainian National Surveys cited in Vynoslavska *et al* (2005: 296)

Majority combines almost-all and majority responses. Minority and very-few responses are omitted. Percentages have been rounded.

Discussion questions

1   Are all ethical values relative to culture and nation-state?

2   Is individualism now a universal value?

3   What factors should inform the design of an ethics training programme?

3 WHAT IS THE CASE FOR A MORE ETHICALLY INFORMED APPROACH TO HRM?

In this section we discuss the four main reasons for a more ethically informed approach to HRM.

Perceived moral decay in western economies

Many HRM and business professionals have become alarmed by what they see as the moral decay of their culture and social values. A lot of publicity has been given to the problem of corporate fraud and malfeasance since the Enron, WorldCom and Parmalat scandals, and the general decline of integrity and honesty in public life. It is small wonder that the question of moral conduct has become an important part of even the business school agenda, in the hope that a concern for right conduct can be encouraged once again.

Declining western economies and emerging Far East economies

The strident market individualism of the western HRM practice has often been outperformed in recent decades by the competitive collectivism of the Japanese and Chinese. Despite the obvious cultural differences between East and West, the principal component of the East's success seems to be managerial common sense and the ability of their managers to build team work and commitment from the workforce by good leadership based around certain values. The worldwide success of books like *Built to Last* have been built upon the quest of businessmen to know how to match the Japanese, and now the Chinese, at their own game (Collins and Porras, 1994).

The failure of MBA courses

Attention in recent years has also been focused on the education of MBA graduates (Mintzberg, 2004). A major criticism is that the MBA student is over-analytical and although competent in all manner of financial and marketing techniques has very little feel for business or understanding of how to manage one. Consequently, many MBAs look for employment outside of industry in financial services or in consultancy. The contrast with the some of the other advanced economies could not be more marked. In many countries there are no MBAs, young businessmen tend to receive a liberal arts and scientific education up to graduate level, then are trained on-the-job by their companies and their own efforts. They are encouraged to become technically expert and to learn from the example of their superiors in the company. Many accounts of the leadership style in these companies emphasise the pivotal role business leaders play in creating values and symbolic meanings for their companies, which make employees feel part of an important community that has a contribution to make for the good of the nation. Again, part of the movement towards the study of business ethics is an attempt to find a language in which to rediscover the values that are neglected in the usual MBA course.

The need for a common good in business and society

As we mentioned above, the success of some companies can be partly attributed to the fact that they pay attention to the management of meanings aimed at certain values and end results. They use moral language and appreciate the need to create a community interest and a vision of the common good. Now it might not be the same one that everyone aims for, but it has a tremendous effect in inspiring hearts and minds. If companies are to become competitive and successful, they must be led by managers who take the responsibility for the company as a community seriously and act with integrity towards their various stakeholders. The notion of stakeholders (see Chapter 12) is a broad one and includes shareholders, employees, management, customers, suppliers, community, and – importantly in the new millennium – the environment. Modern HRM carries responsibilities towards all these constituents and not the least to serving some notion of the common good. In companies, managers need to use moral language and possess the ability to frame arguments that inspire debate about what is right and good. Managers should know about ends as well as means: how to create values as well as create wealth.

In summary, the case for introducing the study of ethics into the HRM curriculum is to enable HRM professionals to engage in analysis and debate about moral and social issues in modern organisations. The full extent of the ethics agenda for HRM is wide and varied and is the subject of many articles in the HRM and business ethics journals. To give an illustration of this new discourse, one aspect of the implications of the ethics agenda for HRM is explored in the next section through a detailed consideration of the concept of organisational justice.

Discussion questions

1   Is it possible to learn from the mistakes of others in business?

2   How are we to define the common good today?

3   Devise an ideal curriculum for an MBA programme.

4 ORGANISATIONAL JUSTICE

Fairness and the good employer

Organisational justice can be conceived as a framework that is designed to regulate and guide managerial behaviour in such ways as to ensure fair treatment for individuals at the pre-employment stage (for example, in the recruitment process), throughout employment from induction to employment termination, and post-employment (for example, in the provision of references for another employer). Another, more narrowly conceived approach is to consider organisational justice as a framework to enable mutual satisfaction in the employment contract through an effective grievance and disciplinary process (Torrington *et al*, 2005). Rules, codes of conduct and codes of practice provide the foundations for organisational justice by serving to underpin and guide managerial and employee behaviour.

The reasons for organisations' seeking to demonstrate fairness in employment stem from the maxim that no employer wants to be perceived as a bad employer. Organisations have a vested interest to promote themselves as good employers to enhance their reputation, to make them an employer of choice or to demonstrate corporate social responsibility (see Chapters 6 and 12). Critical writers such as Legge (2005) have made much of the rhetoric of HRM in promoting the organisation as a caring and sharing employer that is belied by the reality that the organisation does not practise what it preaches. For example, the rhetorical claim is that employees are being empowered whereas the reality means they are doing considerably more work with no commensurate increase in reward or recognition.

Although the benefits of organisational justice – including a better motivated and productive workforce – is explored in greater detail below, it is the potentially damaging consequences and outcomes of perceived unfairness that should focus the attentions of HR managers and line managers alike. Unfair treatment can be exploitative, lead to poor morale and work attitude, induce stress and physical illness, and generate unwanted, negative employee behaviours such as theft or workplace aggression. As we noted in Chapter 2, perceptions of unfair treatment may be an outcome of psychological contract violation, in that one party perceives that the other has failed to fulfil a promised obligation (Rousseau, 1989). Given our emphasis on mutuality in the employment relationship, although managers are self-evidently in a more powerful position than their employees, it is the employees themselves who are the subjects of managerial treatment and, in effect, the real judges of how far HRM policies and practices are fair and just.

Theories of organisational justice

Organisational justice theory posits that perceptions of fairness within an organisation are predicated upon three component parts (Greenberg, 1987), an approach that is widely adopted in the recent literature (Folger and Cropanzano, 1998; Harris, 2000; Saunders and Thornhill, 2003; Tzafrir et al, 2004):

- distributive justice (fairness of outcome)
- procedural justice (fairness of procedures and processes)
- interactional justice (fairness of treatment).

Distributive justice

Distributive justice is perceived fairness arising from organisational allocations and outcomes (Deutsch, 1985; Saunders and Thornhill, 2003). HR specialists have a major stake in employees' perceived fairness of outcomes by providing a major contribution to 'ethical leadership' in the organisation (Winstanley and Woodall, 2000). There are three rules of distributive justice: equity, equality and need (Deutsch, 1985), and the use of each rule is determined by particular goals. Equity is the rule to achieve greater productivity; equality is the rule to underpin harmony; and need is the rule to satisfy the needs of the less fortunate.

Leung et al (2001) identify two forms of distributive justice. *Performance-based distributive justice* is the perceived fairness of one's outcome in relation to one's contribution. *Comparative distributive justice* is the perceived fairness of one's outcome with reference to others and is more widely used in the literature. For example, Greenberg (1987) notes that unfair allocations and outcomes lead to feelings of inequity, so that perceptions of distributive justice are based largely on a comparison with others. Such perceptions are relative not only to absolute measures – such as the size of the annual pay award that is given to the group as a whole – but also to social comparisons, such as the way in which the pay award has been allocated amongst different members of the group. There is always the danger that a disgruntled employee who perceives unduly harsh treatment will try to restore the balance and equity in the employment relationship by other, more negative or deviant means to subvert managerial authority and engage in petty pilfering or reduced work effort.

Procedural justice

Procedural justice is perceived fairness of the means used to determine outcomes (Folger and Greenberg, 1995). Hence it encompasses both procedure and process, such as the efficacy of the performance appraisal system and the way in which appraisals are conducted. Voice or participation allows those affected to exercise some degree of process control or personal influence in the decision-making process (Thibaut and Walker, 1975) (see Chapter 10). Formal rules and written employment practices provide a more tangible and visible manifestation of the organisation's intentions. These are supported by a variety of statutory interventions that underpin various aspects of employment practice – for example, equality and anti-discrimination law in the UK (see Chapter 14).

Leventhal *et al* (1980) identify six rules of procedural justice:

1   Consistency (of procedures to ensure fairness)

2   Bias suppression (procedural development and implementation without reference to the self-interests of the instigators)

3   Accuracy (procedures based on accurate information)

4   Correctability (procedures must have scope for correction)

5   Representativeness (procedures must integrate the needs of all parties)

6   Ethicality (procedures must follow moral and ethical standards).

On the other hand, if one takes Lind's (2000) view that justice is a socially constructed reality, procedures do not necessarily have to be highly formalised. The more important point is in the way the process is carried out than in the efficacy of the procedure itself. Employees need to know they have not been deceived (Herriot *et al*, 2000) – hence the importance of managerial integrity to ensure consistency of application of moral and ethical procedures to generate equity and trust (Saunders and Thornhill, 2003).

Interactional justice

Interactional justice is the quality of interpersonal treatment meted out by the decision-makers (Bies and Moag, 1986), and because this is process-driven, this aspect of organisational justice is commonly treated synonymously with procedural justice (Saunders and Thornhill, 2003). Employees are more likely to accept a decision, whether favourable or unfavourable, if the decision-making process is credible and transparent – for example, in the way recruitment and selection are conducted (Harris, 2000) or performance-related pay is measured and applied (Harris, 2001). Quality of treatment relates both to the explanation and justification for the decision made and to the degree of sensitivity and consideration given in reaching that decision. Employees should be treated with respect and dignity.

Taking the example of the way the employee is treated in a disciplinary interview, management would have to give employees an adequate amount of time to state their side of the story, have demonstrated an ability to respond openly and flexibly to unforeseen issues that arise, and having taken account of all this, be able to explain and justify why a particular sanction was being imposed and was appropriate to the offence in question. Indeed, the matter may turn out not actually to be a disciplinary issue at all because it has arisen from a lack of training or relates to difficult personal circumstances that require sympathetic consideration.

However, Harris (2002) suggests that decisions that take account of employee need are being threatened. Although the expansion of employment law and the growth of workplace litigation have increased the requirement for employers to demonstrate fairness, a potentially negative outcome is adherence to processes developed to demonstrate 'moral neutrality'. In other words, procedures to protect the organisation rather than the individual are developed that have little to do with promoting genuine fairness in the organisation.

Cultural implications of organisational justice

Having already noted how culture impacts upon ethical behaviour, we now turn to examples of the important and wide-ranging effects of culture on justice behaviour in selected countries

(Leung *et al*, 2001; Beugré, 2002). In their research on perceived organisational justice in joint venture hotels in China, Leung *et al* (2001) observed a change in local employees' attitudes over time in the light of their growing experience and continued exposure to these new developments. Having initially regarded their pay as fair even in the light of the very high salaries of expatriate managers, comparative distributive justice has emerged as a predictor of job attitudes and locals perceive their pay as highly unfair. Employees working with overseas Chinese or Japanese managers reported lower distributive justice, procedural justice and integrative justice than those working with western or other Asian managers. Beugré's (2002) case for the wider development and implementation of fair organisational practices raises a number of cultural consequences that are highlighted in Case study 40.

CASE STUDY 40

SOCIAL JUSTICE AND ORGANISATIONAL JUSTICE IN SUB-SAHARAN AFRICA

Dramatic social and political changes in Africa are likely to spill over into the workplace in the form of a quest for justice and empowerment. In an African context, social justice includes more democracy, the rule of law and political governance, especially in the accountability of public officials. The benefits for organisations would include positive employee attitudes and behaviours, such as organisational commitment, trust in management and organisational citizenship that creates strong culture and leads to higher organisational performance. If organisations fail to respond, the consequences are counterproductive behaviours and a weak culture that drives lower productivity.

As in ethics, culture is important in justice perceptions. Three key cultural patterns are important:

High collectivism
People are expected to subordinate their aspirations to those of the relevant social unit. Africans are more likely to use exclusionary justice because they tend to favour the in-group – eg friends and family – rather than the out-group – eg another racial group or expatriates. Local employees employed by multinational corporations may feel a sense of distributive injustice and perceived inequity compared to expatriate employees.

High value of interpersonal ties
An African saying 'What you give is less important than how you give it' is likely to favour greater emphasis on procedural justice and interactive justice than on distributive justice.

High power distance
Autocratic and unaccountable power-holders demand obedience. Decisions may therefore not be accepted because they are fair but because they are enacted by a person of high social status, leading to blind obedience at the expense of inducing productivity and performance.

Source: derived from Deutsch (1985), Hofstede (2001) and Beugré (2002)

Case study tasks

1   How can organisational justice be achieved in South Africa and Zimbabwe, where discriminatory practices favoured a white minority over a black majority?

> 2   Given the importance of distributive justice to performance outcomes, what types of policies and practices should organisations develop, and how should they be implemented, given the cultural barriers suggested?
>
> 3   How can HR managers ensure that line managers are culturally sensitive to organisational justice in different countries?

Discussion questions

1   Is it ethical and just for managers who want to introduce organisational change to focus on the positive effects and downplay the negative effects as a necessary evil to help the company move in the right direction?

2   How many different types of rules can you identify that govern managerial behaviour, and what are the main benefits and drawbacks of each type of rule?

3   How can the HR function and line managers measure the extent to which employees perceive organisational justice?

CONCLUSIONS AND FUTURE ISSUES

Within the scope of this chapter we have only been able to introduce business ethics and give some of the reasons why it deserves more attention in HRM. Three ethical theories used in business ethics analysis were identified and briefly outlined. Several reasons were given for a more ethically informed approach to HRM relating to changes in western society and the need to find a language in which to frame a better notion of the common good. We also reviewed the research on organisational justice and the different meanings of justice in the organisational context. Finally, it should be stressed that it is engagement in the process of analysis and rational argument that is the key benefit to be gained by HRM professionals who explore ethical issues in this context.

In a world of global markets, the relationship between employers and employees must be a voluntary exchange of values on terms acceptable to both sides. However, the thrust of much of the organisational justice literature has been that employees are in an inherently weaker bargaining position compared to employers, and so there has been a push for governments to regulate these matters through employment law. Many laws have been passed on these matters in the area of minimum wages, paid holidays, limits on working time, and health and safety. New issues for future regulation which are of ethical concern will include privacy rights, how to protect whistleblowers, how to deal with problems of sexual harassment, and family-friendly policies.

Successful companies will increasingly be those that recognise that they have responsibilities to a range of stakeholders that go beyond compliance with the law. If in the past the focus was on enhancing shareholder value, now it is on engaging stakeholders for long-term value-creation. In order to survive and be profitable a company must maintain ethical relationships with a range of stakeholders whose values and interests may vary greatly. This means that HRM professionals have to be sensitive and imaginative about ethical issues so they are able to deal with a wide range of issues including greater accountability, human rights abuses, sustainability strategies, corporate governance codes, workplace ethics, stakeholder consultation and management. The corporation must be treated as a community of purpose by its leadership so that attention is paid to the integrity and moral example that pervades the organisation. Of particular importance will be the moral virtues displayed by those in leadership positions in the organisation and the identification this will inspire. But the conception of virtue to be cultivated in this community of purpose must be shared and built from the bottom up on the principle of respect for persons as moral agents. The building of ethical conduct upon these foundations will enable HRM to rise to the challenge of globalisation.

CASE STUDY 41

ENRON – THE BUSINESS ETHICS CASE OF THE MILLENNIUM

After the long run of the rising stock markets in the 1990s came the fall from grace of some of the biggest companies. In particular, the bankruptcy of the Houston, Texas-based energy trading company Enron has raised serious ethical concerns about corporate conduct in the USA and elsewhere. The company was run by a senior team of Chairman of the Board Kenneth Lay, Chief Executive Officer Jeffrey Skilling and Financial Officer Andrew Fastow. After Enron filed for bankruptcy, the senior executives were prosecuted for a wide range of offences concerning accounting and financial fraud to meet aggressive Wall Street earnings forecasts that had helped it maintain its spectacular share price rises during the 1990s. Amongst the many aspects of the financial chicanery that brought about the Enron collapse was the creation of special purpose companies (SPEs) to manage assets off the balance sheet of the main company. This took advantage of US accounting rules that allowed variation from the principle of consolidation of parent and subsidiary accounts. The several thousand SPEs set up by Enron effectively hid the high level of company debt from the main shareholders in Enron and fooled the market into thinking that the company was growing and profitable. They were also a vehicle that helped to further enrich the senior executives, who were receiving share options in Enron and fees for running the SPEs. This intricate labyrinth of financial engineering was toppled when in the late 1990s the dotcom bubble of investment burst and Enron's pattern of sham transactions between itself and its SPEs was exposed and the company's true level of indebtedness – several hundred million dollars – was revealed to the market. Enron was declared bankrupt in 2002.

The Enron collapse raises many business ethics issues and is likely to be the subject of business school case study examination for many years to come. Besides the issues raised regarding this kind of financial chicanery, there are also important issues raised in this case about corporate ethics such as auditor conflicts of interest, the responsibility of banks, whistleblowing procedures, employee pension fund investments and corporate responsibility and corporate governance.

Enron's auditor was Andersen, the Chicago-based accountancy firm and one of the big five auditor firms in the world. Andersen admitted that its auditors misled the shareholders and that it had participated in the destroying of documents in the company's audit trail. Andersen earned fees of $25 million in the year before Enron's collapse, and it had also supplied it with two senior financial executives. It also supplied Enron with $27 million-worth of non-audit services and consultancy work. Naturally, in the light of its misdeeds questions have been asked about the objectivity of its work as an auditor, particularly given its failure to highlight the off-balance-sheet transactions that launched the downward spiral in the share price of Enron when they were uncovered. The degree and extent of Andersen's involvement in this scandal ultimately led to the collapse of confidence in Andersen and to its own demise within a matter of months after the Enron bankruptcy.

A second lesson is to be taken by the banks that financed Enron's rapid growth. It would appear that the banks had a poor understanding of the nature of Enron's business and its reliance on partnerships to shift debt off the balance sheet. Moreover, Enron effectively turned itself into a financial trading company without being properly under the scrutiny of a regulator. It was operating at the frontiers of the financial markets, dealing in some 2,000 financial products that included weather derivatives and bandwidth capacity. It was often the leading operator in markets it had invented.

Some months prior to the Enron bankruptcy a seven-page anonymous memo was sent to the chairman Kenneth Lay setting out major concerns about the accounting practices that might cause the company to implode in a wave of scandals. This memo had been written by Sherron Watkins, an Enron vice-president. A week later she owned up to authoring the letter and had a meeting with Mr Lay in which she further substantiated her claims about the accounting malpractices that had been perpetrated. Her whistle-blowing was internal to the company and did not reach outside financial authorities, but still was a brave act given the competitive nature of its management culture and the likely reprisals that might follow her exposure of her senior colleagues' misdeeds. Her courageous behaviour and letter were only uncovered after the bankruptcy by Congressional investigators, who found her letter to Mr Lay buried in boxes of company documents. She was identified and praised by the House of Representatives committee for being the only senior executive to raise concerns about the company's policies with Mr Lay, although she did not go directly to the financial regulators out of a sense of loyalty to Enron.

Another bitter lesson was learnt by the employees of Enron. Enron's employees' pension fund, worth around $2.1 billion before the collapse, had invested some 60% of its assets in the company's shares – which fell in value from $80 per share in 2001 to almost nothing in 2002. Not only did many employees lose their jobs but many of them lost a good deal of their pension as well. By any normal measures of financial prudence, such a concentration of investment in a single company's shares would be foolhardy. But the fact that the Enron employees had invested their pension funds in their employer's shares added to the risk and left the employees exposed not only to unemployment and the loss of share options, but also to retirement on a much reduced pension. The rules in the USA for such pension plans were designed to encourage employees to hold their company's shares rather than to provide security in old age, and, in effect, allowed the company to restrict share sales by the employees.

Enron had over the years done much to further the cause of corporate social responsibility and had built close links with political parties on both sides of the Atlantic. Both Bush Presidents had been close friends and campaign fundraising beneficiaries of Kenneth Lay, the Enron chairman. Enron was an important contributor to the Greater Houston Partnership business association. It also contributed generously to local charities and even led the regeneration of a depressed area of Houston by financing a new baseball field. Enron gave almost $6 million in political campaign contributions in the 1990s. In the US election prior to its collapse, Enron contributed more than $2.4 million to federal candidates and parties, putting it among the top 50 organisational donors. George W. Bush alone received $114,000 from Enron for his presidential campaign. Enron also contributed to the political campaign funds of the Labour and Conservative parties in the UK. Enron also spent its money in other countries to cultivate political influence and social approval. In India, Enron spent $20 million on educational programmes for local people.

In terms of corporate governance, the Enron board appeared not to have been aware of the risks it was running and the board members only poorly understood the business of the company. This was despite the fact that the Enron board included a former US financial regulator, Wendy Gramm, and its chair of the audit committee was the chartered accountant and former Conservative cabinet minister in the UK, John Wakeham. Enron's collapse in many ways was due to a failure of corporate governance and management. The board of directors did not understand the risks the company was taking and the perverse incentives it had provided to tempt its senior managers into manipulating its earnings and into concealing its debts. In management terms, Enron's failure was also due to the human resources strategy that had militated against a culture of transparency and trust, because its employees were subjected to overweening performance management systems that led to dismissal and demotions for those who failed to meet or exceed the targets, and were afraid to raise their concerns within the company.

Case study tasks

1   What changes in corporate governance and management systems are needed to prevent another Enron from happening?

2   How should conflicts of interest be handled in business?

3   What encouragement should be offered and what procedures ought to be devised for whistleblowing in organisations?

REFERENCES

Aristotle (1961) *The Nicomachean Ethics*. Oxford: Oxford University Press.

Beekun R. I., Westerman J. and Barghouti J. (2005) 'Utility of ethical frameworks in determining behavioural intention: a comparison of the US and Russia', *Journal of Business Ethics*, Vol. 61: 235–47.

Beekun R. I., Stedham Y., Yamamura J. H. and Barghouti J. A. (2003) 'Business ethics in Russia and the USA', *International Journal of Human Resource Management*, Vol. 14, No. 8: 1333–49.

Bentham J. (1971) *Introduction to the Principles of Morals and Legislation*. Oxford: Oxford University Press.

Beugré C. D. (2002) 'Understanding organisational justice and its impact on managing employees: an African perspective', *International Journal of Human Resource Management*, Vol. 13, No. 7: 1091–1104.

Bies R. J. and Moag J. (1986) 'Interactional justice: communication criteria in fairness', in R. Lewicki, B. Sheppard and M. Bazerman (eds) *Research on Negotiation in Organizations* (Vol. 1). Greenwich, CT: JAI Press.

Collins J. and Porras J. (1994) *Built to Last*. New York: Harper & Row.

Deutsch M. (1985) *Distributive Justice*. New Haven, CT: Yale University Press.

Drucker P. (1981) 'What is business ethics?', *The Public Interest*, Vol. 63, Spring.

Folger R. and Cropanzano R. (1998) *Organizational Justice and Human Resource Management*. Thousand Oaks, CA: Sage.

Friedman M. (1970) 'The social responsibility of business is to increase its profits', *New York Times,* 13 September.

Greenberg J. (1987) 'A taxonomy of organizational justice theories', *Academy of Management Review*, Vol. 12, No. 1: 9–22.

Harris L. (2000) 'Procedural justice and perceptions of fairness in selection practice', *International Journal of Selection and Assessment*, Vol. 8, No. 3: 148–57.

Harris L. (2001) 'Rewarding employee performance: line managers' values, beliefs and perspectives', *International Journal of Human Resource Management*, Vol. 12, No. 7: 1182–92.

Harris L. (2002) 'Organisational justice in the workplace: the responsibilities of line managers and human resource management specialists', *Journal of Professional Human Resource Management*, Issue No. 30: 23–8.

Hendry J. (1999) 'Universality and reciprocity in international business ethics', *Business Ethics Quarterly*, Vol. 9, No. 3: 405–20.

Herriot P., Hirsch W. and Reilly P. (1998) *Trust and Transition: Managing today's employment relationship*. Chichester: John Wiley & Sons.

Hofstede G. (2001) *Culture's Consequences* (2nd edition). London: Sage.

Kant I. (1964) *Groundwork of the Metaphysic of Morals*. New York: Harper & Row.

Legge K. (2005) *Human Resource Management: Rhetorics and realities*. London: Palgrave.

Leung K., Wang Z. and Smith P. B. (2001) 'Job attitudes and organisational justice in joint venture hotels in China: the role of expatriate managers', *International Journal of Human Resource Management*, Vol. 12, No. 6: 926–45.

Leventhal G., Karuza, J. and Fry, W. (1980) 'Beyond fairness: a theory of allocation preferences', in G. Mikula (ed.) *Justice and Social Interaction*. New York: Springer Verlag.

Lind E. A. (2000) *Litigation and Claiming in Organizations: Antisocial behavior or quest for justice?* Thousand Oaks, CA: Sage.

Mill J. S. (1972) *Utilitarianism*. London: Dent.

Mintzberg H. (2004) *Managers, not MBAs*. London: FT/Pitman.

Park H., Rehg M. T. and Lee D. (2005) 'The influence of Confucian ethics and collectivism on whistleblowing intentions: a study of South Korean public employees', *Journal of Business Ethics*, Vol. 58: 387–403.

Riedenbach R. E. and Robin D. P. (1988) 'Some initial steps towards improving the ethical evaluations of marketing activities', *Journal of Business Ethics*, Vol. 7: 871–9.

Robertson C. J. and Crittenden W. F. (2003) 'Mapping moral philosophies: strategic implications for multi-national firms', *Strategic Management Journal*, Vol. 24: 385–92.

Rousseau D. M. (1989) 'Psychological and implied contracts in organisations', *Employee Responsibilities and Rights Journal*, Vol. 2: 121–39.

Saunders M. N. K. and Thornhill A. (2003) 'Organisational justice, trust and the management of change', *Personnel Review*, Vol. 32, No. 3: 360–75.

Thibaut J. and Walker L. (1975) *Procedural Justice*. Hillsdale, NJ: Erlbaum.

Torrington D., Hall L. and Taylor S. (2005) *Human Resource Management* (6th edition). Harlow: Pearson Education.

Tzafrir S. S., Harel G. H., Baruch Y. and Dolan S. L. (2004) 'The consequences of emerging HRM practices for employees' trust in their managers', *Personnel Review*, Vol. 33, No. 6: 636–47.

Vynoslavska O., McKinney J. A., Moore C. W. and Longenecker J. G. (2005) 'Transition ethics: a comparison of Ukrainian and United States business professionals', *Journal of Business Ethics*, Vol. 61: 283–99.

Winstanley D. and Woodall J. (2000) 'The ethical dimension of human resource management', *Human Resource Management Journal*, Vol. 10, No. 2: 5–20.

Employment equality

CHAPTER 14

Ben Lupton and Carol Woodhams

CHAPTER OBJECTIVES

When you have read this chapter you should be able to:

- describe the nature and extent of employment inequalities internationally

- distinguish between different policy approaches to reducing inequality – in particular, equal opportunity and diversity-based approaches

- explain and analyse the role of national and international law in addressing labour market inequalities

- outline, and provide examples of, the ways in which historical, social and economic factors impact on labour market inequalities in different countries/regions.

PURPOSE AND SCOPE

Access to employment and the rewards from employment are unequally distributed within countries of the world. Many of these inequalities are not related to people's capabilities but to their gender, race, social class, disability, and a range of other factors. This is not only manifestly unjust but, as we will argue below, it is inefficient, resulting in an under-utilisation of human resources by nations and organisations. In this chapter we seek to explain the basis for employment inequalities in different parts of the world, and the approaches taken to reduce them – by nations through legislation, and by organisations through employment policies and practices.

The chapter starts by examining the nature and extent of employment inequalities and the principles that underlie approaches to tackling them. We introduce and explore the ideas of equality management and diversity management that inform organisational policies in this area. We then explore how international and national legal systems address labour market inequalities. In both of these sections we draw primarily on examples from the United Kingdom, which typifies a western approach to equality and provides a useful basis for international comparison. In the second part of the chapter we broaden the focus to look at equality issues in their international context, examining the extent of employment inequalities in different parts of the world, exploring the different patterns that emerge and seeking to explain them. We look at gender equality in the European Union, China, Eastern Europe (in Case study 45 at the end of the chapter) and race equality in Africa. Throughout the chapter we address a number of the book's key themes, particularly focusing on demographic trends and labour market change, cultural variation, and emerging economies.

1 EMPLOYMENT INEQUALITY: PROBLEMS AND SOLUTIONS

In this section, drawing on examples from the UK, we illustrate the nature and extent of employment inequalities and identify the principles underlying the different ways in which inequality is tackled by organisations.

Employment inequalities: who is affected, and in what ways?

It is in the nature of competitive labour markets that people are not treated equally in their access to work or in the benefits that they gain from employment. Some of these inequalities can be justified as arising from the different skills and experience that individuals bring to their employing organisations, but others are unrelated to people's ability to work effectively. In most – if not all – countries in the world, women, minority ethnic, disabled and older workers are more likely to be found in lower-paid, lower-status jobs with fewer career opportunities, chances of promotion and training.

Examples from the UK labour market will illustrate this point.

Female employment in the UK is now at its highest rate ever, but women's participation-rate is still far from equal. Women comprise 46% of the total workforce and 70% of women are economically active (EOC, 2005a). However, hindered by assumptions of a lack of commitment to work and stereotypical views about their abilities, they are disproportionately found in low-paid occupations such as clerical work, personal services and customer service. This is known as horizontal segregation. Women are also more likely to be found at lower levels of organisations and occupations than men: a phenomenon known as vertical segregation. Only 9% of directors of FTSE 100 companies are women (Vinnicombe and Singh, 2003). As noted in Chapter 12, they also suffer a pay gap in relation to men. Average hourly earnings for women working full-time are 18% lower than for full-time men, and, for women working part-time, hourly earnings are 40% lower (EOC, 2005a). Wage disadvantage is compounded by women's predominance in part-time work (44% of women work part-time in comparison to only 11% of men) (EOC, 2005a).

Black and minority ethnic populations comprise 7.6% of the UK's population (Office of National Statistics, 2002a), but suffer similar patterns of labour market segregation. Men and women from ethnic minority groups have lower levels of economic activity than white people and higher levels of unemployment. This has been a consistent pattern over several decades (CRE, 2005; LFS, 2002). Ethnic minorities, particularly men of Pakistani and Bangladeshi descent, are more likely to be found in industries and occupations (hospitality sector, taxi-driving) which offer fewer opportunities for progression and development (Cabinet Office, 2003).

The weight of historical disadvantage experienced by disabled job-seekers and workers is well documented (Roulstone and Barnes, 2005). In spring 2002, one in five people of working age in the United Kingdom had a long-term disability. Just over half were economically active. This compares with an economic activity rate for the working-age population of 79 per cent. Disabled men are more likely than disabled women to be in employment although the gap between the employment rates is smaller (just over 3 percentage points) than for the population as a whole (11 percentage points). Disabled men are more likely to be unemployed than disabled women, 5% compared with 3% (Office of National Statistics, 2002b).

The UK does not, by international standards, have a particularly poor record on employment equality (see Section 3), but the figures above show some marked inequalities. Furthermore, they are only illustrative of the disadvantages faced by women, ethnic minorities and disabled people – and by other groups in the population that we have not mentioned who suffer in similar ways.

Equality management: theory and practice

The equal opportunities (liberal) model

The dominant western response to labour market disadvantage is based on assumptions that employment opportunities should be fairly distributed, allowing everyone to compete equally on merit (Rawls, 1971). In this liberal model, talent and ability are assumed to be attributes of individuals (Young, 1990), some of whom are hampered unfairly on the grounds of their group membership – for example, by being from an ethnic minority. The assumption is, then, that removal of these collective and group-based barriers will enable the best person to 'win' in competitive employment situations, and more generally, will permit all individuals to make the best of themselves (Fredman, 2002). This approach also allows for some special treatment to enable people in groups that face particular barriers in employment to compete on an equal footing – an approach known as positive action. In practice this allows employers to train, encourage or seek out members of a particular social group in order to redress the effects of previous unequal opportunities (EOC, 2005b). They may, for example, wish to train women for technical work, encourage disabled employees to apply for management posts – or compose advertisements that encourage applications from ethnic minorities, but make it clear that selection will be on merit.

This model is underpinned by an assumption that in a market economy the perfect operation of the labour market is upset by the discriminatory actions of powerful groups against weaker ones. This becomes a matter for legal and organisational policy and correction, as we explore below. The label usually ascribed to this approach is 'equal opportunity' and it is associated with a social justice, or moral, justification for the fair and equal treatment of people. However, this is not the only possible approach.

The equal outcomes (radical) model

The first alternative is a radical approach that seeks to achieve equality of outcomes, as opposed to equality of opportunity, and advocates affirmative action or reverse (or positive) discrimination. Under this model disadvantaged groups are given preferential treatment in appointments and promotions in order to correct existing inequalities until different groups are proportionally represented (Jewson and Mason, 1986). As we will see in Section 2, this approach is unlawful in the UK (with limited exceptions) and many other countries. We will not discuss it further here, but encourage you to consider its merits in the discussion questions.

The diversity model

The second, business-based, alternative makes the case that unfair discrimination interferes not only with the operation of labour markets but also with that of product and service markets, which are damaged by the unequal distribution of employment opportunities. This perspective makes a strong profit- and productivity-related justification for the correction of inequality, suggesting that there is competitive advantage in exploiting the potential of a diverse labour market. Thus, equal opportunity extends into diversity management (Cox and Blake, 1991; Ross and Schneider, 1992). In essence, diversity differs from traditional equal opportunities in ensuring that all individuals within an organisation can maximise their potential, regardless of groups to which they belong. It is an all-embracing concept where the focus is on cultural change and learning, rather than simply on avoiding discrimination. Crucially, managing diversity is seen as a key element of overall business strategy rather than an HR policy. The emphasis is on the business benefits that a strategy of managing workforce diversity might bring. The resource-based view of the firm (Barney, 1991; see also Chapter 2 of this book) suggests that effectively utilising human resources in non-traditional and poorly tapped skill pools may confer competitive advantage (Kandola and Fullerton, 1994). In an environment where increased proportions of women and ethnic minorities are economically active, and the population is getting older, equal opportunities is recast in a positive light as a solution to recruitment difficulties.

Other arguments for diversity focus on enhancing profitability through the utilisation and development of the internal labour market. There is some evidence that diversity in teams inhibits 'groupthink' and enhances innovation (Cox and Blake, 1991), and that recruiting a more diverse workforce may introduce new skills into an organisation – for example, the ability of women to listen, empower, and coach (Hicks-Clarke and Iles, 2003; Schroder et al, 1997). There is also some evidence that promoting diversity within organisations is positively related to career and job satisfaction, how individuals feel about their employer, and how well they perform (Hicks-Clarke and Iles, 2003). Diverse organisations may also prove more attractive to customers, which may become particularly important as the labour market participation and customer market share of minority groups grows (Cox and Blake, 1991; IPD, 1996).

Comparing equality- and diversity-based approaches

On the face of it, then, equal opportunity and managing diversity both have the same goal in their sights – ie to correct labour market disadvantage – but they rely on different justifications for their existence and choose different criteria of success. Diversity management is altogether more positive about the notion of individual difference. Whereas equal opportunity tends to view 'difference' from the standard employee norm as the source only of discrimination, diversity management views each individual as the source of unique histories, experiences and skills that can be positively harnessed to the corporate good. Managing diversity thus regards discrimination as not only unlawful but as an anathema to competitive advantage.

How do equal opportunities and diversity approaches compare in practice?

In the UK, for example, organisations are encouraged as a matter of good equal opportunity practice (and to avoid legal challenge, see Section 2) to adopt formal procedures to ensure that discrimination does not take place. Organisational policies and practices are examined to ensure that they are free from potential discrimination against identified groups. The best way to do this is to minimise subjectivity and standardise decision-making processes, treating minority groups the 'same', as if their point of difference does not exist (Liff and Wajcman, 1996). Good equality practice involves the application of formal rules and procedures uniformly to all employees, irrespective of group characteristics. Implementation of these principles encompasses the key functions of HR management – namely, sourcing and selecting between potential employees, training and developing them, managing them, and rewarding them (Kirton and Greene, 2000).

The practice of diversity management is much less prescriptive than the traditional procedural approach to equal opportunity, and there are many different versions of it (Kirton, 2003). We shall describe it as a number of practices (Cassell, 2001) that build on – rather than conflict with or replace – the equal opportunities approach (Webb, 1997), maximise the benefits of individual difference (Thomas, 1990; Cox, 1992; Jackson and Associates, 1992; Kandola and Fullerton, 1998), and educate others to do the same. Training and development is of key importance because it can be used to communicate the aims of the policy, instruct managers and employees, persuade workers to re-examine their stereotypes of the traditional worker

(Skinner, 1999) and break down divisions (for an example see EOR, 1996). Gathering data on individuals and monitoring their progression – ie knowing who the employees are, their profile characteristics, skills, experience, and qualifications – is also a pivotal practice within a diversity approach (Noon, 1993; Kirton and Greene, 2004). The value of diversity should be recognised at the strategic level and backed up with appropriate high levels of investment.

Discussion questions

1 Think of a country with which you are familiar. Are there any groups other than women, ethnic minorities and disabled people that are disadvantaged in employment?

2 What factors do you think are associated with women's under-representation at senior levels of most organisations in the UK (or a country that you are familiar with)? Think about factors related to the social and education context, but also consider factors related to the behaviour of organisations.

3 Diversity and equal opportunity have very different sets of language associated with their promotion. Think of an organisation you have worked for, or are familiar with. Which approach did it appear to follow?

2 EQUALITY AND THE LAW

So far we have looked at the different approaches to tackling employment equality and the way in which they shape organisations' policies. However, it is not only organisations that may have an interest in addressing inequality: nation-states and supra-national bodies are also active in this area and have legislated to protect disadvantaged groups in employment and to promote equality. In doing so they set the context within which organisations act. In this section we examine the international legal framework, and provide an example of a supra-national framework (that of the European Union) and a more detailed example of national law – that of the UK. The latter – a fairly typical example of a western, liberal, approach to legislating in support of equality – will provide the reader with a useful basis for critical review and international comparison.

The international legal framework

The United Nations and the International Labour Organisation
Protection from discrimination has been taken forward in international law through the actions of the United Nations (UN), the provisions of the International Labour Organisation (ILO) (see Chapter 11) and various regional declarations and constitutions. Most legal frameworks enshrine a right to non-discrimination as opposed to a right to equality. The United Nations Universal Declaration of Human Rights 1948, for example, states (Article 1(3)):

'Everyone is entitled to all the rights and freedoms set forth in this declaration without discrimination of any kind, such as

> **race, colour, sex, language, religion, political opinion, national or social origin, property, birth or other status.'**

The intention of the UN is to create a 'universal respect for human rights and fundamental freedoms' (UN Charter Article 55(c)), but the Charter is not legally binding on member states, and it is only those that are endorsed and ratified by state signatures that have legal force. Further, these formulations have been criticised as 'vague and aspirational' (Sargeant, 2004: 47).

From its foundation, the ILO campaigned on discrimination, particularly racial discrimination, broadening more recently to turn its attention to lesbian and gay workers, workers who are HIV-positive and older workers. The definition of discrimination contained in the ILO Discrimination (Employment and Occupation) Convention 1958 is broad and not restricted to intentional discrimination: discrimination can be direct or indirect (see definition below) – what matters is the outcome of action. Again, the intention of the ILO is commendable but it lacks sufficient enforcement mechanisms to drive compliance and has to rely on campaigns of exposure that have often been ignored. As a result, in practice, the ILO has limited impact on the activities of independent nations.

Regional bodies – the EU example
Regional supra-national bodies can have more influence in this area. The 25 member states of the EU are subject to considerable influence on their national equality laws arising from their collective decisions as a union of nation-states (see also Chapter 11). The principles underpinning the EU's framework of discrimination have their origins in economic equality and internal market integration. However, the decisions of the European Court of Justice now emphasise the importance of equality as a fundamental social right – but still focus on anti-discrimination as opposed to positive promotion.

Equality between the sexes, in particular, is an underlying principle of EU law. The EU seeks to achieve this in part through legislation in the form of Directives which member states are required to incorporate into their national law (Sargeant, 2001). For example, Article 2 of the Equal Treatment Directive deals with direct and indirect sex discrimination and harassment, and there also Directives on, *inter alia*, parental leave and the protection of pregnant workers. The EU also seeks to promote equality through policy development. For example, in 1997 the strengthening of equality between men and women became the 'fourth pillar' of the employment guidelines – the other three were adaptability, employability and entrepreneurship (Rubery 2002). In 1999, as part of its employment strategy, the EU went further by issuing a guideline requiring that member states consider the impact of all employment policies on gender equality – an approach known as 'gender mainstreaming' – the idea being to integrate concerns with gender equality into other areas of employment policy (Rubery, 2002; Rubery *et al*, 2003).

International and EU law, then, set out anti-discriminatory guiding standards but do not prescribe forms of incorporation into the local context. At a national level, anti-discriminatory legislation and equal opportunity employment practice are pursued with varying amounts of commitment and vigour in different countries. Local responses are adapted to fit frameworks derived from socio-historical and legal traditions to provide solutions to locally defined disadvantage. Across the world, legislation on sex discrimination is most common, followed by laws on race discrimination.

National equality legislation – an example: the UK

Underlying principles

British laws on employment equality are typical of those of many western nations in their extent and coverage. They provide a good example of the potential and limitations of a widespread and influential approach. In the UK, anti-discrimination legislation is primarily a moral/ethical response to historic patterns of vertical and horizontal sex-based segregation in the labour market. It is designed to ensure that people compete on a 'level playing-field' by seeking to deter discrimination against specified groups. It does so by providing a mechanism (employment tribunals) for individuals to seek redress and financial compensation from organisations and individuals who discriminate against them. UK law is therefore essentially liberal (see above) in its approach. Special treatment (ie positive action) is lawful to the extent that individuals in disadvantaged groups can be equipped with the means to compete equally, and encouraged to do so, as long as all people are treated equally when employment decisions are made. Nevertheless, this is the only positive promotion of equality of opportunity within a primarily minimalist framework.

Major UK equality laws

The Equal Pay Act (1970, amended in 1986) is designed to ensure equal pay between men and women for the same or like work, and was a response to a long-standing concern that women were being paid less for doing the same work as or similar work to men. By the time the Equal Pay Act was implemented (in 1975), the Sex Discrimination Act (1975) with its complementary focus on anti-discriminatory principles in broader employment matters was also on the statute books. This piece of legislation owed its origins to the changed climate of opinion about the position of women that occurred as part of a social movement in the 1960s and 1970s. It covers discrimination on grounds of sex, marital status and, latterly, gender reassignment. It recognises and covers instances of direct and indirect discrimination. Direct discrimination occurs where a person from one group is treated less favourably than people not in that group. Indirect discrimination occurs when criteria (for example, in a recruitment campaign) are applied to everyone but are substantially harder for people in one group to comply with. For example, a requirement that all employees in a particular job be 1.8 metres (5 foot 11 inches) tall would be indirectly discriminatory against women, on the grounds that fewer of them could comply (and therefore unlawful, unless the height requirement could be objectively justified).

The social context for the Race Relations Act (RRA) 1976 lay in post-war labour shortages that could not be filled by the indigenous UK population, coupled with a recognition of the inexcusable discrimination against immigrants (primarily from the Caribbean and the Indian subcontinent) in all areas of public life (Daniel, 1968). The RRA (1976) covers discrimination on grounds of colour, race, nationality or ethnic or national origin. Its wording is almost directly equivalent to that of the Sex Discrimination Act.

Disabled people were without effective protection against discrimination until the introduction of the Disability Discrimination Act 1995. This Act conforms to the same basic anti-discriminatory ideology of other equality statutes while extending the criteria of discrimination to encompass a limited entitlement to positive action (employers are required to make 'reasonable adjustments' to accommodate disabled people). Latterly, and primarily in response to the EU's Framework Directive 2000, protection from discrimination has been extended to cover sexual orientation and religious belief through the Employment Equality (Sexuality and Religion and Belief) Regulations 2003, and age in the Employment Equality (Age) Regulations 2006.

Limitations of UK equality legislation

As we have seen, then, the UK has a fairly extensive and ever-increasing framework of anti-discrimination legislation. Nevertheless, the provision has some weaknesses related to how inequality is understood and approached in our society. In Britain the law is essentially concerned with formal equality of opportunity, with less emphasis placed on the direct eradication of social disadvantage – and this is demonstrated through several features. Firstly, there is a limited obligation on employers to positively promote equality, although this is increasing, as evidenced by the Race Relations (Amendment) Act 2000 and the Disability Discrimination Act 2005. Secondly, the law in Great Britain allows for limited positive action. It does not permit the achievements of quotas through affirmative action (akin to positive discrimination) as expressly permitted in Northern Ireland, South Africa, Canada, India and the USA, and encouraged within Article 26 of the International Covenant for Civil and Political Rights from the UN. Thirdly, in the UK complaints are treated individually, and this lacks the remedial power of class action which in the United States, as an example, permits individuals who have been affected by identical discrimination to be given the same remedy. Finally, the law in Great Britain lacks the enforcement potential of, say, the Fair Employment (Northern Ireland) Act 1989, which utilises not only criminal penalties but also the system of loss of grants and contracts to punish bad practice. For these reasons the design and enforcement of anti-discrimination legislation have been criticised as weak (Davies, 2004; Fredman, 2002). Patterns of employment segregation remain in respect of all protected groups, and changes to patterns of labour market disadvantage are levelling off.

CASE STUDY 42

EQUALITY LAW CHALLENGE

As we have seen, the purpose and structure of discrimination law differs between countries. Have a look at the following brief scenarios which would *almost certainly* be considered unlawful under UK discrimination legislation. Would they also be unlawful in your country, or in a country that you know well?

1 a day-care nursery that seeks to recruit a female nursery nurse (direct discrimination: Sex Discrimination Act)

2 a retailer that refuses to consider flexible employment hours to enable a disabled employee to make hospital visits (direct discrimination: Disability Discrimination Act)

3 a manufacturer that offers the opportunity for overtime to its full-time employees before offering it to its part-time employees (indirect discrimination: Sex Discrimination Act)

4 a local authority that insists that all employees for all positions have minimum of a GCSE in English (indirect discrimination: Race Relations Act)

5 a retailer that is requiring all existing employees to provide cover for its new Sunday opening hours (indirect discrimination: Equality Regulations – religion)

6 a Health Authority that is opening up promotion opportunities only to women of South Asian origin in order to redress the under-representation of this group at senior levels of the organisation (direct discrimination: Sex Discrimination and Race Relations Acts)

7 a train operator that is offering concessionary travel passes only to employees' spouses (indirect discrimination: Equality Regulations – sexuality)

> ### Discussion questions
>
> 1   Legal responses to inequality are driven by a set of social, political and economic circumstances. Consider a country that you are familiar with. Are there any groups in that society that you think are without adequate protection from discrimination?
>
> 2   Do you think that an approach of positive discrimination and quotas, designed to remedy historic disadvantage that some groups have suffered, is justified?
>
> 3   Diversity management realises a competitive advantage by making the most of the differences between employees. Under the UK's current system of legislation (or that in a country you are more familiar with), what might be the dangers of this approach?

3 EQUALITY ISSUES IN INTERNATIONAL CONTEXT

So far we have examined different approaches to labour market inequalities and ways in which legal systems, and organisational policies and practices, can be deployed to achieve greater equality and to realise the benefits of diversity. In doing so, we drew on some examples of law and practice in the UK. It will be clear that the UK experience of inequality, and its legal and organisational responses, are to a great degree shaped by that country's history and values, and the nature of its economic and political system. The same applies in other countries.

In the remainder of the chapter we explore how the historical, political and social factors have impacted on equality/inequality in three different parts of the world. Firstly, we examine the issue of gender equality in the EU. We then explore the same issue in China in the context of that country's transition from a centrally controlled labour market to one incorporating elements of a western-style free market. Finally, we look at the issue of race equality in Africa. We have been selective, but the examples that we have chosen will help illustrate how local context impacts on labour market inequalities and informs the design of policies intended to tackle them.

Gender equality in the EU

With its interconnected economies, some level of cultural similarity (by global standards) and mature and stable political systems, we might expect to find a great deal of similarity in European countries both in their approach to gender equality and in levels of equality. Indeed, for those countries in the EU – with its single market and over-arching political and legal systems – one might expect these similarities to be particularly striking. Furthermore, in view of the length of time the issue has been of concern at the policy level of the EU, we might also expect to see minimal gender-based inequality. As we shall see, the reality is less straightforward.

EU countries perform well on measurements of gender equality. For example, 12 of the top 20 countries in the UN's gender development index (UNDP, 2002) are in the EU. However, this conceals some marked differences. When the World Economic Forum (WEF, 2004) used a range of social and economic indicators to rank 58 countries from across the globe on the size of their gender-equality gap, EU countries were widely dispersed in the rankings. Sweden came first (ie had the smallest gap), Denmark was fourth and Finland fifth. The UK and France were eighth and thirteenth respectively, with Spain 27th, Italy 45th and Greece 50th.

Comparisons between EU countries on equality measures

Drawing comparisons between countries in respect of their levels of gender inequality is not straightforward and depends on the measures of inequality that are chosen (Walby, 1996; Platenga and Hansen, 1999; van der Lippe and van Dijk, 2002). Interpretation is also problematic. For example, high levels of participation in part-time work may be viewed positively as encouraging equality for women by making it easier for them to combine childcare commitments with paid work. But in countries where this kind of work is traditionally poorly paid, it could have a negative effect on equality. Despite the various difficulties, figures for the EU on the employment participation, segregation and pay of women, in comparison with men, make for some interesting comparisons.

Participation rates for women working full-time in the EU show an upward trend (Walby, 1996; van der Lippe and van Dijk, 2002), but there are still marked national differences. Scandinavian countries have the highest levels of female participation – for example, Sweden (75.8% of women work) – whereas the countries of southern Europe have the lowest – for example, Italy (47.9%) (Eurostat: Labour Force Survey, 2002). A similar pattern emerges in respect of the availability of part-time work although the Scandinavian countries are outperformed by the UK and the Netherlands. Fewer than 10% of employees work part-time in Greece, Italy and Spain. The type of work arrangement varies across Europe, slightly reduced hours being more common in Scandinavian countries, 'half-time' work prevalent in Britain and the Republic of Ireland, and full-time work (or no work at all) the typical pattern in many southern European countries (see also Chapter 4).

The data on employment segregation (horizontal and vertical) reveal some interesting patterns. EU women are over-represented in service sectors (82.1% of women work in the service sector, compared with 55.7% of men). Thirty-four per cent of EU women are working in the lowest-paying occupations as opposed to 19% of men. Women in the EU are also less likely than men to work in managerial occupations: women's representation in these occupations is, on average, only 54% of that of men. However, this figure varies markedly: here the Scandinavian countries (with the exception of Finland) are outperformed by many countries including France, Belgium, the Republic of Ireland, and the accession countries of Eastern Europe (Eurostat: Labour Force Survey, 2002).

As for pay, across the EU women are paid on average around four-fifths of the male average (Eurostat: www.eurostat.com) and although this gap is narrowing, it is doing so slowly. Again there are interesting variations between the pay-gaps of different member states. The Scandinavian countries are in mid-table, faring worse than might be expected on this indicator, probably as a result of the high concentration of women in the public sector. The UK also does poorly, probably as a result of the high concentration of women in low-skill part-time work.

Approaches to equality within the EU and their impact

As noted in Chapters 4 and 11, differences in government policy in member states exist despite the common framework of the EU. This reflects the different interpretation and implementation of EU Directives arising from national social and political ideologies (Rubery et al, 2003). These ideologies also underpin governments' approaches to social policy. Van der Lippe and van Dijk (2002), drawing on Gornick and Jacobs (1998), identify three broad ideologies in relation to social policy: conservative, liberal and social-democratic. The con-servative ideology sees women's role as being in the home and men's in paid work, and social policy supports this (an approach typical of some southern European countries). The liberal approach advocates equal rights for men and women and supports that with anti-discriminatory legislation, but is reluctant to intervene more directly (an approach broadly typical of the UK). The social-democratic approach (typical of Scandinavian countries) identifies a need to intervene actively to support women's access to employment – for example, by providing parental leave and supporting childcare.

As van der Lippe and van Dijk (2002) point out, and as the WEF figures above indicate, levels of gender equality tend to be highest in the social democratic countries, lower in the liberal ones, and lowest in the conservative ones. Differences in the provision of, and support for, childcare across the EU provide an interesting example – such provision is important in the pursuit of gender equality because it facilitates women's participation in the labour market and broadens the choices available to them (Walby, 1996). France, Belgium and the Scandinavian countries have higher levels of public-funded childcare than those found elsewhere in the EU (Platenga and Hansen, 1999). That said, the differences in provision of publicly funded childcare are narrowing significantly as those countries that had traditionally done little in this area move towards meeting the EU's target of provision for 33% of children under age three and 90% of children between three and school age (Rubery, 2002).

There are no simple explanations as to why and how gender equality differs within the EU. As Platenga and Hansen observe (1999: 362), 'The current status of equal opportunities ... should be interpreted as a highly complex process in which economic, sociological, political and cultural factors all play a part.' The historical dimension should not be underestimated. As Rubery (2002) points out, one of the main factors underlying differences in member states is their very different starting points on the route towards gender equality. Nonetheless, some important themes and patterns have emerged in the foregoing discussion, and it appears that countries within the social democratic tradition who invest in social policy provisions that support women in the labour market tend to have the highest degree of gender equality.

CASE STUDY 43

GENDER EQUALITY IN BRITAIN AND FRANCE

As we have seen, the national historical and cultural context plays an important role in shaping the patterns of gender equality in different countries (see also Lyness and Kropf, 2005). Crompton and Le Feuvre (2000) illustrate this in their examination of gender equality in the banking sector in Britain and France. Britain has a longer history than France of giving civil rights to women – for example, the right to vote (1920, as opposed to 1944) and the right for married women to exist as independent citizens. However, as these authors note, French policies of supporting motherhood and the right and duty of all citizens to work (as part of policies for population and economic growth) led to the provision of support for mothers who work, and their formal equality as employees under the law, half a century before the equivalent measures were introduced in Britain. Paid maternity leave was introduced in France in 1913 and the French state supports childcare for most pre-school children in a way which still far outstrips the marginal support offered in Britain.

As Crompton and Le Feuvre (2000) show, this led to women in France having similar unbroken career patterns to men and having access to the professions, in contrast to women's interrupted careers in Britain (with all the disadvantages in employment that that entailed) and their historical exclusion from areas of well-paid work. In their study of banking, these authors show that in Britain, as recently as the 1960s, married women were paid on separate (lower!) pay-scales, or in some cases were required to resign on marriage, whereas in France this was not the case. However, the employment legislation enacted in Britain since the 1970s has provided British women with much stronger rights as individuals in employment, and also provided a much more conducive environment for positive action to improve the position of women at work. This may explain why Crompton and Le Feuvre found that women in the banking sector in Britain were more likely to reach senior positions than those in France. The case suggests that although women in France have been encouraged and supported by the state to enjoy continuous employment, when they are in employment they experience an environment, legal and cultural, which is less conducive than that in Britain to the development of their careers on an equal basis with men.

Case study tasks

Think of a country that you are familiar with, and consider some of the issues that are illustrated by the above case.

1   What have been the prevailing views about the role(s) that women and men are expected to take in society? How, if at all, are these changing?

2   How, if at all, does the state support women at work? Think of legal rights and also support through policy – for example, provision of childcare.

3   What has been the impact of the state support that you have identified? What more could be done?

Gender equality in China

Historical context

In understanding gender equality in China it is necessary to consider three important contextual factors. The first is the Confucian philosophy in which women were 'subservient and undervalued and had no place in public life' (Kitching, 2001: 39). Confucian values remain prevalent to this day (Patrickson, 2001) and continue to exert influence (Maurer-Fazio and Hughes, 2002). As Cooke observes (2001: 347), 'China is a country of traditional values in which the ideology of male superiority still prevails in all aspects of life.' The second is the socialist ideology. China's post-1949 society and economy were 'the antithesis of a free-market system' (Maurer-Fazio and Hughes, 2002: 711). The state owned the organisations and workers and assigned the latter to the former. There was no labour 'market' as such. The third is the impact of the period of economic reform that commenced in the late 1970s, in which China commenced its transition towards a market economy. Workers began to be able to choose whom they worked for, and managers whom they employed and how much they would be paid.

Socialist China placed gender equality at the centre of its political and ideological project. The state legislated to protect the rights of women in work and acted directly to promote female employment. The legacy is a high female participation rate – 47% in 1997 (Cooke, 2001) – and a particularly high employment rate of women in their child-bearing years, reflecting state provision to support working mothers. However, Cooke points out that this apparently positive picture hid a less attractive reality of discrimination against women in employment.

The impact of economic and labour market reform

There is a suggestion that the position of women has deteriorated during the reform period. Cooke (2001) and Dong *et al* (2004) report widespread discrimination against women in recruitment in the new labour markets. The latter found that horizontal occupational segregation was significant in rural enterprises. Women were more likely to be found in production and less likely to be found in administration and sales. This reflected managers' preferences, which in turn reflected gendered norms around work. For example, managers preferred women to work in textiles, clothing and food preparation and men in steel production and farm tool manufacture. They also found that women experienced less control over their work, were less likely to see their experience reflected in higher wages, and were less likely to own shares in their enterprises.

Segregation has worked to the detriment of women in the new economy, with women less likely to be found in the better-paid state sector. Women were also particularly vulnerable to the reduction in the size of the state sector, and Cooke (2001) reports a decline in female participation rates resulting partly from this. The lowering of state support for childcare has made women more expensive to employ, and the lack of monitoring of private and foreign firms has meant that employment rights are much more difficult to enforce than in the times when the state was the sole employer. As Maurer-Fazio and Hughes put it (2002: 713), 'The reduction in government involvement in the labour market meant that managers had more freedom to engage in discriminatory practices.'

How has the gender wage gap been affected by the reform period? Both Dong *et al* (2004) and Liu *et al* (2000) found evidence for an increased wage gap. Maurer-Fazio and Hughes (2002) report that it is largest in the liberalised sector and lowest in the state sector, suggesting, as these authors put it (*ibid*: 727), that 'at first glance labour market liberalisation in China appears not to work to women's advantage ...'. However, they go on to to point out that women (and men) are better paid in the liberalised sector than elsewhere, and that most of the wage gap can be accounted for by wage structure factors rather than discrimination. Market-led economies tend to have higher inequalities in wages generally (not just between men and women) than centralised ones, as human capital characteristics (skills, etc) are rewarded. China's state-controlled and liberal sectors are a microcosm of this contrast and the wage differentials in each sector reflect this. Overall, Maurer-Fazio and Hughes are sceptical of the evidence for increased discrimination against women resulting from the reforms. They also point out that the ratio of female to male earnings in China is still high by international standards, attesting (in their view) to the durability of the effect of the policies under Communism.

CASE STUDY 44

WOMEN'S MANAGERIAL CAREERS IN CHINA

Women's progress in managerial and professional work in China is 'not impressive' (Leung, 2002: 606) with women 'clustered at the lower end of the ladder' (2003: 323). A number of factors have been identified as inhibiting women's progress. One factor is the stereotypical view held by senior male managers about the suitability of women for senior positions, either because of their attitudes and abilities – 'women have been criticised for their lack of confidence, narrow-mindedness, lack of leadership charisma, low self-esteem, fear of success ...' (Cooke, 2003: 323) – or because male managers 'suspected they might become pregnant and ignored them' (Leung, 2002: 612) or might be more committed to their family than to their career. A second issue is the range of difficulties that women face when they reach senior positions, being regarded as insufficiently feminine, characterised as being overly competitive and ambitious, and criticised for neglecting their family. Cultural difficulties remain for a woman earning more than her husband, which may lead to a wife's withdrawing from promotion opportunities, and also high-flying women may find it harder to find a husband (rumour suggests), or may perceive it as being such, which may also provide a deterrent to progression (Cooke, 2003).

Chinese women are not only disadvantaged in the formal employment arena, but also in the informal arena. Leung (2002) shows how the important notion of *guanxi* in Chinese society impacts differently on men and women managers. *Guanxi* 'refers to the intensity of ongoing relations between two parties' (*ibid*: 605) and involves the development of relationships of mutual dependence between people through exchange of favours and developing reciprocal obligations. In work settings it plays an important role in maintaining harmonious relations, but also as a means of gaining and retaining power, prestige and status at work. Leung shows how men have greater access to *guanxi* with senior male managers than women, who in turn have fewer senior women managers to build relationships with. Yet when they do develop relationships with senior men they may be characterised by colleagues as developing inappropriate relationships with men to support their advancement. Leung also shows how women tend to use *guanxi* to foster supportive collegiate relationships whereas men tend to use it in a utilitarian way to secure advancement.

Case study tasks

1   To what extent are the barriers that women managers face in reaching senior positions in China similar to those in a different country that you are familiar with?

2   In the country that you considered in Task 1, are there other barriers, or other factors, that account for women's under-representation at senior levels?

3   Does the notion of *guanxi* have any equivalents in employment settings in a country that you are familiar with? Does it have different impact on men and women?

Race equality and diversity in Africa

The majority of African nations are highly ethnically diverse – a legacy of colonialism, which had the effect of creating 'arbitrary' national boundaries encircling many different ethnic groups (Nyambegera, 2002). Although a great deal is known about the political and social impact of this diversity, much less is known about its impact on the sphere of employment (with the exception of South Africa). What evidence there is suggests a tendency towards ethnic homogeneity in organisations and work groups – for example, Nyambegera (2002) reports that the harbours and railways authorities in Kenya were staffed almost exclusively by two ethnic groups – often reflecting differences in power and privilege along ethnic lines, or resulting from favouritism, reserving jobs for kith and kin, or from a positive desire to seek homogeneity in order to reduce conflict and generate harmonious and productive relationships. Muuka and Mwenda report the existence of the Wako-ni-Wako employment culture in Zambia: 'another name for tribalism, nepotism and regionalism all rolled into one' (2004: 39). Buegré (2004) reports that in the Ivory Coast preferential treatment to fellow tribe members is considered to be an obligation, and may have the added benefit of building up a power-base in the organisations. He also explains how a shared ethnic background affects the relationship between managers and subordinates, to the benefit of the latter (in terms of security of employment, 'perks', etc) and to the detriment of employees who do not share this background. Debrah *et al* (2004) argue that this 'particularism', which is expressed in favourable treatment along ethnic lines in HR decisions around recruitment, progression and pay, is an enduring feature across Africa despite evidence of multinational corporation introducing more systematic and sophisticated recruitment practices (Ramgutty-Wong, 2004). With the exception of South Africa, there is little evidence for the kind of western legislative regime encountered earlier in the chapter existing or impacting on this.

South Africa

South Africa is an interesting country to consider in terms of race equality and diversity on account of its decades of 'institutionalised workplace discrimination' (Horwitz *et al*, 2004: 2) under apartheid. Post-apartheid, the state has legislated to prevent discrimination in employment through, for example, the Employment Equity Act 1998. This Act legislated against unfair discrimination, but also required all but the smallest employers to prepare an equity plan in which they set out their agenda to work towards non-discriminatory practices. This approach is liberal in its attempts to create a level playing-field, but at the same time more interventionist than equivalent legislation in many western democracies in seeking to ensure that positive steps are taken to reduce inequalities. Notwithstanding these legal interventions since the fall of apartheid, the South African labour market remains highly unequal along racial lines – as Horwitz *et al* put it: 'the consequence[s] of years of systematic discrimination' (2004: 9). For example, unemployment rates vary greatly along racial lines (black African 41.2%, Coloured 23.3%, Indian 17.1% and whites 6.3%: Kingdon and Knight, 2004) as do average monthly incomes (black Africans R1,865, Asian and Coloured R7,265, whites R9,108). Allanson *et al* (2002) show that these inequalities increased in the immediate post-apartheid years. Such differences are unlikely to be attributable wholly to discriminatory employment practices, and therefore are unlikely to be reduced quickly (and exclusively) by anti-discrimination legislation. In good part they are likely to be the result of structural features of the South African labour market that are a legacy of the apartheid years – for example, differences in skills, educational levels and experience between the different racial groups (Allanson *et al*, 2002). However, Kingdon and Knight's (2004) analysis suggests that not all of the differences can be accounted for in this way and the possibility remains that continuing discriminatory practices may underlie some of them.

What impact has the diversity paradigm had in South Africa?

Horwitz *et al* (2004) argue that it has had limited impact, the focus being on a liberal equal opportunities approach underpinned by anti-discrimination legislation. They report that many South African companies are not racially diverse, and where different groups are represented 'the blacks were expected to adopt the culture of the white dominant group' (2004: 13). Proponents of the diversity approach might argue that a focus on compliance with legislation alone would have limited success. The failure to recognise a business case for diversity impacts on organisations' willingness to act. The resulting lack of diversity is likely to be detrimental to business success, in that it would fail to foster a culture in which difference is valued, so that organisations fail to draw on the talents of all their workers and reflect their customers. However, Horwitz *et al* (2004) do provide an example of a South African organisation which has been active in promoting diversity – a bank which introduced a 'cultural diversity awareness programme', which formalised gatherings and meetings across racial groups, and required managers to spend time in an African township to gain a better grasp of the requirements of their customers.

Discussion questions

1 In most European countries women's average earnings fall between 75% and 95% of men's average earnings. What causes this difference? Does it matter? Why/why not?

2 What are the factors in China's transition from a centrally controlled to a market economy that are likely to improve/disadvantage the employment position of women?

3 South Africa has some of the strongest equality legislation in the world. Consider a country that you are familiar with – what would you see as the advantages and disadvantages of introducing more stringent and far-reaching equality legislation?

CONCLUSIONS AND FUTURE ISSUES

This chapter has illustrated the widespread inequalities in employment in countries across the world, and shown that an understanding of these requires an appreciation of the historical, cultural, political and legal context. It may be that approaches to employment equality, and levels of equality, will converge (upwards) as globalisation exports western approaches to equality management, and as former socialist countries and developing nations complete the transition to liberal market economies. We have revealed a number of difficulties with this analysis. Firstly, widespread inequalities in western nations have persisted despite decades of liberal interventions. Secondly, the impact of the liberal model has varied on account of the differing historical and cultural conditions in ostensibly very similar countries. Thirdly, the transition from state-controlled to liberal market economies has not necessarily led to greater equality.

We might question both the effectiveness and transportablility of the western approach. The liberal equality framework has been criticised for its ineffectiveness in securing managerial commitment (Collinson et al, 1990; Jenkins, 1986; Jenkins and Solomos, 1987) and in achieving change (Cockburn, 1991; Jewson and Mason, 1986; Liff, 1989; Richards, 2001; Webb and Liff, 1988). Although the majority of employers would claim to be 'equal opportunity employers' (Breugal and Kean, 1995; Cockburn, 1991; Jewson and Mason, 1986; Yates, 1995), policies often turn out to be little more than 'empty shells' (Hoque and Noon, 2004; Woodhams and Lupton, 2005). Strengthening the law, and enforcement, may help, but even highly developed legislative regimes are unlikely to have a rapid effect in eradicating the effects of systemic sources of historical disadvantage (see Section 3).

Liberal approaches may be bound to fail in cultures where the underlying assumptions of equality between the sexes and races, and of the importance of open and transparent competition, do not hold. For example, Patrickson reports how approaches to managing people in many Asian countries 'reinforce the paternalistic type of family culture predominant in Asia' (2001: 8), women typically playing a supporting role that carries lower status. They suggest that people 'do not believe that discriminatory behaviour (as defined through western eyes) is unacceptable', and that 'much of the discrimination is invisible, unremarked and unchallenged' (ibid: 8). Challenge may be difficult in cultures that place great store on harmony and respect for authority.

What of the alternatives to liberal quality? Whereas the radical approach prioritises outcomes over process (Jewson and Mason, 1986), it does not fit well with the dominant public understanding of 'equality' (Liff, 1999), and the promotion of positive/affirmative action is likely to attract significant backlash (see Zhu and Kleiner, 2000). As for diversity, some authors suggest that the diversity approach is neither new nor different from equal opportunities (Liff, 1997; IPD, 1996), others that legitimising a business rationale for equal opportunities risks legitimising discriminatory decisions also (Dickens, 1994). The diversity movement arguably depoliticises equal opportunities and draws attention away from group inequalities (Vince, 1996). Herman Ouseley, quoted in Overell (1997), makes this point:

> **'Diversity approaches encourage managers to ignore the realities of inequality and discrimination that create such [difficult] conditions for people from certain groups [and this] will mean that the status quo is maintained.'**

Inequalities in employment are likely to persist in societies which are themselves inherently unequal along gender, race and other lines. Our review in this chapter suggests that these inequalities are difficult to dislodge because they are embedded in different cultures and political systems. Many western countries that have had a 'run' at removing inequalities through liberal legislation have found progress to be slow. However, we should not lose sight of the fact that there have been real advances in the employment position of women and ethnic minorities in many western countries. A strong liberal legislative regime, supported by discourses around equality and diversity, supportive public policy, and positive action by employers, may represent the best route towards sustained, if steady, progress. If so, this offers hope that, in future, organisations and nations will be able make more productive use of their human resources and that *all* individuals will be able to maximise their potential in employment.

CASE STUDY 45

GENDER EQUALITY IN THE FORMER COMMUNIST COUNTRIES OF EASTERN EUROPE AND RUSSIA

Gender equality was an ideological commitment in the Communist countries of Eastern Europe (Ogloblin, 1999; Jurajda, 2003; Pollert, 2003), such that women were meant to have full access to education and work. However, the extent to which this resulted in equality in paid work is less clear. Certainly, the commitment to full employment meant that participation rates for women were high in comparison with many western countries – for example, almost 90% in the Soviet Union (Ogloblin, 1999). Women had the same educational opportunities (and achievements) as men, and thus in theory the same access to work requiring higher-level qualifications. As Pollert notes (2003: 334), 'Women entered qualified professions in larger numbers than in the west,' and state support was given for women – for example, in terms of extended maternity leave and the availability of part-time work – although, as Pollert points out, the reality was not always as impressive as the rhetoric. Wages in the Soviet Union and other centrally planned economies were largely set by the state, and the principle of equal pay for equal work underpinned this (Ogloblin 1999; Jurajda, 2003).

However, in other areas women fared less well. There was a significant gender wage gap under Communism. For example, in Czechoslovakia in 1988 women's average earnings were approximately 70% of men's, a figure similar to that in many western economies. This was due, in significant part, to horizontal occupational segregation. As Ogloblin (1999) explains, this was because the state, despite its avowed commitment to equality, regarded men and women as 'different' workers, encouraging them into areas of work that were considered appropriate, typically in 'caring' occupations in health and education, in contrast to men who were channelled into engineering and construction. Work related to production tended to be more highly valued and rewarded under Communism than service work, thus contributing to women's lower earnings. Furthermore, although women were expected to work, they were also expected to be the main carers – a fact which Grappard (1997) and Pollert (2003) term the 'double burden'. This led to the similar sets of assumptions about commitment to employment and barriers to progress as in many market economies, and to a pattern of vertical segregation typical of the western world, men occupying the higher echelons of what were otherwise 'female' professions. It is fair to conclude that while there were significant differences between the approach to gender equality in Communist and western countries, and some different outcomes, both resulted in gendered labour markets, and left men's power and privileges 'deeply entrenched' (Pollert, 2003: 335). That said, measures of gender equality showed the Communist countries of Europe outperforming the market economies (Pollert, 2003), leading this author to conclude that despite the difficulties identified above, 'women enjoyed significant gender equality advantage in comparison with other industrialised countries' (*ibid*: 335).

How has the transition from centrally controlled to market economies impacted on the relative position of women?

Evidence from a variety of countries suggests that the gender wage gap has tended to remain fairly stable through transition (Gerry *et al*, 2004; Jurajda, 2003; Adamchik *et al*, 2003; Pollert, 2003; Ogloblin, 1999), although Brainerd (1998) reports a significant increase in the immediate post-transition years in Russia. Pollert (2003) points out that the emergence of the private sector (which tends to be better paid, and more male-dominated) may also be a factor in maintaining the wage gap. Later analysis by Brainerd (2000) suggests an increase in the gap in Russia and the Ukraine and a decrease in other Eastern European countries, indicating that it is important not to homogenise these countries, which have often had very different experiences of transition (Orazem and Vodopivec, 2000). The complex picture may reflect the countervailing forces of, on the one hand, liberalisation of the labour market from equality-minded (in theory) central control and the increase in inequality in the labour market generally, and the introduction of western-style anti-discrimination legislation on the other.

Other indicators suggest that the gender equality position of transition economies has deteriorated. Withdrawal or reduction of state support for working women with children has been a feature in some countries – for example, Hungary and Poland (Pollert, 2003). Where provisions have continued, employers, freed from the burdens of state regulations, have used them as an excuse to discriminate against women, who are perceived as more costly to employ and as providing less continuity of employment – a common pattern in western countries. There has also been a decline in levels of female employment in the transition countries. For example, women's employment declined by 40% in Hungary from 1985 to 1997 (Pollert, 2003). Large cuts in public service in the post-Communist era have disproportionately affected women, who, as we have seen, were more likely to be employed there. Nonetheless, the data in referred to in Section 3 show the transition countries in the EU performing quite well on some equality measures, perhaps reflecting a residual effect of the Communist years.

What of the future?

Some writers (quoted in Pollert, 2003) have reported a retrenchment against notions of gender equality, which may have its roots in a reaction against the dual burden created by the Communist espousal of equality, and may have been exacerbated by men exploiting the advantages of the new liberal market. The reality is rather more complex (Pollert, 2003). One possible force in favour of greater equality may be the accession of some of the transition countries to the EU, with its legal framework and recent agenda of gender mainstreaming. Anticipating this, some of the transition countries have introduced anti-discriminatory employment legislation along western lines. For example, the Czech Republic legislated against direct and indirect discrimination on grounds of sex, dismissal of pregnant women and to promote equal pay for work of equal value. As we have seen in relation both to western democracies and Communist states, the provision of legal rights is no guarantee of increased equality. Progress towards gender equality has been 'poorest in countries following free-market tenets' (Pollert, 2003: 350) and strongest in social democracies. To the extent to which the transition countries with their liberal labour markets and weak labour movements resemble the former, the prospects for greater gender equality are not overwhelmingly positive.

Case study tasks

1   Given the overall rise in women's earnings in the transition to market economies, why, if at all, should commentators be concerned about the relative position of women compared to men?

2   How successful do you think legislative interventions along the lines of the EU framework will be in improving the position of women in the transition economies? Explain your answer.

3   It was suggested by one author in the case study that social democracy offers the best hope for gender equality in the transition countries. What are the features of the approach to gender equality in social democracies? What is the evidence to show that this type of approach provides better equality outcomes? How convinced are you by the argument?

REFERENCES

Adamchik V., Hyclak T. and King A. (2003) 'The wage structure and wage distribution in Poland, 1994–2001', International Journal of Manpower, Vol. 24, No. 8: 916–34.

Allanson P., Atkins J. and Hinks T. (2002) 'No end to racial wage hierarchy in South Africa?', Review of Development Economics, Vol. 6, No. 3: 442–59.

Brainerd E. (1998) 'Winners and losers in Russia's economic transition', American Economic Review, Vol. 88, No. 5: 1094–1116.

Brainerd E. (2000) 'Women in transition: changes in gender wage differentials in Eastern Europe and the former Soviet Union', *Industrial and Labour Relations Review*, Vol. 54, No. 1: 128–62.

Bruegal I. and Kean H. (1995) 'The movement of municipal feminism: gender and class in the 1980s local government', *Critical Social Policy*, Vol. 15: 147–69.

Buegré C. (2004) 'HRM in Ivory Coast', in K. Kamoche, Y. Debrah, F. Horwitz and G. Muuka (eds) *Managing Human Resources in Africa*. London: Routledge.

Cabinet Office (2003) *Ethnic Minorities in the Labour Market*. London: Cabinet Office.

Cassell C. (2001) 'Managing diversity', in T. Redman and A. Wilkinson, *Contemporary Human Resource Management*. Harlow: Pearson.

Cockburn C. (1991) *In the Way of Women*. Basingstoke: Macmillan.

Collinson D., Knights D. and Collinson M. (1990) *Managing to Discriminate*. London: Routledge.

Cooke F. (2001) 'Equal opportunity? The role of legislation and public policies in women's employment in China', *Women in Management Review*, Vol. 16, No. 7: 334–48.

Cooke F. (2003) 'Equal opportunity? Women's managerial careers in governmental organisations in China', *International Journal of Human Resource Management*, Vol. 14, No. 2: 317–33.

Cox T. (1992) 'The multi-cultural organisation', *Academy of Management Executive*, Vol. 5, No. 5: 34–47.

Cox T. and Blake S. (1991) 'Managing cultural diversity: implications for organisational competitiveness', *Academy of Management Executive*, Vol. 5, No. 3: 45–56.

CRE (1992) *Second Review of the Race Relations Act 1976* London: Commission for Racial Equality.

CRE (2005) 'Key points about racial inequality in the labour market', available at www.cre.gov.uk/research/statistics_labour.html#keypoints [accessed 12.12.05].

Crompton R. and Le Feuvre N. (2000) 'Gender, family and employment in comparative perspective: the realities and representations of equal opportunities in Britain and France', *Journal of European Social Policy*, Vol. 10, No. 4: 334–44.

Daniel W. W. (1968) *Racial Discrimination in England*. Baltimore: Penguin.

Davies A. C. L. (2004) *Perspectives on Labour Law*. Cambridge: Cambridge University Press.

Debrah Y., Horwitz F., Kamoche K. and Muuka G. (2004) 'Conclusions: towards a research agenda', in K. Kamoche, Y. Debrah, F. Horwitz and G. Muuka (eds) *Managing Human Resources in Africa*. London: Routledge.

Dong X.Y., MacPhail F., Bowles P. and Ho S. (2004) 'Gender segmentation at work in China's privatized rural industry: some evidence from Shandong and Jiangsu', *World Development*, Vol. 32, No. 6: 979–98.

EIRO (2004) 'Family-related leave and industrial relations', *European Industrial Relations Observatory On-line*, http://www.eiro.eurofound.eu.int/2004/03/word/cs_parental_annex.doc [accessed 8 August 2005].

EOC (2005a) *Facts about Men and Women, 2005*. Manchester: Equal Opportunity Commission.

EOC (2005b) *Code of practice*, www.eoc.org.uk/Default.aspx?page=15640&lang=en

EOR (1996) 'Women in the Post Office', *Equal Opportunities Review*, No. 66: 13–19.

Fredman S. (2002), *Discrimination Law*. Oxford: Oxford University Press.

Gappard U. (1997) 'Theoretical issues of gender in the transition from socialist regimes', *Journal of Economic Issues* Vol. 3: 665–86.

Gerry C., Kim B.-Y. and Li C. (2004) 'The gender wage gap and wage arrears in Russia: evidence from the RLMS', *Journal of Population Economics*, Vol. 17, No. 2: 267–9.

Hicks-Clarke D and Iles P. (2003) 'Gender diversity and organisational performance', in M. J. Davidson and S. L. Fieden (eds) *Individual Diversity in Organisations*. Chichester: John Wiley & Sons.

Hoque K. and Noon M. (2004) 'Equal opportunity policy and practice in Britain: evaluating the "empty shell" hypothesis', *Work, Employment and Society*, Vol. 18, No. 3: 481–506.

Horwitz M., Nkomo S. and Rajah M. (2004) 'HRM in South Africa', in K. Kamoche, Y. Debrah, F. Horwitz and G. Muuka (eds) *Managing Human Resources in Africa*. London: Routledge.

IPD (1996) *Managing Diversity: An IPD position paper*. London: Institute of Personnel and Development.

Jackson S. E. and Associates (1992) *Diversity in the Workplace: Human resource initiatives*. New York: Guilford Press.

Jenkins R. (1986) *Racism and Recruitment: Managers, organisations and equal opportunity in the labour market*. Cambridge: Cambridge University Press.

Jenkins R. and Solomos J. (eds) (1987) *Racism and Equal Opportunity Policies in the 1980s*. Cambridge: Cambridge University Press.

Jewson N. and Mason D. (1986) 'Theory and practice of equal opportunities policies: liberal and radical approaches', *Sociological Review*, Vol. 34, No. 2: 307–34.

Johnston W. B and Packard A. H. (1987) *Workforce 2000: Work and workers for the 21srt century*. Indianapolis: Hudson.

Jurajda S. (2003) 'Gender wage gap and segregation in enterprises and the public sector in late transition countries', *Journal of Comparative Economics*, Vol. 31, No. 2: 199–222.

Kamoche K., Debrah Y., Horwitz F. and Muuka G. (eds) (2004) *Managing Human Resources in Africa*. London: Routledge.

Kandola R. and Fullerton J. (1994) *Managing the Mosaic – Diversity in action*. London: IPD.

Kingdon G. and Knight J. (2004) 'Race and the incidence of unemployment in South Africa', *Review of Development Economics*, Vol. 8, No. 2: 198–222.

Kirton G. (2003) 'Developing strategic approaches to diversity policy', in M. J. Davidson and S. L. Fielden (eds) *Individual Diversity in Organisations*. Chichester: John Wiley & Sons.

Kirton G. and Greene A. M. (2000) *The Dynamics of Managing Diversity*. London: Butterworth-Heinemann.

Kitching B. (2001) 'China', in M. Patrickson and P. O'Brien (eds) (2001) *Managing Diversity: An Asian-Pacific focus.* Milton, Qld: Wiley.

Leung A. (2002) 'Gender and career experience in mainland Chinese state-owned enterprises', *Personnel Review*, Vol. 31, No. 5: 602–19.

LFS (2002) *Employment Rates by Ethnic Origin and Age*. Labour Force Survey, Summer 2002.

Liff S. (1989) 'Assessing equal opportunity policies', *Personnel Review*, Vol. 18: 27–34.

Liff S. (1997) 'Two routes to managing diversity: individual differences or social group characteristics', *Employee Relations*, Vol. 19: 11–26.

Liff S. and Wajcman J. (1996) '"Sameness" and "Difference" revisited: which way forward for equal opportunities initiatives?', *Journal of Management Studies*, Vol. 33, No. 1: 79–95.

Liu P.-W., Meng X. and Zhang J. (2000) 'Sectoral gender wage differentials and discrimination in the transitional Chinese economy', *Journal of Population Economics*, Vol. 13: 331–52.

Lyness K. and Kropf M. (2005) 'The relationships of national gender equality and organisational support with work-family balance: a study of European managers', *Human Relations*, Vol. 58, No. 1: 33–62.

Maurer-Fazio M. and Hughes J. (2002) 'The effects of market liberalisation on the relative earnings of Chinese women', *Journal of Comparative Economics*, Vol. 30, No. 4: 709–31.

Muuka G. and Mwenda K. (2004) 'HRM in Zambia', in K. Kamoche, Y. Debrah, F. Horwitz and G. Muuka (eds) *Managing Human Resources in Africa*. London: Routledge.

Noon M. (1993) 'Racial discrimination in speculative application: evidence from the UK's top 100 firms', *Human Resource Management Journal*, Vol. 3, No. 4: 35–7.

Nyambegera S. (2002) 'Ethnicity and human resource management practice in sub-Saharan Africa: the relevance of the managing diversity discourse', *International Journal of Human Resource Management*, Vol. 13. No. 7: 1077–90.

Office of National Statistics (2002a) 'Economic Activity Status of Disabled People: by sex, 2002', *Social Trends*, 33.

Office of National Statistics (2002b) *Ethnicity: Population size* from www.statistics.gov.uk/cci/nugget.asp?id=273 [accessed 12.12.05].

Ogloblin C. (1999) 'The gender earnings differential in the Russian transition economy', *Industrial and Labor Relations Review*, Vol. 52, No. 4: 602–29.

Orazem P. and Vodopivec M. (2000) 'Male-female differences in labour market outcomes during early transition to market: the cases of Estonia and Slovenia', *Journal of Population Economics*, Vol. 13: 283–303.

Overell S. (1999) 'Ouseley in assault on diversity', *People Management*, 2 May: 7–8.

Patrickson M. (2001) 'Introduction to diversity', in M. Patrickson and P. O'Brien (eds) (2001) *Managing Diversity: An Asian-Pacific focus*. Milton, Qld: Wiley.

Platenga J. and Hansen J. (1999) 'Assessing equal opportunities in the European Union', *International Labour Review*, Vol. 138, No. 4: 351–79.

Pollert A. (2003) 'Women, work and equal opportunities in post-Communist transition', *Work, Employment and Society*, Vol. 17, No. 2: 331–57.

Prasad P. and Mills A. J. (1997) 'From showcase to shadow: understanding the dilemmas of managing workforce diversity', in P. Prasad, A. J. Mills, M. Elmes and A. Prasad (eds) *Managing the Organisational Melting Pot: Dilemmas of workplace diversity*. Thousand Oaks, CA: Sage.

Ramgutty-Wong A. (2004) 'HRM in Mauritius', in K. Kamoche, Y. Debrah, F. Horwitz and G. Muuka (eds) *Managing Human Resources in Africa*. London: Routledge.

Rawls J. (1971) *A Theory of Justice*. Cambridge, MA: Belknap.

Richards W. (2001) 'Evaluating equal opportunities initiatives: the case for a "transformative" agenda', in M. Noon and E. Ogbonna (eds) *Equality, Diversity and Disadvantage in Employment*. London: Palgrave.

Ross R. and Schneider R. (1992) *From Equality to Diversity*. London: Pitman.

Roulstone A. and Barnes C. (eds) (2005) *Working Futures? Disabled people, policy and social inclusion*. Bristol: The Policy Press.

Rubery J. (2002) 'Gender mainstreaming and gender equality in the EU: the impact of the EU employment strategy', *Industrial Relations Journal*, Vol. 33, No. 5: 500–22.

Rubery J., Grimshaw D., Fagan C., Figueredo H. and Smith M. (2003) 'Gender equality still on the European agenda – but for how long?', *Industrial Relations Journal*, Vol. 34, No. 5: 477–97.

Sargeant M. (2004) *Discrimination Law*. Harlow: Longman.

Sargeant M. and Lewis D. (2005) *Employment Law*. Harlow: Pearson Education.

Schroder B., Blackburn V. and Iles P. A. (1997) 'Women in management and firm financial performance: an exploratory study', *Journal of Management Issues*, Vol. 9, No. 3, Fall: 359–72.

Skinner D. (1999) 'The reality of equal opportunities: the expectations and experiences of part-time staff and their managers', *Personnel Review*, Vol. 28, No. 5/6: 425–38.

Thomas R. R. (1990) 'From affirmative action to affirming diversity', *Harvard Business Review*, Vol. 68, No. 2: 107–17.

United Nations Development Programme (2002) *Gender-Related Development Index (GDI) Rank*, http://www.hdr.undp.org/statistics/data/indic/indic_217_1_1.html [accessed 5 August 2005].

van der Lippe T. and van Dijk L. (2002) 'Comparative research on women's employment', *Annual Review of Sociology*, Vol. 28: 221–42.

Vince R. (1996) 'Employing critical thinking to develop theories of managing diversity', Proceedings of the British Academy of Management Conference, Aston, 16–18 September.

Vinnicombe S. and Singh V. (2003) *The 2003 Female FTSE Index*. Cranfield University: The Cranfield Centre for Developing Women Business Leaders.

Walby S. (1996) 'Comparative analysis of gender relations in employment in Western Europe', *Women in Management Review*, Vol. 11, No. 5: 9–18.

Webb J. (1997) 'The politics of equal opportunity', *Gender, Work and Organisation*, Vol. 4, No. 3: 159–69.

Webb J. and Liff S. (1988) 'Play the white man: the social construction of fairness and competition in equal opportunity policies', *Sociological Review*, Vol. 36: 543–51.

Woodhams C. and Lupton B. (2005) 'Equal opportunities policy and practice in small firms: the impact of HR professionals', *Human Resource Management Journal*, Vol. 16, No 1.

World Economic Forum (2004) *Women's Empowerment: Measuring the global gender gap*. http://www.weforum.org/pdf/Global_Competitveness_Reports/Reports/gender-gap.pdf [accessed, 8 August 2005].

Yates J. (1995) 'Approaches to equal opportunities', paper presented at the British Academy of Management Conference: Revitalising Organisations – the Academic Contribution. Sheffield University, 11–13 September.

Young I. (1990) *Justice and the Politics of Difference*. Princeton: Princeton University Press.

Zhu J. and Kleiner B. (2000) 'The value of training in changing discrimination behaviour at work', *Equal Opportunities International*, Vol. 19, No. 6/7: 5–9.

Themes and reflections

CHAPTER 15

Hamish Mathieson, Rosemary Lucas and Ben Lupton

The main aim of this book has been to critically examine topical international issues in HRM within a thematic conceptual framework. In contrast to texts in which the focus is on the processes of managing HR strategies and practices within the context of the multinational company (MNC) or a particular geographical region, our approach has been to address HR issues in relation to three primary cross-cutting themes: globalisation, convergence and divergence, and cultural variation. Within these are located sub-sets such as technological change, the rise of the 'knowledge economy', and labour market change. The concept underpinning the book has been the weaving of these primary themes into 13 main chapters grouped under the five headings *Employment and HRM*, *Work organisation, flexibility and culture*, *Recruiting, managing and developing people*, *Regulation and employment relations*, and *Corporate governance, justice and equity*, with the four subsidiary and related themes appearing in the context of particular chapters. In this chapter we focus on the three primary themes and illustrate them with reference to some of the significant issues that have emerged.

GLOBALISATION

'Globalisation' refers to the phenomenon of increasing worldwide interconnectedness and integration of economic and political activity. Its main features are the growing levels of international trade in goods and services, the increasing volume of international financial transactions and the transformation of financial markets, an acceleration of the rate of foreign direct investment, and an increased incidence of labour migration (Williams and Adam-Smith, 2006: 61–2). The principal sponsors of globalisation are international organisations such as the International Monetary Fund (IMF) and the World Trade Organisation (WTO), which promote an Americanised economic model that prescribes market liberalisation as the basis of global economic development. Globalisation is greatly facilitated by the transformation in information and communications technologies and by the activities of MNCs.

Our chapters variously track the implications of globalisation for international HR. Chapter 3 notes how western models of strategic HRM such as 'best practice' and 'best fit' are designed to contribute to improving firms' performance and overall business success. Nevertheless, there are tensions between the opposing tendencies implied in each model – the former often implying a 'soft' approach based on long-term asset-building, quality-enhancing and value-added measures, whereas the latter may entail a 'hard' approach that involves cost-cutting, cost-minimisation and greater efficiency. These dichotomies are reflected in later chapters. In the area of work organisation Chapter 4 asserts that the primary motor driving employers' concern for change has been the globalisation of markets, which has sharpened product market competition and further emphasised the need to achieve and sustain competitive advantage. In serving these aims firms are seeking more flexible workers whose jobs and pay are rendered less secure in order to reduce operating costs and increase market share. Similar pressures may be attributed to the rise in importance of employee performance on company HR agendas. Chapter 8 discusses the role of performance management as an over-arching tool in enhancing the stock of an organisation's human capital. At a micro-level the authors show how globalisation places increased emphasis on the need to develop appropriate performance management systems for managers in MNCs. The implication is that that successful performance management should be based on respect for the individual, procedural fairness and transparency of decision-making, and not constituted as a new form of 'Taylorism' that seeks to control the labour process. The effect of global competition is also reflected in Chapter 5. As such pressures have intensified, so have the efforts of companies to secure employee contribution and commitment by the manipulation of corporate culture. Acculturation of employees is a particular feature of HR strategies in globalised MNCs. Globalisation is identified in Chapter 6 as one factor in the internationalisation of the workforce, with far-reaching implications for traditional 'ethnocentric' models of recruitment and selection.

In the broad field of managing and developing performance, globalisation features as an important driver of employer initiatives. In an examination of learning and development practice, Chapter 7 points out that globalisation has the potential to result in 'low-road' HR practice based on cost minimisation or alternatively in a 'high-road' strategy stressing investment in people. Globalisation is also held to have significant implications for the regulation of employment relationships given that traditionally this is a field in which systems have been developed within national contexts. Chapter 10 argues that globalisation has the potential to shift the balance of power in the employment relationship in the employers' favour, thus presenting considerable challenges for effective collective employee representation and voice. In the analysis of employment law in Chapter 11 it is suggested that we are at a crossroads where the degree to which local employment law regimes bow to the requirements of globalisation is a major issue for politicians. The influence of globalisation has also been considered in the context of systems of corporate governance. Chapter 12 shows that globalisation is a significant pressure behind company initiatives in proclaiming their social responsibility credentials. Recognition of public approval for their activities, particularly in the developing world, can be seen as essential to continuing as profitable businesses. In its review of fair treatment at work, Chapter 14 also considers the role of globalisation as a vehicle that could potentially spread western models of equality at work around the world. Conversely, Chapter 9 suggests that a successful global reward strategy must ensure a balance between organisational consistency and local compatibility that can be achieved from an informed understanding of national economic conditions, the legal environment, labour market issues and pay practices.

CONVERGENCE AND DIVERGENCE

To what extent does the globalisation of markets and supply chains imply convergence in HR policy and practice? Chapter 2 suggests that pressure for convergence derives from two sources. One is the role of MNCs. Where organisations possess a strong corporate culture seen as vital to maintaining competitive advantage, this is likely to be translated into standardisation of operating methods, work organisation and employment policies. Although terms of employment may be set locally, there may, in addition, be corporate coordination exercised according to over-arching guiding principles embedded in corporate values. The extent of coordination will, however, depend on the degree of differentiation or integration of policy on HR matters. In the case of highly integrated companies corporate office will be active in effecting regular meetings of HR staff, utilising internal benchmarking around best practice, and fostering international policies. A second convergence pressure source is the European Union (EU) which seeks through processes of 'social dialogue' between bodies representing employers and employees and by legislation to establish a community-wide framework of employment standards.

The salience of convergence in HR practice is reflected through the book. For example, Chapter 5 discusses the attempts of MNCs to export their corporate cultures worldwide. Second, the role of the EU and organisations such as the International Labour Organisation (ILO) in promoting a measure of regional and international convergence in employment standards is discussed in Chapters 6 and 14 in their considerations of discrimination in recruitment and selection and fair treatment at work.

On the other hand there is considerable evidence of persisting divergence in HR practice. Two sorts of factors explain such trends. First there are *labour market considerations* which include employment legislation and institutional frameworks. Illustrations of the power of these factors may be drawn from the text. As Chapter 3 notes, we should caution against assuming that western models of HRM necessarily resonate in countries manifesting very different national and organisational contexts, and that a better understanding of these differences will help us move beyond western-centric HRM. In its discussion of employment flexibility Chapter 4 shows how the UK diverges from France because of the way in which the respective governments of the two countries regulate their labour markets. It points out that the relatively deregulated environment in the UK has had the effect of prioritising employer needs over employee needs in employment flexibility. Another example of the role of national institutional arrangements in constraining convergence is the case reported in Chapter 10 concerning the reactions of British Airways and German-based Lufthansa to common pressure to restructure in order to adapt to change in the external environment occasioned by liberalisation. A contrast is made between the approach adopted in the 'coordinated market economy' of Germany and the 'liberal market economy' of the UK. Although both countries' airlines experience the effects of globalisation, the differing institutional contexts have led to quite different implications for employee voice in the restructuring process in Germany and the UK. The significance of different legal frameworks for employment regulation is emphasised in Chapter 11, which asserts that the trend to convergence through EU and ILO initiatives continues to be largely outweighed by diversity in legal systems throughout the world and by pressures for deregulation as countries seek competitive advantage in world markets.

The second major factor in explaining divergence is *national culture* – and it is to that we now turn.

CULTURAL VARIATION

Chapter 2 asserts that although the employment relationship is influenced by a range of contextual factors, the role of national culture may be seen as pre-eminent. Cultural values and assumptions shape the way business and political systems have developed and also impact on the labour market. Above all they are a profound influence on both worker behaviour and management practice. Subsequent chapters illustrate the mediating effects of culture on tendencies to convergence. In Chapter 5 we find that the attempt by MNCs to achieve cross-border replication of centrally devised corporate culture have only been partly successful given the strength of local cultures, leading rather to a pattern of variable and hybrid corporate cultures. The authors also point to the possibility of local resistance, perhaps channelled through trade unions, to the imposition of corporate culture. Chapter 7 takes up the issue of the sensitivity of HR policies in varying cultural contexts against the background of a tendency to de-emphasise cultural factors in favour of generic idealised views of IHR practice. In this vein Chapter 8 questions the appropriateness of extending performance management systems developed within a predominantly American cultural milieu to other cultures. In other practice areas Chapter 6 points to the importance of national culture in terms of the extent to which employees will engage with aspects of corporate recruitment and selection processes. Likewise, Chapter 9 discusses the need for sensitivity in adapting reward management policies to varying cultural conditions. Chapter 10 looks at how the translation of cultural values into the ways management and workers interact and the relative status of labour, capital and the state acts either to enhance or impede the articulation of employee voice in different national contexts. In its discussion of equality at work Chapter 14 shows that the impact of a western liberal equality model varies significantly according to the local context in which it is implemented. Finally, on a broader canvas, Chapter 13 explores the ethical dimension of cross-border cultural convergence and divergence. It indicates that at best managers working across national boundaries may face barriers to progress, and at worst overt hostility to decisions deemed to be culturally unethical.

HRM CHALLENGES FOR THE FUTURE

In looking at HRM in an international context, a picture of simultaneous convergence and divergence is apparent. Forces of convergence are undoubtedly shaping HR policy and practice around the world as MNCs – particularly the dominant American ones – have exported their model of management practice. The convergence model has clear utility in seeking to analyse globalisation. But it only tells some of the story. For globalisation is also accompanied by, and contributes to, divergence and diversity as countries and organisations seek to differentiate themselves in order to succeed in the race to attract foreign direct investment or new business. Although labour markets become more interconnected through globalisation, they are also becoming more culturally diverse. Scase (2002) has remarked that the paradox of globalisation is that as we become more similar we also become more different from each other. From the viewpoint of HRM practitioners and scholars the importance of managing and understanding cultural diversity ought therefore to be at the forefront of our endeavours in the future.

REFERENCES

Scase R. (2002) *Living in the Corporate Zoo: Life and work in 2010*. Oxford: Capstone.

Williams S. and Adam-Smith D. (2006) *Contemporary Employment Relations: A critical introduction*. Oxford: Oxford University Press.

INDEX

(all references are to page number)

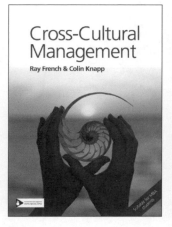